Understanding the Order of Melchizedek

Robin Main

Copyright © 2017 Robin Main

All rights reserved.

ISBN: 0-998-59824-0
ISBN-13: 978-0-998-59824-6

**Cover Image: Fiery Wheel With His Wheel
By Robin Main**

DEDICATION

Judy Roehl
My beautiful mom and co-laborer in Christ

All my life, I was privileged to have an up-close and very personal relationship with the best servant that I have ever seen. My mom was the epitome of selfless love and service as well as utter devotion to the Lord, His people and her family. Judy… Judy… Judy… proofed each and every one of the enclosed books over and over again while freeing up my time to minister to the Lord and His people through doing laundry, dishes or whatever was needed. I am forever and deeply grateful for the incredible gift God gave to me… y-o-u.

CONTENTS

	Acknowledgments	i
	Preface	iii
	Book 1 – Melchizedek's Time, Appearance & First Ministry	1
1	Introduction	3
2	King of Righteousness	11
3	King of Peace	19
4	First Occurrence of Melchizedek in Scripture	23
5	Time of Melchizedek's Appearing	29
6	Technology of Communion	37
7	The Perfection of the Order of Melchizedek	41
8	Common Union	57
	Book 2 – Practical Keys to Unlocking Melchizedek	61
1	Introduction	63
2	Overcoming Babylonian Kings	69
3	The Original Melchizedek	71
4	Technology of the Wine and Bread	87
5	Raising Up One Man	93
6	What We Must Not Do	97
7	Order Speaks	103

8	Treasurer of the Most Intimate	109
9	Life's Pure Perfection	115
10	Power Over Death	121
	Book 3 – Taking On Common Union	127
1	Introduction	129
2	With This Bread & Wine, I Thee Wed	135
3	With This Bread & Wine, We Thee Wed	137
4	Behold, A New Living Creature	141
5	Behold, The New Living Creature is the Cherubim	145
6	Wing of Royal Priests Flying by the Spirit	151
7	His New Living Creature's Purpose	155
8	Creature Waiting for the Manifestation of Mature Sons	159
	Book 4 – Hitting the Bull's Eye of Righteousness	171
1	Introduction	173
2	Have We Already Been Made the Righteousness of God in Christ?	179
3	Mysteries of the Deep Red	187
4	Baptism of Fire	191
5	Steps for the Bride's Baptism of Fire	195
6	Holy Priesthood Offering Spiritual Sacrifices	199
7	Never Cut Off the Body from the Head	205

8	Becoming a Burnt Offering	209
9	Purify the Soul	215
10	Faithfulness Test	221
11	Brokenness of One's Soul	227
12	Continual Living Sacrifice	235

	Book 5 – Formation of the New Living Creature	243
1	Introduction	245
2	The Chariot Throne's Appearance of a Man	251
3	Behold, the Living Creature is the Cherubim	255
4	Cherubim Guarding the Tree of Life	259
5	Cherubim on the Ten Copper Chariot Lavers	267
6	Cherubim on the Walls	283
7	Cherubim on the Veil	289
8	Cherubim on the Ark of the Covenant in the Tabernacle	297
9	Cherubim on the Ark of the Covenant in Solomon's Temple	305

	Book 6 – Window into the Wheels Within Wheels	313
1	Introduction	315
2	To Be or Not To Be	317
3	Gyroscopic Wheel Within Wheels	321
4	Living Creature Transportation – Beryllium #1	325
5	Living Creature Communication – Beryllium #2	329

6	Living Creature Medicine – Beryllium #3	335
7	Living Creature Space Exploration – Beryllium #4	341
8	Living Creature Safety – Beryllium #5	347
9	Living Creature Energy – Beryllium #6	353
10	Living Creature Defense and Security – Beryllium #7	359
	Book 7 – Place of Sapphires	**367**
1	Introduction	369
2	Place of Sapphires	373
3	Three Sapphire Truths	387
4	The Shamir Stone	395
5	Cubes of Sapphires	407
6	Bone of My Bone. Flesh of My Flesh.	417
7	Twilight and Sabbath	423
	Book 8 – Blazing New Wine of Hanukkah: Bridal Restoration of DNA	**427**
1	Background	429
2	Introduction	437
3	Healing a Man Born Blind	443
4	Journey to Become His Bride: Hanukkah Battles	449
5	Purification of the Temple & Re-Dedication of God's Altar	465

6	DNA Restoration of Christ's Body	469
7	Fullness of the Messiah Bodily: Metatron	483
8	The Good Shepherd of Hanukkah	499
9	Beauty and the Beast: Christ's Bride and the Antichrist	505
10	General Guidelines to Celebrating Hanukkah	511
11	Hanukkah Devotions	521
12	Informal Bibliography	539

ACKNOWLEDGMENTS

Special thanks to my brilliant editor

Judy Ellan Roehl

ROBIN MAIN

PREFACE

This book is a compilation of the seven books in *Sapphire Throne Ministries' Understanding the Order of Melchizedek Series* as well as an eighth book that's a major key for God's people maturing into the fullness of the Order of Melchizedek, the fullness of the Bride of the Messiah, and the fullness of the Heavenly One New Man in the Messiah – Metatron.

A very unique chapter entitled the "Fullness of the Messiah Bodily: Metatron" has been added to the eighth book – *Blazing New Wine of Hanukkah* – which reveals a vital key for growing into the 100-percent fullness of the Messiah bodily. Another major addition is found in "The Original Melchizedek" Chapter of *Book 2 – Practical Keys to Unlocking Melchizedek*. The new section is called "Assignment of Death." Here I share my own ascended experience in overcoming an Assignment of Death, as a king and priest of the Most High God.

Even though there are additions, modifications and corrections in this edition, the integrity of the previously published books is mostly kept in-tact. Some concepts are so significant to the Order of Melchizedek that they are mentioned more than once, like communion, righteousness, perfection, et cetera. Not only do we all learn from repetition, but I have strived to add various unique elements each time a noteworthy concept connected to understanding the Order of Melchizedek is mentioned.

If the Order of Melchizedek is new to you and you feel that this material is over-your-head, the following are a few suggestions to help you press toward the high calling of God in Christ Jesus and to help you grow into the measure of the stature of the fullness of Christ:

[1]   Choose to be humble and teachable.

[2] Choose to seek first His Kingdom and His righteousness (Matthew 6:33).

[3] Ask for a growing hunger and thirst for His kingdom and righteousness.

[4] Ask our Heavenly Father for the Seven Spirits of God to be your tutors

[5] Daily Bread – Pay attention to the Pattern Son, Messiah Yeshua (Jesus Christ), as you study the Word of God.

[6] Daily Communion – Intimately connect to the Father, the Son, and the Holy Spirit through the communion elements.

[7] Daily Crucifixion – Die to anything not like Yeshua.

Within the pages of *Understanding the Order of Melchizedek*, you will discover that the word "order" in the Order of Melchizedek literally meaning WORD. In addition to chewing on a substantial portion of daily bread (i.e., the Word of God), please take daily communion as well, which conveniently has daily crucifixion included due to the need to rightly examine oneself before taking communion.

Once you are humming with Daily Bread, Daily Communion and Daily Crucifixion with the Seven Spirits of God personally tutoring you; then dive into the *Sapphire Throne Ministries (STM)* materials, such as this book, both *MEL GEL Study Guides* and the *Ascension Manual*. All *STM* materials are a result of over 15 years heavy-duty ascended study – 3 to 12 hours (or more) a day of pressing into His Presence and His Word (Spirit and Truth). Know that there's a divine acceleration in this Kingdom Day. What took me 15 years may only take you a couple years, or 15 months, or 15 days. I love how the Lord our God works best when we freely give and freely receive, so we can all rise as One New Man in Christ and as the Bride of Christ. I pray that my ceiling can become other's floor.

Book 1

Melchizedek's Time, Appearance & First Ministry

Cover Art: "Hitting Melchizedek's Time" by Robin Main

© February 1, 2016. All Rights Reserved

Text Copyright © 2016 Robin Main. All Rights Reserved

ROBIN MAIN

1 - INTRODUCTION

We are in the perfect time when the Order of Melchizedek is appearing. It is the divinely right time for Melchizedek to arise.

This book's primary focus is on the time of Melchizedek's appearing, how he appears as well as the first ministry of Melchizedek mentioned in the Bible. We will especially give attention to the two titles given to Melchizedek in Scripture: King of Righteousness and King of Peace.

Before we go into the time, appearance and first ministry of Melchizedek according to Genesis 14, let's make it perfectly clear that Yeshua Ha Mashiach (Jesus Christ) is the only high priest of the Order of Melchizedek; and therefore, its head (Hebrews 2:17; 4:14-15; 5:1,5,10; 6;20; 7:26; 8:1; 9:11; 10:21). I have run into several individuals who seem to think that Jesus Christ being the High Priest of the Order of Melchizedek negates the reality of people entering into this order. I chalk this up to religious orders not being a common thing these days.

"Melchizedek" is more of a title than a name when it comes to the sons of the Living God. When Scripture says that Yeshua has been *"called of God a High Priest after the Order of Melchizedek" (Hebrews 5:10)*, a group of people united in a formal way under the banner of the "Order of Melchizedek" is implied. Groups like the Order of Saint John may not be very familiar to many of us in our day, but various religious orders where people have been required to take solemn vows have existed for a very long time. These have been communities under a religious rule. In Genesis 14's case, it was the King of Righteousness's rule. It was this man who was also a priest of Most High God that ruled Salem, which was the predecessor of Jerusalem.

Just like the Order of St. John is an order of chivalry, so is the Order of Melchizedek an order of perfection. If you study all the occurrences of the word "perfection" in Scripture, you get a picture of PERFECT talking about completion, accomplishment or consummation of something, especially in character -- being complete in labor, complete in growth, complete in mental character and complete morally. In the Greek, it speaks of a full age or mature man, which is the manifestation of the sons of God spoken of in Romans 8:19. *"For the anxious longing of the creation waits eagerly for the revealing of the sons of God" (Romans 8:19 $_{NASB}$)*. At its root, the word "perfect" in Scripture speaks of setting out for a definite point or goal – to be just like Jesus – and its fulfillment to the uttermost. For more on the Order of Melchizedek being an order of perfection, please check out the "The Perfection of the Order of Melchizedek" Chapter.

What if I told you that the kings and priests of the Order of Melchizedek are supposed to be masters of time and space just like Yeshua? "The Coming of Melchizedek" section of the Dead Sea Scrolls (11Q13) reveals that by the power of Melchizedek, dominion on earth shall pass from Satan (i.e., Belial) to the righteous Sons of Light. What is this dominion on earth? Could it be earth's entire domain, including time and space? Deep thoughts to ponder, and deeper still to make them a walking-talking reality.

Let's zero in on Melchizedek as it applies to those personally commissioned into the Order of Melchizedek. Just like the Bride of Christ is a corporate entity, so is the Order of Melchizedek; but before we can go corporate, each one of us need to grasp how to apply being part of the Order of Melchizedek on a personal level. Please note that *Sapphire Throne Ministries' Taking On Common Union* book was the first book I wrote about the corporate manifestation of the Order of Melchizedek.

COMMISSIONED INTO THE ORDER OF MELCHIZEDEK

You have probably heard that everyone belongs to the Order of Melchizedek once they accept Jesus (i.e., Yeshua) as their Savior. This is simply not true. We need to follow the Pattern Son – Yeshua – the High Priest to see how the Order of Melchizedek becomes a reality here on earth. Remember, Moses was divinely instructed when he was about to make the Tabernacle (God's Dwelling Place): *"See that you make all things according to the pattern shown you on the mountain"* (Hebrews 8:5).

That mountain was where heaven touched earth. Many more people are focusing and going to the heavens (which is excellent and good), but if our character on earth can't contain His Kingdom and flow in Kingdom exploits, we literally can't facilitate bringing heaven to earth.

To be commissioned into the Order of Melchizedek a person needs to have entered God's Kingdom. How do I know this? I asked Abba (i.e., Father God): "When does Your commissioning for the

Melchizedek Army begin?" He told me: "When people enter the Kingdom of God."

The following are four conditions for entering the Kingdom of God:

[1] BORN OF WATER AND SPIRIT - *"Jesus answered, 'Most assuredly, I say to you, unless one is BORN OF WATER AND THE SPIRIT, he cannot ENTER THE KINGDOM OF GOD (John 3:5 NKJV)*. God's people have to have been born of water and the spirit to be commissioned into His royal priesthood.

[2] RECEIVE AS A LITTLE CHILD - *"[14] Let the little children come to Me, and do not forbid them; for of such is the kingdom of God. [15] Assuredly, I say to you, whoever does not RECEIVE THE KINGDOM OF GOD AS A LITTLE CHILD will by no means enter it" (Mark 10:14-15 NKJV)*. We must have the simplicity of a child trusting that we will receive the Kingdom of God.

[3] HARD FOR THOSE WHO TRUST IN RICHES - *"[23] Then Jesus looked around and said to His disciples, 'How hard it is for those who have riches to ENTER THE KINGDOM OF GOD!' [24] And the disciples were astonished at His words. But Jesus answered again and said to them, 'Children, how HARD it is FOR THOSE WHO TRUST IN RICHES TO ENTER THE KINGDOM OF GOD! [25] It is easier for a camel to go through the eye of a needle than for a rich man to ENTER THE KINGDOM OF GOD" (Mark 10:23-25 NKJV)*. It's extremely significant that the phrase "enter the Kingdom of God" is mentioned three times regarding it being difficult for those who have and/or trust in riches to enter the Kingdom of God. We need to take our cue from the advice Yeshua gave to the rich young ruler prior to

these verses. We obtain treasures in heaven by denying and dying to what you want in order to follow Yeshua: *"Then Jesus, looking at him, loved him, and said to him, "One thing you lack: Go your way, sell whatever you have and give to the poor, and you will have treasure in heaven; and come, take up the cross, and follow Me" (Mark 10:21 NKJV).*

[4] **THROUGH MANY TRIBULATIONS -** *"Strengthening the souls of the disciples, exhorting them to continue in the faith, and saying, "WE MUST THROUGH MANY TRIBULATIONS ENTER THE KINGDOM OF GOD" (Acts 14:22 NKJV).* Suffering is simply part of our crucifixion process that enables us to enter into the death, burial and resurrection life of the Kingdom of God. Nothing better develops Christ's Character within us like distress, sufferings and tribulations. *"[12] Beloved, do not think it strange concerning the fiery trial which is to try you, as though some strange thing happened to you; [13] but rejoice to the extent that you partake of Christ's sufferings, that when His glory is revealed, you may also be glad with exceeding joy" (1 Peter 4:12-13 NKJV).* As we offer our sufferings and sacrifices to Him, we are crucified in union with Christ in an ever-increasing greater measure, so we can live by the faith of the Son of God (Galatians 2:20). *"I now rejoice in my sufferings for you, and fill up in my flesh what is lacking in the afflictions of Christ, for the sake of His body, which is the church" (Colossians 1:24 NKJV).*

Know that the Order of Melchizedek is the highest spiritual order on earth that manifests heaven – making the kingdoms of this earth, the kingdoms of our God (Revelation 11:15). Scripturally, when we are born-again, we merely SEE the Kingdom of God (John 3:3) and are immature sons at this point. According to John 3:5 when we are born of water and the Spirit, we ENTER the kingdom of God. It is during this step that Manifested Sons or the Maturing Sons are produced. This is where the New Living Creature of the One New Man in Christ (i.e., the Messiah) who is a wing of His Melchizedek Army begins to take shape. In its fullness, there will be a company within the Order of Melchizedek who are Christ's having crucified their flesh. They are the ones that have truly earned the title – Crucified Ones. They are those who led by the Spirit and INHERIT the Kingdom of God (Galatians 5:19-21; 1 Corinthians 6:9-10). This third level where one inherits the Kingdom of God is where Mature or Maturing Sons become His Pure and Spotless Bride.

The One New Man in Christ, the Order of Melchizedek and the Bride of Christ are three corporate manifestations of the Body of Christ that eventually leads whosoever wills into a purified state. These corporate manifestations of the Body of Christ are also progressive maturation steps as well. First, the One New Man in Christ made up of everyone born from above. The goal of the One New Man in Christ is to come into the fullness of the Order of Melchizedek. Being made after the Order of Melchizedek is our second corporate step in our "moving unto perfection" process. Those who pursue the fullness of the Order of Melchizedek are led into the third and highest corporate manifestation in the Body of Christ, which is His beautiful Bride, which is the 100-percent fullness of the Heavenly One New Man in the Messiah (i.e., Metatron) at the same time. Please remember that there is no male or female in the spirit. *"^{26} For you are all sons of God through faith in Christ Jesus. ^{27} For as many of you as were baptized into Christ have put on Christ. ^{28} There is neither Jew nor Greek, there is neither slave nor free, there is neither male nor female; for you are all one in Christ Jesus" (Galatians 3:26-28 $_{NKJV}$)*. Just as a woman can be a Son in the spirit, so can a man be part of Christ's Bride.

One of my first introductions to the Order of Melchizedek in the Spirit was connected to the Bride of Christ. I speak about this in the Taking on Common Union book. In a nutshell, when I personally took communion with Yeshua in a corporate setting, He led the communion by vowing: "With this bread and wine, I thee wed." I followed suit in the reverential awe of the Lord.

After this sacred encounter, I began to take communion daily, like my mentor and spiritual mom. I took it daily for years. Every time, after the holy, reverential fear encounter, I would engage by proclaiming: "With this bread/wine I thee wed." Eventually, I began to hear a deep primordial sound that my mentor – Nancy Coen – had called the One Note: "ooooooonnnnnnnneeeeeeeee…." The Priesthood of One Love of the Order of Melchizedek needs to tune into that one note. We need to be ONE, as Yeshua and the Father are ONE.

All this time, I kept on receiving revelation about the Bride and Melchizedek almost simultaneously. I was getting so confused, because these concepts seemed so intertwined in the Spirit. So… I sought the LORD for a long time, asking Him: "What is the difference between Melchizedek and Your Bride?" One day I heard Him say a one-liner: "Melchizedek is the predecessor to the Bride." When a person is made after the Order of Melchizedek, it is their responsibility to lead their own inner fire bride forth.

Before we continue in this vein, we need to lay some basic ground work about Melchizedek first. Know that this book lays a foundation to build upon for subsequent revelations about the Mystery of Melchizedek.

*****

2 – KING OF RIGHTEOUSNESS

Let's travel to the King of Righteousness to answer the question: Who is Melchizedek? In Hebrew, "Melchizedek" is translated as the King of Righteousness. Hebrews Chapter 7 speaks of Melchizedek being both the "king of righteousness" as well as the "king of peace":

"[1] For this Melchizedek, king of Salem, priest of the Most High God, who met Abraham returning from the slaughter of the kings and blessed him, [2] to whom also Abraham gave a tenth part of all, first being translated "KING OF RIGHTEOUSNESS," and then also king of Salem, meaning "king of peace" (Hebrews 7:1-2 NKJV).

Righteousness is a dove-tail joint where Melchizedek and the Bride of Christ meet. One is the king of righteousness (Hebrews 7:2). The other is given bright and clean fine linen to wear equivalent to the righteous deeds of the saints (Revelation 19:7-8).

Fundamentally, righteousness is a State of Being. Please remember this fundamental fact of righteousness. Righteousness is not a State of Doing, but a State of Being.

The Hebrew word for "righteousness" is *tsedeq* (Strong's OT:6664). It's what right naturally, morally, or legally. Abstractly, *tsedeq* can mean equity; or figuratively, it can mean prosperity. *Tsadeq* can be translated as just, or justice, or a cause. A cause is a reason for action. It's a motive. A cause is also an agent that brings something about, like God's Throne. *"Clouds and thick darkness surround Him; righteousness and justice are the foundation [habitation] of His Throne" (Psalm 97:2 NASB).*

Therefore, righteousness is literally a place where God is at home. Righteousness is a permanent structure in which He dwells, which is supported by the root meaning behind the word *tsedeq*. When we dig to the Hebraic root of "righteousness," we see that it means TO BE, or to cause to make right in a moral or forensic sense. "To be" is the primitive root to "righteousness," which also means to cleanse or clear self, to be just, or do justice, or turn to righteousness.

"To be or not to be" really is the right question when it comes to righteousness. As stated previously, righteousness is literally a State of Being. My mentor teaches that we have been created as human beings, not human doings. We have to first be, not do; but if we don't do what we say, even the world knows that we're hypocrites.

Have you ever noticed that many Christians name and claim "I am the righteousness of God in Christ Jesus;" then shortly thereafter treat people terribly? There's a major disconnect in the Body of Christ when people manifest demonic activity and at the same time claim to be righteous. Ian Clayton calls this a form of pseudo-spirituality without any reality. Righteousness flows from intimacy. Yes. The Bride is clothed in righteousness, but what that really means is that she is enthroned in righteousness.

Many of us have been taught that righteousness has nothing to do with what we do. That paradigm needs to shift a quark or two.

> "*¹³ For everyone who partakes only of milk is unskilled in the Word of Righteousness, for he is a babe. ¹⁴ But solid food belongs to those who are of full age, that is, those who by reason of use have their senses exercised to discern both good and evil*" (Hebrews 5:13-14 NKJV).

Melchizedek is all about the Word of Righteousness. In fact, the word "order" in the Order of Melchizedek fundamentally means "word." Don't forget that *"all Scripture is inspired by God and profitable ... for training in righteousness; that the man of God may be adequate, equipped for every good work"* (2 Timothy 3:16). Therefore, we can easily say that the Order of Melchizedek is connected to the Word of the King of Righteousness. Furthermore, we can say that the Bride will resonate at the same righteous frequency as her Beloved Bridegroom. Those things in our lives that are not plumb with God's measuring line of righteousness (according to His Word) will cause us to resonate at a lower frequency than a pure and spotless one.

After several months of studying the concept of "righteousness" in the Bible, I concluded that the topic was so huge that it's appears to be almost endless. The bottom line for God's Bridal Company being formed here on earth, as it is in heaven, is that James 2:21-23 shows us that "completed faith" or "perfect faith" is reckoned by God as righteous. It's where a believer has matured into a full age son in a particular area of their lives where they have become an actual manifestation of the Living Word. It's a place where these people's actions line up with their words as well as with God's Eternal Word.

Let's dive a little deeper into awakening to righteousness, seeking righteousness, pursuing righteousness and doing righteousness. You can either have faith in Christ, faith through Christ or the very same faith of Christ. As we move unto perfection (i.e., maturity) from salvation to sanctification to purification, you will experience these various quantum levels of faith.

Having faith in Christ or faith towards God is good and right, but it is merely the first step in our journey unto perfection. Hebrews 6:1 tells us that "faith toward God' is an elementary teaching of the Anointed One. "Faith through Christ" is more difficult than "faith toward God." It takes more active participation to have faith through someone than to have faith toward someone; therefore, the second quantum step of faith can be seen as "faith through Christ": *"⁸ Yet indeed I also count all things loss for the excellence of the knowledge of Christ Jesus my Lord, for whom I have suffered the loss of all things, and count them as rubbish, that I may gain Christ ⁹ and be found in Him, NOT HAVING MY OWN RIGHTEOUSNESS, which is from the law, BUT THAT WHICH IS THROUGH FAITH IN CHRIST, THE RIGHTEOUSNESS WHICH IS FROM GOD BY FAITH; ¹⁰ THAT I MAY KNOW HIM AND THE POWER OF HIS RESURRECTION, and the fellowship of His sufferings, being conformed to His death, ¹¹ if, by any means, I may attain to the resurrection from the dead"* (Philippians 3:8-11 $_{NKJV}$). The final and most difficult quantum step of faith is having the exact same faith of Christ. It's where those made after the Order of Melchizedek are made into the image of the Son of God (Hebrews 7:3):

- *"I am crucified with Christ: nevertheless I live; yet not I, but Christ lives in me: and the life which I now live in the flesh I live by the FAITH OF THE SON OF GOD, who loved me, and gave himself for me" (Galatians 2:20 $_{KJV}$).* "

- *Here is the patience of the saints; here are those who keep the commandments of God and the FAITH OF JESUS" (Revelation 14:12 $_{NKJV}$).*

At the second level, which is having "faith through Christ", we seek righteousness, pursue righteousness and do righteousness:

- *"But SEEK FIRST His Kingdom and HIS RIGHTEOUSNESS; and all these things shall be provided to you" (Matthew 6:33).*

- *"Seek the LORD, all you humble of the earth who have carried out His ordinances (justice); SEEK RIGHTEOUSNESS, seek humility. Perhaps you will be hidden in the day of the LORD's anger"* (Zephaniah 2:3 NASB).

- *"Now flee from youthful lusts, and PURSUE RIGHTEOUSNESS, faith, love and peace, with those who call on the LORD from a pure heart"* (2 Timothy 2:22).

- *"But flee from these things [love of money], you man of God; and PURSUE RIGHTEOUSNESS, godliness, faith, love, perseverance and gentleness"* (1 Timothy 6:11 NASB).

- *"Thus says the LORD, "Preserve justice, and DO RIGHTEOUSNESS, For My salvation is about to come and My righteousness to be revealed"* (Isaiah 56:1 NASB).

- *"Break away from your sins by DOING RIGHTEOUSNESS"* (Daniel 4:27 NASB).

Please note that a person does not seek or pursue something that they already have. There are many examples of a continual pursuit of righteousness in Scripture. Take for example: *"Blessed are those who hunger and thirst for righteousness, for they shall be satisfied"* (Matthew 5:6 NASB). Then it goes on to exhort believers: *"[10] Blessed are those who are persecuted for the sake of righteousness, for theirs is the kingdom of heaven. [11] Blessed are you when men cast insults at you, and persecute you, and say all kinds of evil against you falsely, on account of Me. [12] Rejoice and be glad, for your reward in heaven is great"* (Matthew 5:10-12 NASB).

Righteousness is probably one of the most undervalued and misunderstood commodities of the Kingdom of God. Think about it. God instructs us to seek first His righteousness. He tells us to hunger and thirst for righteousness, and that we are blessed when we are persecuted for righteousness sake. This means that the righteous place we dwell "in Christ" gets enhanced through persecution. We can also say that the end or purpose behind us being persecuted for His Name's sake is to exhibit the character of Christ, which is founded both in righteousness and justice (Psalm 97:2).

Don't forget that Scripture reveals that the unrighteous shall not inherit the Kingdom of God (1 Corinthians 6:9). We like to project that means unbelievers, but it's not. It is anyone who doesn't walk in the Spirit and who manifests the works of the flesh (Refer to 1 Corinthians 6:9-1; Galatians 5:17-21).

Scripture tells us that every man is given a measure of faith after we are exhorted to present our bodies as living sacrifices and to be transformed by the renewing of our mind in order to prove which level of the will of God we operate. Does your life prove:

[1] God's good will,

[2] His acceptable will or

[3] His perfect will? (See Romans 12:1-3).

Believe it or not, it's the righteousness of God being revealed at these three quantum levels of faith that proves what echelon of His will we are operating on. *"For in it [the gospel of the Messiah] the righteousness of God is revealed from faith to faith; as it is written, 'The just shall live by faith'"* (Romans 1:17 NKJV).

The righteousness of God is revealed faith to faith, because true righteousness from God Himself is the motive for our faith working through love. Romans 6 reveals that we are slaves to the one whom we obey, whether to sin unto death or to obedience unto righteousness (Romans 6:16). Christ's righteousness in us via the Holy Spirit will bring about the process for our becoming the righteousness of God in Christ Jesus here on earth (2 Corinthians 5:21), as we partner with Him in order to become *"a perfect man, unto the measure of the stature of the fullness of Christ" (Ephesians 4:13 KJV)*.

As we obey the leading of His Spirit within, it will happen just as it did with Yeshua: *"Although He was a Son, He learned obedience from the things which He suffered" (Hebrews 5:8 NASB)*. This is the context we need when we read in Romans Chapter 6 that the obedience of His "servants of righteousness" results in righteousness, which then results in their holiness (Romans 6:19). Please notice that being holy as He is holy is a command, not a suggestion: *"[14] As obedient children, not conforming yourselves to the former lusts, as in your ignorance; [15] but as He who called you is holy, you also be holy in all your conduct, [16] because it is written, 'Be holy, for I am holy.' [17] And if you call on the Father, who without partiality judges according to each one's work, conduct yourselves throughout the time of your stay here in fear; [18] knowing that you were not redeemed with corruptible things, ... [19] but with the precious blood of Christ, as of a lamb without blemish and without spot" (1 Peter 1:14-19 NKJV)*.

Let's all receive the seal of righteousness, like Abraham did before he was circumcised, which is upon all who believe (Romans 3:22). Let's all walk in the steps of faith, which is the righteousness of faith, knowing that the evidence of the trying of our faith will be found at the appearing of Messiah Yeshua (Romans 4:11-14; 1 Peter 1:7). Let's all be faithful and true by making our faith perfect through doing what we believe (James 2:22). By the way, doing righteousness belongs to the third level of faith, which equates to literally having the same faith of Christ or the faith of the Son of God (Galatians 2:20).

Those people made after the Order of Melchizedek are called to rule and reign in Christ, as kings of righteousness. We are to grow in becoming the righteousness of God in Christ Jesus just as a prince learns to reign before being crowned king.

*****

3 – KING OF PEACE

"*¹⁸ And MELCHIZEDEK KING OF SALEM brought out bread and wine; he was the priest of the Most High God. ¹⁹ And he blessed him, saying, Blessed be Abram to God Most High, possessor of heaven and earth; ²⁰ And blessed be the Most High God, who had delivered your enemies into your hands. And Abram gave him tithes of everything*" (Genesis 14:18-20 Aramaic).

Wherever we find the term "kings and priests" in the Word of God, it's connected to the first occurrence of "Melchizedek." Fundamentally, Scripture tells us that the Genesis 14 Melchizedek was both a priest and king.

Hebrews 7:2 tells is the King of Salem means the King of Peace. Nancy Coen taught me that Yeshua is the Prince of Peace. When you couple this with the fact that Yeshua is the High Priest of the Order of Melchizedek, who is called the King of Peace, we understand that the Eternal Order of Melchizedek is about crowning the Prince of Peace, as the King of Peace in our lives, and the fullness thereof.

"*¹⁴ But God forbid that I glory, save in the cross of our Lord Jesus Christ, by whom the world is crucified unto me, and I unto the world. ¹⁵ FOR IN CHRIST JESUS... AVAILETH ... a NEW CREATURE. ¹⁶ AND AS MANY AS WALK ACCORDING TO THIS RULE,*

PEACE BE ON THEM..." (Galatians 6:14-16 KJV).

King of Salem can also mean PERFECT KING. We will delve into the Melchizedek concept of "perfect" and "perfection" more soon. Melchizedek is a king that rules perfectly. Melchizedek, as KING OF PEACE, symbolizes *shekinah*, which is the Dwelling Presence of God or the *Shekinah* Glory. *Shekinah* is also known in mystical circles both as *malkut* "kingdom" and *tsedeq* (righteousness). Melchizedek, as *Shekinah*, is *shalem* ("perfect, complete").

Let's look at Salem itself. It says in *Psalm 76:2* that *"In Salem is His Tabernacle, and His Dwelling Place in Zion."* God's Tabernacle in Salem can be interpreted as the *Shekinah* in Salem (in a state of perfection).

During a *Mystic Mentoring (in Christ)* Group Ascension, we were led according to the Father's Heart to explore the original City of Peace – Salem. We experienced that it's the city of immortals where the Great Cloud of Witnesses live, and the 600 Mighty Men of David reside. We had an ancient man point us the way to some pillars. When we got there, we realized that the pillars were the hairy legs of the Mighty Men. We had to choose to become as big as the Mighty Men for His glory in order to take dominion and authority over kingdoms. There was a big gate to this city. During our ascension, we journeyed across time and space to step into a horizontal twirling whirlwind-like structure that smoothed off our rough edges, so we could go through the narrow gate. When our Group Ascension was done, we were told that we could come back to Salem anytime to get equipped, because that particular group now carries the DNA that this gate recognizes. It's a combo where we can walk straight through.

What I'd like to point out from our Mystic Mentoring Group Ascension to Salem is there was a rainbow light show at the Gate of The City of Peace. Please recall that *"In Salem is His Tabernacle"* (*Psalm 76:2*). God's Tabernacle is in Salem as well as God's *Shekinah* Glory is in Salem.

Christian and Jewish Mysticism recognizes *shekinah* as the divine rainbow that radiates colors in two directions. The eyes of the Lord are over the righteous like the rainbow round about His Sapphire Throne (Ezekiel 1:28). He's watching His Word to see that it's fulfilled. Yeshua walked in this crossover place of heaven and earth at the same time; and as Son of Man, He was completely filled with the Seven Spirits of God: *"And the spirit of the Lord shall rest upon Him, the spirit of wisdom and understanding, the spirit of counsel and might, the spirit of knowledge and of the fear of the Lord" (Isaiah 11:2)*.

Scripture tells us that when we abide in Christ, we walk in the same manner as He did (1 John 2:6). This means that one of the ultimate realities for God's Devout Ones is we are supposed to be made perfect and complete, like the High Priest of the Order of Melchizedek being completely filled with the Seven Spirits of God here on earth, as it is in heaven.

Currently, we are in an opportune time to get beyond God simply visiting us. You know His Presence coming and going… coming and going… coming and going… We are in a perfect time for the glory of His Dwelling Presence to come and remain. The root to Hebrew word *shekinah* literally means to settle, inhabit or dwell. God's *shekinah* glory manifests in His Temple. Never forget that God's people are the Temple of the Spirit of Living God (1 Corinthians 6:19).

Christian Mystics tell us that Shekinah is not found among sinners. The state of our souls does affect how His light shines through our lives. In fact, Ezekiel Chapter 8 speaks of four things which cause God's *Shekinah* to not remain. God first asks Ezekiel "Do you see what they do?" to get him to focus on the issues that the Lord Himself is bring up. Then God adds: *"That I should go far off from My sanctuary?" (Ezekiel 8:6)*.

If you desire to abide in Christ, live in His *shekinah* glory and be made into the exact image of Yeshua; then you must examine your life according to the Ezekiel 8 crux for His Dwelling Presence. Please refer to my book *SANTA-TIZING: What's wrong with Christmas and how to clean it up* for more information => https://www.amazon.com/SANTA-TIZING-Whats-wrong-Christmas-clean/dp/1607911159. I also wrote about here => http://wp.me/p158HG-Dx and here https://sapphirethroneministries.wordpress.com/2013/12/17/to-dismiss-christ/.

*****

4 – FIRST OCCURRENCE OF MELCHIZEDEK IN SCRIPTURE

The first occurrence of Melchizedek in Scripture is in Genesis Chapter 14. Pay attention, because any time something occurs first in Scripture, it sets precedence:

1 And it came to pass in the days of Amraphel king of Shinar, Arioch king of Ellasar, Chedorlaomer king of Elam, and Tidal king of nations,

2 that they made war with Bera king of Sodom, Birsha king of Gomorrah, Shinab king of Admah, Shemeber king of Zeboiim, and the king of Bela (that is, Zoar).

3 All these joined together in the Valley of Siddim (that is, the Salt Sea).

4 Twelve years they served Chedorlaomer, and in the thirteenth year they rebelled.

5 In the fourteenth year Chedorlaomer and the kings that were with him came and attacked the Rephaim in Ashteroth Karnaim, the Zuzim in Ham, the Emim in Shaveh Kiriathaim,

6 and the Horites in their mountain of Seir, as far as El Paran, which is by the wilderness.

7 Then they turned back and came to En Mishpat (that is, Kadesh), and attacked all the country of the Amalekites, and also the Amorites who dwelt in Hazezon Tamar.

8 And the king of Sodom, the king of Gomorrah, the king of Admah, the king of Zeboiim, and the king of Bela (that is, Zoar) went out and joined together in battle in the Valley of Siddim

9 against Chedorlaomer king of Elam, Tidal king of nations, Amraphel king of Shinar, and Arioch king of Ellasar — four kings against five.

10 Now the Valley of Siddim was full of asphalt pits; and the kings of Sodom and Gomorrah fled; some fell there, and the remainder fled to the mountains.

11 Then they took all the goods of Sodom and Gomorrah, and all their provisions, and went their way.

12 They also took Lot, Abram's brother's son who dwelt in Sodom, and his goods, and departed.

13 Then one who had escaped came and told Abram the Hebrew, for he dwelt by the terebinth trees of Mamre the Amorite, brother of Eshcol and brother of Aner; and they were allies with Abram.

14 Now when Abram heard that his brother was taken captive, he armed his three hundred and eighteen trained servants who were born in his own house, and went in pursuit as far as Dan.

15 He divided his forces against them by night, and he and his servants attacked them and pursued them as far as Hobah, which is north of Damascus.

16 So he brought back all the goods, and also brought back his brother Lot and his goods, as well as the women and the people.

17 And the king of Sodom went out to meet him at the Valley of Shaveh (that is, the King's Valley), after his return from the defeat of Chedorlaomer and the kings who were with him.

18 Then MELCHIZEDEK KING OF SALEM BROUGHT OUT BREAD AND WINE; HE WAS THE PRIEST OF GOD MOST HIGH.

19 And he blessed him and said: "Blessed be Abram of God Most High, Possessor of heaven and earth;

20 And blessed be God Most High, Who has delivered your enemies into your hand." And he gave him a tithe of all.

21 Now the king of Sodom said to Abram, "Give me the persons, and take the goods for yourself."

22 But Abram said to the king of Sodom, "I have raised my hand to the LORD, God Most High, the Possessor of heaven and earth,

23 that I will take nothing, from a thread to a sandal strap, and that I will not take anything that is yours, lest you should say, 'I have made Abram rich'—

24 except only what the young men have eaten, and the portion of the men who went with me: Aner, Eshcol, and Mamre; let them take their portion."

(Genesis 14:1-24 NKJV).

Before Abram could receive the ministry of Melchizedek, he had to first conquer the Babylonian Kings here on earth. Genesis 14 illustrates a kingdom truth in our day. In this Kingdom Day, the seed of Abraham will come out of Babylon. We will temporarily go back into the world (i.e., Egypt); but then we will return to our Promised Land. There we must first dethrone the same Babylonian kings that

Abram did. The Babylonian kings' names indicate that we must overthrow:

- darkness,
- deception,
- savagery,
- mercilessness,
- false positions, and
- producing after the Tree of Knowledge of Good and Evil.

These are practices and mindsets within each one of us – His kings and priests – that need to be crucified. Yeshua was crucified in the place of the skull – Golgotha – and He wore a crown of thorns on His head, which represents the cares of this world and the deceitfulness of riches being crucified. We know that he who believes that Yeshua is the Son of God, and in His death, burial and resurrection overcomes the world. We also know that the Melchizedek Company is made like unto the Son of God, so pay attention when you study Scripture to the phrase "Son of God," because His Royal Priestly Order of Melchizedek will walk in the same manner of the Son of God manifesting the excellencies of His Everlasting Kingdom.

Please do not over-spiritualize the battle to dethrone our own Babylonian kings! The battle to overcome Babylonian mindsets and practices is a very up-close and personal battle where the One New Man in Christ must choose to do what is right in God's eyes alone.

The Jewish Sages identify this Melchizedek as Shem, the righteous son of Noah. Initially, I dismissed Shem being Melchizedek, because I was taught that Melchizedek had some distinct qualities that I had assumed Shem did not have. Most notably, Hebrews 7:3 tells us that Melchizedek had no mother, no father, no beginning of time, and no end of time; and in my limited mindset I reasoned that Shem had all of these because he was a man on this earth.

Consider how Hebrews 7:16 tells us that there is another priest (priesthood) that arises after the power of an endless life. There is a day when those who are continually maturing into the very image of God will forsake our earthly genealogy (i.e., the DNA that comes from our earthly mothers and fathers) and exchange it for a heavenly genealogy of Christ, which is the very DNA of God. This will happen through a crucified life… our being a continual living sacrifice. A person can only be joined to God, if they carry His likeness according to Spirit and Truth, which is His very DNA. Please refer to the three transformative agents always present in the perfection of the Order of Melchizedek, which we go into later in this book. Another possibility to the interpretation of "without genealogy" is the ascended state of how we all were with God before the very foundations of the world.

When the Holy Spirit prompted me to re-examine what I believed, I was amazed at what was revealed. First of all, the Hebrews probably would have kept the best track of their own history. Why was Shem identified with Melchizedek? Just like Nimrod is identified with King Amraphel, so is Shem recognized as Melchizedek. When people are associated with different names, each name signifies a different part of their nature.

Scripture appears to be silent about many facts about Melchizedek when, in fact, there are many keys to unlock the heaven-on-earth reality of the Order of Melchizedek that are hidden and encoded in Scripture, which are now being unveiled by His spirit of revelation and understanding.

In Ian Clayton's *Abraham In the Stars* teaching, he reveals some Jewish history that was thrown out of Christianity when the Emperor Constantine had his way in the fourth century. Ian speaks about how "Shem met Abraham at the beginning of his life. Therefore, we need to understand who Shem was. Shem was one of Noah's sons who built the City of Salem. The city of Salem became a hallowed (holy) city that got trans-dimensionalated into another realm. Shem mentored Abraham about the True City of Zion. That's why Abraham left his mother and father to go to a city whose founder and builder is God, because Shem has shown Abraham the way to the city. Even though Abraham was going to a physical city, there was a spiritual reality he was very aware of."

This is true in life. Every physical reality is always accompanied a spiritual reality. Therefore, when we consider that the battle to overcome Babylonian mindsets and practices is a very up-close and personal battle, please don't leave out an important detail. When Abram fought the Babylonian kings in Genesis 14, Shem's own son – Chedorlaomer, the king of Elam – was leading the opposition. Not only did Shem get the spiritual reality in the battle to overcome Babylonian kings, which even included his own son, Shem celebrated it. Talk about a crucified life!

One other close and personal battle in overcoming Babylonian mindsets and practices has to do with Amraphel the king of Shiner. The Hebrew Sages identify Amraphel as Nimrod – the leader of the tower builders in Babel who led the world rebellion against heaven's Ruler. "Amraphel" is the one whose command brought darkness on the world. In addition to Babel meaning "confusion," its primitive root means to mix. Mixture is the essence of Babylon. NOTE: Much of the mixture in today's "church" is rooted in Nimrod's Babylon and comes to us via Constantine in the fourth century. The Lord's pure and spotless Bride will come out of all of the mixture. By the way, Shem's brother Ham was Nimrod's grandfather.

We can't escape the close and personal battle to overthrow the Babylon's kings in our own life. It is the only way we overcome them.

5 -TIME OF MELCHIZEDEK'S APPEARING

Notice that the time of Melchizedek's first appearing in Scripture was a time of great warfare.

This was a time before the destruction of Sodom and Gomorrah in the days of Abraham and Lot. The Elamite King Chedorlaomer had subdued the local tribes and cities of the Jordan River valley. For twelve years, the people of the Jordan served Chedorlaomer. In the thirteenth year, the Cities of the Plain rebelled against his rule (Genesis 14:4).

According to Jewish history, the revolt started with their refusal to pay tribute to King Chedorlaomer. In response, Chedorlaomer gathered three other northern kings in the fourteenth year to show the might of Elam and to start a campaign against Bera, the king of Sodom. Four other southern kings joined Bera king of Sodom: (1) King Birsta, ruler of Gomorrah (2) King Shemeber, ruler of Zeboiim (3) King Shinab, ruler of Admah, and (4) King (not named) of Bela (Zoar). Therefore, there were four northern kings of the earthly rule against five southern kings fighting for their freedom.

En route, Chedorlaomer's armies and allies plundered the tribes and cities along the way for their provisions. They plundered the Rephaims in Ashteroth Kamaim, the Zuzims in Ham, the Emims in Shaveh Kiriathaim, the Horites in Mount Seir, the Amalekites in Kadesh at En-mishpat, the Amorites in Hazezontamar, and the Canaanites of the Jordan plain. Once Chedorlaomer's northern forces engaged the southern kings, they overwhelmed them by driving them into the tar pits that littered the Siddim Valley (Genesis 14:10). Those who escaped fled to the mountains, including the kings of Sodom and Gomorrah (Genesis 14:10).

Once Chedorlaomer put down the rebellion at the Battle of Siddim, he went to Sodom and Gomorrah to collect booty. Some of the citizens of Sodom and Gomorrah were taken captive, including Abraham's nephew Lot (Genesis 14:12). When Abram received word from one that had escaped, he immediately armed his trained servants. Three hundred and eighteen faith-filled warriors born in Abram's own household (Genesis 14:13-14). Abram and his 318 caught up with Chedorlaomer in the city of Dan, which mean "the judge," They continued to pursue the Elamite forces north of Damascus to Hobah where Abram and one of his divisions slaughtered Chedorlaomer and the kings with him at the King's Valley – Shaveh (Genesis 14:17).

Remember, before Abram got his name changed to Abraham, he had to first conquer FOUR Babylonian kings. The number FOUR is inextricably connected to creation. The Babylonian kings that Abram and all us have to overcome are connected to creation too. Think of the FOUR corners of the earth, the FOUR directions on a compass, the FOUR seasons, and the FOUR rivers that flow from Eden. Think of the FOUR spheres of the earth: geosphere (ground), hydrosphere (water), biosphere (life), and atmosphere (air). Think of the FOUR elements of the earth: earth, air fire, and water. On the FOURTH day of creation, God made the lights in the firmament. The sun was made to rule the day on earth, and the moon was made to rule the night with the stars joining in the nightly display of light, which is the basic demarcation of time. We are literally told that the sun, moon, and stars are *"for signs, and for seasons, and for days, and years" (Genesis 1:14)*. Significantly, the FOURTH commandment is to remember and keep the seventh day sabbath holy (Exodus 20:9-11). The sabbath is connected to creation. It's the day that God ended the work of creation and He rested, as an example to us all.

It's extremely important that conquering four Babylonian kings is connected to the seventh day sabbath. It's also extremely significant that 318 men, plus Abram, conquered the Babylonian kings. When we boil the number "318" bottom to its simplest form, we get $12 = 3 + 1 + 8$. Add 1 to 12, as in adding Abram to the 318 men; and we come up with the number "13." Thirteen is not an unlucky number or superstitious number, as the world has tried to pervert it. Thirteen is the number for love and for Melchizedek.

There are records in the *Dead Sea Scrolls* of the "Songs of the Sabbath Sacrifice." The songs sung in God's Temple on the seventh day Sabbath were sung to Melchizedek. There are 13 Sabbath Songs. We get the picture of a corporate community going through a 13-week cycle where they recite the Sabbath Songs, and are led through a progressive experience. This community gives spirit and life to the heavenly temple until the worshippers experience the holiness of the *Merkabah* (i.e., God's Chariot Throne) and the Sabbath sacrifices conducted by angelic high priests. The intense preoccupation with angelic priest in the "Songs of the Sabbath Sacrifice" suggests that the angelic priests are related to the glorification of the Melchizedek Priesthood. Melchizedek in Genesis Chapter 14 taught Abram all about this.

The Qumran Community, connected to the *Dead Sea Scrolls*, claimed to be the true priests of God. Therefore, their devout hearts keep meticulous track of what a true priest of God was – angelic priests. The angels ascending and descending on the Son of Man in

John 1:51 were both angelic messengers and human messengers who stand before the Throne of the Holy One. They have also been born in the Holy of Holies. These are the ones who have entered the Kingdom of God (John 3:5), and have been commissioned into the Order of Melchizedek who are *"equal to angels and are sons of God, being sons of the resurrection" (Luke 20:36)*.

Resurrection life for the sons of God on earth (i.e., kings and priests of the Order of Melchizedek) is a type of *"theosis."* This *theosis* is a transformation of human being back into our original created state – a divine being made in the image of God (Genesis 1:27). We all need to shift our mindsets about "resurrection" from a post mortem experience to a living and active transformation of God's people into our original "angelic" state. Enoch actually models this reality for us. In 2 Enoch 22, Enoch is transformed into an angel, resurrected, and then sent back to earth. This is our journey back to the future where we are gradually transformed into the very image of God.

NEW DISPENSATION

The time of Melchizedek's appearing is not only during a time of great warfare, but it's a *karios* time of God that happens every two thousand years where there's a global shift in the divine order of earthly things. The promises that have regulated human affairs for the past two thousand years are not going away, but shifting by a quark or two in order to prepare God's people for our coming King. God is in charge of this, and any, shift in the divine order of earthly things; and it affects everything we do and who we are. The kings and priests of the Eternal Order of Melchizedek are literally being made into a new state of being (in Christ). This new state of being will result in the gathering together in one all things in Christ (Ephesians 1:10) – which in a word is ONE(NESS).

The purpose of this divine global shift in earth's administration is to make adjustments, so His resurrected body of believers of the One New Man in Christ and His pure and spotless bridal company can come into their fullness. Another word for administration is "dispensation."

The biblical pattern for each new dispensation as it relates to Melchizedek is first a precious son volunteers to become a worshipful, sacrificial burnt offering; then gradually a new dwelling place for God is built. Know that the Creator of our universe started with something wholly natural, but eventually His divine building pattern will culminate in something entirely spiritual. *"⁴⁶ The spiritual is not first, but the natural; then the spiritual ... ⁴⁹ Just as we have borne the image of the earthly, we will bear the image of the heavenly ... ⁵⁰ flesh and blood can not inherit the Kingdom of God; nor does the perishable inherit the imperishable"* (1 Corinthians 15:46, 49-50 NASB).

The first account of a son volunteering to be a sacrifice is when God asked Abraham to take his only son up Mount Moriah and offer him there as a burnt offering, as a voluntary act of worship (Genesis 22). NOTE: Abraham was 137-years-old, and Isaac was 36-years-old at the time. There were several iterations of God's dwelling place after *"akedah"* (i.e., Abraham sacrifice of Isaac) that were built, with one version overlapping the next:

- Wilderness Tabernacle (Built by Moses) – Portable earthly image that served as a copy and shadow of heavenly things to come (Exodus 25:40; Hebrews 8:5).

- Solomon's Temple.

- Herod's Temple

The next time a precious son volunteers to become a burnt offering is Yeshua. With Yeshua's death, burial, and resurrection, a great slide from the natural toward the supernatural began. Even though there was a new beginning inaugurated at the cross to facilitate a transformation of God's temple, historically, there was a gradual turning so God's people could transition into the new dispensation. The promise of the new dispensation inaugurated at the cross was, and still is, the adoption of sons (i.e., restoration of fellowship). *"⁴ But when the fullness of time had come, God sent forth His Son, born of a woman, born under the law, ⁵ that we might receive the adoption of sons" (Galatians 4:4-5 NIV)*. It's an eternal promise; therefore, it will continue.

Right now, we have a fresh dispensation dawning, which encompasses and expands on everything that has gone before it: *"that in the dispensation of the fullness of time He might gather together in one all things in Christ, both which are in heaven and which are on earth – in Him" (Ephesians 1:10 NIV)*.

It should be another quantum leap in the spiritual direction, which should result in something enveloped by something completely heavenly. Something like: a holy city, the Lamb's wife, the Bride of the Messiah, the New Jerusalem *"coming down from God out of heaven" (Revelation 21:2)*. Something like: the mature HEAD of Christ (Revelation 1:14) spiritually being joined to His mature BODY of believers (Ephesians 4:15-16; 1 Corinthians 12:12-27).

The time of Melchizedek's appearing was a time when God's desire was to raise up ONE MAN to bless the nations of the earth, and this ONE NEW MAN is part of the Order of Melchizedek.

It's extremely significant that the pattern in Scripture is One New Man offers himself as a Burnt Offering, which is connected to ascension, because a Burnt Offering is also called an Elevation Offering. The word "burnt" in Hebrew is *olah*, and it means "going up." The Hebraic roots of the word "offering" communicates "coming near." Therefore, when we sincerely offer ourselves or anything dear to ourselves to the LORD for the purpose of drawing close, we personally go up to meet with the God of mercy.

The Burnt Offering is also called an Elevation Offering, because it raises one's spiritual level. A Burnt Offering was considered to be superior to all others, because it was a completely voluntary sacrifice offered in its entirety by fire to the LORD Himself. The spiritual principle that is still behind the Burnt Offering is: *"Behold, I have come to do Thy will" (Psalms 40:7-7; Hebrews 10:7).* There is a mystery revealed when one breaks down the three Hebrew Letters for "*olah.*" That mystery is that a true *olah* (Burnt Offering) is that which the Shepherd brings forth. We don't get to choose what's get crucified, He does. His fiery refining process is evident when our attitudes and behaviors don't line up with His plumb line – the Word of God. The Great Shepherd of our souls will guide each of us in the best path to become just like Him.

*****

6 – TECHNOLOGY OF COMMUNION

The key to unlocking the Order of Melchizedek is "intimacy with God." Being one with Him and thinking His thoughts.

There is power resonating from the words: "Eat My flesh and drink My blood." Inside communion is the key to eternal life. *"⁸ Though He were a Son, He learned obedience by the things suffered;⁹ and having been perfected, He became the author of eternal salvation to all who obey Him, ¹⁰ called of God as High Priest according to the order of Melchizedek" (Hebrews 5:8-10 KJV).*

Question: Is there a difference between salvation and eternal salvation? The perfection of the sons called of God according to the Order of Melchizedek and them learning obedience through things suffered are huge keys to eternal life. Communion is a catalyst for this.

Through communion, immortality will swallow up mortality. It's key to the restoration of all things. *"¹⁵ In the likeness of Melchizedek, there arises another priest¹⁶ who has come not according to… a fleshly commandment, but according to the POWER OF AN ENDLESS LIFE" (Hebrews 7:15-16 NKJV).*

Hidden within the bread and wine – the body and blood of the Messiah – is the secret to doing the greater works of John 14:12. *"My food is to do the will of Him who sent Me and to finish His work" (John 4:34)*. When Yeshua said, *"For My flesh is true food, and My blood is true drink" (John 6:35)*, He was about to introduce an extremely powerful technology in His Spirit. Had Yeshua (who is our pattern for the Order of Melchizedek) wanted us to take on communion monthly or yearly, He would have used a different concept. In order for our spirit to live and stay strong, we should take communion every day, just like our body needs to eat every day.

The elements of the bread and wine appear the same in the natural, but in the invisible realm the Body and Blood of Yeshua are absolutely there. Our spirit will really drink His Blood, and we will become one with His Body (bone of His bone, flesh of His flesh). Our Promised Land is a supernatural life here on earth where heaven is a tangible reality. The bread and wine cause the supernatural Kingdom of God to descend upon and among us. Our spirit will literally absorb the life of God, and we become blended together little by little until we are totally consumed within Him. Until we are gloriously possessed by Him, literally becoming not only one spirit, but one body (1 Corinthians 6:17; Ephesians 4:4).

When we take daily communion, it requires that we examine our hearts and behaviors. It is through His mystical body (i.e., us) that God governs and brings His Kingdom to earth. Discerning the body correctly (both personally and corporately) is essential to our relationship with the Father. Taking communion every day opens our eyes to that fact that the body of the LORD was broken for us not only on the cross, because of His great love for us, but it remains in a broken state until sin is done away with (broken when sin manifests in the Body of Christ).

So, not only is communion a great tool to infuse eternal life; but it's a vital ingredient in our being free from our body of sin. One of the reasons God hates sin so much is that it blocks our communion with Him. Therefore, He provided a spiritual technology so powerful that it would redeem everything that sin had destroyed. Not only that, but the spiritual technology had to satisfy the cry of His own righteousness and justice, which demands payment for transgression. Only one thing holds this power - communion. This one thing is the love of God that flows from the fountain of redemption through the shed blood of the Lamb.

Please notice that Abram received the bread and wine from Melchizedek just prior to Abram's name being changed to Abraham (Genesis 17:5). The bread of communion is also the bread of heaven – manna. *"He who has an ear, let him hear what the Spirit says to the churches. To him who overcomes I will give some of the hidden manna to eat. And I will give him a white stone, and on the stone a NEW NAME written which no one knows except him who receives it" (Revelation 2:17).* Hidden manna and a white stone with a new name are the overcoming promises to the Church of Pergamum. The one who speaks to the Church of Pergamum has a double-edged sword: *"¹² These things says He who has the sharp two-edged sword: ¹³ I know your works, and where you dwell, where Satan's throne is. And you hold fast to My name…" (Revelation 2:12-13 NKJV).* Please recall that our food is to do the will of Him who sends us – the Father – and to finish the work, just as Yeshua did.

The other church in the Book of Revelation that speaks of "I know your works" is the Church of brotherly love in Philadelphia: *" ⁷And to the angel of the church in Philadelphia write, 'These things says He who is holy, He who is true, 'He who has the key of David, He who opens and no one shuts, and shuts and no one opens'. ⁸ I know your works. See, I have set before you an open door, and no one can shut it; for you have a little strength, have kept My word, and have not denied My name. ⁹ Indeed I will make those of the synagogue of Satan, who say they are Jews and are not, but lie — indeed I will make them come and worship before your feet, and to know that I have loved you. ¹⁰ Because you have kept My command to persevere, I also will keep you from the hour of trial which shall come upon the whole world, to test those who dwell on the earth.* ⁱⁱ *Behold, I am coming quickly! Hold fast what you have, that no one may take your crown.* ¹² *He who overcomes, I will make him a pillar in the temple of My God, and he shall go out no more. I will write on him the name of My God and the name of the city of My God, the New Jerusalem, which comes down out of heaven from My God. And I will write on him My new name.* ¹³ *He who has an ear, let him hear what the Spirit says to the churches."' (Revelation 3:7-13 NKJV).*

We will follow in the steps of faith of Abraham who dethroned the Babylonian kings before he could receive the ministry of Melchizedek. In order to be commissioned by Yeshua Himself into the Highest Order of Melchizedek, we must dethrone the Babylonian practices and mindsets within.

There's a technology in the spiritual dimensions of communion that's a mystery which will transform your life into its fullness. To rightly re-member Christ's Body, we need to daily have a personal transformation, which contributes to a corporate transformation, but we must always start with ourselves.

*****

7 – THE PERFECTION OF THE ORDER OF MELCHIZEDEK

There are components always present in the perfection of the Order of Melchizedek. First, let us look at the concept of "PERFECTION," which is intimately associated with the Order of Melchizedek.

It is not perfectionism! It's all about completion, fulfilling, being made perfect or complete in labor, complete in growth, complete mentally and complete in moral character to a Mature or Full Age Man (i.e., Manifested Son). Melchizedek perfection is about setting out for a definite point or goal – the uttermost – with results in being made into the exact image of Yeshua Ha Machiach (Jesus Christ). I highly suggest that you study the words "perfect" and "perfection" in Scripture.

The Promise of Perfection is eternally connected to:

- Almighty God
- The Son's (Christ's) Cross
- His Sapphire Throne
- Melchizedek Priesthood

Notice that Hebrews 7:11 implies that the Order of Melchizedek is an Order of Perfection: *"¹¹ If therefore PERFECTION were by the Levitical priesthood, … what further need was there that another priest should rise after the Order of Melchizedek, and not after the order of Aaron? ¹² For the priesthood being changed, there is made of necessity a change also in the law"* (Hebrews 7:11-12 KJV).

Both Jeremiah 31:33 and Ezekiel 36:26-27 foretold of the change in the law that came with the change in the priesthood:

- *"But this is the covenant that I will make with the house of Israel after those days says the LORD: I will put My law in their minds, and write it on their hearts; and I will be their God and they shall be My people"* (Jeremiah 31:33; Hebrews 8:10).

- *"²⁶ I will give you a new heart and put a new spirit in you; I will remove from you your heart of stone and give you a heart of flesh. ²⁷ And I will put my Spirit in you and move you to follow my decrees and be careful to keep my laws"* (Ezekiel 36:26-27).

Instead of "the law" (i.e., the commandments of God, being written on stone or paper or any other substance), the law has been put in our minds and written upon our hearts.

One of the most significant foundations of the Order of Melchizedek is the worship-filled rest stance that kings and priests operate out of. The "Melchizedek Section" of the *Dead Sea Scrolls* relates "The Songs of the Sabbath Sacrifice" to Melchizedek. The twelfth song of the cherubim was said to be almost indistinguishable from the wheels of God's Chariot Throne. We are told that the worship was silent, and one cannot physically hear the praise; but it is evident in brass-like flashes of light emerging from the throne. NOTE: These Seventh Day Sabbath Songs include both priestly and princely (royal) praise.

UNDERSTANDING THE ORDER OF MELCHIZEDEK

The Seventh Day Transfiguration of Man is the One New Man in Christ made up of mature and maturing sons. Never forget that His Melchizedek Company is *"made like unto the Son of God" (Hebrews 7:3).*

The concept of "perfection" used in Hebrews 7:11 is unique to Hebrews 7:11. *"If therefore PERFECTION were by the Levitical priesthood ... what further need was there that another priest should rise after the Order of Melchizedek, and not after the order of Aaron?"* (Hebrews 7:11 KJV).

Just as the Order of St. John is an order of chivalry, the Order of Melchizedek is an order of perfection. We can say that because of Hebrews 7:11. Let's take the time to delve into the meaning of the Hebrews 7:11 "perfection" according to *The Strong's Concordance* to lay a vital foundation:

- STRONG's NT:5050 - Greek word τελείωσις *teleiōsis*. (*tel-i-o-sis*). From NT:5448. *Teleiōsis* communicates the **act of completion, verification**, or of **expiation**, absolution :- perfection, performance.

- STRONG's NT:5448 – Greek word *physioo* (*foo-see-o-o*). From NT:5449 in the primary sense of **blowing**; to inflate.

- STRONG's NT:5449 – Greek word *physis* (*foo'-sis*). From NT:5453; **growth** (by **germination** or **expansion**), i.e., by implication - natural production (lineal descent); by extension - a genus or sort; figuratively **native disposition, constitution** or usage: man, mankind, nature, natural.

- STRONG's NT:5453 – Greek word *phyō* (*foo'-o*). A primary verb only used in the implied sense to **germinate** or **grow** (**sprout, produce**) both literally and figuratively. Spring or **spring up**.

Let's dig a little deeper into the *Strong's Concordance* layers of Hebrews 7:11 "perfection" by gazing more intently on the various components of:

[1] *teleiōsis*,

[2] *physioō*,

[3] *physis*, and

[4] *phyō*.

[1] **Teleiōsis** is the unique concept of "perfection" that applies specifically to the Order of Melchizedek in Hebrews 7:11. We begin with the Greek concept of *teleiōsis*, which communicates the act of completion. Completion is the process of completing something as well as the state of being complete. As an adjective, "completion" means having all necessary parts, elements or steps. It means that something has been fully carried out. Something is total, absolute, and full. As a verb, "completion" communicates what the Melchizedek Order of Perfection does. They bring something to an end, especially into a perfected state. Royal priests make things whole or perfect.

Teleiōsis also speaks of verification, which is a state of being verified. To verify something is to confirm in law by oath as well as to establish the truth accuracy, or establish the reality of something. The Order of Melchizedek confirms that *"the law of the LORD is perfect converting the soul" (Psalm 19:7a)*. They establish the truth and accuracy of the Word of God here on earth, as it is in heaven, by demonstrating its reality.

Additionally, *teleiōsis* is of expiation, which speaks of the Order of Melchizedek is a finishing generation. "Expiation" means to put an end to, and to extinguish the guilt incurred by anything, including

The Fall. It means to make amends, or to attain atonement.

[2] *Physioō* – A level deeper into the layers of Hebrews 7:11 "perfection" reveals that *teleiōsis* comes from the Greek word *physioō*. In its primary, *physioō* communicates a sense of blowing. To blow something is to move it with force and speed. It carries the concept of moving or being carried by wind. Think of the violent rushing wind that filled the whole house on Pentecost in Acts 2:2-4. It was a place where a group of believers were seeking Him, as one. Think about how Yeshua stood in the midst of His disciples, and said *"Peace be unto you;" then He blew on them so they could receive the Holy Spirit (John 20:19-23)*. Also, think of us being created a full-blown living soul (Genesis 2:7).

This Greek definition of *physioō* "perfection" comes with a nugget and a warning. First the bad news. The warning is that *physioō* can also means to swell up, puff up, to make proud or haughty. So… we need to guard ourselves from getting puffed up or haughty in our perfection process, especially since we supposed to take on the character of Christ, which is humility. The nugget is that *physioō* carries the concept to make something natural, or to cause a thing to pass into nature. It is connected to the Order of Melchizedek making the kingdoms of this earth, the kingdoms of our God. It is connected to the restoration of all things. The Order of Melchizedek brings heavenly realities into earth. The Lord's Prayer says: *"Your kingdom come. Your will be done on earth, as it is in heaven" (Matthew 6:10)* for good reason.

[3] *Physis* – Another level deeper into the layers of Hebrews 7:11 "perfection" shows us that *physioō* is from the Greek word *physis*. *Physis* is about growth either by germination or expansion. Growth is a stage in the growing process. Increase, expansion, and outgrowth are part of the growing process. Since the Order of Melchizedek is based on an endless life, immortality and resurrection life are two of its fruits (Hebrews 7:16).

The Order of Melchizedek's growth by expansion is intimately connected to the *"expanse"* or the *"firmament in the midst of the waters" (Genesis 1:6)*. Whenever you come into contact with "expanse" or "firmament" in Scripture make a Melchizedek note: *"²² Now over the heads of the living beings there was something like an EXPANSE, like the awesome gleam of crystal (ice), spread out over their heads. ²³ Under the EXPANSE their wings were stretched out straight, one toward the other; each one also had two wings covering its body on the one side and on the other. ²⁴ I also heard the sound of their wings like the sound of abundant waters as they went, like the voice of the Almighty, a sound of tumult like the sound of an army camp; whenever they stood still, they dropped their wings. ²⁵ And there came a voice from above the EXPANSE that was over their heads; whenever they stood still, they dropped their wings. ²⁶ Now above the EXPANSE that was over their heads there was something resembling a throne, like lapis lazuli in appearance; and on that which resembled a throne, high up, was a figure with the appearance of a man" (Ezekiel 1:22-26 NASB)*.

Another dimension of *physis* is lineal descent. The holy royal priesthood lineal descent comes directly from our Pattern Son – Messiah Yeshua. In fact, only God commissions people into His eternal Order of Melchizedek.

Physis is also associated with our native disposition where we are citizens of heaven. The Order of Melchizedek administrates His heavenly Kingdom in such a way that it comes to earth, and it is accomplished through His will being done. These Sons of Righteousness are servants to all of creation through first serving the King of Kings. Their servant hearts are continually set in readiness to literally do what they see the Father doing (John 5:19).

Another native disposition of the Order of Perfection is the distinguishing quality of manifesting the same likeness as Christ Jesus (Messiah Yeshua). Think of the "I AM" statements of Yeshua, and know that the order's attitude of restoration, redemption and restitution flows from the place of being "in Christ." The Order of

Melchizedek is a group of kings and priests marked by one love – the Father's Love – as well as the humility that comes with being progressively made after the Order of Melchizedek. We are a company whose nature is maturing, or has matured, into the very character of Christ through taking up our cross and joining Him (Matthew 16:24; Mark 8:34; Luke 9:23). The Order of Melchizedek is group of individuals who know true communion with the Father, the Son and the Holy Spirit.

Physis speaks of constitution, which is an established law. "Constitution" is also the structure, composition, physical makeup or nature of something as well as the act of establishing, making or setting up. Christ's Crucifixion was, and still is, an act of establishing. In fact, the Greek word for "crucified" is connected to standing, abiding, continuing, establishing, holding up, et cetera. It's not a coincidence that Yeshua the High Priest of the Order of Melchizedek was crucified standing up. We are *"to know nothing ... except Jesus Christ, and Him crucified" (1 Corinthians 2:2)*. Our crucified stance causes us to abide in *alef-tav* (the beginning and end). *John 19:41* says: *"Now in the place where He was crucified there was a garden."* We must become completely Crucified Ones to be in that primordial place and space, as it was in the Garden east of Eden. Just remember that when a person picks up their own cross, they have to drop everything else.

Additionally, *physis* speaks of nature. Nature is the inherent character or basic constitution of a person or thing. It's its essence or disposition. The creative force of the Order of Melchizedek in the universe is the power of the Most High God. Melchizedek – *Malki-Tzedek* (מַלְכִּי־צֶדֶק) – is called the priest of the Most High God (Genesis 14:18). The Most High God is called *El Elyon* (אֵל עֶלְיוֹן) in Hebrew, which means the "Ascended God." Therefore, Melchizedek is the priest of the Ascended God. *Proverbs 30:4* says *"Who has ascended into heaven and descended? Who has gathered the wind in his fists? Who has wrapped the waters in His garment? Who has established all the ends of the earth? What's His Name or His son's name? Surely you know!"*

First and foremost, this verse is speaking about *El Elyon* and His Son – Yeshua Ha Machiach (Jesus Christ) – who is the High Priest forever after the Order of Melchizedek. Please remember that His Son is made up of a Mature Head – Messiah Yeshua – and His Mature Body. The *physis* nature points to man's original natural condition, which is divine due to man being made in God's image (Genesis 1:27). The *physis* nature also points to the genetically controlled qualities of an organism. It's DNA. Recall in the "First Occurrence Melchizedek in Scripture" Chapter that the enigmatic phrase *"without father or mother, without genealogy, without beginning of days or end of life"* can either refer to kings and priests exchanging their human genealogy for their original divine genealogy (carrying God's likeness – His very DNA) or His royal priesthood returning to the ascended state of how we all were with God before the very foundations of the world.

Finally, *physis* reveals what is natural for the Order of Melchizedek. Being filled with the fullness of the Seven Spirits of God is the natural culmination for the Order of Perfection – the Perfect Man – whose soul is filled unto the measure of the stature of the fullness of Christ (Ephesians 4:13). The Seven Spirits of God is equivalent to the seven-fold nature of Christ, which Yeshua walked in here on earth: The Spirit of the Lord, the Spirit of Wisdom, the Spirit of Understanding, the Spirit of Counsel, the Spirit of Might, the Spirit of Knowledge, and the Spirit of the Fear of the Lord (Isaiah 11:1-2). Heaven's will and the Seven Spirits of God enabled Yeshua to fulfill His high and holy calling, and so this will be for those of the Order of Melchizedek and of the Bride. Nita Johnson reveals that the Seven Spirits of God are part of the government of God – His ruling and reigning Kingdom – and they are resident in mature saints who bring increase of His government of peace and righteousness (Isaiah 9:7). Believers who mature into their royal priesthood function will have Christ's Being lived out through them by means of the Seven Spirits of God. These Spirits will promote God's administrated will or government on earth through His end-time Royal Priesthood.

Anyone who wills to do so can have this place in Him. The operation of the Seven Spirits of God enables revelation to flow unabated in the Priesthood of the Order of Melchizedek. This revelation reveals the deep, secret and hidden truths of God's Kingdom, life in the Spirit, and God's plans and purposes found in Christ.

A new kingdom chip is being implanted into the Order of Melchizedek, and we are beginning to see this new breed arise in greater numbers than ever before. In the scrolls of those being born in this Kingdom Day is the inborn nature of the New Living Creature of the Order of Melchizedek who is the One New Man in Christ. These inborn into the Order of Melchizedek will move in stuff that we haven't even had a hint about. They will be like diamonds in the sky. This Diamond Generation will have no competition or jealousy. They will be open, not secretive. They will display the excellencies of our God. There is a tide of the Kingdom of God rushing into upon us all. The water is rising, rising, rising…

The original intent of God at Mount Sinai was to make the people of God a nation of priests. Since the Order of Melchizedek is based on an endless life and there is a both a heavenly and earthly Melchizedek Army, I believe that the Priesthood of Melchizedek is the original and eternal priestly order. Remember Melchizedek, king of Salem, priest of the Most High God predated the Aaronic or Levitical Priesthood: *"[4] Now consider how great this man was, to whom even the patriarch Abraham gave a tenth of the spoils. [5] And indeed those who are of the sons of Levi, who receive the priesthood, have a commandment to receive tithes from the people according to the law, that is, from their brethren, though they have come from the loins of Abraham; [6] but he whose genealogy is not derived from them received tithes from Abraham and blessed him who had the promises. [7] Now beyond all contradiction the lesser is blessed by the better. [8] Here mortal men receive tithes, but there he receives them, of whom it is witnessed that he lives. [9] Even Levi, who receives tithes, paid tithes through Abraham, [10] so to speak, for he was still in the loins of his father when Melchizedek met him. [11] Therefore, if perfection were through the Levitical priesthood (for under it the people received the law), what further need was there that another priest should rise according to the order of Melchizedek, and not be called according to the order of Aaron?" (Hebrews 7:4-11 NKJV).*

The physical and natural existence of the Order of Melchizedek is a holy, priestly nation that will literally cause the kingdoms of this earth to become the kingdoms of our God (Revelation 11:15). YHVH will reign in and through this Melchizedek Company forever with Messiah Yeshua as King of Kings of Kings and High Priest of His royal order of the Queen's Guards. Those in the Order of Melchizedek are not artificial, but totally genuine. They exhibit the higher qualities of the first command: Love the Lord God and love others as yourself. They are begotten of the Father, just like Yeshua His only begotten Son. They have an essential relationship with the Father, the Son and the Holy Spirit. Those made after the fullness Order of Melchizedek will obviously display the Order of Perfection.

[4] *Phyō* – Last, but not least when we dig into the deepest layer of Hebrews 7:11 "perfection," we understand that *physis* is from the Greek word *phyō*. *Phyō* is a primary verb, which only implies germination or growth. It's a sprout or actual produce both literally and figuratively. Think about spring or spring up. Isaiah 44:1-6 speaks about pouring out water on him who is thirsty and God's Spirit on Jacob and his descendants. They will spring up.

FIRST OCCURRENCE OF "PERFECTION"

Notice that the first occurrence of the word "perfection" in Scripture is Job 11:7. *"⁷ Can thou by searching find out God? Can thou find out the Almighty unto PERFECTION? ⁸It is as high as heaven; what can thou do? Deeper than hell; what can thou know?" (Job 11:7-8 KJV).* Notice how Job 11:7 says *"find out the Almighty unto perfection,"* which highlights the eternal connections to the Promise of Perfection: Almighty God, the Son's (Christ's) Cross, His Sapphire Throne, and the Priesthood of Melchizedek.

This time "perfection" is the Hebrew word *takliyth* (pronounced *tak-leeth'*). It's all about completion. By implication, it's speaking about an extremity, like an end or to end. Its primitive root *kaw-law'* adds to our understanding words like: accomplish, determine, destroy, be done, finish, fulfill, bring to pass, wholly reap, make clean, etc.

The Ancient Hebrew Word Picture (pictograph) for *tak-leeth'* perfection tells us that perfection of the Almighty is made manifest in, to, and through us, as we join together with the Lamb in the midst of the throne through the blood of the everlasting covenant. This everlasting blood covenant urges us back to the future through Jesus Christ our great shepherd who was the Lamb slain before the foundation of the world, and makes us perfect in every good work to do His will, which speaks of His Kingdom and opens us up to its abundant life and action. (Revelation 7:17; Hebrews 13:20-21)

Please check out the *Place of Sapphire* book for more on *tak-leeth'* perfection.

The Order of Melchizedek alive on earth in this Kingdom Day is a finishing generation. As we have seen, they are an Order of Perfection. This perfection of Almighty God is made manifest, as we join together with the Lamb in the midst of the throne through the blood of the everlasting covenant, which urges us back to the future through Jesus Christ - the Lamb slain before the foundation of the world. He is the Good Shepherd that makes us perfect in every good work to do God's will. The Order of Perfection, which is His Melchizedek Army, speaks of His Kingdom and opens people and things up to its abundant life and action.

THREE COMPONENTS ALWAYS PRESENT IN THE PERFECTION OF THE ORDER OF MELCHIZEDEK

There are three components always present in the perfection of the Order of Melchizedek:

[1] Daily Communion,

[2] Daily Crucifixion, and

[3] Daily Bread.

DAILY COMMUNION

In the *Blazing New Wine od Hanukkah* book, there's a chapter called "DNA Restoration of Christ's Body." Within that chapter, we emphasize that the Blood and Body of Yeshua is the reality of Daily Communion: *"[53] Then Jesus said to them, "Most assuredly, I say to you, unless you eat the flesh of the Son of Man and drink His blood, you have no life in you. [54] Whoever eats My flesh and drinks My blood has eternal life, and I will raise him up at the last day. [55] For My flesh is food indeed, and My blood is drink indeed. [56] He who eats My flesh and drinks My blood abides in Me, and I in him"* (John 6:53-56 NKJV).

Why did Yeshua say in 1 Corinthians 11:24-25: Do this in remembrance of Me? The Order of Melchizedek's goal is to bear the record of the testimony of God's DNA in one's body. "Taking communion" or as I like to say it "taking on common union" is doing what the High Priest of the Order of Melchizedek did.

When a person gets a bone marrow transplant, the DNA in their blood is different than the DNA of their external skin. To change the record of our testimony to become the very DNA of God, daily communion causes the record in the marrow of our bones to change. Yeshua is speaking once again to His Beloved: *"Bone of my bones, and flesh of my flesh"* (Genesis 2:23 KJV).

Through communion, our bones start producing the correct record in our blood first. Then as we make the right choices, our body gets conformed into His image, which was first born in our blood. So, as each one of us rightly examine ourselves, we become more and more one with Christ and His Body (1 Corinthians 11:28). This process allows an ever-brightening arc of His Presence to form between your blood and your body until its outward expression of an inward reality manifests in shining pure white light. The blood and body of Yeshua is what enables the kings and priest of the Order of Melchizedek to return to our primordial Living Beings of Light State.

We, as a mature body of believers, can only be joined to the Mature Head Jesus Christ if we carry His likeness and His DNA. The bread and wine cause His Supernatural Kingdom to descend upon and among us. Our spirit literally absorbs the life of God as we partake communion, and little by little we become blended together until we are totally consumed within Him and possessed by Him. That word "joined" comes from the same word for when a man and woman become intimate with one another.

Please see the previous chapter entitled "Technology of Communion" for information about communion.

DAILY CRUCIFIXION

Daily Crucifixion is about the cross being applied to our flesh, so we can join Him here on earth in the finished work of the cross (Matthew 16:24-26). Conveniently, crucifixion is included in daily communion, because it requires us to examine our hearts and behaviors according to perfect kindness and love; and then, confess and repent of anything that does not align with His plumb line.

Once our bones produce His record in our blood, we must "rightly examine ourselves" to be conformed into His image in our bodies. We have to offer up ourselves daily as a living sacrifice to burn up our sin nature (i.e., flesh), specifically as a burnt offering.

Moving unto perfection is a crucifixion process (Hebrews 6:1). The wisdom of God insists on our daily permission to crucify our sin nature. He only completes the work of co-crucifixion with Christ with our approval (Galatians 2:20). At some point, I believe we will divinely transcend the time element in all this – divinely accelerate and divinely transform – but my guess is that the amount and degree that we accelerate and transform will depend on our daily crucifixion choices and process. Great grace!!! We can catch up in a moment; but never let that be your excuse to not to get on His altar and deal with your flesh/sin nature, because it can become a habit where a person can become stunted in one's growth. Too many Christians over spiritualize the crucifixion process. I hear things like: We just need to see the ascended reality and go there. Yes! Yes, we need to see ascended reality to become it, but we also need to get on His altar, as directed by the Great Shepherd, so His coals of love can burn up everything that hinders us from getting there!

DAILY BREAD

Daily Bread super charges daily communion and daily crucifixion. Daily Bread is the Word of God. Specifically, it is the Word of Righteousness mentioned in Hebrews 5:13, because the Order of Melchizedek can literally be translated as THE WORD OF THE KING OF RIGHTEOUSNESS, which is the frequency that a Bridal Heart is aiming at.

The Bride will resonate at the same frequency as the Bridegroom. One of Yeshua's names is the Word of God (Revelation 19:13).

We are also told *"¹ In the beginning was the Word, and the Word was with God, and the Word was God... ¹⁴ And the Word was made flesh, and dwelt among us, (and we beheld His glory, the glory as of the only begotten of the Father) full of grace and truth"* (John 1:1,14 KJV).

*****

8 – COMMON UNION

As we progressively learn about Melchizedek, we can look back and progressively gain more insight into any revelation knowledge shared. For instance, these three Melchizedek Components – communion, crucifixion (cross), and bread (the Word of God) – were revealed to me through the first Corporate Ascension I had with of a group called *Corporate One North*. We met almost every week for four years. Together, we ascended and descended on the Son of Man (by the price He paid on the cross – the Blood of the Lamb) by His Spirit through the Revelation 4:1 Door to go to the place of the Father. For two-and-a-half years, we only reported what we saw, heard, or perceived in the Spirit to learn heaven's language and the new rhythms of the Spirit. The last year and a half the LORD allowed us to process the ascension, as we went along. When I say, "process the ascension," I mean add scriptures, science or anything else that the Spirit prompts to help us interpret what the Spirit of the Living God is saying. By the way, we always tried to stay together with the oneness element being a constant during all our Group Ascensions. Through this I was shown that we operated as a wing of His Melchizedek Army flying by the Spirit with one another – a New Living Creature of the One New Man in the Messiah with Bridal overtones.

Please allow me to share the scribed notes from that first *Corporate One North* Group Ascension, which we entitled "Common Union – Communion." Please choose to enter in by the Spirit with this heavenly report:

The first thing we saw in the Spirit was some eagles with fire on the outer tips of their wings who were crying: "Prepare the way of the Lord." It was a Company of Eagles each carrying a New Creature Prototype in a bubble with a horse underneath it. When the bubble popped, the New Creation rested atop a horse.

We then saw a giant arrow that looked like a gigantic javelin that hit the bull's eye of a target. This giant arrow had similar fiery feathers to it, as the eagles did. We all gathered around the huge arrow. The eagles gathered around too with the tips of their wings touching.

Surrounding us was a great cloud of witnesses. Yeshua was right in the middle of the bull's eye. He put his robe around us all, after He had personally greeted each one of us. He makes us ONE in His robe of righteousness.

We then saw a red stepping stone floating in the air. We move forward, as One, under His robe in the direction of the Red Stone. It appeared to be a very large gem. As we stood with Him on this Red Stone, there were light rays bursting forth in all directions, as the red gemstone glowed and pulsated. It felt alive. We reached down to the stone and put some of this multifaceted jewel of wisdom in our hand. We felt the red substance go down and radiate light after we ate it.

This Red Rock was like a knife that started cutting on the inside. The RED reminded us of the Blood of Christ – the crucifixion. We saw a cross in Yeshua's hand that He used like a sword to cut away parts of us that are not of the knowledge of Him. Yeshua said: "May the Spirit of the Cross be on you." We see the Lord as fierce, but not angry. He's zealous. We hear Him say: "Damn to the flesh! Damn to the flesh! Damn to the flesh!"

We see His hair all messed up and it's like He cleansed out His Temple. Then we hear Him say: Not by might, nor by power, but by My Spirit, says the Lord." We ate the red substance. It was like taking communion. This was our common union. After we ate common-union with Him, our weight on the red stone increased exponentially, which caused the red gemstone to become buoyant.

*****

UNDERSTANDING THE ORDER OF MELCHIZEDEK

Book 2

Practical Keys to Unlocking Melchizedek

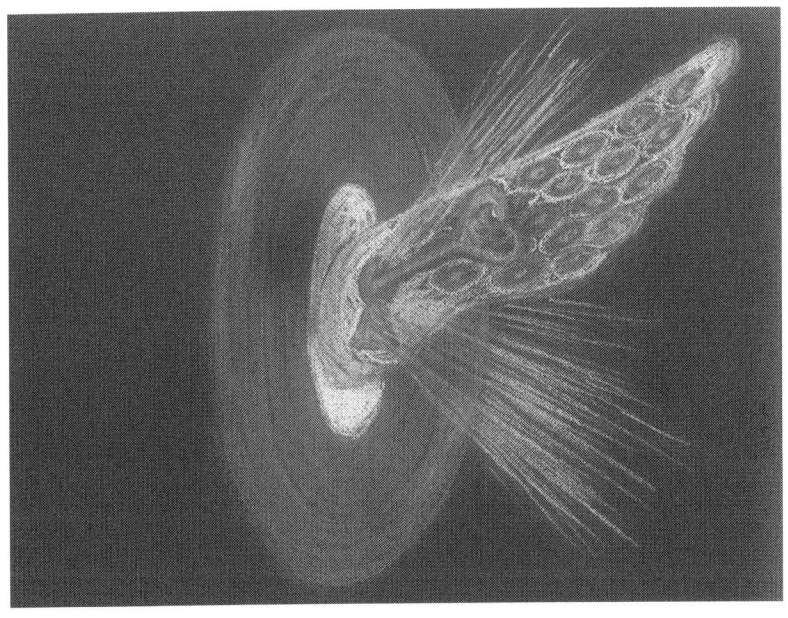

Cover Art: "Unlocking Melchizedek's Glory" by Robin Main

© September 7, 2014. All Rights Reserved

Text Copyright © 2014 Robin Main. All Rights Reserved

1 – INTRODUCTION

This book is a great way to be introduced to understanding the Order of Melchizedek in general. Within, we will visit the first Melchizedek mentioned in Scripture, understand the *karios* times that God raises up the Order of Melchizedek, necessary practices for this order of kings and priest as well as a few heavenly works on earth that will be birthed through His royal priesthood.

In Hebrew, "Melchizedek" means King of Righteousness. Let's emphasize up front that Yeshua Ha Machiah (Jesus Christ) is the only High Priest of the Order of Melchizedek (Hebrews 2:17; 4:14-15; 5:1,5,10; 6;20; 7:26; 8:1; 9:11; 10:21). We also find in Scripture two other people specifically associated with the Order of Melchizedek. We have Melchizedek mentioned in *Genesis 14:18: "And Melchizedek king of Salem brought forth bread and wine: and he was the priest of the Most High God."* The first four chapters of this book goes more into these details. We also have King David associated with the Order of Melchizedek: *"The LORD hath sworn, and will not repent, Thou art a priest for ever after the Order of Melchizedek" (Psalm 110:4 KJV)*. King David had a lot to say about Melchizedek, and how this order operates; but it is not seen in the plain sense interpretation of Scripture. The Spirit of the Living God will illuminate how the Tabernacle of David reveals how the wings of God's End-Time Melchizedek Army flies in another book.

"Melchizedek" is more of a title than a name for the sons of the Living God. When Scripture says that Yeshua has been *"called of God a High Priest after the Order of Melchizedek" (Hebrews 5:10)*, a group of people united in a formal way under the banner of the "Order of Melchizedek" is implied. Recall that groups like the Order of Saint John may not be very familiar to many of us in our day, but various religious orders where people have been required to take solemn vows have existed at least since the days of Genesis 14. These have been communities under a religious rule. In Genesis 14's case, it was the King of Righteousness's rule over Salem, which historians say was the predecessor of Jerusalem. More precisely, I believe that it was some sort of prototype for the New Jerusalem. This ancient hallowed city ruled by the King of Righteousness who was also a priest of the Most High God was in many ways not of this earth. That was why Abraham *"looked for a city which hath foundations, whose builder and maker is God" (Hebrews 11:10 KJV)*.

Just note that wherever we find the term "kings and priests" in the Word of God, it's connected to the first occurrence of "Melchizedek," because fundamentally Scripture tells us that the Genesis 14 Melchizedek was both a priest and king. As kings we rule, and as priests we stand in the courts of heaven as part of the Council of the Lord.

In the book where we are told that everyone who reads it and hears it are blessed, there are two direct references to the term "kings and priests":

> [1] *"⁴ Grace to you and peace from Him who is and who was and who is to come, and from the seven Spirits who are before His throne, ⁵ and from Jesus Christ, the faithful witness, the firstborn from the dead, and the ruler over the kings of the*

earth. To Him who loved us and washed us from our sins in His own blood,⁶ and HAS MADE US KINGS AND PRIESTS TO HIS GOD AND FATHER, to Him be glory and dominion forever and ever. Amen" (Revelation 1:4-6 NKJV).

[2] *"⁵ But one of the elders said to me, 'Do not weep. Behold, the Lion of the tribe of Judah, the Root of David, has prevailed to open the scroll and to loose its seven seals.' ⁶ And I looked, and behold, in the midst of the throne and of the four living creatures, and in the midst of the elders, stood a Lamb as though it had been slain, having seven horns and seven eyes, which are the seven Spirits of God sent out into all the earth. ⁷ Then He came and took the scroll out of the right hand of Him who sat on the throne. ⁸ Now when He had taken the scroll, the four living creatures and the twenty-four elders fell down before the Lamb, each having a harp, and golden bowls full of incense, which are the prayers of the saints. ⁹ And they sang a new song, saying: 'You are worthy to take the scroll, And to open its seals; For You were slain, And have redeemed us to God by Your blood Out of every tribe and tongue and people and nation, ¹⁰ And have MADE US KINGS AND PRIESTS TO OUR GOD; AND WE SHALL REIGN ON THE EARTH'" (Revelation 5:5-10 NKJV).*

Revelation 5 is a key passage to understanding the Lion of the Tribe of Judah's Order of Melchizedek, and how it is manifesting in our day. Notice that in Revelation 5:9-10, the four living creatures and twenty-four elders declare three things, when they fall prostrate before the Lamb, which connects humans to the ancient Order of Melchizedek:

[1] You have redeemed us to God by Your blood.

[2] You have made us kings and priests to our God.

[3] And we shall reign on the earth.

For more information on the human element to the Living Creature, please refer to the *Taking on Common Union* and the *Formation of the New Living Creature* books. This information is also available in the first 25 minutes of the *Melchizedek Arising 2 – Formation of New Living Creature YouTube* video at https://www.youtube.com/watch?v=1BElDZaaFqo. Know that when we talk about the Order of Melchizedek, we are actually focusing on the Living Creature of Ezekiel 1 and the Cherubim of Ezekiel 10 fame as well.

Just so you know, there is not one verse that shows where His people enter the Order of Melchizedek. We must take a common sense and holistic approach to understand this concept. I got the revelation for this concept when I asked Abba: "When are people initially commissioned into the Order of Melchizedek?" He told me a one-liner: "When they enter the Kingdom of God." This is such a significant concept. Let's revisit it:

- *"Assuredly, I say to you, whoever does not RECEIVE THE KINGDOM OF GOD AS A LITTLE CHILD will by no means enter it" (Mark 10:15 NKJV).*

- *"And the disciples were astonished at His words. But Jesus answered again and said to them, "Children, HOW HARD IT IS FOR THOSE WHO TRUST IN RICHES TO ENTER THE KINGDOM OF GOD!" (Mark 10:24 NKJV).*

- *"Jesus answered, 'Most assuredly, I say to you, UNLESS ONE IS BORN OF WATER AND THE SPIRIT, HE CANNOT ENTER THE KINGDOM OF GOD" (John 3:5 NKJV).*

- *"Strengthening the souls of the disciples, exhorting them to continue in the faith, and saying, 'We must THROUGH MANY TRIBULATIONS ENTER THE KINGDOM OF GOD" (Acts 14:22 NKJV).*

This totally makes sense, because maturing sons of the Living God are being made kings. In order to be made kings, they first have to enter the Kingdom of God. Yeshua's sacrifice on the cross was the once-for-all perfect sacrifice that makes a way for whosoever wills to have access to many heavenly realities. Once we accept the gift of salvation, it takes persistence on our part and focus on the Author and Perfecter of our faith to join Him in the heavenly work here on earth to become just like Him. As we move unto perfection (become a mature son of God), we are learning to be His kings and priests.

Notice that *Revelation 1:6* says *"And has made us kings and priests unto God and His Father." Revelation 5:10* also repeats: *"And has made us unto our God kings and priests, and we shall reign on the earth."* That phrase "has made us" speaks of a progressive work where people endeavor to make our heavenly position our earthly condition.

The particular segment of God's family that are referred as His royal priesthood has made the first step of entering the Kingdom of God according to the requirements in His Word (John 3:5, 1 Peter 2:9) with the goal of manifesting the fullness of being made kings and priests to God here on earth, as it is in heaven.

<u>Side Note</u> – You and I know people who have gotten saved by grace through faith (Ephesians 2:8-9) who never move on from that initial step. Yes. These people are part of His family when they accept His gift of salvation, but those who are part of the Order of

Melchizedek have chosen to move beyond the entryway state of salvation where they simply "see the Kingdom of God" (John 3:3).

Know that the actions of those in the Order of Melchizedek will speak volumes. Just like Abraham, our completed faith or perfected faith will be revealed (James 2:20-23).

Stay tuned because we will see how the fullness of the Order of Melchizedek are generals in His Melchizedek Army who have been personally commissioned by the High Priest of the Order of Melchizedek Himself. These are the ones who are destined to literally inherit the Kingdom of God (1 Corinthians 15:50). These are the ones who keep the faith of Jesus and the commandments of God (Revelation 14:12), specifically not doing the works of the flesh (Galatians 5:19-21; 1 Corinthians 6:9-10).

Remember Yeshua is called the Prince of Peace (Isaiah 9:6). He is also the High Priest of the Order of Melchizedek. Melchizedek is also called the King of Peace in Hebrews 7:2 Behold a mystery that my mentor taught me. His generals in the Order of Melchizedek will have crowned the Prince of Peace as their King of Peace. This is literally the New Creature who are Crucified Ones that walk according to His rule with peace literally being on them: *"¹⁵ For IN CHRIST JESUS ... AVAILETH ... A NEW CREATURE. ¹⁶ And as many as WALK ACCORDING TO THIS RULE, PEACE BE ON THEM, and mercy, and upon the Israel of God" (Galatians 6:15-16 _{KJV})*.

*****

2 – OVERCOMING BABYLONIAN KINGS

Recall that before Abram could receive the ministry of Melchizedek in Genesis 14, he had to first conquer some Babylonian Kings.

Abram's journey in Genesis 14 illustrates a kingdom truth in our day. In this Kingdom Day, God's people will come out of Babylon. We will temporarily go back into the world (i.e., Egypt), but then we will return to our Promised Land. There we must first conquer the rulership of the Babylonian practices and mindsets in our own lives before we can receive the ministry of Melchizedek. We must dethrone the same Babylonian kings that Abram did.

The Babylonian kings' names indicate that we must overthrow darkness, deception, savagery, mercilessness, false positions, and producing after the Tree of Knowledge of Good and Evil. * These are the mindsets within each one of us – His kings and priests – that need to be crucified.

Please remember that Yeshua was crucified in the place of the skull – Golgotha – and He wore a crown of thorns on His head, which represents the cares of this world and the deceitfulness of riches being crucified. We know that he who believes that Yeshua is the Son of God, and in His death, burial and resurrection overcomes the world. We also know that the Melchizedek Company is made like unto the Son of God, so pay attention when you study Scripture to the phrase "Son of God," because His Royal Priestly Order of Melchizedek will walk in the same manner of the Son of God manifesting the excellencies of His Everlasting Kingdom.

* Genesis 14:1 – Amraphel king of Shinar, Arioch king of Ellasar, Chedorlaomer king of Elam, and Tidal king of Goiim.

REFERENCES: Genesis 14; Matthew 13:22; 27:33; Hebrews 7:3; 1 John 2:6; 5:5.

*****

3 – THE ORIGINAL MELCHIZEDEK

Once Abram victoriously conquered the Babylonian Kings in Genesis 14, the King of Sodom went out to meet him at the Kings' Valley (the valley of *Shaveh*). He then escorted Abram to the city of Salem, i.e. ancient Jerusalem, where they were met by its king – Melchizedek.

The Jewish Sages identify this Melchizedek as Shem, the righteous son of Noah. Initially, I dismissed Shem being Melchizedek, because I was taught that Melchizedek had some distinct qualities that I had assumed Shem did not have. Most notably, Hebrews 7:3 tells us that Melchizedek had no mother, no father, no beginning of time, and no end of time; and in my limited mindset I reasoned that Shem had all of these because he was a man on this earth. Note: The basis of the priesthood of Melchizedek is everlasting life (Hebrews 7:16).

When the Holy Spirit prompted me to reexamine what I believed, I was amazed at what was revealed. First of all, the Hebrews probably would have kept the best track of their own history. Why was Shem identified with Melchizedek? Just like Nimrod is identified with King Amraphel, so is Shem recognized as Melchizedek. When people are associated with different names, each name signifies a different part of their nature. "Melchizedek" is more of a title than a name for people created in God's image. Understand that there is both an earthly and heavenly dimension to it.

Scripture appears to be silent about many facts about Melchizedek when, in fact, there are many keys to unlock the heaven-on-earth reality of the Order of Melchizedek that are hidden and encoded in Scripture, which are now being unveiled by His spirit of revelation and understanding.

Please note that Yeshua is not Melchizedek, but the High Priest of the Order of Melchizedek. How do I know this? I had a third heaven experience with both Yeshua and Melchizedek on January 19, 2012. As I was preparing for time of deliverance for my pastor who had an Assignment of Death against him, I was soaking in His Presence in a bubbling eddy of the River of Life when all of sudden Yeshua pulled me down to the bottom. There He opened a golden door. We entered this long hallway with unusual portraits of military personnel on the wall. A regal gentleman came up to us. He had on a golden breastplate of the priesthood of the Order of Melchizedek with triple concentric circles. I saw the label "General," as a nameplate on the upper left side of his golden breastplate and it had five stars under it. Yeshua personally introduced me to His highest general of the Melchizedek Order – Shem. He was extremely handsome and eternally young, yet his hair had a touch of gray, as a symbol of his wisdom. Yeshua, Shem and I talked very casually for a while when Yeshua announced that they were both going to commission me into the Order of Melchizedek. They both placed a golden triple concentric circle gem-encrusted breastplate on me. It was just like Shem's, except under the nameplate "General" was one star. Then Yeshua placed His hand on my heart and Shem placed his hand over Yeshua's hand to impart to me and commission me into the Eternal Royal Order of Melchizedek. Already overwhelmed at this wonderful surprise, Yeshua started giving me other gifts, including a golden shepherd's staff.

Please note a couple things. The purpose of the Order of Melchizedek is to minister to God, and primarily flows from heaven to earth out of that reality. Only the King of Kings Himself can commission those in this royal priesthood, which is a military order. When we enter the kingdom by being born (baptized) by the Spirit, we are initially commissioned as a royal priest. At the "general" level, Yeshua personally comes to a person to commission them due to the weightiness of this kingdom honor. Yeshua is the pattern in the Order of Melchizedek, because Melchizedek is made like unto the Son of God (Hebrews 7:3). Due to the priesthood of Melchizedek being based on everlasting life, it is the only legal voice in the universe (besides God Himself) that can overcome an Assignment of Death. And even then, it is God within them which enables His kings and priests to do the work. By the way, an Assignment of Death is when a spirit of death has been specifically tasked to carry out its function. Once an Assignment of Death is released, it will manifest in a person's death if not nullified.

ASSIGNMENT OF DEATH

I am being prompted to share my experience of overcoming an Assignment of Death, as a king and priest of the Most High God and as a commissioned general of the Melchizedek Army. This section will be unique to *Understanding the Order of Melchizedek* compilation of books. The following are my scribed notes for our January 19, 2012 setting the captives free ascension deliverance session:

Since the time was limited for this handpicked group, the mission was critical (life and death), and it was our first time experiencing this sort of thing, Yeshua took me to His back office in His library in heaven and rolled out a scroll. He gave me the following instructions to bring understanding and get the group on the same page.

Yeshua told me that the bottom-line for what we are dealing with is that when a religious spirit combines with a martyrdom syndrome, it is almost impossible for that person to be delivered from the deception that he is "suffering for the gospel." Any rejection or correction received from others at this point is perceived as the price he must pay "to stand for the truth." This wacked out and warped perspective drives this person even further from the truth and any possible correction. How do you speak to a deaf man? *"For nothing is impossible with God" (Luke 1:37)*. This martyr syndrome can be a manifestation of the spirit of suicide. Galatians 2:20 tells us that we are "crucified with Christ" according to His ways and His cross. When we deny ourselves, take up our cross, and follow Him (Matthew 16:24), we need to understand that our cross is His cross. Self-crucifixion is part of the Babylonian Kingdom of Self, which is also called self-abasement. It is earthly, sensual and demonic, like selfish ambition and jealousy (James 3:15-16). The point of the cross is the resurrection, not the grave. We must always choose the Way and the Truth and the Life, even if we are on the way out. Choose Yeshua. Never choose death! Never! It's not of the Kingdom of God!

It is a deadly delusion to believe that holding onto a vision from God is equivalent to holding unto God Himself. This is especially so if that vision or work for God has unconsciously become a personal sacrifice (cross) that's being used to gain God's approval or His love. If that vision/work is judged by passing under God's rod and found wanting, the person bound with a religious spirit/martyrdom syndrome who is holding onto that work dies with it.

We want all works of the flesh to die in you, in me and everyone, so that we can walk according to His Spirit. However, we don't want the people to die with them. Three witnesses have confirmed that there's an "Assignment of Death" on my pastor's life. An Assignment of Death will manifest in a person's death if it's not completely nullified.

In February 2002, I had my own up-close and personal encounter with an Assignment with Death. Just prior, I had been warned that I was going to have a close encounter with death and to take it seriously. Coincidentally, I had a physical exam a few days later and my left arm was aching. The physician assistant checked me out, and simply gave me the warning to immediately go to the emergency room if my symptoms got worse. A few days later, I checked myself into the emergency room and got diagnosed with all the symptoms of a heart attack. I had called a spiritually-attuned friend to meet me there. She was sitting next to me once the doctors put an oxygen mask on me after the diagnosis. As soon as the doctor left the room, I asked her what she was getting. She told me that all she got was I was to come out of all agreement with death. I told her that I thought I had, but oh well. Sure. What did I have to lose? As I sincerely and wholeheartedly came out of all agreement with death, because my life literally depended on it, my friend saw a Spirit of Death be released from taking my breath away. Immediately, I began to improve and confound the doctors. They checked me into the cardiac unit where they almost killed me. There, I tried to cover everyone I knew, so they would not be the recipient of that Spirit of Death. Somehow, I knew the Spirit of Death was released from its death assignment on me, but it was still looking for a place to fulfill its assignment. I tried to cover everyone I knew. After I was released from the hospital the next day, I was home with my family humbled, grateful, and tired. I opened the newspaper to find in the obituaries my physician assistant's husband. As I was struck with horror and sadness while reading about their six-year-old twins, I cried out to God: "Why didn't you tell me!" I had forgotten to cover my doctor and physician assistant. God told me that my physician assistant's husband had agreement with death, else that Spirit of Death could not have fulfilled its assignment. He also instructed me that if an Assignment of Death is not completely nullified, it will manifest in someone's death.

From this extremely hard lesson, I will never forget that an Assignment of Death has to be nullified. So, when we received revelation that my pastor had an Assignment of Death, I knew what we needed to do. We just didn't know how, so we sought the El Shaddai in the matter and followed His lead. He gave me four specific people that needed to be there. Two of them had to leave early, so the Lord led us to have a total of six people participate in this particular Deliverance Group Ascension. Unbeknownst to me at the time, that's the Living Creature number in Ezekiel 1.

We blew the shofar to start the Deliverance Group Ascension to announce to the gates of hell that we were coming and to also prepare ourselves. We first worshipped El Shaddai and took communion.

I am feeling led to share this Setting the Captives Free Ascension as it came to us. During the Deliverance Group Ascension, we saw a shepherd seated with a wooden shepherd's rod on His right side. It's the Great Shepherd in the midst of the throne (Revelation 7:17). We saw an ocean on one side and the gates of hell that won't prevail against the church on the other side.

There was a morning mist coming off the right side of the gates of hell; then there was an expanse of land to the Lord's left. There were people on the land. It was us. We were facing the gates of hell. We were given some type of huge wings that are muscular and substantial, not merely feathery. We test our wings as a group. These wings are the wings of our heart that move accordingly. We are a wing of the end-time Melchizedek Army flying by the Spirit with one another.

We ask the Lord, "What do you want to do?" Yeshua points to the gates of hell. We see come type of swirling, bright light in the shape of a laurel wreath crown, but we know that it's a circle on its side. The lower part of the "wreath" revolves counterclockwise, because we are about to undo what has been done. We hear a whining sound mixed with stringed-instruments. Then two gigantic wings shoot out of the sides of this "thing," like a wall. There's a magnetism in the wheel that's drawing us. It's leading us, because the spirit of the Living Creature was in the wheels (Ezekiel 1:20-21). These humongous wings are at least fifty times the size of the gates of hell. These wings are part of a heavenly battering ram connected to God's heart.

We see an old-fashioned padlock on the gates with hordes behind it. We ask the Lord, "Do you have any weapons for us today?" I was reminded of several weapons I was given that day once I sank down to the bottom of the River of Life and was brought through a golden door. We all stood up and we all received a large golden shepherd's staff/rod in our right hand that can only be used corporately according to the Father's heart. We also received a cloaking garment in our left hand, which we were directed to throw over our right shoulder.

We were then instructed to put up both arms to receive the golden breastplate of Melchizedek with a triple concentric circles insignia embossed on the front. In the most center circle of Melchizedek's emblem was a white-faceted stone that represents a pure heart. In the middle circle was a hollowed out red-faceted precious stone, which was cut out to leave room for the white stone. This red stone represents Christ's Blood. The Outermost and largest circle was a blue-faceted stone, which represents the Sapphire Throne of the All-Consuming Fire.

Then, we were instructed to lift up our heads and open our mouths to receive a heavenly drop of Christ's Blood. This one drop of blood contained all of the Word of God. The final equipment needed was a golden belt with a golden globe in the middle of it, which enables us to go anywhere on earth. It never comes off. It's a belt of truth.

We see that Yeshua is in two places at once. He is seated, and he is standing by us. Jesus approached each one of us and asked us: "Are you willing?" We respond "Yes!" in unison. Then, Yeshua gives each of us one word: truth, magistrate (a judge), dancer, life, dance, and servant.

We smell a strong sweetness in the air, like a honeysuckle or a honeycomb. We know that this fragrance is a spirit of unity that's a blanket over us.

We can see both sides: the heavenly and the demonic. The demonic turn into a bunch of tribal crazies. We see demonic hordes pounding their spears on the ground loud and in unison. It was almost funny when we look at the huge swirling symbol of victory with humongous wings that's an overwhelming wall. This heavenly battering ram with wings and all of us having wings are both keys of the kingdom for the gates of hell to not overpower Christ's Church: "*[18] Upon this rock I will build My church; and the gates of Hades will not overpower it. [19] I will give you the keys of the kingdom of heaven; and whatever you bind on earth shall be bound in heaven, and whatever you loose on earth shall have been loosed in heaven*" (Matthew 16:18b-19 NASB).

Jesus takes His shepherd's staff and signals us to move forward to the gates. The whirling sound of the heavenly battering ram gets more intense and the contraption goes faster. Sparks begin to fly and starts to ignite. It becomes a ball of fire! It's the All-Consuming Fire! It dissolves the gates of hell. The little demons in the front row are melting. There are bigger demons behind the little ones.

Jesus motions us to advance behind the heavenly winged battering ram. We hear that we are to go to a graveyard, because they have already made a memorial.

We see ourselves in the Pastor's Graveyard. There are mounds of fresh icky dark dirt. One of the witnesses to the Assignment of Death on my pastor's life had previously seen one demon digging his grave and another demon etching his tombstone. She told us that he's in the Pastor's Graveyard. There really is such a place. We see a headstone etched in another language than English. This graveyard is void of demons.

The pastor's deception makes it seem that everything is okay. They don't realize that they have been deceived. This is not a nice place. We look up and see black birds circling. The black birds are watching. We cloak ourselves to remain hidden. We see a little white gate, and we understand that we need to go toward the back, left corner. As we pass various graves, we see headstones that from a distance we could not see, because the light's so dim here. We hear demonic laughter. We perceive that the laughter is because these pastors have no idea they've been deceived. Their ears can't hear the truth. This Pastor's Graveyard is a Region of Captivity.

We sense in our hearts that as we walk through the graves that we are to speak the word, "Life!" Hear Jesus say: "I love raising people from the dead." We sense that we are going to retrieve all the pastors. We gather in a circle around the graveyard and grasp our golden shepherd staffs in our right hands. We follow Yeshua's lead. He raises His shepherd's staff over His head, so that the rod is perpendicular to the ground. We understand that we are supposed to shout the word "Life!" in unison, as we bring our shepherd staffs to hit the ground. We are immediately joyful and see light.

We hear: "It's time for the wings!" We all uncloak ourselves. We unfurl our wings. We stand wingtip to wingtip, as we surround this region. We are floating. We are dancing. Jesus is standing in the middle of the Pastor's Graveyard; He's tall, erect and clothed in white. He's the Word. Jesus says, "I've longed for this." We see Jesus coming to each of us. He lays His hands on each heart and reminds us of the belt of truth.

Jesus begins to lead and speak these words to us:

- I AM the Head. Connect Me to My Body, because I give life abundantly.

- Wake up sleeper, rise from the graves.

- My judgment (justice) is true. I AM the righteous judge.

- If hearts are willing to be lifted up in complete surrender to Me, they will never be the same."

- *"^{26} It is not this way among you, but whoever wishes to become great among you shall be your servant, ^{27} and whoever wishes to be first among you shall be your slave; ^{28} just as the Son of Man did not come to be served, but to serve, and give His life a ransom for many"* (Matthew 20:26-28 NASB). That's why I came at the beginning of this journey as a shepherd, because through that complete surrender I'm going to lead.

- *"^{1} The LORD is my shepherd, I shall not want. ^{2} He makes me lie down in green pastures; He leads me beside quiet waters. ^{3} He restores my soul; He guides me in the paths of righteousness for His name sake. ^{4} Even though I walk through the valley of the shadow of death, I fear no evil, for You are with me; Your rod and Your staff, they comfort me. ^{5} You prepare a table before me in the presence of my enemies; You have anointed my head with oil; My cup overflows. ^{6} Surely goodness and lovingkindness will follow me all the days of my life, and I will dwell in the house of the LORD forever"* (Psalms 23:1-6 NASB).

- Speaking over the graves: *"O death, where is your victory? O death, where is your sting?"* (1 Corinthians 15:55 NASB). A song about this is sung over the graves: "Death has lost its sting… He has redeemed." (sung three times)

- *"^{14} Righteousness and justice are the foundation of Your throne; Lovingkindness and truth go before You. ^{15} How blessed are the people who know the joyful sound! O LORD, they walk in the light of Your countenance. ^{16} In Your name they rejoice all the day, and by Your righteousness they are exalted. ^{17} For You are the glory of their strength, and by Your favor our horn is exalted. ^{18} For our shield belongs to the LORD, and our king to the Holy One of Israel" (Psalm 89:14-18 $_{NASB}$).*

Before we are given permission to dance on these grave, the chains need to be broken.

"^{8} Now do not stiffen your neck like your fathers, but yield to the LORD and enter His sanctuary which He has consecrated forever, and serve the LORD your God, that His burning anger may turn away from you. ^{9} For if you return to the LORD, your brothers and your sons will find compassion before those who led them captive and will return to this land. For the LORD your God is gracious and compassionate, and will not turn His face away from you if you return to Him" (2 Chronicles 30:8-9 $_{NASB}$).

They are already rumbling in their graves. The Scriptures (Word) are breaking their chains.

We seek God for the order that He'd like these Scriptures read and get:

[1] 1 Corinthians 15:55,

[2] Psalms 23,

[3] Psalms 89:14-18,

[4] Matthew 20:26-28, and

[5] 2 Chronicles 30:8-9.

We proclaim what Jesus said prior to giving these Scriptures beginning with "I AM the Head. Connect Me to My Body, because I give life abundantly...." as well as these Scriptures and then add the word "Life!"

We see all the pastors rise up. The group proclaims, "Return to the Lord!" We gather around the pastors and take them up with our wings. Jesus says, "You came for one, but I came for all."

We land where we started a little above the expanse. When we rose up with the pastors in our wings, we saw that we took the place of the birds of prey. We were dancing in the air. The pastors have just come out of the grave. The Lord is doing the healing and our job is to love them. We hug the pastors. The resurrected pastors need to embrace God's mercy. Revelation is coming to them, and jack-slapping them. The Lord is giving healing.

We hear the black birds being loud and angry, because they were in charge of that region of captivity. Yeshua instructs us send them back and close the door. Even though we know that we are silencing the black birds by saying, "Be still and know that He is God," we actually silence them without words by simply pointing our wingtips. The message behind our pointing is "be still and know that He is God." We see the spiral hovering battering ram seal up the gates of hell again with sparks.

Then we begin to personally minister to my pastor in the Spirit.

At the very end of this Deliverance Group Ascension, we were led to legislate these heavenly realities to earth through four decrees:

- We decree that the chains holding the pastors in the grave are broken and they have been set free and given new life.

- We decree that the Body of Christ will come under the Head, who is the Righteous Judge, their Good Shepherd, the Truth and the Life, their Servant and their Savior.

- We decree that these pastors from the grave will see God's face and hear, "I am your source."

- We decree that the pastors who were in the grave are restored according to 2 Chronicles 30:8-9 _{NASB} - *"⁷ Now do not stiffen your neck like your fathers, but yield to the LORD and enter His sanctuary which He has consecrated forever, and serve the LORD your God that His burning anger may turn away from you. ⁸ For if you return to the LORD, your brothers and your sons will find compassion before those who led them captive and will return to this land. For the LORD your God is gracious and compassionate, and will not turn His face away from you if you return to Him"*

GENESIS 14 MELCHIZEDEK – SHEM

Shem being Melchizedek of Genesis 14 fame makes sense on several levels. Shem was known as the righteous son of Noah; therefore, it's not much of a stretch to believe he could have been called a King of Righteousness. For example, just as the Messiah can sit on the Throne of David, He can be High Priest of the Order of Melchizedek.

Especially when we consider that Shem led the overthrow of the apostate world ruler of his time – Nimrod – we can extrapolate that Shem easily could have been exalted to such a status himself. Even though Shem was Abraham's great-great-great-great-great-great-great-grandfather, the priesthood of Melchizedek is earned, not inherited. Don't get me wrong, just as Abraham believed and was counted righteous, so did Melchizedek. In fact, Melchizedek must have epitomized a priesthood of believers who draw near to God with a sincere heart in full assurance of faith (Hebrews 10:22), else he would not have been considered righteous.

NOTE: The king of Elam is identified as Shem's son. Although Chedorlaomer was the leader of the Babylonian alliance, the king of Shinar – Amraphel – is mentioned first in the Bible (Genesis 14:1), because he was the senior king of the four. Significantly, the Jewish Sages identify Amraphel as Nimrod. The *Jewish Encyclopedia* shares: "Some say Amraphel was his real name, and he was called Nimrod – 'the chief rebel' as leader of the tower-builders, 'who led the world rebellion' against heaven's Ruler. Others say Nimrod was his real name, and he was called Amraphel as the one who commanded them to cast Abraham into the fire." One of the etymologies for the name Amraphel is explained as that of one whose "command brought darkness [destruction] on the world."

Did you know that long before Shadrach, Meshach and Abendego was thrown into a fiery furnace for refusing to worship idols, Abram endured a literal baptism of fire too? Abram's father – Terah – manufactured and sold idols. When Abram smashed all his dad's wares in a zealous fit of righteous indignation, Terah complained to Nimrod. When King Nimrod had Abram thrown into a fiery furnace, Abram's brother was challenged to choose sides between Abram and Nimrod. By all accounts, death appeared to be swallowing Abram up in the fire. Haran was afraid to choose sides, so he decided to wait until he saw who came out victorious. His choice was between the physically strong and seemingly all-powerful Nimrod and his spiritually-attuned brother, who followed in the righteous footsteps of those who survived the flood.

When Abram was miraculously saved from the furnace, Haran sided with his brother, whereupon the furious Nimrod had Haran thrown in the furnace. Due to his lack of conviction and commitment to what was righteous, Haran was not miraculously saved from the flames. He died in *Ur Kasdim*, which literally means the fire of the land of *Kasdim* (i.e., Chaldea or Babylon).

Today, we are called to the same stance. We must refuse to accept idol worship no matter what anybody else thinks. We must rise to the challenge of the Kingdom of Heaven suffering violence in our own lives and taking it back by force (Matthew 11:12).

UNDERSTANDING THE ORDER OF MELCHIZEDEK

*****

4 – TECHNOLOGY OF THE WINE AND BREAD

There is power resonating from the words: "Eat My flesh and drink My blood." Inside communion is the key to eternal life.

The first time that bread and wine are mentioned in Scripture, we see a priest of the Most High – Melchizedek – King of Salem. He brings out bread and wine to Abram in Genesis 14:18. By this point, Abram had obeyed the Lord in leaving Babylon. He already had come to the land that God had shown him (Genesis 12:1). He had continued on to Egypt for a short time due to famine in the promised land (Genesis 13:1). By the way, this speaks of him going back into the world during a time of testing when spiritual things were neither quick, easy or abundant.

This time when Abram received the bread and wine from Melchizedek was just prior to Abram's name being changed to Abraham (Genesis 17:5). Has anyone received their name changed yet?

Recall that the Babylonian Kings needed to be dethroned by Abram before he could receive the ministry of Melchizedek. We must also first conquer the rulership of the Babylonian practices and mindsets in our own lives before we can be commissioned by God Himself into the Highest Order of Melchizedek.

The principle of communion in the breaking of the bread and the pouring out of the wine is about overcoming to the end to the subduing of self in order to receive your new name:

> *"He who has an ear, let him hear what the Spirit says to the churches. To him who overcomes I will give some of the hidden manna to eat. And I will give him a white stone, and on the stone a NEW NAME written which no one knows except him who receives it" (Revelation 2:17 $_{NKJV}$).*

Yeshua said that the communion elements were literally His Body and His Blood: *"^{26} And as they were eating, Jesus took bread, blessed and broke it, and gave it to the disciples and said, 'Take, eat; THIS IS MY BODY.' ^{27} Then He took the cup, and gave thanks, and gave it to them, saying, "Drink from it, all of you. ^{28} For THIS IS MY BLOOD of the new covenant, which is shed for many for the remission of sins" (Matthew 26:26-28 $_{NKJV}$).*

There is a technology in the spiritual dimensions of communion that's a mystery which will transform your life into its fullness. Hidden within the bread and wine – the body and blood of Yeshua – is the secret to doing the greater works of John 14:12. By taking communion daily, it opens up your spiritual eyes to see Yeshua face-to-face in a greater measure as well as enabling you to possess your spiritual and material inheritance in His Kingdom.

When Yeshua declared in *Matthew 26:29*: *"But I say to you, I will not drink of this fruit of the vine from now on until that day when I drink it new with you in My Father's kingdom,"* He is speaking of the time when we enter the Kingdom of God through an authentic salvation experience (genuine repentance and commitment to follow Yeshua the Messiah as Lord and Savior) and the Spirit of God unites with the spirit of man transforming that person into a new creation. From that moment on, Christ in you, the hope of glory, will grow and be strengthened through spiritual food, which is the flesh and blood of Yeshua as well as the Word of God.

The elements of the bread and wine will always appear the same in the natural, but in the invisible realm the Body and the Blood of Yeshua are really there. Our spirit will literally drink of His Blood and we will become one with His Body (i.e., His Flesh). Our spirit will literally absorb the life of God. We will become blended together little by little until we are literally one.

Our Promised Land is a supernatural life where heaven is a tangible reality. The bread and wine cause the supernatural Kingdom of God to descend among us. It's a link that unites heaven and earth. The unfathomable mystery of heaven and earth being united in the same body is portrayed in Yeshua when He walked this earth as the Son of God.

When Yeshua was conceived, the Heavenly Father's nature was fused with that of the woman. Blood can only be transmitted through the seed of man to the egg of the woman. In Yeshua's case, the Father put His life in the form of blood into the womb of Mary. He used the instrument of His blood to unite human and divine nature. Eternity penetrated time and inhabited a body for the first time at

Yeshua's conception. This is eternal life. Not only are we talking about a life that does not die, but the very nature of God penetrating our humanity and uniting us with Him. The Son of God became flesh and dwelt among us. He continues to become flesh through His Body, specifically those in the Order of Melchizedek that are made like unto the Son of God (Hebrews 7:3).

Yeshua did not speak rashly, when He said: *"For My flesh is true food, and My blood is true drink" (John 6:35)*. He was about to introduce an extremely powerful technology of His Spirit. In order for our spirit to live and stay strong, it must eat every day just like our body. He was establishing continual invigorating fellowship, not a ritual. Had the Lord wanted us to take on communion monthly or yearly, He would have used a different concept other than bread that we consume for daily sustenance.

When we take communion daily, it requires that we examine our hearts and behaviors. It is through His mystical body (i.e., us) that God governs and brings His Kingdom to earth. Discerning the body correctly is essential to our relationship with the Father. Taking communion every single day opens our eyes to the fact that the body of the Lord was broken for us not only on the cross because of His great love for us, but because we need to grasp what our sin(s) produce in the physical body of Christ. Hear His voice: *"This is my body which was broken because of you."* Your sin and my sin crucified the Son of God.

As the primitive church broke bread, they remembered what their sins had done to the body of the Lord. In Hebrew, the words "in memory of me" means vividly reliving an event as if it were happening at that moment. Breaking bread daily in their houses was something that deeply impacted how they knew and loved Yeshua.

So not only is communion a great tool to infuse eternal life into us, but it's a vital ingredient to our being free from our body of sin. One main reason that God hates sin so much is because it blocks our communion with Him. God had to provide some spiritual technology so powerful that it would redeem everything that sin had destroyed. Not only that, but it must also satisfy the cry of His own righteousness and justice, which demands payment for transgression. Only one thing held this power. This one thing was the love of God that flows from the fountain of redemption through the shed blood of the Lamb.

I can go on and on, but I will refer you to one of the best resources I've come across for the taking on communion, which is Ana Mendez Ferrell's book: *Eat My Flesh Drink My Blood*.

Just know when we consult that whole counsel of Scripture that God has established an everlasting foundation that those who are under the protection of the blood of the sacrifice cannot be touched by death (Exodus 12:12-13). In this Kingdom Day, we will see this corruptible putting on incorruption, and this mortality putting on immortality (1 Corinthians 15: 53). Those who truly believe in the Name of the Son of God will know eternal life being a priest forever in the Order of Melchizedek (1 John 5:13; Hebrews 5:6; 6:20; 7:17,21).

*****

5 – RAISING UP ONE MAN

The time of Melchizedek's appearance in Scripture was a *karios* (i.e., right time) of God that only happens every 2,000 years. It's a time when God desires to raise up ONE MAN to bless the nations of the earth as well as it being the opportune moment when all the old passes away for everything to become new. It's a time of shifting when the Lord visits the earth to bring a new concept.

Kairos is an ancient Greek word meaning the right or opportune moment (the supreme moment). The ancient Greeks had two words for time: *chronos* and *kairos*. While the former refers to chronological or sequential time, the latter signifies a time lapse, a moment of indeterminate time in which everything happens.

So far, we have had three *karios* "ages" or "dispensations":

[1] Age of Israel,

[2] Age of the Church, and

[3] Age of the Kingdom.

Please note that all three of these are eternal concepts. Note that the Kingdom Age has just begun around the year 2000 AD. Also note that the Biblical pattern for each new global shift in His divine administration of earthly things (i.e., dispensation) is first a precious son volunteers to become a worshipful burnt offering before a new dwelling place for God is built. (Please refer to "Come Up Here!" http://wp.me/p158HG-x5 and "Royal Road to New Life" http://wp.me/p158HG-vV for more information). In *chronos* time, it is our responsibility to activate these *karios* seeds that LOVE has imparted.

Let's back up just a little bit to quickly review the time of Genesis 14. Remember that it was a time after great warfare, and the Babylonian kings were destroyed. In order to receive our Order of Melchizedek commissioning from Yeshua Himself, we must also defeat those same Babylonian kings in our own lives.

My mentor – Nancy Coen – has taught about the raising up of one man for years. I share the following revelation with her permission. God's raising up ONE MAN actually started with Noah, not Abraham. Noah was raised up to build a boat in the middle of a desert when no one had seen rain before. We know that story of Noah obeying God, and the first bringing of the rain.

Next, Abraham was raised as ONE MAN where he was told to leave everything he knew behind, even though he didn't know where he was going. As a result, monotheism was birthed into the earth.

Next, came the Age of the King and the ONE MAN called David who had a heart after God's own heart.

Then came John the Baptist who was the VOICE OF ONE preparing the way for the Lord. He told people everywhere to repent for the remission of sins. He came in the spirit of Elijah and spirit of reformation.

Jesus epitomized the ONE MAN who was sinless. He fulfilled the Law (Matthew 5:17) and became the author of eternal salvation for all those who obey Him (Hebrews 5:9).

Today, another ONE NEW MAN is being raised up during the Age of the Kingdom where we will all be taught of God. He is stirring up the gift and VOICE OF ONE being taught by the Holy Spirit. The fullness of the ONE NEW MAN IN CHRIST is where the visible and invisible church are in ONENESS agreement. The key to the mystery of ONE is in the word "IN":

"Believe Me that I am IN the Father and the Father IN Me, or else believe Me for the sake of the works themselves" (John 14:11 NKJV).

Each one of the previous ONE MAN in Scripture has a vital lesson for the New Living Creature of Crucified Ones coming forth in our day. God Himself is raising up a Corporate Man of Mature Sons. This Corporate One New Man in Christ will look like, talk like, walk like, and be exactly like Christ crucified and risen:

[1] We will obey the Lord totally by faith in an unprecedented way.

[2] We will leave everything we have known behind without knowing where we are going.

[3] We will operate as his prophets, priests and kings in the earth with a heart that is after God's own heart.

[4]   We will be the VOICE OF ONE declaring repent for the remission of your sins, and we will restore all things in the anointing and spirit of Elijah (reformation).

[5]   We will fulfill the law like Yeshua did (Revelation 14:12), and be holy and He is holy.

In this Kingdom Day, it's the *karios* time for His Chariot Throne to manifest. Those who are His divine human messengers. These are the ruling and reigning ones who are part of God's End-Time Melchizedek Army who fly by the Spirit with one another according to the perfect will of the Father. His sovereign will is made manifest because the Order of Melchizedek operates from a position of rest, as the Seventh Day Transfigured One New Man in Christ who is His Messenger. (For more information of His Messenger, check out the *Taking on Common Union* booklet.)

*****

6 – WHAT WE MUST NOT DO

The kings and priests of the Order of Melchizedek are His Kingdom agents who will facilitate the restoration of all things.

One basic Kingdom Principle that God's people need to understand is that a prince has no kingdom power until he is crowned king. The majority of His people have not crowned Yeshua as their King (yet). We still have things that we want to hold unto, which still require a death to self. In the Kingdom of God, the King of Kings owns everything and has rulership over it.

Before we go any further, I'd like to share something simple, yet very vital, that Nancy Coen shares. I am so thankful for such a genuine, kind, and generous mentor who blows people away with so much revelatory kingdom power. I share the following with her permission and honor her for teaching me and so many souls the ways of The Kingdom.

The following are some basic character checks for those called to operate as His Reigning Ones.

To walk in the Melchizedek anointing, we must NOT:

[1]   BE JUDGMENTAL – Every measurement that we apply to another person is being measured back to us (Matthew 7:1-2). This is such a critical point because the foundation as well as the habitation of God's Throne is righteousness and judgment (Psalm 89:14; Psalm 97:2); therefore, any unrighteous judgment on our part disqualifies us from being His Kingdom agents. We need to see the finished work in a person through the Blood of Yeshua Ha Machiach (Jesus Christ). We have to see everything and everybody from the perspective of the sovereign (perfect) will of God.

[2]   BE EXCLUSIVE – God's people are called to mutually benefit one another, which means we need to be non-exclusive. The days of keeping your revelation to yourself is over, if you are part of the Order of Melchizedek. We will receive in direct proportion of our giving things away for His glory.

[3]   ENTERTAIN PRIDE OR ARROGANCE – The Melchizedek Company will not be guilty of spiritual pride, nor will they have an air of superiority over those "less informed." Remember that Yeshua humbled himself, and became obedient to the point of death of the cross (Philippians 2:8). We will not glorify ourselves. Like Yeshua, the Father will declare over each one of us that we are His beloved mature son after we have learned obedience

through the things suffered; and He will personally send the Great High Priest of the Order of Melchizedek – the Son of God – to commission us into His Royal and Holy Eternal Priesthood (Hebrews 5:5-10).

[4] ENTERTAIN UNFORGIVENESS – Forgiveness to a Christian is like breathing is to the body. The Word of God tells us if we want to receive forgiveness, we must forgive others (Matthew 6:14). Forgiveness is so crucial in these dark times, because unforgiveness leads to bitterness, and bitterness leads to a spirit of offense, and a spirit of offense causes a person's love to grow cold, which is the antithesis of His manifestation of perfection – love (Matthew 24:10-12).

[5] BE UNTEACHABLE – Being unteachable is actually a subset of being prideful. If you desire to rule and reign with Christ, you must hold loosely to anything and everything, except for God Himself. God's people have so many distorted paradigms and unholy traditions of men that if we are to lay hold of the divine positioning as the Sons of God, we must die to anything that He deems as unfit or unholy, as articulated by His Spirit and His Word. If you think all your theology and practices perfectly align with Scripture, you should humble yourself and pray for a teachable heart, because this thought is a sure indication that you're off. It's kind of like self-righteousness. As soon as you say I'm not

self-righteous, you are.

[6] OPERATE IN COMPARISON – We exult ourselves when we compare ourselves with another. Don't compare yourself with another person; because when God created you, He broke the mold. You are unique, and your unique manifestation of Christ in you is needed in the Body of Christ.

[7] ISOLATE – Even though we can operate as part of His Melchizedek Army as individuals, the militaristic redemptive kingdom power comes in a much greater measure corporately. In fact, relational ONENESS is not only a major key to the Restoration of All Things, it's a major key to a person being made perfectly WHOLE. Without the corporate aspect, a person cannot be filled up with all the fullness of the measure of the stature of Christ (Ephesians 4:13). The enemy has worked overtime to get God's people to disconnect and put up walls of self-protection, but praise the Lord! In this Kingdom Day, it's Isaiah 61 time!!! It's time to set the captives free!!!

There are many more things we could focus on, but these are seven touch points that will help His Crucified Ones come into their fullness.

Primarily, we need to focus on the author and perfecter of our faith (Hebrews 12:2). I encourage each one of you to practice walking in the heavenly realm daily. I call this "Daily Ascension," because in this Kingdom Day we are being made into the Sons of God who ascend and descend on the Son of

Man and who fly by the Spirit with one another to the right hand of the Father – His Throne Room. When we see Him like He is, we will become like Him (1 John 3:2).

We will soon discuss more thoroughly how those in God's Melchizedek Army walk in the crossover place where they have access to heaven and earth at the same time.

*****

7 – ORDER SPEAKS

The basic essence of the Order of Melchizedek can be boiled down to the words "order" and "Melchizedek." Maybe I shouldn't be surprised that I haven't heard about the "ORDER" in Melchizedek before, but I am.

Come! Let's see what the most important path for God's family is. This most ancient ORDER in "the Order of Melchizedek" reveals the highest way of life for a person who moves in and out of His house. By the way, I just articulated the Ancient Hebrew Word Picture (Pictograph) for the word "order."

The word "order" in the "Order of Melchizedek is the Hebrew word *dibrah*, which occurs 5 times in Scripture. Its first and fundamental definition is literally "a word." When we couple this fact with the first declaration of the "Order of Melchizedek" was made in the Tabernacle of David, we put two practical keys in our pocket that helps unlock the mystery of His Kingdom involving Melchizedek:

"The LORD has sworn and will not relent, You are a priest forever according to the order of Melchizedek" (Psalm 110:4 NKJV).

"So he swayed the hearts of all the men of Judah, JUST AS THE HEART OF ONE MAN, so that they sent this word to the king: "Return, you and all your servants!" (2 Samuel 19:14 NKJV).

Please allow me to explain. The fourth time that "*dibrah*" is used in the Word of God is in *Ecclesiastes 7:17 – "In the day of prosperity be joyful, but in the day of adversity consider: God also hath set the one over against the other, to the end that man should find nothing after Him."* I am using this obscure verse, because it's a great illustration of the Order of Melchizedek being A WORD.

I don't know about you, but the LORD has set one person after another over me that I felt was against me. Be encouraged. When God sets one over against the other, it is for the purpose of the end of that man or woman, so that they find NOTHING. Say what? It sounds strange that a person will find NOTHING until we study "nothing" in Scripture.

Primeval earth was hung on nothing (Job 26:7), and so is the dust of your earth, which is the primordial state of a person's body and soul (Genesis 2:7). James 1:2-4 tells us that the trying of a person's faith, especially by someone who is over and against them, is a perfect work of patience, which leaves a Melchizedek Candidate perfect and entire, wanting NOTHING.

If you want to discover some secret keys about Melchizedek that are hidden in plain sight, study "nothing" in Scripture and the concepts associated with it. For instance, NOTHING concerns priests of the Order of Melchizedek who sprang out of Judah – the Throne of David (Hebrews 7:13-14).

Please bear with me as we blow a few erroneous paradigms away, because if we do not "get" the first and fundamental concept that the Order of Melchizedek is a word and understand its basic application, we will miss the highest way of life for God's family and its most important ancient path.

Since Yeshua was baptized with fire on the cross, we have been taught that *"the law made nothing perfect" (Hebrews 7:19)*, which is true... but now we are making a quantum leap to the other side of His double-edge sword. Consider that our primordial souls were created in His image, as perfect before the Fall; therefore, we can say in a sense that NOTHING IS PERFECT. By the way, I can prove this through Scripture, but I am going to let you search this out for yourself.

We are told in Hebrew 7:15-16 that after the visible likeness of Melchizedek arises another priest who is made after the power of an endless life – eternal life. Then before we are told *"the law made nothing perfect,"* we are told of the *"disannulling of the commandment going before" (Hebrews 7:18)*. This "disannulling" phrase stopped me in my tracks, because it appeared to contradict some other things I had just studied.

Suffice it to say that when we boil "disannulling" down to its root and consult the entirety of Scripture, Christians can understand that we have inherited lies, which have been carried over from the Nicene Council in the fourth century. You may say: What's this have to do with me? If you are called to be part of His Melchizedek and Bridal Companies, a lot!!! When Christianity began to be institutionalized in the fourth century, it was their modus operandi to indiscriminately mix the holy with the profane. In order for the institutional church to get away with this at the time, they told its members that the "old" way of the law was done away with, which was a slight twist of a righteous real. By the way, the word "wicked" means a slight twisting of a righteous real.

> *"Do we then make void the law through faith? God forbid: Yea, we establish the law"* (Romans 3:31).

The realm of the Spirit is entirely based on the Word of God, and we move in the spiritual realm through our faith in what God has spoken. When the manifested sons of God of a wing of His Melchizedek Army ascend and descend on the Son of Man – Yeshua – to see heavenly things, they are experiencing His word with the purpose of being made ONE with it here on earth, as it is in heaven.

The GRACE that much of Institutional Christianity said did away with the law is also based on God's Word – crucified, buried, and risen. The One who walked full of grace and truth demonstrated for us a perfect life that was contrary to the demands of "religion." Yeshua transcended the law by living a life in the fullness of love. He even told us: *"Do not think that I came to destroy the Law or the Prophets. I did not come to destroy but to fulfill"* (Matthew 5:17 $_{NKJV}$). Please note that "fulfill" is the opposite of abolishing or doing away with something.

There are two roots to the word "disannul" or "disannulling." The first root communicates the sense of union while the second root speaks of a horizontal and passive posture of rest as well as various worship stances. This worship-filled rest picture is punctuated with the concepts of intimacy, conceiving and being made into the image of the Messiah.

For the law made nothing perfect. The Order of Melchizedek will perfectly know, as I am perfectly known (1 Corinthians 13:12).

The power of an endless life is articulated in *John 17:2 – "This is eternal life, that they may know Thee."* That word "know" comes from the translation of a Jewish idiom for sexual intercourse between a man and a woman. The Hebrew word *yadah* points to this most intimate relationship. It's the word used when Adam experienced Eve, or Adam knew Eve.

This higher degree of intimacy IS the better covenant and better promises that Christ unlocked on the cross. Like the Great High Priest of the Order of Melchizedek, we sit with Him on the right hand of the throne of the Majesty in heaven (Hebrews 8:1). We are ministers of the sanctuary of the New Jerusalem that's coming from heaven to earth. The new heavens and the new earth within the Order of Melchizedek are established by the Lord of Love Himself, not by man (Hebrews 8:2). His "new" covenant with physical and spiritual Is-real has already been prophesied in Jeremiah 31. It foretold the change in the law that came with the change in the priesthood (Hebrews 7:12):

> *"But this is the covenant that I will make with the house of Israel after those days says the LORD: I will put My law in their minds, and write it on their hearts; and I will be their God and they shall be My people" (Jeremiah 31:33; Hebrews 8:10).*

So, when you see the word "disannul" or "disannulling" in Scripture, substitute the concept of an intimate worshipful rest stance in your mind, instead of getting rid of one of the most significant foundations of the Order of Melchizedek. The ORDER in the "Order of Melchizedek" is speaking about manifesting His word. This is not much of a stretch since the PATTERN of the Order of Melchizedek is our

Great High Priest the Word of God Himself: *"And He was clothed with a vesture dipped in blood: and His name is called The Word of God" (Revelation 19:13 KJV)*.

The way of life for royal priests is paved with ONE who is intimately positioned in the Spirit in the midst of the Tabernacle of David, as they abide at the frequency of His Word. The Order of Melchizedek speaks! Word up!

You are meant to be a Sent One who walks in the highest ways of life flowing in His perfect rhythms of Spirit and Truth. So, let's all take that quantum leap to restore the ORDER in the Order of Melchizedek.

> *"² You are our epistle written in our hearts, known and read by all men; ³ clearly you are an epistle of Christ, ministered by us, written not with ink but by the Spirit of the living God, not on tablets of stone but on tablets of flesh, that is, of the heart" (2 Corinthians 3;2-3 NKJV)*.

*****

8 – TREASURER OF THE MOST INTIMATE

YHVH foreknew and foreordained that His Order of Melchizedek would come to the Kingdom for such a time as this (Esther 4:14).

"To every thing there is a season, and a time to every purpose under the heaven" (Ecclesiastes 3:1 KJV). What He has made beautiful in this Kingdom Day is His wings of His Melchizedek Army who ascend and descend on Yeshua – the Son of Man – by the Spirit of the Living God to the right hand of the Majesty in heaven. In No Man's Land (a place that the Melchizedek Company resides), we find out God's works from the beginning until the end, because He set eternity in our hearts (Ecclesiastes 3:11).

Time is a mystery. The Melchizedek section of the *Dead Sea Scroll* (11Q13 – cave 11, Qumran physical scroll 13) speaks that Melchizedek will instruct the world about all the periods of history for eternity and the statutes of the truth.

Know that even though there are seven Feasts of the Lord spelled out in Leviticus 23, which God Himself says: *"These are My feasts" (Leviticus 23:12)*, there are two additional feast that are in the Bible: Purim commemorated in the Book of Esther and Hanukkah (John 10:22-23).

Know that with each of the Lord's Feast a portal opens in the heavenlies. There are greater graces articulated in His various Biblical Feasts that His people can tap into during these times. These greater graces are always available; but somehow, they are brought nearer, as we cycle through the times He has set up in His Word. The years which the LORD has given to His people are set according to His Biblical Feasts. The months which the LORD has given to His people are set by His new moons, and weeks are set by His seventh day Sabbaths. These are the times and the seasons set up by the Lord Himself as articulated in His Word.

If the ORDER in the Order of Melchizedek is going to abide in an intimate rest worship stance, they must resonate at the frequency of His word. By the way, the *Dead Sea Scrolls* also speaks of the songs sung over the Sabbath Sacrifices, which are still resonating throughout eternity seeking for a place where they can manifest and rest.

> *"² The word preached did not profit them, not being mixed with faith in them that heard it. ³ For we which have believed do enter the rest ... ⁴ For He spake in a certain place of the seventh day on this wise, And God did rest the seventh day from all His works. ⁹ There remaineth therefore a rest to the people of God. ¹⁰ For he that is entered into His rest, he also has ceased from his own works, as God did from His" (Hebrews 4:2-4, 9-10 KJV).*

The "Songs of the Sabbath Sacrifice" were sung to Melchizedek, who is called the chief angelic priest in one fragment. Recall that the New Living Creature of the One

New Man in the Messiah (Christ) is called the Cherubim in Ezekiel 10, and that word "Cherubim" can either be a divine angelic or divine human messenger according to the Hebrew Scripture and the Greek Septuagint. For more information, please refer to the *Taking on Common Union* book.

Basically, the Eternal Order of Melchizedek operates from a position of REST as the Seventh Day Transfigured Son -- the One New Man in the Messiah. In the twelfth song of the Cherubim, which we are told are almost indistinguishable from the wheels of God's chariot throne (Ezekiel 1), the priests used to worship YHVH silently. We are told that one cannot hear this praise, but it is evident in brass-like flashes of light emerging from His throne. These Ancient Sabbath Songs included priestly and princely angelic praise of the divine king as well as praise issuing from the vestibules. A vestibule is a passage, hall or room between the outer door and the interior building, which gives access to something new.

At the dawning of this New Kingdom Age, the Order of Melchizedek operates as the king's chamberlain or treasurer of the most intimate. Please recall from the previous chapter that there are some secret keys about Melchizedek that are hidden in plain sight when we study "nothing" and the concepts associated with it in Scripture. Let's gaze into some mysteries of Purim.

> *"Now when the turn of Esther, the daughter of Abihail, the uncle of Mordecai, who had taken her for his daughter, was come to go in unto the king, she required NOTHING but what Hegai the king's chamberlain, the keeper of the woman, appointed. And Esther obtained favor in the sight of all them that looked upon her" (Esther 2:15 KJV).*

The Lord's Melchizedek Company is the predecessor for the un-paralleled beauty of His Pure and Spotless Bridal Company. They both have pure hearts surrounded by Yeshua Ha Machiach (Jesus Christ)'s Blood, which passes through the righteous judgments that emanate from His Sapphire Throne. These royal priests of Melchizedek prepare the way for the Bride to join the King of Kings.

One of the Bridal Preparation functions that Melchizedek operates in is displayed in his role as the king's chamberlain. My *Webster's Collegiate Dictionary (10the Edition)* tells me that a chamberlain is an attendant on a sovereign in his bedchamber. He is a chief officer in the household of a king who is the treasurer of his most intimate possessions. As guardians entrusted with the receipt, care, and disbursement of the king's treasures, the Eternal Royal Priests of Melchizedek are governmental officers who are in charge of receiving, keeping and disbursing the king's resources.

This incredible kingdom key to the wealth of heaven being dispersed to the sons of God on earth is given only to those whose character have been refined in His Baptism of Fire to the place where His Sons of Light can stand in the council of God and take responsibility for being seated in His government. When we restore the ORDER in the "Order of Melchizedek," we hit the mark of the highest way of life for God's family, which is flowing in the perfect rhythms of Spirit and Truth. The most ancient path of ORDER points us to manifesting a Living Word, as HE is the Word made manifest. In fact, the meaning behind the king's chamberlain's name – Hegai – speaks of four things: meditation, word, groaning (birthing) and separation. These are all key, because they are the instructions of the one in charge of the house of the women – the house of the Bride of Christ (Esther 2:3). We are to do NOTHING, except what the king's chamberlain appoints.

What also is so wonderful is that Esther's father's name – Abihail – speaks of loving God with all your strength, which is the Bridal Portion of loving God with all one's resources. The Hebrew word for "strength" articulates for us to passionately love the Lord vehemently; wholly, speedily, especially when repeated; diligently, especially, exceedingly, greatly, louder and louder, mightily, utterly; to rake together; a poker for turning and gathering embers; a firebrand (i.e., torch).

Purim is currently a twisted counterfeit – a type of Mardi Gras – of a righteous real. What I mean when I say that Purim is a twisted counterfeit of a righteous real is that we need to untwist it. We need to keep that which is holy and get rid of that which is profane: drunkenness, debauchery and revelry. Many of the current practices of Purim are related to a Mardi Gras spirit, which needs to be redeemed and refocused by His Sons of the Kingdom on the preparation of the Bride and deliverance aspects of this feast that's in His Word.

The Eternal Order of Melchizedek is called for such a time as this to restore His Kingdom Order to this Biblical Feast. Both Hanukkah and Purim are not feasts forever, because they have a culmination. That culmination is the church becoming His Bride through the acceptance of being cleansed from sin by Yeshua's Blood as well as being cleansed from the world by the application and manifestation His Eternal Word.

We are the curators of the king's most intimate treasure AND we are His most valued possession. The commitment to being married to the King of Kings and the Lord of Lords is not to be taken lightly is almost an understatement. His queen will most excellently represent the King. You have been called to His Exalted Kingdom for such a time as this. His scepter is currently being extended to those who say, "I do" with all their heart, soul and strength.

*****

9 – LIFE'S PURE PERFECTION

The Order of Melchizedek has the look and sound of PERFECT, because they are ONE with PERFECTION Himself and the PATTERN SON – Yeshua Ha Machiach (Jesus Christ) who is the High Priest of His royal order of priests. Hebrews 7:11 indirectly declares that PERFECTION is by the Melchizedek Priesthood:

> *"If therefore perfection were by the Levitical priesthood… what further need was there that another priest should rise after the Order of Melchizedek, and not be called after the order of Aaron?" (Hebrews 7:11 KJV).*

Many people have a negative concept about PERFECTION, because they think of the onerous burden of being a perfectionist. Please be patient, as we flip this concept on its head and redeem it. Excellence for the King is always a desirable quality, but instead of flowing from a burdensome taskmaster spirit, the look and sound of MELCHIZEDEK PERFECTION flows from a place of rest.

Recall from "Treasurer of the Most Intimate" that the Order of Melchizedek abides in a restful intimate worship stance, as we resonate at the frequency of His word. Before Yeshua literally became our all-sufficient sacrifice on the cross, there were different songs sung over the various sacrifices. The *Dead Sea Scrolls* record that the "Songs of the Sabbath Sacrifice" were sung to Melchizedek. This prophetically speaks about the Eternal Order of Melchizedek operating from a position of REST as the Seventh Day Transfigured Son – the One New Man in the Messiah (Matthew 17:1-2; Ephesians 2:15).

So, let's take a closer look at Life's Pure Perfection that's now manifesting here on earth, as it is in heaven. The particular type of PERFECTION pointed out in Hebrews 7:11 is unique to this verse, and speaks about the completion of prophecy and the verification of its reality. The original intent of God on Mount Sinai was to make His people a nation of priests – a holy nation – but they rejected this call. Besides Moses, the incident of the Golden Calf caused the uncompromising tribe of Levi to step up to the plate to be intimately acquainted with Him and His ways. By the way, this is a Biblical pattern of the first-born (begotten) being chosen – you and I individually – before a corporate company radically shows that we are for God by whole-heartedly following Him through taking up the cross of our flesh daily to join Him and learning obedience by the things we suffer (Matthew 16:24; Hebrews 5:8).

You've probably heard the saying that the Old Testament is the New Testament concealed while the New Testament is the Old Testament revealed. I believe that the Melchizedek priesthood has been YHVH original design all along. The Melchizedek Priesthood predates the Levitical one. When Abram met Noah's son – Shem – and gave him a tenth of all, the King of Righteousness (i.e., Shem) had already set up a priestly order. Shem, the original Melchizedek on earth, had this right being the first King of Salem. Please refer to Genesis 14 and "The Original Melchizedek" Chapter. I find it interesting that Melchizedek is first identified by his name – King of Righteousness, which is the essence of a completely moral and right character – and then by the place that he was given dominion – King of Salem (i.e., Ancient Jerusalem and prophetically the New Jerusalem).

The royal priestly nation of the Order of Melchizedek in this Kingdom Day will fulfill Revelation 11:15, like the first Melchizedek and company did, except this time it's the time of culmination. In addition to the PERFECTION speaking about the completion of prophecy and the verification of its reality (in Hebrews 7:11), it declares that the Melchizedek Priesthood is a finishing generation, and we are returning to our primordial state (as we were before The Fall in the Garden, only better because we have been redeemed and we freely volunteer to become part of His PRIESTHOOD OF ONE LOVE). We will overthrow the Babylonian kings in our own lives first to make the kingdoms of this earth, the kingdoms of our God.

There are secret keys involving Melchizedek that are hidden in plain sight when we study "nothing" and "no man" and the concepts associated with them in Scripture.

Hebrews 5 reveals a NO MAN'S LAND where priests of the Most High are called by God Himself and ordained by Him for men in things pertaining to God. These royal priests taken from among men have compassion on those lacking knowledge and the wayward due to their own frailties; and thus, they are able to offer up passionate prayers and tearful supplications. They glorify not themselves, but the Father through whom they are begotten sons. As His promised sons, we learn obedience by the things we suffer, so we can be made perfect after the Order of Melchizedek. These are the ones who are heard of the Father, because of their reverential fear of the Lord.

Additionally, Hebrews 7 reveals a NO MAN'S LAND where there is a different tribe of people that springs out of Judah and rises after the visible likeness of Melchizedek who gives attendance at Altar of the Most High God. These are the ones who are made after the power of an endless life, because they are easily understood and recognized as manifesting HIS ETERNAL LIVING WORD (law) that's in their minds and written on the tablets of their hearts (Hebrews 8:10). Please refer to the "Order Speak" Chapter.

Hebrews 7:19 tells us that the law made NOTHING PERFECT. "Nothing" in Scripture is a primordial state that points us to:

[1] What the dust of our earth (living soul) hangs on (Genesis 2:7; Job 26:7).

[2] What is true (1 Kings 22:16; 2 Corinthians 13:8).

[3] The trying of our faith (Psalm 17:3; James 1:4).

[4] A crucified life and humility (Philippians 1:20; 1 Corinthians 2:2).

[5] The good portion of the Father, which are the treasures hidden in darkness in the secret place of His throne (John 16:23-34; John 18:20; Philippians 4:6).

[6]   The Tablets in the Ark of His Presence (2 Chronicles 5:10).

[7]   The provision of manna in God's Wilderness (Numbers 11:6; Deuteronomy 2:7).

[8]   Priests of the holy royal priesthood of Melchizedek (Malachi 2:6; Hebrews 7:14,19).

This is not an all-inclusive list, but a sampling of the themes related to NOTHING in Scripture, which are related to kingdom priests of the Most High God. That word "perfect" in Hebrews 7:19 paints a picture for the Eternal Order of Melchizedek to focus on the Most High God like a telescope – intently and paying attention to details. It also re-iterates the character of the King of Righteousness.

The word "perfect" in Hebrews 7:19 is also referred to in Yeshua's last instructions to His disciples before He went to the cross: *"I in them and Thou in Me, that they may be made PERFECT IN ONE; and that the world may know that Thou hast sent Me, and hast loved them, as Thou hast loved Me" (John 17:23 KJV)*. "PERFECT" is the Greek word *teleioo*, which conveys the notion of being complete, accomplishing, consummating in character, fulfilling, and making perfect. It comes from the Greek word *teleios*, which communicates a deeper truth of being complete in labor, complete in growth, complete in mental character, complete in moral character, and being of full age, as an adult son (Ephesians 4:13). Diving deeper. The root of both of these Greek words is *telos*, which connects the concept of fulfilling; i.e., what it means to be a full age mature son to the idea of setting out for a definite point or goal, the point aimed at as a limit, the conclusion of an act or state (a result, a purpose), or the uttermost.

Being made after the Order of Melchizedek is a top-down heaven-to-earth arrangement that facilitates one's utmost character development, as well as equipping us for the unlimited royal order of His End-Time Melchizedek Army.

Therefore, to be PERFECT in the Kingdom of God or to walk in MELCHIZEDEK PERFECTION means that His Royal Priesthood sets out for the goal to become just like the Word of God, Yeshua, who is the Great High Priest of the eternal Order of Melchizedek in accordance to a restful most-intimate worship stance. Don't forget that the "Entering His Rest" Chapter – Hebrews 4 – which directly precedes the revelation of the Order of Melchizedek culminates with encouraging all of us to come boldly to His Throne of Grace. Great grace is an essential ingredient in us being made PERFECT in ONE.

I think you're perfect! SEE it and BE it!!!

NOTE: NO MAN'S LAND is the place where people daily yield to LOVE and His crucifixion process, which enables their Kingdom of Self to disappear and the Kingdom of God to appear. The dust of our earth is hung (put to death) on NOTHING. May we BE NOTHING, except Jesus Christ crucified, so we can bear much fruit for without our Beloved King we can DO NOTHING.

*****

10 – POWER OVER DEATH

In this Kingdom Day, we are literally seeing another priesthood arise, which is made after the power of an endless life (Hebrews 7:15-16). Not only was King David associated with the Royal Order of Melchizedek (Psalm 110:4), but so was Elijah.

The key to how we know that Elijah was part of the Order of Melchizedek is held in the picture of the chariot of fire that appeared, which took Elijah up into heaven by a whirlwind (2 Kings 2:11-12). Ezekiel 1:4-5 tells us that a fiery whirlwind came out of the north with a likeness of the four living creatures. In verse 5, it also significantly tells us that the likeness of the four living creatures is the likeness of a man. What man? The New Living Creature of Melchizedek who is the One New Man in Christ (Ephesians 2:15). We will not be going into the depth of explanation necessary here. If you have not already read the *Taking on Common Union* book yet, please do because it makes clear the "cherubim" classification of the New Living Creature of Melchizedek.

The One New Man in Christ has an application on both an individual and corporate level. Individually, you and I, need to be wed in a fourfold way, so that Christ's Being can be lived out through us by means of the Seven Spirits of God according to the perfect will of the Father. After each of us are firing to-the-best-of-our-ability on all cylinders, we connect corporately. The key is "to-the-best-of-our-ability" for remember His fiery chariot throne is also a throne of grace.

Now recall that Elijah was used by God to raise a boy from the dead:

> "[8] *Then the word of the LORD came to him, saying,* [9] *"Arise, go to Zarephath, which belongs to Sidon, and dwell there. See, I have commanded a widow there to provide for you...* [15] *So she went away and did according to the word of Elijah; and she and he and her household ate for many days.* [16] *The bin of flour was not used up, nor did the jar of oil run dry, according to the word of the LORD which He spoke by Elijah.* [17] *Now it happened after these things that the son of the woman who owned the house became sick. And his sickness was so serious that there was no breath left in him.* [18] *So she said to Elijah, "What have I to do with you, O man of God? Have you come to me to bring my sin to remembrance, and to kill my son?"* [19] *And he said to her, "Give me your son." So he took him out of her arms and carried him to the upper room where he was staying, and laid him on his own bed.* [20] *Then he cried out to the LORD and said, "O LORD my God, have You also brought tragedy on the widow with whom I lodge, by killing her son?"* [21] *And he stretched himself out on the child three times, and cried out to the LORD and said, "O LORD my God, I pray, let this child's soul come back to him."* [22] *Then the LORD heard the voice of Elijah; and the soul of the child came back to him, and he revived.* [23] *And Elijah took the child and brought him down from the upper room into the house, and gave him to his*

mother. And Elijah said, "See, your son lives!" [24] *Then the woman said to Elijah, "Now by this I know that you are a man of God, and that the word of the LORD in your mouth is the truth"* (1 Kings 17:8-9, 15-24 NKJV).

It's time for the Spirit of Elijah resident in the New Living Creature of the One New Man in the Messiah to come forth and resurrect the dead sons of the widow woman – the Bride of Christ.

We are in historic times. Today, on April 15, 2014, it is the Feast of the Lord called Passover. As you probably know, last night there was the first of a 2014-2015 Blood Moon Tetrad , which will land on the Lord's Feast Days of Passover and Tabernacles. It is the eighth Blood Moon Tetrad since Yeshua (Jesus) walked the earth (30 AD), and at the exact same time on our Gregorian calendar we are experiencing eight consecutive numerical palindrome days The NEW BEGINNINGS are being dramatically declared in the heavens. Right before Yeshua went to the cross, He celebrated Passover(i.e., Pesach) with His disciples. During the Feast, Yeshua partook of the first cup, which symbolizes sanctification as well as the second cup that represents judgment. During the third cup, Yeshua declared: "This cup is the cup of my blood," which still symbolizes redemption. This was a foreshadow of His crucifixion later that day by which His shed Blood would buy redemption for the entire world. The fourth cup of Elijah was not drunk by Yeshua the night before His crucifixion, but He promised those close to Him: *"I say to you, I will not drink of this fruit of the vine from now on until that day when I drink it new with you in My Father's kingdom"* (Matthew 26:29 NKJV). The fourth cup of His Kingdom is manifesting anew NOW!!!!! It's the cup of Elijah!

Elijah's cup – the Cup of the Kingdom – is reserved for such a time as this, because this fourth cup is for all who believe as we lovingly obey our Beloved King. Scripture tells us once we accept the gift of the death, burial and resurrection of Yeshua, which is the gift of salvation by faith through grace, His Kingdom is at hand (Matthew 10:7). It is near. It is within you (Luke 17:21). So, let us all enter His Kingdom, and all drink the fourth cup. Let's drink the Cup of the Kingdom with Yeshua who is the hope of glory who now resides within us and is unfolding outwardly in this hour.

Some believers do not set out a cup for Elijah at their Passover Table. My family does; because even though John the Baptist was a fulfillment of Elijah coming to prepare the way of the Lord in Yeshua's Day, there is still a greater corporate Spirit of Elijah coming forth in this Kingdom Day to restore all things.

The greater fulfillment of a corporate Spirit of Elijah is hinted at in *Matthew 17:11* in the words: *"Elijah truly shall first come, and RESTORE ALL THINGS."* Have "all things" been restored yet here on earth? Nope. *Malachi 4:5* prophesies: *"Behold, I will send you Elijah the prophet before the coming of the great and dreadful day of the LORD. And he will turn the hearts of the fathers to the children, And the hearts of the children to their fathers, Lest I come and strike the earth with a curse."*

Peter also prophetically speaks about the restoration of all things: *"[19] Repent therefore and be converted, that your sins may be blotted out, so that times of refreshing may come from the presence of the Lord, [20] and that He may send Jesus Christ, who was preached to you before, [21] WHOM HEAVEN MUST RECEIVE UNTIL THE TIMES OF RESTORATION OF ALL THINGS, which God has spoken by the mouth of all His holy prophets since the world began" (Acts 3:19-21 NKJV)*. If we put Matthew 17:11 together with Acts 3:19-21 and add Malachi 4:5 to the mix, we see that there is a corporate spirit of Elijah resident in the New Living Creature of Melchizedek who are part of the priesthood of ONE LOVE restoring the hearts of the Fathers to their children, and the children to their Fathers.

Not only does the restoration of all things include the redemption of His time and His celebrations, but it's also mortality putting on immortality: *"So when this corruptible shall have put on incorruption, and this mortal shall have put on immortality, then shall be brought to pass the saying that is written, Death is swallowed up in victory" (1 Corinthians 15:54 NKJV).*

I've already recounted my "Assignment of Death" story in the previous book. Let's recap. In 2012, the LORD shared with several people that a pastor had an "Assignment of Death." I knew from a previous experience that if this "Assignment of Death" was not taken care of completely, it would literally manifest in someone's death. I also knew that the LORD held the key, so I sought Him and sought Him and sought Him. He told me that He needed four people to always be present during a Group Ascension to take care of this "Assignment of Death," and He told me the exact people that He wanted. We were each equipped as a Melchizedek Company with a golden breastplate, a golden shepherd's staff, a cloaking garment, one drop of Christ's Blood, a set of wings, and a golden belt with a globe in its midst that enabled us to go anywhere on earth.

Long story short, Yeshua came to us as the Great Shepherd and took us to the gates of hell. He led the procession, but required our participation. A form of the Living Creature acted like a heavenly battering ram that blew the gates of hell to bits and incinerate the first row of demons that were acting like tribal crazies. We found out after our divine encounter that the demon with the "Assignment of Death" for that pastor was burnt up when we stormed the gates of hell. This heavenly battering ram with the wings and all of us with the wings were two views of the same reality. We were the keys to the kingdom of heaven for the gates of hell to not overpower Christ's Church: *"[18] I also say to you that you are Peter, and upon this rock I will build My church; and the gates of Hades will not overpower it. [19] I will give you the keys of the kingdom of heaven; and whatever you bind on earth shall be bound in heaven, and whatever you loose on earth shall have been loosed in heaven" (Matthew 16:18-19 NASB)*.

Therefore, from this experience I know that four royal priests here on earth who are equipped by Him, as a Melchizedek Army who obediently fly by His Spirit with one another, have the power over death. It's based in the power of LOVE in laying down our lives for another as well as the resurrection power resident in the precious Blood of the Lamb.

So, let's bless the LORD our God, King of the universe who has delivered us from the power of darkness and conveyed us into the Kingdom of the Son of His love (Colossians 1:13). We are tasting and seeing that the Lord is good in the land of the living, and by the Spirit we see the Son of Man coming in His Kingdom within each one of us (Matthew 16:28). We pray that the Son of Man will send out His angels to gather out of His Kingdom all things that offend (Matthew 13:41), so we can attend the Wedding Supper of the Lamb (Matthew 22:1-14). Therefore, let everyone this day drink the Kingdom Cup, which is Elijah's Cup, as we honor His Kingdom come, His will being done, on earth as it is in heaven in you and me and the world. Let everyone raise your Cup of the Kingdom and toast: "To endless life!"

UNDERSTANDING THE ORDER OF MELCHIZEDEK

Book 3

Taking On Common Union

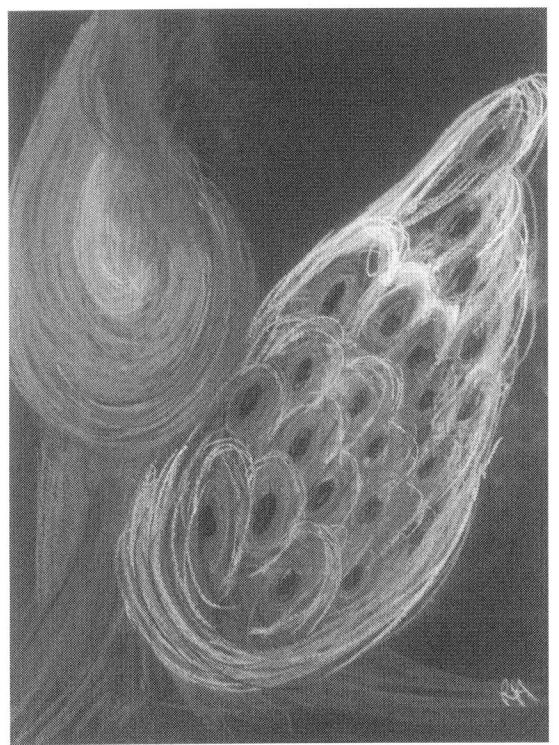

Cover Art: "Fiery Living Creature" by Robin Main

© July 24, 2014. All Rights Reserved

Text Copyright © 2014 Robin Main. All Rights Reserved

1 – INTRODUCTION

In this Kingdom Day, taking communion is transforming into TAKING ON COMMUNION, because common union is the ultimate prize of our high calling of God in Christ Jesus.

Taking on common union starts when by faith through grace, we accept Yeshua Ha Machiach (Jesus Christ) as our Lord and Savior; but this is merely the beginning where believers begin to SEE THE KINGDOM OF GOD (John 3:3). If we want to go beyond merely seeing the Kingdom of God, Scripture tells us that we need to be born (i.e., baptized) by water and the Spirit to ENTER THE KINGDOM OF GOD (John 3:5), which is where we begin to work out our salvation with fear and trembling (Philippians 2:12). INHERITING THE KINGDOM OF GOD is a quantum leap beyond entering Hs Kingdom. Galatians 5:19-21 and 1 Corinthians 6:9-10 lists the works of the flesh that believers must NOT do to inherit the Kingdom of God. 1 Corinthians 15:50 puts an exclamation point to it:

"[19] Now the works of the flesh are obvious, which are: adultery, sexual immorality, uncleanness, lustfulness, [20] idolatry, sorcery, hatred, strife, jealousies, outbursts of anger, rivalries, divisions, heresies, [21] envyings, murders, drunkenness, orgies, and things like these; of which I forewarned you, even as I also forewarned you, that THOSE WHO PRACTICE SUCH THINGS WILL NOT INHERIT THE KINGDOM OF GOD" (Galatians 5:19-21 HNV).

"[9] Do you not know that THE WICKED SHALL NOT INHERIT THE KINGDOM OF GOD? Be not mislead; neither the immoral nor idolaters nor adulterers nor the corrupt men who lie with males [10] Nor extortioners nor thieves nor drunkards nor railers nor defrauders shall inherit the Kingdom of God" (1 Corinthians 6:9-10 Lamsa's Aramaic).

"Now this I say, my brethren, that FLESH AND BLOOD CANNOT INHERIT THE KINGDOM OF GOD; neither does corruption inherit incorruption" (1 Corinthians 15:50 Lamsa's Aramaic)

Those who attain Bridal Fullness of TAKING ON COMMON UNION are those who literally *"keep the commandments of God, and the faith of Jesus" (Revelation 14:12)* in an eternal life-giving way.

At every progressive step of TAKING ON COMMON UNION, we are positioned by grace through His Blood and His Endless Love in such a way that the Lord leads all who obey Him into the very midst of His Kingdom. In fact, the term "in the midst" is a key phrase in the KJV of Scripture, which reveals what it means to take on common union.

In the midst of God's Kingdom is a throne. In the midst of the throne is a Lamb:

"For THE LAMB WHICH IS IN THE MIDST ON THE THRONE shall feed them, and shall lead them unto living fountains of waters: and God shall wipe away all tears from their eyes" (Revelation 7:17 KJV).

"And I beheld, and lo, IN THE MIDST OF THE THRONE AND OF THE FOUR BEASTS, AND IN THE MIDST OF THE ELDERS, STOOD A LAMB as it had been slain, having seven horns and seven eyes, which are the seven Spirits of God sent forth into all the earth" (Revelation 5:6 KJV).

Notice how Revelation 5:6 tells us that the Lamb of God is also IN THE MIDST of "four beasts" and "the elders" with the previous chapter emphasizing that these four beasts are IN THE MIDST of the throne set up in heaven:

"⁶ And before the throne there was a sea of glass like unto crystal: and IN THE MIDST OF THE THRONE, and round about the throne, WERE FOUR BEASTS FULL OF EYES before and behind. ⁷ And the first beast was like a lion, and the second beast like a calf, and the third beast had a face as a man, and the fourth beast was like a flying eagle" (Revelation 4:6-7 KJV).

This book is a result of my own personal journey of TAKING ON COMMON UNION and the mysteries of God that unfolded before me. Many moons ago, our Beloved introduced me to the four beasts in the midst of His Throne with a bridal flare. It began with a unique and a wedded way for taking communion. May this book be a tool in your quest to truly know Him and the power of His resurrection, as His Pure and Spotless Bride (Philippians 3:10).

Not only is His Throne in the midst of God's Kingdom, but this throne can be mobile. Just know that there is a vital connection between the Bride of Christ and the four beasts (also known as the Living Creature or the four living creatures in the book of the Ezekiel). As you will see, the Living Creature (described in Ezekiel 1 and Ezekiel 10) can symbolize not only an individual who is becoming ONE (or has become ONE) with the Father, the Son and the Holy Spirit, but also a group of individuals endeavoring to hit the same bull's eye – the perfect will of the Father (Romans 12:2; Hebrews 10:7).

Please note that the perfect will of the Father is Throne Room Ministry where its purpose is for the kingdoms of our earth to become the kingdoms of our God (Revelation 11:15). When sold-out hearts come corporately together as ONE for His Kingdom come and His will being done here on earth, as it is in heaven, God's Chariot Throne is propelled by the Spirit of the Living God that operates through His New Creation – the Living Creature. This New Living Creature is a Corporate One New Man in Christ made up of mature/maturing sons who form wings of God's Melchizedek Army flying by the Spirit with one another.

In the *Hitting the Bull's Eye of Righteousness* book, we see how the Order of Melchizedek is the predecessor of the Bride. Keep this in mind when you think of the Lamb in the midst of God's Kingdom. Not only is there a Lamb and four beasts in the midst of God's Kingdom, but there is a Lamb with His Bride:

- *"⁴ And the twenty-four elders and the four living creatures fell down and worshipped God who sits on the throne saying, 'Amen. Hallelujah!' ⁵ And a voice came from the throne, saying, 'Give praise to our God, all you His bond-servants, you who fear Him, the small and the great.'⁶ Then I heard something like the voice of a great multitude and like the sound of many waters and like the sound of mighty peals of thunder, saying, 'Hallelujah! For the Lord our God, the Almighty, reigns.* ⁷ *Let us rejoice and be glad and give the glory to Him, for the marriage of the Lamb has come and His Bride has made herself ready.* ⁸ *It was given to her to clothe herself in fine linen, bright and clean; for the fine linen is the righteous acts of the saints.'* ⁹ *Then he said to me, 'Write, "Blessed are those who are invited to the marriage supper of the Lamb."' And he said to me, 'These are true words of God'" (Revelation 19:4-9 NASB)*

- "That He might present to Himself the church in all her glory, having no spot or wrinkle or any such thing: but that she would be holy and blameless" (Ephesians 5:27 NASB).

IN THE MIDST OF GOD'S KINGDOM IS A THRONE WHERE THERE IS A KING AND QUEEN. Know that His most valued possession is His True Queen of Heaven. That the commitment of being married to the King of Kings is not to be taken lightly is almost an understatement. His Queen will most excellently represent the King.

*****

2 – WITH THIS BREAD & WINE, I THEE WED

When I helped organize daily prayer for a citywide event in the year 2000, the Lord led a time of communion. He desired each participant to look solely at Yeshua and privately take the communion elements with Him, as one, yet corporately.

As I quieted myself down and slightly raised my portion of bread, I immediately heard a clear still, small voice say, "With this bread, I Thee wed." I don't remember what I was thinking at the time, but it certainly wasn't along that line. It was such a revelatory moment. So, I raised my bread a little higher and solemnly whispered, "With this bread, I thee wed." Then I took the bread of heavenly common union and became one with it.

Next, I raised my cup. Again, I immediately and unmistakably heard inside my spirit, "With this wine, I Thee wed." With total reverential awe, I whispered: "With this wine, I thee wed."

Our God is so detailed. It was the third day of the week when I heard: "With this bread and wine, I thee wed." I found out years later that Tuesdays (i.e., the third day of the week) is the day when weddings took place in ancient Israel. Our Beloved is coming to marry His pure and spotless Bride in this prophetic third day.

Webster's Collegiate Dictionary, 10th Edition:

WED ~*verb* : to take for wife or husband by a formal ceremony : MARRY : to join in marriage : to pledge : to enter into matrimony

MARRY ~*verb* : to join as husband and wife : to give in marriage : to take a spouse : WED : to unite in close and unusually permanent relation

UNITE ~*verb* : to put together to form a single unit : to cause to adhere : to link by a legal or moral bond : to possess (as qualities) in combination : to become one or as if one : to become combined by or as if by adhesion : to act in concert [more at ONE]

COMBINE ~*verb* : to bring into such close relationship as to obscure individual characters : MERGE : to cause to unite into a single number or expression : BLEND : to possess in combination

*****

3 – WITH THIS BREAD & WINE, WE THEE WED

After several years of my taking communion elements daily, a holy shift happened. The taking OF communion (common union) changed to the taking ON common union.

One morning after receiving a vision of Yeshua walking among the Seven Spirits of God, I heard the Father say: "Today, we come together for holy matrimony." Since I had been declaring "With this wine and bread, I thee wed" over my daily communion for years, I was a bit perplexed and at the same time extremely expectant. I waited silently in awe. Then without any external instruction, all four of us – the Father, the Son, the Holy Spirit and I – spontaneously recited in unison: "With this bread and wine, we thee wed." We all took the communion of holy matrimony.

My heart-cry the previous night was that the seven-fold nature of Christ (that's represented before the throne as seven torches) would take possession of me. From the depths, I cried out to be completely possessed by the life of

God. I wanted to walk in the fullest impartation of the Seven Spirits of God, like Yeshua did when He walked the earth.

I had been reading Nita Johnson's book *Melchizedek: The New Millennium Priesthood* at the time. It literally struck me that Melchizedek saints will have Christ's Being lived out through them by means of the Seven Spirits of God. The Spirits – the divine spiritual depiction of the seven-fold nature of Christ – will promote God's administered will or government on earth through this end-time priesthood.

All that is given through the marvelous gift of the Seven Spirits of God is designed to bring the Bride into a place where she is without spot or wrinkle. These carriers of God's Divine Presence have been willing to have the world removed from their soul come-what-may in order to gain the Seven Spirits of God, so they can rule and reign throughout the earth. God needs them to break the strongholds that are crippling the earth.

The torn veil at Christ's crucifixion re-instituted the original royal priesthood made in the Order of Melchizedek with Christ Jesus – the Lamb of God Himself – being its High Priest. In this Kingdom Day, we are taking a giant quantum leap forward, which God has prepared for us from the beginning of time. Truly, all that matters right now is your decision to set your heart like flint to let the world go. If what awaits you at the end of the path is manifest common union with Christ and the infilling of the fullness of Jesus Christ, isn't it worth it?!

Through this great royal priesthood, the Lord will birth the "Bridal Company" in the earth that conforms to the Living Word and the Spirit of Christ. Right now, the Order of Melchizedek is beginning to march throughout the earth, as the predecessor of the Bride. Won't you join us in selling out all for Jesus?!

> "^{38} *Now the just shall live by faith: but if any man draw back, My soul shall have no pleasure in him* [note: God has a soul]. ^{39} *But we are not of them who draw back unto perdition; but of them that believe to the POSSESSING of the soul*" *(Hebrews 10:38-39).*

POSSESS = Strong's NT:4047 *peripoiēsis* - a preservation : possession, one's own property : an obtaining : acquisition : saving.

REFERENCES: Genesis 14:18; Psalm 110:4; Isaiah 9:7; 11:1-2; Hebrews 5:4-6; Hebrews 6:19-20; Hebrews 7:1-28; Revelation 4:5.

*****

4 – BEHOLD, A NEW LIVING CREATURE

The mysterious elements in Scripture are found when we study God's Word like a man who brings out of his household treasures both old and new. I am going to reveal one of the highly treasured aspects of the picture the Lord gave when the Father, the Son, the Holy Spirit and I spontaneously recited in unison: "With this bread and wine, we thee wed." By the way, this is a huge key to the unveiling the mysteries surrounding the Order of Melchizedek.

Almighty God handed us a key to a treasure that is connected to the Living Creature portrayed in the faces of *Ezekiel 1:10:* "*As for the likeness of their faces, each had the face of a man; each of the four had the face of a lion on the right side, each of the four had the face of an ox on the left side, and each of the four had the face of an eagle.*"

The Father is represented by the face of the bull or the ox, which is communicated through the ancient Hebrew letter of *alef/aleph*. The Son is represented by the face of the lion who is the Lion of the Tribe of Judah (Revelation 5:5).

The Holy Spirit is represented by the face of the eagle that soars in the Spirit. Finally, put yourself in place of the face of the man; and thus, we see a new revelatory dimension that the four living creatures is a New Living Creature.

The One New Man in Christ has an application on both an individual and corporate level. Individually, you and I, need to be wed in a fourfold way, so that Christ's Being can be lived out through us by means of the Seven Spirits of God according to the perfect will of the Father. Let's hover on the individual application on how God is going to rule and reign in and through His Purified (Crucified) Ones. We each need to be firing to-the-best-of-our-ability on all cylinders before we connect corporately. The key is to-the-best-of-our-ability for remember His fiery chariot throne is also a throne of grace.

> "*⁴ And I looked, and, behold, a whirlwind came out of the north, a great cloud, and a fire infolding itself, and a brightness was about it, and out of the midst thereof as the color of amber, out of the midst of the fire. ⁵ Also out of the midst thereof came the likeness of four living creatures. And this was their appearance; they had the likeness of a man" (Ezekiel 1:4-5 KJV).*

> "*¹⁹ And when the living creatures went, the wheels went by them: and when the living creatures were lifted up from the earth, the wheels were lifted up. ²⁰ Whithersoever the spirit was to go, they went, thither was their spirit to go; and the wheels were lifted up over against them: for the spirit of the living creature was in the wheels. ²¹ When those went, these went; and when those stood, these stood; and when those were lifted up from the earth, the wheels were lifted up over against them: for the spirit of the living creature was in the wheels" (Ezekiel 1:19-21 KJV).*

REFERENCES: Ezekiel 1; Hebrews 4:16: Revelation 1:4.

UNDERSTANDING THE ORDER OF MELCHIZEDEK

*****

5 – BEHOLD, THE NEW LIVING CREATURE IS THE CHERUBIM

"I kept looking until thrones were set up, and the Ancient of Days took His seat; His vesture was like white snow and the hair of His head like pure wool. His throne was ablaze with flames, its wheels were a burning fire" (Daniel 7:9 NASB).

In our last chapter, we glanced at the Living Creature (i.e., four living creatures) depicting a dimension of the One New Man in Christ on a personal level where an individual is joined to the Father, the Son, and the Holy Spirit in a four-fold way, so that Christ's Being can be lived out through a person by means of the Seven Spirits of God according to the perfect will of the Father. This is not something done automatically when we are born again from above, but a progressive work of oneness wrought through a person aiming at the goal of becoming holy, as He is holy. Rightly searching one's heart and taking things to the cross daily while taking on communion (common union) are essential ingredients to becoming a living breathing manifestation of a New Living Creature in Christ. God knows, and He will tell you when you have reached a certain level of hitting this mark of the high calling of God in Christ Jesus. He is the only One that can.

Before we apply this picture on a corporate level, let's examine this New Living Creature more thoroughly. Ezekiel 1:20-21 tells us that the spirit of the Living Creature is in the wheels. In the last chapter, we alluded to the picture of the "wheel within a wheel" in the Book of Ezekiel, which symbolizes God ruling and reigning through His Purified (Crucified) Ones. Notice that the wheels on His chariot throne in Daniel 7:9 are described as a burning fire.

Hebrews 1:7 speaks of the Most Holy One making His ministers a flame of fire. Many people dismiss this verse as applying only to angels, but they would be missing a vital, albeit mysterious, ingredient. The word for "angels" in Hebrew 1:7 is the Greek word *aggelos*, which is from the Hebrew and means "sent one" or "messenger." But here's a hidden fact that will blow your mind! Both the Hebrew Scriptures and Greek Septuagint tell us that the sent one or messenger can be either a divine angelic or divine human messenger.

The Living Creature of Ezekiel 1 are also called "Cherubim" in Ezekiel 10. The specific points that connect the Living Creature of Ezekiel Chapter 10 to Chapter 1 are the following. By the way, I am sharing the King James Version of Ezekiel Chapter 1 and Chapter 10 due to it being the most accurate English translation of the confusing Hebrew in this case:

[1] Each of the living creatures have four faces apiece:

- *"⁶And every one had four faces, and every one had four wings. ¹⁰ As for the likeness of their faces, they four had the face of a man, and the face of a lion, on the right side: and they four had the face of an ox on the left side; they four also had the face of an eagle" (Ezekiel 1:6,10 KJV).*

- *"Every one had four faces apiece, and every one four wings; and the likeness of the hands of a man was under their wings" (Ezekiel 10:21 KJV).*

[2] Each of the living creatures had four wings with the likeness of the hands of man under their wings:

- *"And they had the hands of a man under their wings on their four sides; and they four had their faces and their wings" (Ezekiel 1:8 KJV).*

- *"Every one had four faces apiece, and every one four wings; and the likeness of the hands of a man was under their wings" (Ezekiel 10:21 KJV).*

[3] Each of the living creatures went straight forward:

- *"And when they went every one straight forward: whither the spirit was to go, they went; and they turned not when they went" (Ezekiel 1:12 KJV).*

- *"And the likeness of their faces was the same faces which I saw by the river Chebar, their appearances and themselves; they went every one straight forward" (Ezekiel 10:22 KJV).*

[4] Seen by the river Chebar:

- *"Now it came to pass in the thirtieth year, in the fourth month, in the fifth day of the month, as I was among the captives by the river Chebar, that the heavens were opened, and I saw visions of God" (Ezekiel 1:1 KJV).*

- *"[20] THIS IS THE LIVING CREATURE that I saw under the God of Israel by the river Chebar; and I knew that THEY WERE THE CHERUBIM. [22] And the likeness of their faces was the same faces which I saw by the river Chebar, their appearances and themselves; they went every one straight forward" (Ezekiel 10:20,22 KJV).*

The details behind these four points will have to wait. For now, note that when you see the word "angel," "cherub," or "cherubim" in Scripture, think of it like a red flag going up in a good way to alert us to the possible presence of a deep kingdom mystery connected to our being a New Living Creature in Christ. Not only is this mystery preserved in the bowels of Scripture, but also in a commentary about Melchizedek in the 11Q13 section of the *Dead Sea Scrolls*.

"[4] And I looked, and, behold, a whirlwind came out of the north, a great cloud, and a fire infolding itself, and a brightness was about it, and out of the midst thereof as the color of amber, out of the midst of the fire. [5] Also out of the midst thereof came the likeness of four living creatures. And this was their appearance; they had the likeness of a man" (Ezekiel 1:4-5 KJV).

"[26] And above the firmament that was over their heads was the likeness of a throne, as the appearance of a sapphire stone: and upon the likeness of the throne was the likeness as the appearance of a man above upon it. [27] And I saw as the color of amber, as the appearance of fire round about within it, from the appearance of his

loins even upward, and from the appearance of his loins even downward, I saw as it were the appearance of fire, and it had brightness round about. ²⁸ As the appearance of the bow that is in the cloud in the day of rain, so was the appearance of the brightness round about. This was the appearance of the likeness of the glory of the LORD. And when I saw it, I fell upon my face, and I heard a voice of one that spake" (Ezekiel 1:26-28 KJV).

"¹ Then I looked, and, behold, in the firmament that was above the head of the cherubim there appeared over them as it were a sapphire stone, as the appearance of the likeness of a throne. ²⁰ THIS IS THE LIVING CREATURE that I saw under the God of Israel by the river Chebar; and I knew that THEY WERE THE CHERUBIM. ²¹ Every one had four faces apiece, and every one four wings; and the likeness of the hands of a man was under their wings. ²² And the likeness of their faces was the same faces which I saw by the river Chebar, their appearances and themselves; they went every one straight forward" (Ezekiel 10:1, 20-22 KJV).

REFERENCES: Leviticus 27:14; Ezekiel 1; Ezekiel 10; Daniel 7:9-10; Matthew 16:24; Ephesians 1:4; Philippians 3:14; 1 Peter 1:15; Hebrew 1:7.

*****

6 – WING OF ROYAL PRIESTS FLYING BY THE SPIRIT

Once a person is manifestly joined to the Father, the Son and the Holy Spirit, as a New Living Creature, they still need to press on into greater levels of their high calling of God in Christ to be completely ONE not only with God Himself, but with others. This is a divine work which connects the Head – Jesus Christ who is the Messiah – to His Body. This work of connecting the Messiah's Head to His Body is wrought not by might, nor by power, but by His Spirit (Zechariah 4:6) as well as at the intersection where His will and your will are one. We need to understand how powerful the crucified concept is of *"not My will, but thine, be done" (Luke 22:42)*. God's Kingdom comes where His perfect will is heard, understood, and done.

The corporate level of His new creation of the One New Man in Christ is portrayed several ways. Let's focus on the Living Creature's wings today. Ezekiel 1:9 tells us that the four living creatures' wings touch one another as they move straight ahead without turning.

To understand the significance of the New Living Creature's wings, we need to take a Hebrew peek. The most common (and first) occurrence of the word "wings" in Scripture is the Hebrew word *kanaph* (pronounced kaw-nawf'). *The Strong's Concordance* tells us that it's an edge or extremity, specifically of a wing or an army. This definition really got my attention, because I had just come off a third-heaven group experience where the Great Shepherd (i.e., Yeshua) led an excursion to take captivity captive for a group of pastors where the Lord divinely imparted some spiritual equipment to each one of us for our journey: a golden Melchizedek breastplate with triple-concentric circles in the midst, a golden shepherd rod, and a set of wings. Significantly, He told me ahead of time that four people needed to be present for the type of thing that we all wanted to accomplish. So, when I saw the above definition for *kanaph*, I immediately received a greater revelation: *Kanaph* speaks of a precise wing of God's end-time Melchizedek Army flying by the Spirit with one another.

Next, I flipped over to my *Webster's Collegiate Dictionary (10the Edition)* and looked up the definition for "wing":

> **WING** ~*noun* : one of the movable feathered or membranous paired appendages by means a creature is able to fly : power of flight : means of flight or rapid progress : a flank of an army : one of the offensive positions on either side of a center position (Christ) : a unit of the U.S. Air Force higher than a group and lower than a division : two or more squadrons of naval airplanes : a dance step marked by quick outward and inward rolling guide of one foot : insignia consisting of an outspread pair of stylized bird's wings which are awarded on completion of prescribed training to a qualified pilot or aircrew member.

Then I dug even deeper by searching for revelation in the Ancient Hebrew Word Picture (pictograph) of the word *kanaph*. An Ancient Hebrew Word Picture is when you put the different pictures that the Hebrew letters represent together to understand a deeper meaning of a Hebrew word. By the way, I try not to not lean on my own understanding, as I set a Hebrew Word Picture before the Lord in a meditative way. For example: *Kanap*h's Ancient Hebrew Word Picture is made up of three Hebrew letters: *kaf, noon,* and *pey. Kanaph* in Hebrew looks like – כנף. Let's break the pictures of kaw-nawf' down:

כ - pictograph of the Hebrew letter *kaf* is a wing or open hand that symbolizes:

    1) to allow,

    2) to cover, and

    3) to open.

נ - pictograph of the Hebrew letter *noon* or *nun* is a fish darting through the water that symbolizes:

    1) action, and

    2) life.

ף - pictograph of the Hebrew letter *pey* is a mouth. It symbolizes:

    1) to speak,

    2) to open, and

    3) the beginning, like a river.

Having just studied the word "throne" in Scripture, I understood that the picture for *kaf* as a wing meant a kingdom covering or being enthroned. Therefore, *kanaph*'s Ancient Hebrew Word Picture tells us several things:

[1] Wings are the beginning of covered (enthroned, kingdom) life and action.

[2] Wings speak of kingdom life and action as well as open things up to it.

[3] Wings open things by speaking life

When the wings of the Living Creature touch one another, it is a picture of a wing of God's end-time Melchizedek Army touching the heart of a matter – or – in other words, a wing of royal priests hitting the bull's eye of the Father's perfect will. It portrays God's Kingdom moving straight ahead when a group of Crucified Ones fly by the Spirit with one another according to His throne. It's the place where His word goes forth and doesn't return void, but accomplishes exactly what is in the heart of the Father, here on earth as it is in heaven.

What do you say? Shall we point some wings?! Shall His royal priests open things to God's kingdom life and action?! You betcha!!!

REFERENCES: Leviticus 27:14; Ezekiel 1, Ezekiel 10; Zechariah 4:6; Matthew 16:24; Luke 22:42; Ephesians 1:4; Philippians 3:14.

*****

7 – HIS NEW LIVING CRETAURE'S PURPOSE

Since a life without purpose is worthless, let's examine the purpose of a wing of the Order of Melchizedek flying in the Spirit together. The "cherubim" classification of the New Living Creature of Melchizedek holds several keys for us. First, please recall that a "cherubim" can be either a divine angelic or divine human messenger – sent one – according to Hebrew Scripture and the Greek Septuagint. *"This is the Living Creature that I saw under the God of Israel by the river of Chebar; and I knew that they were the Cherubim" (Ezekiel 10:20 KJV).*

IN THE MIDST OF GOD'S KINGDOM is a throne and in the midst of the throne are the living creatures that are sometimes called Cherubim. The living creatures have to do with creation. They mark the heavenly sweet spot for our returning to our primordial state on earth, as it was in the Garden before the Fall.

Let us see what Scripture has say about the Cherubim overall.

SCRIPTURE COMMUNICATES THAT CHERUBIM:

[1] Cherubim mark the spot for us returning to our pristine, primeval state (Genesis 3:24).

[2] Cherubim are guardians of the holiness of God *"to keep the way of the Tree of Life" (Genesis 3:24)*, and therefore, they must express His holiness.

[3] Cherubim mark the Dwelling Place of God, because He *"dwells between the cherubim" (Numbers 7:89; 1 Samuel 4:4; 2 Samuel 6:2; 2 Kings 19:15; Psalm 80:1; Psalm 99:1; Isaiah 37:16)*.

[4] Cherubim are carriers of God's throne, which is the seat of His divine glory as well as His royal power (1 Chronicles 28:18; Ezekiel 1:26-28; Ezekiel 10:1).

CHERUBIM ARE FOUND IN 3 MAJOR CONTEXTS IN THE BIBLE:

[1] Cherubim stand at the entrance of the Garden of Eden with a flaming sword, which turns every way to keep the way to the Tree of Life (Genesis 3:24).

[2] In God's Dwelling Place (i.e., The Tabernacle, The Temple and The New Jerusalem), Cherubim are the most frequently sculpted, engraved, and embroidered figures made according to a heavenly pattern given by the Lord Himself (Exodus 26:1, Exodus 26:31-33; Exodus 36:8, Exodus 36:35; 1 Kings 6:29-35;

[3] Cherubim are attendants of Almighty God and His throne. Cherubim make up the foundation of His fiery chariot throne that bears God's Kingdom here on earth (Daniel 7:9; Ezekiel 1:22-28; Ezekiel 10:1). God's royal priests set out for the goal to become just like Yeshua -- the High Priest of the eternal order of Melchizedek. We will soon see how His Melchizedek Company is the Messenger that will facilitate the kingdoms of this world becoming the kingdoms of our Lord, and His Christ (Revelation 11:15).

REFERENCES: Genesis 3:24; Exodus 26:1, Exodus 26:31-33; Exodus 36:8, Exodus 36:35; Numbers 7:89; 1 Samuel 4:4; 2 Samuel 6:2; 1 Kings 6:29-35; 2 Kings 19:15; 1 Chronicles 28:18; 2 Chronicles 3:7; Psalm 80:1; Psalm 99:1; Isaiah 37:16; Ezekiel 1:22-28; Ezekiel 10:1; Daniel 7:9; Revelation 11:15.

SPECIAL NOTE OF WARNING: In the last chapter, I mentioned a third-heaven group ascension experience that ultimately led to proclaiming liberty for a group of pastors. It was glorious! I want to encourage everyone to go through the Revelation 4:1 open door in heaven by the Blood of Jesus Christ of Nazareth (Hebrews 10:19), but I'd also like to mention a word of caution. All of us must go there completely surrendered to His will and His ways. We can ask the Lord if we can do such-and-such and He may lead us to do so, but please never initiate any divine encounters out of your own soul. The Revelation 4:1 Heavenly Door is meant to take us into the Third Heaven where His throne and other realms of the Most High God exist. If we soulishly try to go there with our own imaginations and our own agendas, we will end up in a place where the prince of the power of the air reigns. The Lord has shown a person in our *Corporate One North* group a place in the lower heavens that mimics and slightly twists a Third Heaven Experience. This is NOT where the Revelation 4:1 Door is supposed to lead to. Another thing that will cause experiences to not go as high as we need to go is when we have idols in our hearts unbeknownst to ourselves. A simple grace-filled way to protect ourselves from "getting off" in this manner is to simply focus on Yeshua and only report what the individuals in your group see, hear, or perceive in the Spirit. We must NEVER try to ascend to the Third Heaven with our own agenda. Humility and simplicity are key.

*****

8 – CREATURE WAITING FOR MANIFESTATION OF MATURE SONS

The New Living Creature, which is a wing of the Order of Melchizedek flying in the Spirit together, waits for the manifestation of mature sons.

"For the earnest expectation of the CREATURE waiteth for the manifestation of the sons of God" (Romans 8:19 KJV).

Today, we usually hear the phrase "All creation waits for the manifestation of the sons of God," which is true and accurate, but more specifically this verse is speaking about the restoration of all things is waiting for a royal priesthood to arise, shine and rule the earth, as co-heirs in Christ. All of creation groans for the ones who will be delivered from the bondage of corruption into the glorious liberty of the children of God (Romans 8:21-22).

We truly are what we are waiting for. In fact, the entire world is on the edge of its seat – groaning – desperately looking for the Corporate One New Man in Christ to become a public demonstration of His power. The key that unlocks the formidable appearance of the Royal Order of Melchizedek (with Jesus Christ as its High Priest) is mature sonship.

The second leg of our three-part journey of *"moving onto perfection" (Hebrews 6:1)* is called the son's portion, but more accurately it should be defined as the mature son's portion for that's the ultimate goal at this part of our Kingdom trek. Our quest to be just like Jesus is "painfully beautiful" at this juncture.

The son's portion is the place where our bonds in Christ are readily perceived by our senses and recognized by our minds (Philippian 1:13). Second Corinthians 5:14 tells us that the love of Christ should instruct, control or constrain us. Therefore, the bonds in Christ are obvious within a believer at this stage when one endeavors to become a mature man (Ephesians 4:13) or when one shoots even higher to become part of Christ's pure and spotless Bride (Matthew 25: 1-13; Ephesians 5:27; Revelation 21). Remember that both men and women are called to be Adult Sons and the Bride of Christ, because in the Spirit there's no male or female (Galatians 3:28). By the way, the third and hardest leg of the "moving unto perfection" journey is the bridal portion. For now, please note that sons are chosen to build a house for God's sanctuary (1 Chronicles 28:10) while His Bride literally makes up His house. She is the glorious exalted space where He can and will dwell: *"²And I John saw the holy city, New Jerusalem, coming down from God out of heaven, prepared as a bride adorned for her husband. ³ And I heard a great voice out of heaven saying, Behold, the tabernacle of God is with men, and He will dwell with them, and they shall be His people, and God Himself shall be with them, and be their God" (Revelation 21:2-3 KJV).*

Let's keep focused on the full-grown son's portion. Please note that the magnificent corporate purpose of mature sons being bonded in Christ is to unite via an attractive force as His Bride, and then to embed this cohesive force into a matrix called the One New Man in Christ, which is a phenomenal truth.

The maturing son's portion is a place where we are moving beyond proving what's merely good to a more restrained place of proving what's acceptable, approved or pleasing in God's sight, so we will no longer be conformed to this world in a greater measure (Romans 12:2).

Let the words of my mouth and the meditation of my heart be acceptable in Your sight, O LORD, my rock and my Redeemer. (Psalm 19:14 NASB).

We tend to forget that it was partaking of the Tree of the Knowledge of good and evil that caused man to fall from their exalted state of daily communion with God. When we are working out what is acceptable to the Lord our God in our Kingdom within, God works to rein in our mouths, hearts and deeds to align perfectly with His words, His thought and His works. Incremental solidified change results in transformation, which can be a lengthy process at best unless God does something sovereign. Be forewarned: When God is tuning a person's life to that which is acceptable in His sight, anything that grieves His heart will surface. Mixture will be sifted out here.

Most believers, if not all, have things to perfect at this level. If you think that you don't, it's the quickest signal that you do because having a humble, teachable heart is a preeminent hallmark of a maturing or mature son of God (Proverbs 2-7). Growing, maturing sons continually endeavor to work out their salvation with fear and trembling

(Philippians 2:12), according to the righteous and just standards of God's throne (Psalm 89:14).

When we declare platitudes, like: I'm already holy, I'm already righteous, I'm already a mature son, I'm already His Bride, or I'm already an overcomer, we need to realize that God is already examining those very areas of our life to see if they measure up. Any one of the above manifestations are heavenly positions that believers have access to "in Christ," but it's God's appraisal of our earthly condition that determines the level of a person's or a group's maturity.

Ephesians 4:13 tells us that "a mature man" is determined by the standard of the measure of the stature which belongs to the fullness of Christ. Jesus Christ's fullness is always 100-percent. Your or my fullness is not. Not yet. I dare you to ask the Lord, "How much of the fullness of the stature of Christ do I have?" Our goal is for these heavenly positions to become walking-talking realities here in the land of the living; but for now, I see too often that these glorious heavenly positions, like being an Adult Son or the Bride, are used as emphatic declarations that keep us unknowingly stunted.

Everyone (both in the Church and the world) recognizes a genuine manifestation of God's power and any heavenly position manifestly held here on earth. If we're honest with ourselves, we will see that blanket platitudes are red flags that signal where God would like to refine us. Trite remarks usually indicate areas where we're protective, defensive, and unwilling to dive deeper into the Way and the Truth and the Life. When someone utters, I'm already such-and-such but their life doesn't always demonstrate that reality, the only people who buy into their confession are like-minded individuals. Everyone else can discern the fact that your State of Being doesn't measure up to what you tout. Christ's Church needs to recognize that our hypocritical assumptions are painfully obvious to the most casual observer.

> *"He began saying to His disciples first of all, 'Beware of the leaven of the Pharisees, which is hypocrisy'" (Luke 12:1b NASB).*

Most of us are more immature than we'd like to admit. Just remember that if you cannot or will not admit the truth of your current condition here on earth, you'll never be set free in that area of your life because it's the truth that set us free (John 8:32). But praise be to God that He never denies genuine heart cries! Oh, that we might turn, and be healed!

Wade Taylor writes in *"Make the Right Choices"*: "Our 'willing obedience' is the determining factor in our becoming an overcomer. Being an overcomer is not that we do. Rather, it relates to the intent and issues of our heart, which determines our actions.... as long as we walk in submission and obedience, it can be said that we are an overcomer." I agree, except I'd extend this statement to include holiness, righteousness, mature sons, the Bride, etc. For this subject, let's just say that our willing obedience to the One who sits on the throne and unto the Lamb is the determining factor in our becoming a mature son.

Two chief characteristics of a son of God is that they serve God with a whole heart (1 Chronicles 28:9) as well as keeping God's commandments (Proverbs 7:1-2: 1 John 2:3-6; Revelation 14:12). We are not talking about something yucky and legalistic, but a State of Being that resonates at the same frequency as the Word of God – Jesus. Please be encouraged, because this is a divine work of sanctification that's done not by your might, or your power, but by His Spirit (Zechariah 4:6). All that God requires from you and I is that we put our best foot forward in obeying His Word and surrendering to

His Spirit.

Thankfully, the Lord our God will give us all the grace that we need (2 Corinthians 9:8; Hebrews 4:16).

"For I am confident of this very thing, that He who began a good work in you will perfect it until the day of Christ Jesus" (Philippians 1:6 NASB).

Even though the son's portion came in the Fullness of Time when Jesus came to earth and purchased it on the cross (Galatians 4:4-6), we must experientially appropriate the redemptive gift of sonship the same way that it was acquired. Our journey of "moving unto perfection" is a crucifixion process. Dying daily is the only way we actually develop into mature, full-grown sons of God (Matthew 10:37-39, Matthew 16:24; Mark 8:34, Mark 10:21; Luke 9:23, Luke 14:27). The wisdom of God insists upon our permission to crucify our sin nature, and He will only complete the work of co-crucifixion with Christ with our approval. Volunteering freely in the day of God's power is a continual daily sanctioning of *"not my will, but Yours be done" (Matthew 6:10)*. Paul shows us the culmination of being an Adult Son is living a crucified life:

"I have been crucified with Christ; and it is no longer I who live, but Christ lives in me; and the life which I now live in the flesh I live by faith in the Son of God, who loved me and gave Himself up for me" (Galatians 2:20 NASB).

It's the Good Shepherd of our souls who chooses the best sacrifice that will go on His Altar, not us. So, when you find yourself in a miserable place where you just want out (you want to run for all your worth), just stop, take a breath, stand, and keep your eyes focused on the prize – the Author and Perfecter of your faith, who for the joy set before Him endured the cross (Hebrews 12:2).

> *"² My brethren, count it all joy when ye fall into divers temptations (encounter various trials); ³ Knowing this, that the trying of your faith worketh patience. ⁴ But let patience have her perfect work, that ye may be perfect and entire (complete), wanting nothing" (James 1:2-4 KJV).*

When you focus on the Way and the Truth and the Life (John 14:6), He revelatory leads you beside the still waters around the Tree of Life, which will enable you to recognize and process the grueling situation(s) you find yourself in according to His Kingdom come. As you keep focused on Him when you encounter various trials, the Lord our God will restore your soul (Psalm 23:3). He will guide you in the paths of righteousness for His Name sake (Psalm 23:3), and He will prepare a feast of goodness, kindness and love before you in the presence of your enemies (Psalm 23:5). And thus, you are well on your way on the path of life (i.e., righteousness) where one of the most arduous tests is overcoming evil with good (Romans 12:21):

> *"⁴⁴ But I say to you, love your enemies and pray for those who persecute you, ⁴⁵ so that you may be sons of your Father who is in heaven; for He causes His sun to rise on the evil and the good, and sends rain on the righteous and the unrighteous. ⁴⁶ For if you love those who love you, what reward do you have? Do not even the tax collectors do the same? ⁴⁷ If you greet only brothers, what more are you doing than others? Do not even the Gentiles do the same? ⁴⁸ Therefore you are to be perfect, as your heavenly Father is perfect." (Matthew 5:44-48 NASB).*

Only the highest caliber of saints allows their sin natures to be completely crucified. Through the ages, saints who've endured the cross to live in this high and lofty place of common union with the Most High God have been few and far between. People like Enoch, Moses, the Apostle John and Paul were totally separated from the world, which allowed them to live an overcoming life in a crossover place with God, so sacred and beautiful that it begs description. Even though resurrection life (complete crucifixion of worldly and fleshly passions) is not a new grace, it's been preferred by and fixed on by a small number of extremely devout saints. One of the new things that God is going to do in our day is to extend this crucified life grace (authentic death, burial, resurrection life reality) to a large company of believers:

> "*[10] That I may know Him and the power of His resurrection and the fellowship of His suffering, being conformed to His death; [11] in order that I may attain to the resurrection from the dead. [12] Not that I have already obtained it or have already become perfect, but I press on so that I may lay hold of that for which also I was laid hold of by Christ Jesus*" (Philippians 3:10-12 NASB).

We must remember that difficult crucifying circumstances are the painfully beautiful agents that form you into His very image where you are filled with tangible effervescent joy, unwavering powerful love, profound life-giving wisdom, et cetera. All of you, for all of Him. It's really quite a bargain.

Let's shift for a moment, please remember that the Biblical pattern for each new dispensation is first a precious son volunteers to become a worshipful, sacrificial burnt offering; then gradually a new dwelling place for God is built. This means we need to look more into what God says about a precious or mature son.

Almost every time the word "son" is used in the New Testament, it comes from two Greek words:

1. *teknon*: babies or immature sons,

2. *huios*: mature sons (used in Revelation 21:7)

Immature sons of God – *teknons* – tend to go after their own heart's desires, and are less likely to follow the leading of the Holy Spirit. So basically, a mark of the spiritually immature is that they have not yet learned to act only on the Spirit's leading. Another mark of spiritual immaturity is most often *teknons* react, or respond, emotionally or intellectually to various trials they face as well as seeking to protect themselves; therefore, they are *"always learning and never able to come to the knowledge of the truth" (2 Timothy 3:7)*. We can only come to the knowledge of the truth by applying it.

Character is forged by facing difficult circumstances, not running away from or hiding from the truth. Truth must be allowed to have its way in our lives if we are going to mature. The Hebrew pictograph for the word "humble" reveals that humility comes when we destroy our walls of self-protection. While the Hebrew pictograph for the word "pride" tells us that we are in pride when we lift ourselves up in our own strength.

God's Kingdom focuses on growing and maturing sons (*huios*). Physical growth for people is a function of time. Intellectual growth is a function of learning. While spiritual growth is a function of obedience. If Jesus was a mature Son (*huios*), yet He learned obedience by the things He suffered (Hebrews 5:8), then we should expect to have to walk in the same manner as He did (1 John 2:6):

" ⁶ Do you not know that when you present yourselves to someone as slaves for obedience, you are slaves of the one whom you obey, either of sin resulting in death, or obedience resulting in righteousness? ... ¹⁹ I am speaking in human terms because of the weakness of your flesh. For just as you presented your members as slaves to impurity and to lawlessness, resulting in further lawlessness, so now present your members as slaves to righteousness, resulting in sanctification [holiness]" (Romans 6:16,19 NASB).

From these verses we see a pattern where obedience to God's divine will results in our righteousness, which results in our holiness. Please allow me to pull out some prevalent Biblical themes with regard to mature sons of God without doing an exhaustive study. Mature or Adult Sons:

1. Are heirs of God's Kingdom (Romans 8:17; Galatians 3:29; Hebrews 11:8-10).

2. Serve God with a whole heart and willing mind, i.e., soul (1 Chronicles 28:9).

3. Are chosen to build a dwelling place for God's sanctuary (1 Chronicles 28:10).

4. Hear, treasure, and observe God's commandments (Proverbs 1:8; Proverbs 2:1; Proverbs 4:1; Proverbs 5:7; Proverbs 7:1,24).

5. Love their enemies and they pray for their persecutors (Matthew 5:44-45).

6. Are continually led by the Spirit of God (Romans 8:14).

7. Make up the overcoming bridal company (Revelation 21:7).

Mature or maturing sons of the Living God make up the overcoming bridal company; however, all mature sons are not necessarily part of the pure and spotless Bride (Matthew 25:1-13; Ephesians 5:27). One does not guarantee the other. There are wise virgins and foolish virgins within the church. To be part of Christ's Bride, one must literally go through their own close and personal baptism of fire (i.e., complete crucifixion) where the All-Consuming Fire who sits on the sapphire throne (Ezekiel 1:26-27, Ezekiel 10:1; Hebrews 12:29) righteously judges our earth. On this side of heaven in the land of the living, God will be testing the quality of each bridal candidate's works by fire (1 Corinthians 3:12-15), so she can be properly clothed for the Marriage Supper of the Lamb with bright and clean fine linen, which is a robe of righteousness (Isaiah 61:10-11), or as Revelation 19:8 tells us that this fine linen is literally the righteous acts of the saints.

Please do not dismiss this truth lightly. Becoming part of the Bride of Christ is not a salvation issue, it's about the most intimate, eternal relationship with the King of kings. It's an eternal reward issue where no one will be exempt. True Christians will either be found by the Judge of heaven and earth, the King of the Ages, to be a wise virgin or a foolish one and I wouldn't just assume that you are counted in the wise column. Too much is at stake to assume and presume anything; and unfortunately, Christ's Church has taught us for decades that everyone who is part of the church is part of the pure and spotless Bride. This is not a Scripturally accurate picture. Please refer to the *"Here Comes The Bride"* Chapter in my book: *SANTA-TIZING: What's wrong with Christmas and how to clean it up* for more information => http://www.amazon.com/SANTA-TIZING-Whats-wrong-Christmas-clean/dp/1607911159/.

" ¹⁴ But God forbid that I should glory, save in the cross of our Lord Jesus Christ, by whom the world is crucified unto me, and I unto the world. ¹⁵ FOR IN CHRIST JESUS … AVAILETH … A NEW CREATURE" (Galatians 6:14-15 KJV).

In conclusion, even though the son's portion came in the Fullness of Time when Jesus came to earth and purchased it on the cross, we must appropriate the redemptive gift of sonship the same way that it was acquired. Our journey of "moving unto perfection" is a crucifixion process. Dying daily is the only way we develop into mature, full-grown sons of God. The wisdom of God insists upon our permission to crucify our sin nature, and He will only complete the work of co-crucifixion with Christ with our approval.

REFERENCES: Matthew 10:37-39; Matthew 17:11; Matthew 16:24; Mark 8:34; Mark 10:21; Luke 9:23; Luke 14:27; Romans 8:19-23; Galatians 4:4-6; Galatians 6:14-15; Ephesians 2:13-16; Hebrews 5:10; Hebrews 6:20; Hebrews 8:1.

*****

UNDERSTANDING THE ORDER OF MELCHIZEDEK

Book 4

Hitting the Bull's Eye of Righteousness

Cover Art: "Hitting the Bull's Eye of Righteousness"

by Robin Main

© August 21, 2014. All Rights Reserved

Text Copyright © 2014 Robin Main. All Rights Reserved

1 – INTRODUCTION

RIGHTEOUSNESS. It doesn't seem like it would be a controversial subject, but it is. Today, it's common to hear the phrase: "I am the righteousness of God in Christ Jesus." 2 Corinthians 5:21 may be one of the most misquoted Scriptures of our day:

"For He hath made Him to be sin for us, who knew no sin; THAT WE MIGHT BE MADE THE RIGHTEOUSNESS OF GOD IN HIM" *(2 Corinthians 5:21 KJV).*

This should not surprise us, because what is said to cloth the Bride? The righteous deeds or acts of the saints: *"Let us rejoice and be exceedingly glad, and let us give the glory to him. For the marriage of the Lamb has come, and his wife has made herself ready.* IT WAS GIVEN TO HER THAT SHE WOULD ARRAY HERSELF IN *bright, pure, fine linen: for the* FINE LINEN IS THE RIGHTEOUS ACTS OF THE HOLY ONES" *(Revelation 19:7-8 HNV).*

What does Melchizedek's name mean in the plain sense? King of Righteousness, which describes an essential element of his nature: "*¹ FOR THIS MELCHIZEDEK, king of Salem, priest of the Most High God, who met Abraham returning from the slaughter of the kings and blessed him, ² to whom also Abraham gave a tenth part of all, FIRST BEING TRANSLATED "KING OF RIGHTEOUSNESS," and then also king of Salem, meaning "king of peace" (Hebrews 7:1-2 NKJV)*.

What is a fundamental part of the foundation of God's Throne? Righteousness. *"RIGHTEOUSNESS and justice are THE FOUNDATION OF YOUR THRONE. Lovingkindness and truth go before your face" (Psalm 89:14 HNV)*.

When we think about how "righteousness" is a key ingredient for the Order of Melchizedek, the Bride of Christ and the foundation of God's throne, we get a huge clue as to why this manifest reality meets resistance. If the enemy of our souls can convince us that we already are the righteousness of God in Christ Jesus and don't need to do anything in this regard, then we cease to examine those areas of our lives that don't line up with the plumb line of Scripture:

> "*¹⁶ Therefore thus says the Lord GOD: 'Behold, I lay in Zion a stone for a foundation, A tried stone, a precious cornerstone, a sure foundation; Whoever believes will not act hastily. ¹⁷ Also I will make justice the measuring line, and RIGHTOUSNESS THE PLUMMET; The hail will sweep away the refuge of lies, and the waters will overflow the hiding place" (Isaiah 28:16-17 NKJV)*.

Abba showed a friend and myself a prophetic picture of RIGHTEOUSNESS as a literal plumb line. A plumb line is a line directed to the center of gravity of the earth - your earth and mine. It is a vertical line that goes straight to His Throne Room. It also measures the depth of something by examining it minutely and critically, so the House of God can be exactly vertical and true.

When we saw this vertical plumb line hanging by His frequency before us in the Spirit, the frequency appeared to be a multi-strand spiraling white light with a thin red line (outline) that started on the right side. It resembled a swirling heavenly wave of light, like a double-helix DNA structure, except it appeared as if there were all 12-strands of light, not merely two. As we stood in front of His plumb line, we bent before it. We were judged with His righteous judgments (Psalm 19:9). Then we heard something like three Big Ben booms, and the precious Blood of the Lamb set us vertically upright. Immediately, we began to climb the plumb line holding onto His frequency. As we climbed higher and higher, our garments changed from the top down. Our garments were not made out of a cloth material, but a light that was becoming a brilliant concentrated white light all over. Our inner line is becoming ONE with the plumb line frequency. Notice that it is by the Blood that we have the grace to climb higher. I would like to encourage us all to keep climbing and becoming one with the Plumb - *"becoming the righteousness of God in Christ Jesus"* (2 Corinthians 5:21). The Bride will vibrate at the same frequency as her Bridegroom.

The root meaning behind the Hebrew word for "righteousness" is "to be." RIGHTEOUSNESS is a Righteous State of Being where our actions line up with our beliefs and our words. Please note that in the same chapter that tells us that faith without works is dead, it shows us the completed faith of Abraham where we are told that by works His faith was made perfect (James 2:22): *"[20] But do you want to know, O foolish man, that faith without works is dead? [21] Was not Abraham our father justified by works when he offered Isaac his son on the altar? [22] Do you see that faith was working together with his works, and by works faith was made perfect?* ²³ *And the Scripture was fulfilled which says, "Abraham believed God, and it was accounted to him for righteousness." And he was called the friend of God.* ²⁴ *You see then that a man is justified by works, and not by faith only.* ²⁵ *Likewise, was not Rahab the harlot also justified by works when she received the messengers and sent them out another way?* ²⁶ *For as the body without the spirit is dead, so faith without works is dead also." (James 2:20-26* NKJV*).*

Righteous acts or deeds are works done according to the perfect will of the Father (Romans 12:2; Hebrews 10:7), which begins in the faith realm. There is simply no other way to know the perfect will of God: *"*³⁶ *For you have need of endurance, so that after you have done the will of God, you may receive the promise:* ³⁷ *'For yet a little while, And He who is coming will come and will not tarry. Now the just shall live by faith; But if anyone draws back, My soul has no pleasure in him.'* ³⁸ *But we are not of those who draw back to perdition, but of those who believe to the saving of the soul." (Hebrews 10:36-39* NKJV*).*

It is credited to you and me as righteousness when we manifest the perfect character of Christ in the present moment through the fullness of His indwelling Spirit where we live and move and have our being in Him (Acts 17:28). Righteousness is one of the elements the Kingdom of God is built upon; and it has all to do with our State of Being, not an activity. Righteousness is doing what is virtuous and right in His eyes where one's actions perfectly match the Word of God (the hidden manna in one's life). It's where our being resonates at the same frequency as the WORD OF GOD. It's where we LET THERE BE LIGHT!

As you can see, even though our righteousness in Christ is a present reality in every believer's life where we have been given a deposit of our heavenly position in Christ, it is still something that has to be "walked out" in our lives, which my mentor – Nancy Coen – teaches is a person's earthly condition. Quite honestly, there are things in most, if not all, of our lives that are not "righteous" that still needs the purging of His refiner's fire. The goal is for our heavenly position to become our earthly condition.

What better way to disconnect His kings and priest from attaining the fullness of becoming His Kings of Righteousness than for them to believe it's already done? What better way to short circuit your priestly call to lead your inner fire bride to be clothed in righteousness? Remember: *"⁸ If we say that we have no sin, we deceive ourselves, and the truth is not in us. ⁹ If we confess our sins, He is faithful and just to forgive us our sins, and to cleanse us from all unrighteousness" (1 John 1:8-9 NKJV).*

Daily crucifixion, confession and repentance should be a fundamental part of a believer's life. Don't let anyone deceive you elsewise. Stay tuned. Our next chapter tackles the tough question: "Have We Already Been Made the Righteousness of God in Christ?" in greater detail. May the eyes of your understanding be enlightened. May you with an open face behold the glory of the Lord, and be changed into His same image from glory to glory.

*****

2 – HAVE WE ALREADY BEEN MADE THE RIGHTEOUSNESS OF GOD IN CHRIST JESUS?

Have we already been made the righteousness of God in Christ? Good question! Here are two more questions to think about as well. If Christians have already been made the righteousness of God in Christ Jesus here on earth, then we need to ask ourselves: "Why don't believers demonstrate His righteousness in all we do?" And why would Jesus tell us to seek first His Kingdom and His righteousness, if we already embody that reality (Matthew 6:33)?

Possibly the best way to answer this question is to know that all the Scriptures that contain the phrase "in Christ" are heavenly positions that we have access to when we first believe that Jesus came in the flesh and the Father raised Him from the dead. This is an incredible and wonderful reality! The LORD of LOVE also gives us an initial deposit of Himself here on earth, and it is our job (as good stewards) to grow that initial deposit, so that we can become (be made into) the exact same image as Yeshua. The maturation steps for becoming holy, as He is holy are:

[1] salvation.

[2] sanctification, and

[3] purification.

The process of wholly becoming (i.e., manifesting on earth) the heavenly position fully paid for on the cross belongs in the purification stage of a believer's walk, which is the righteousness of God in Christ Jesus by the way. This is not always a clear-cut process, and sometimes our sanctification will bleed over into our purification. Another series of three to consider in all this is:

[1] obedience leads to

[2] righteousness, which leads to

[3] holiness (Romans 6:16, Romans 6:19).

The verse about "righteousness" that Christendom tends to name and claim without realizing its full potential here on earth is 2 Corinthians 5:21. You've heard it touted, and it is a good and proper foundation that we all need to begin with: "I am the righteousness of God in Christ Jesus." However, that verse doesn't say what's been touted. It says: *"For He made Him who knew no sin to be sin for us, that WE MIGHT BECOME THE RIGHTEOUSNESS OF GOD IN HIM" (2 Corinthians 5:21 NKJV)*. The Greek verb for "might become" means to begin to be, to come upon a new stage in life, or the process of becoming, to undergo change or development.

Additionally, it is very helpful to understand "fullness" in Scripture. Please allow me to lay some groundwork in this regard.

FULLNESS DEPOSIT

A supernatural calm came over me, as a woman yelled in my face: "I have all the fullness of Christ within me!" I thought something like, "Major disconnect" and "Wow! The fullness of Christ doesn't act like that." I try to stay as teachable as possible, because I know that we can all err. As Mark 12:24 puts it, it is because we do not know the Scriptures nor the power of God. If you know of anyone who doesn't have gaps in knowing the Scriptures or the power of God, I really want to meet them! In this Kingdom Day, we will each be filled with all the fullness of God according to the breadth, length, depth and height of the love of Christ in our lives (Ephesians 3:17-19).

This bizarre yelling encounter led me to study the word "fullness" in Scripture. Numbers 18:27 sets a precedence for the word "fullness," because the first occurrence of a word in Scripture always does. The word "fullness" in Numbers 18:27 is Strong's OT:435 *mel-ay-aw'*. First, let's comprehend that Numbers 18:27 is talking about the *terumah* in Hebrew, which is a heave offering. Primarily, it's a true contribution from the heart. Yeshua is our heave offering (our *terumah*). He is our wholehearted contribution. Our Beloved Messiah taught us that the *terumah* offering that Moses gave in Numbers 18:25-31 was essentially a willing heart; therefore, the congregation of the Living God is formed by having a willing heart. We are called to be wholehearted by having a heart to do the perfect will of the Father. If you and I are to walk in the same manner as Jesus did, we are to do everything with all our heart (1 John 2:6; Deuteronomy 6:5).

Let's take a closer look at the context and background of the Numbers 18:27 "fullness":

" ²⁵ Then the Lord spoke to Moses, saying, ²⁶ 'Speak thus to the Levites, and say to them: 'When you take from the children of Israel the tithes which I have given you from them as your inheritance, then you shall offer up a heave offering of it to the Lord, a tenth of the tithe. ²⁷ And your heave offering shall be reckoned to you as though it were the grain of the threshing floor and as the FULLNESS of the winepress. ²⁸ Thus you shall also offer a heave offering to the Lord from all your tithes which you receive from the children of Israel, and you shall give the Lord's heave offering from it to Aaron the priest. ²⁹ Of all your gifts you shall offer up every heave offering due to the Lord, from all the best of them, the consecrated part of them'" (Numbers 18:25-29 NKJV).

A *terumah* is separated from the grain at the threshing floor and from the grape juice and/or olive oil as it ripens in a vat. In Biblical times, when the Levites received their 10-percent share from the other Israelites, it was required that they raise up their "tithe from the tithe" (i.e., "tenth of the tithe") as a gift to God Himself before it was given to His priests. The "tithe from the tithe" had the status of a *terumah*, which meant that only a *Kohen* (descendant of the first High Priest Aaron) may eat it, and it had to be kept in a state of purity.

Notice that the *terumah* applies to grain, wine and oil. The oil symbolizes the pouring out of the Spirit of the Living God while the grain and grape juice symbolizes Yeshua's communion elements given first by a royal priest of the Order of Melchizedek (Genesis 14:18). The Old Testament *terumah* picture of the "tithe on the tithe" is a foreshadowing of the New Testament reality of the 10-percent earnest or deposit of the Holy Spirit that happens when by grace through faith Christ dwells in the heart of one who believes (Ephesians 2:8; Ephesians 3:17):

- *"Now He that wrought us for this very thing is God, who gave unto us the EARNEST OF THE SPIRIT" (2 Corinthians 5:5 ASV).*

- *"[13] In whom ye also trusted, after that ye heard the word of truth, the gospel of your salvation: in whom also after that ye believed, ye were SEALED WITH THAT HOLY SPIRIT OF PROMISE, [14] WHICH IS THE EARNEST OF OUR INHERITANCE UNTIL THE REDEMPTION OF THE PURCHASED POSSESSION, unto the praise of His glory" (Ephesians 1:13-14 KJV).*

Shortly, we will discuss the phrase "until the redemption of the purchased possession." For now, let's stand amazed at the deep meaning of the Ancient Hebrew Word Picture for the word "fullness" that was hidden thousands of years before Christ died for you and me on the cross, which puts an exclamation point to the 10-percent deposit (earnest) of the Holy Spirit Scriptures. The Ancient Hebrew Word Picture for *mel-ay-aw'* fullness communicates that the water (i.e., the Holy Spirit and/or the Word) reveals the Shepherd (Yeshua) who shows us the Father. We should definitely raise our hands for the heave offering graciously given to us at the cross! Let's worship the Lamb of God who is most worthy of our praise!

For those of you who are still wondering about our being filled with all the fullness of Christ, please remember that there's a heavenly position of the 100-percent fullness of Christ and your manifest earthly condition of that heavenly position. Jesus Christ's fullness of the Spirit was, is, and will always be 100-percent. Your fullness of His Spirit is not. Not yet, anyway. Any work of the Spirit in our lives grows as we obey the Father, and walk in the truth, faith and grace of the

Son. Stay tuned, because a soon coming attraction is there is a Kingdom time and Kingdom place where *"we all will come in the unity of the faith, and of the knowledge of the Son of God, unto a perfect man, unto the measure of the stature of the fullness of Christ" (Ephesians 4:13 KJV)*. Notice how it says, "we all come… unto the measure of the stature of the fullness of Christ," because this is both an individual and corporate work of His Spirit by the Blood according to the Father's heart.

FULLNESS IS A 10 % DEPOSIT UNTIL…

Why does Scripture's first reference to the word "fullness" speak of a "tithe on the tithe" or a 10-percent deposit (Numbers 18:27)?

It seems kind of counter-intuitive; but for those who believe that God is the author of what is written in the Bible and oh so good, He is making a significant point. God's initial concept of "fullness" in His Word doesn't scream from the mountain tops that I AM 100-percent full all the time. Our incredible and gracious King of Kings is showing us a way to become filled up with all the fullness of God (Ephesians 3:19).

> *"[13] In whom ye also trusted, after that ye heard the word of truth, the gospel of your salvation: in whom also after that ye believed, ye were SEALED WITH THAT HOLY SPIRIT OF PROMISE, [14] WHICH IS THE EARNEST OF OUR INHERITANCE UNTIL THE REDEMPTION OF THE PURCHASED POSSESSION, unto the praise of His glory" (Ephesians 1:13-14 KJV).*

Did you catch that? Those who trust the Messiah after they hear the gospel of salvation are sealed with the earnest of the Holy Spirit UNTIL the redemption of the purchased possession. An earnest is like the guarantee or deposit one puts down on a home. In fact, the Numbers 18 "tithe on the tithe" concept is the origins of the 10-percent tithe model as well as the 10-percent Holy Spirit deposit mentioned in both Ephesians 1:14 and 2 Corinthians 5:5.

Without going into quite a bit of detail, please know that when one studies the words "redemption," "purchase," and "possession" a mysterious and glorious picture unfolds that speaks of one made like unto the Son of God (Hebrews 7:3). This one is made after the Order of Melchizedek. The journey of those who are manifesting being part of the royal priesthood of ONE will literally increase the 10-percent tithe of the Holy Spirit within them in amount, magnitude, and degree to the fullness of the stature of Christ by living a crucified life unto the knowledge of the Son of God via the Seven Spirits of God.

As we daily take up our cross and follow Him, the veil within (between our soul and spirit) will be torn one thread at a time from top to bottom until you and I are filled up with the full measure of the Seven Spirits of God in our soul, just like Jesus was. Therefore, fullness is a 10-percent deposit of the Holy Spirit until the redemption of the purchased possession when we will manifest being holy, as He is holy.

The divine Melchizedek/Bridal journey will cause the 10-percent tithe of the Holy Spirit within His holy blood-bought vessels to grow in amount, magnitude, and degree to the fullness of the measure of the stature of Christ, as led by the Spirit of God according to the perfect will of the Father.

Romans 14:17 tells us that *"The Kingdom of God is … righteousness and peace and joy in the Holy Spirit."* These three are spiritual dimensions within a person that the Lord seeks to grow within His Kingdom vessels. Please remember this DEEP RED mystery of His Kingdom that will be realized by His Crucified Ones (i.e., mature sons): They will return to their primordial position where their body will be clothed in righteousness, their soul will be completely filled with the *shekinah* glory of God where it's the permanent Dwelling Place of God, and their spirit will be in constant communion with their Creator. Please refer to the "Baptism of Fire" Chapter.

One's body cannot be fully clothed with righteousness "UNTIL THE REDEMPTION OF THE PURCHASED POSSESSION (Ephesians 1:14), which I believe is the filling up of the soul of a person with the 100-percent fullness of the Seven Spirits of God, which is how Jesus walked in the nature of Christ on earth. I am totally open to learning from the Spirit and the Word in this regard, because I think that we have only caught a smidgen of the vastness of this kingdom truth.

*****

3 – MYSTERIES OF THE DEEP RED

In this Kingdom Day, it's a time for the transformation of birds of a feather that flock together. Right now, there is Company of Eagles of His Strategic Air Command being released in the earth where each is a wing of the Order of Melchizedek flying by the Spirit with one another. Keep at the top-of-your-mind that this New Living

Creature of royal priests will only glory in the cross of Yeshua Ha Machiach (Jesus Christ).

Come! Let us go to the DEEP RED space where we have direct contact with the Father. Let us go to the place where the triple concentric circles of the Melchizedek Breastplate are positioned, as a contact lens, on the Father's Bloodshot Eye to see this DEEP RED mystery of the Kingdom of God.

Imagine, if you will, the full stature of the crimson flow. What would that be? We are told in Ephesians 4:15 that it is necessary for the Mature Body of Christ to grow up into Him in all things. Colossians 1:24-25 portrays each member of His

Body must fill up the afflictions of Christ in their flesh for His Body's sake to fulfill the word of God.

Believers need to grasp what it means to walk in the exact same manner as Yeshua did. Scripture says that it pleased our Heavenly Father that all fullness should dwell in Yeshua having made peace through the blood of His cross to reconcile all things unto Himself (Colossians 1:19-20). If all fullness dwelt in Yeshua through the blood of the cross, then it is a good clue how we all will corporately realize becoming a mature ONE NEW MAN to the measure of the stature of the fullness of Christ (Ephesians 4:13). In Christ, we are brought near through the blood of Christ, and reconciled to God through the cross (Ephesians 2:13, 16).

How are we reconciled through the cross? Ephesians 2:16 says in ONE BODY. This is first an individual work in a believer's life that must also be carried out corporately, so Yeshua's Mature Head can attach to His Mature Body (Revelation 1:14). When the Son of Man comes again in His fullness bodily, His head – complete with white hair – can only be joined to a Body that is equally developed (i.e., full grown).

The WAY OF RIGHTEOUSNESS consists of progressive crucifixion steps, which are the spiritual sacrifices still required of God's Holy Priesthood (1 Peter 2:5). This is the process by which we will hit the bull's eye of righteousness. Before we dive into this meaty subject, let's take a quick fundamental look at what the book of Romans says about the RIGHTEOUSNESS OF GOD.

The Righteousness of God is by the FAITH OF JESUS CHRIST unto all that believe in His shed blood for the remission of their sins. A man is justified solely by faith as a redemptive gift of grace, which reigns through righteousness unto eternal life via Yeshua Ha Machiach.

Let's take a closer look at this last statement. Romans 3:28 tells us that a man is justified by faith without the deeds of the law; and then, Romans 3:24,31 brings to light that a man is justified freely by the redemptive grace that is in Christ Jesus, which establishes the law. Say what? How can this be?

If we look at the root of the Greek word "justified," it means that when one is truly justified, they show what is right, free, innocent and holy. Even though deeds are never the basis of our being justified or righteous, it is our deeds that show the substance of who and what we are.

James 2:22-23 discloses that it is by works that faith is made perfect or complete. If we are crucified daily in union with Christ according to the plumb line of righteousness (the Word of God), our outward appearance will be transformed into that same image from glory to glory, until we plainly reveal the righteous character of Christ.

*****

4 – BAPTISM OF FIRE

One of the DEEP RED mysteries of God's Kingdom being revealed in our day has to do with the BAPTISM OF FIRE, which will refine His Bride into a pure and spotless state. When we discuss RIGHTEOUSNESS, many times we will be jumping back and forth from the Messiah's Bride – who is made ready by being clothed in righteousness – to the Order of Melchizedek, which personifies the King of Righteousness and Peace.

Previously, we discussed that the Melchizedek birds of a feather that are now flocking together only glory in the cross of Jesus Christ. The cross was Yeshua's third and final baptism – His Baptism of Fire (Matthew 3:11).

Please bear with me as I lay a little ground work. Divine series of three in Scripture are keys for the hour that we live in. When you see three items listed in your Bible, sit up and take notice. Biblical threes list things from easiest to hardest; but more importantly, they reveal the way of life that propels us toward maturity. I prefer to use the phrase *"move onto perfection" (Hebrews 6:1)* to the word "maturity." Divine threes are typically progressive in nature with one building on what was previously gained or attained. Usually these steps that move us unto perfection also overlap (where God can be working on two or three different levels within us at the same time, since parts of any one of us can be more mature than others). Yeshua's three baptisms articulated in Matthew 3:11 is a good example. Being baptized by water is easier, and usually precedes, being baptized by the Holy Spirit, which is definitely easier than being baptized by fire by going to a cross.

Mark 9:49 NKJV says: *"For everyone will be seasoned with fire."* Everyone? Everyone. Each person who desires to be part of the Order of Melchizedek and the Bride of the Messiah must walk where He walked, even to the utmost crucifixion of our flesh.

I sought the Lord for years asking Him: How is a person clothed in righteousness as Your Bride? As I was studying the word "throne" in Scripture a couple years ago, Jeremiah 33:18 struck me like a bolt of lightning. He showed me that the way of being enthroned or clothed in righteousness was progressive crucifixion steps, which are the spiritual sacrifices still required of God's Holy Priesthood (1 Peter 2:5). This is the process by which we will actually hit the Father's bull's eye of righteousness.

The moving unto perfection crucifixion process outlined in Jeremiah 33:18 will completely circumcise our carnal nature. Remember our Savior needs our permission to crucify our sin nature. Once we have endured the cross and our flesh has been mortified, Yeshua purges one's soul with fire to at last make our soul His permanent dwelling place. *Hebrews 10:39* says it like this *"have faith to the possessing of the soul."*

Behold, an awesome treasure of the DEEP RED MYSTERY OF HIS KINGDOM: Crucified (mature) sons will return to their primordial position:

[1] BODY – Clothed in righteousness.

[2] SOUL – Completely filled with the *shekinah* glory of God where it's the permanent Dwelling Place of God (NOTE: *Shekinah* in Hebrew means "to dwell").

[3] SPIRIT – Continually in constant communion with their Creator.

Once a soul endures the cross to the point of purification – the All-Consuming Fire purging – he or she is clothed or enthroned in righteousness. Our next chapter begins to go into the steps for the Bride's Baptism of Fire outlined in Jeremiah 33:18.

REFERENCES: Psalm 16:11; Jeremiah 33:18; Matthew 3:11; Matthew 16:24; Mark 9:49; John 14:6; 1 Peter 2:5; Hebrews 6:1; Hebrews 7:2; Hebrews 10:39; Revelation 19:7-8.

*****

5 – STEPS FOR THE BRIDE'S BAPTISM OF FIRE

"Call to Me and I will answer you, and I will tell you great and mighty things, which you do not know" (Jeremiah 33:3 NAS).

Through the Eternal Order of Melchizedek, the Lord will birth His Bridal Company in the earth, which will completely conform to the Living Word and the Spirit of Christ. Right now, a Royal Priesthood is beginning to march anew throughout the earth, as the predecessor of the Bride. These are ones who were once far off; but are, even now, being brought nearer and nearer until they literally become ONE with the Almighty, as they willingly lay down their flesh in order to receive all of Calvary's dividends.

Let's look at the passage that shows us the way we can be enthroned (i.e., clothed) in righteousness. Jeremiah 33:18 reveals three progressive crucifixion steps, which are spiritual sacrifices still required of God's Holy Priesthood (1 Peter 2:5). This is the process by which Crucified Ones will hit the Father's bull's eye of righteousness. This is the procedure that will hone the essence of the Messiah's Bride, so she can be named: "The Lord is our righteousness." Just remember that His Beautiful Bride will be the embodiment of who she is married to.

> " *¹⁴ 'Behold, days are coming,' declares the LORD, 'when I will fulfill the good word which I have spoken concerning the house of Israel and the house of Judah. ¹⁵ 'In those days and at that time I will cause a righteous Branch of David to spring forth; and He shall execute justice and righteousness on the earth. ¹⁶ 'In those days Judah will be saved and Jerusalem will dwell in safety; and THIS IS THE NAME BY WHICH SHE WILL BE CALLED: THE LORD IS OUR RIGHTEOUSNESS.' ¹⁷ For thus says the LORD, 'David shall never lack a man to sit on the throne of the house of Israel; ¹⁸ and the Levitical priests shall never lack a man before Me to offer burnt offerings, to burn grain offerings and to prepare sacrifices continually'" (Jeremiah 33:14-18 NAS).*

The crucifixion process outlined in Jeremiah 33:18, which will completely circumcise one's sin nature is:

[1] offer burnt offerings,

[2] burn grain offerings, and

[3] prepare sacrifices continually.

These are the steps of the Baptism of Fire that His pure and spotless Bride will be required to go through, so she will be able to live and move and have her being in a continually surrendered state to do the Father's perfect will. These transformative stages will facilitate the New Jerusalem being called: *"The Lord is our righteousness" (Jeremiah 33:16).*

Right now, the Bride of Christ is hungry for righteousness. She is seeking first His Kingdom and His righteousness above all else. In a dry and thirsty land, His Bride thirsts for the refreshing, joyous life that only righteousness brings. The Water of Life that flows from His throne is imprinted with righteousness, justice, holiness and truth; and it is the Lamb of God – our Great Shepherd – that guides us to these springs of living water (Revelation 7:17).

Nehemiah 3:1 reveals that Jerusalem's Sheep Gate needs to be repaired first. We don't know exactly why, but we do know that it was the priest's inheritance to make offerings by fire to the Lord. To me, this speaks of the need in our day for kings and priests to set the stage, so people can bring their offerings to the Lord. By the way, it was only at the Sheep Gate that God's priests were sanctified with the word and prayer. These are necessary components to the Bride's purification.

When Jerusalem's Sheep Gate was repaired in Nehemiah's day, Eliashib was the High Priest who led the consecration and building of God's Holy City. This is a picture of what we need to do today to set apart His people to build His Bride, which is the Holy City, the New Jerusalem (Revelation 21:2,9). Eliashib's name means "The Almighty will restore." The Ancient Hebrew Word Picture for Eliashib's name speaks of the all-consuming work of El Shaddai done within His Body is the progressive work of the Father that moves us forward, so we can be built into His permanent dwelling place (i.e., be His Bride).

Before we go into the details for our initial step in the Bride's Baptism of Fire, let's understand a precedence set by God Himself when it comes to offerings made by fire. Abel was the first one to bring an "offering by fire" to the Lord. In

Hebrew, the original text of Genesis 4:4 reveals that not only did Abel bring the firstborn of his flock, he also brought himself (offered his heart) while Cain only brought his offering. This is what made Abel's sacrifice acceptable, and Cain's not. Whenever we speak of an offering, always think of yourself first and foremost.

REFERENCES: Genesis 4:4; Psalms 48:2; Psalms 89:14; Psalms 110:1-4; Jeremiah 33:14-18; Amos 9:11; Matthew 16:24; Acts 15:16; Galatians 2:20; 1 Peter 2:5; Revelation 21:1-9, Revelation 22:1.

*****

6 – HOLY PRIESTHOOD OFFERING SPIRITUAL SACRIFICES

For such a time as this, the Master of the Wedding Banquet is revealing what the Bride of the Messiah (i.e., Christ) needs to do in order to be ready. Hidden within the bowels of Scripture are the instructions for God's Holy Priesthood on how to make spiritual sacrifices, which will culminate in them becoming a glorious part of His Pure and Spotless Bride.

> "*⁴ Coming to Him as to a living stone, rejected indeed by men, but chosen by God and precious, ⁵ you also, as living stones, are being built up a spiritual house, A HOLY PRIESTHOOD, TO OFFER UP SPIRITUAL SACRIFICES ACCEPTABLE TO GOD THROUGH JESUS CHRIST" (1 Peter 2:4-5 NKJV).*

Before we go into the three progressive crucifixion steps for the Bride's Baptism of Fire, we need to understand the concept of "spiritual sacrifices" according to the Messiah's instruction. Please be patient as we lay some foundations, so

His Crucified Ones can literally see how to hit the Father's bull's eye of righteousness.

Some Christians believe that the instructions of Moses on the priests, the altar, and the sacrificial system are not true for us today. That's not what Yeshua said: *"For if you believed Moses, you would believe Me; for he wrote about Me. But if you do not believe his writings, how will you believe My words?" (John 5:46-47 NKJV)*. Yeshua has also told us that: *"Do not think that I came to destroy the Law or the Prophets. I did not come to destroy but to fulfill" (Matthew 5:17 NKJV)*. That word "fulfill" means to fill it full of meaning. Will we do things exactly as the Levitical priests did in their day? No, but God's Holy Priesthood will apply those Biblical principles and ask the Spirit of the Living God how we can fill them full of meaning in our day. By the way, we will not be going into what Judaism or Christianity has taught. We will only stick to the things that Yeshua tells us if you believe these things, then you will believe Me.

The Levitical Sacrificial Service was an audio-visual aid to explain certain profound, basic principles on how His people should relate to God, how we are supposed to live with one another, and how to be reconciled with one another. Within the instructions of the priests, the altar, and the sacrificial system are the basic of our faith. Without these ancient foundations, the cross of Christ means nothing.

The very beginning of the Levitical Sacrificial System starts with the first word in the Book of Leviticus – *vyihkra*. The Hebrew letter *"alef"* in this word is made small, and if one dissects this word Hebraically, a person understands: If you are going to be called of the Lord, your strength must be made small, so His strength may be made large in your life. Any person called of the Lord will share this testimony. Recall that John the Baptist (who was a Levite) gave this exact testimony in being a forerunner of the Messiah: *"He must increase, but I must decrease" (John 3:30 NKJV)*. In a sense, John the Baptist was saying I must go away (disappear), so He can come forward (appear).

The following are five reasons Jesus of Nazareth gives on why we need to have sacrifices, and why we still have a priestly sacrificial system:

[1] TABLE FELLOWSHIP – God's Altar was the place where sacrifices were burnt in His Temple. The Brazen Altar was considered to be the Lord's Table. The hospitality of the Lord is basically the hospitality of your homes. When someone is coming over, they ask their host: What can I bring to join you at your table? Then the host will specify what's appropriate to bring. The Altar is the place where God said, I will meet with a man and we will do business together. Even the business world makes agreements over a good meal. God has set standards, protocols, and manners that will be done at His Table. It's that simple. If you want to come near to God and approach His Table, simply ask; because it's open to whomsoever will. LOVE will whole-heartedly welcome you, and He will specify something you can bring to the table to join Him (Luke 22:29-30; 24:30; 1 Corinthians 10:21).

[2] RESTORATION OF FELLOWSHIP – God's Altar is for the restoration of fellowship, because sin separates us from God. These are instructions on how to turn

your direction in order to come closer to the Lord. It is here that the Messiah instructs us: "*²³ If you bring your gift to the altar, and there remember that your brother has something against you, ²⁴ leave your gift there before the altar, and go your way. First be reconciled to your brother, and then come and offer your gift*" (Matthew 5:23-24 NKJV).

[3]   WORSHIP OF GOD – The adoration of God Almighty is illustrated by every sacrifice, which had to be lifted up, so they could be elevated unto the Altar. When we come to the Lord, we lift up our hands when we bring any gift or sacrifice to the Lord. These gifts and sacrifices don't earn God's love. They are simply reflections of your loving, respectful, obedient heart. What do people do at sporting events when a great play is made? They cheer, raise their voice and their hands. They show exuberance, excitement and respect (John 4:23-24; 1 Timothy 2:8).

[4]   REDEMPTIVE WORK OF THE MESSIAH – The whole principle of sacrifice teaches the substitution and ultimate work of the Messiah on the cross. Because of God's Altar, we know that something of value can take the place of another and be found acceptable, as a just conclusion. The entire concept of "giving" is first based on God's sacrificial system in Scripture. Your sacrifice must come from your domestic herd. It has to cost you. It has to come from you. Remember, I mentioned that a sacrifice is really representative of you offering yourself?

The one of the ultimate lesson on "giving" in the Word of God embodies the Father gave His only begotten Son (John 3:16).

[5] ESTABLISHMENT OF FEASTS – All the feasts prescribed by the Lord Himself were based on certain gifts brought to God's Altar. If you believe in celebrating the Lord the way He originally prescribed, then start off with the instructions given to the priests. By the way, you may want to consider that Scripture says His *"Word stand forever" (Isaiah 40:8)*, and God Himself says, *"these are My feasts" (Leviticus 23:2)*. In 2 Chronicles 8:13, the primitive root for the yearly feasts that are His set appointments is the Hebrew word *ya-ad*. This primitive root implies that during God's set appointments with His people, the Lord is summoning His people to meet Him at His Table at His stated time. It also tells us during His Biblical feasts that LOVE is directing us into a certain position, so He will be able to engage us for marriage (i.e., to be betroth).

REFERENCES: Leviticus 1:1,23; 2 Chronicles 8:13; Psalm 119:48; Isaiah 40:8; Lamentations 3:40-41; Matthew 5:17,23-24; Matthew 9:10; Luke 22:29-30; Luke 24:30; John 3:16-18; John 4:23-24; John 5:46-47; 1 Corinthians 10:21; 1 Timothy 2:8; 1 Peter 2:4-5.

*****

7 – NEVER CUT OFF THE BODY FROM THE HEAD

The mysteries of God's Kingdom have always existed, but their vast reality has barely been delved into until such a time as this. The Lord is unveiling much more about a mystery, which He calls His Pure and Spotless Bride. Her code name is the New Jerusalem (Revelation 3:12; 21:2) or the One New Man in Christ (Ephesians 2:15).

Please don't get hung up on gender specific terms; because both men and women are called to be Sons of God, the Bride of Christ, and the One New Man. Let's contemplate how the perfect resurrection of Christ's Body will inaugurate the age of the Bride of Christ, or the New Jerusalem, or the One New Man in Christ – these three being one as diverse aspects of the same consummation. In Him and in fellowship with one another, we are essentially being built according to His time and His way into an eternal dwelling place for the King of Kings.

A radically new dispensation has arrived upon the scene of human history every two thousand years since the dawn of man's time (Biblically speaking). The first two-thousand-year mark in man's time saw Abraham walked up Mount Moriah to worship God by offering up his son Isaac. Many experts agree that God's physical temple in Jerusalem – the city of our great king – was built upon the same Mount Moriah. Two-thousand years later (which is also approximately two thousand years ago for us), another fullness of time came when Yeshua was born so we might be reconciled to God: *"⁴ But when the fullness of time had come, God sent forth His Son, born of a woman, born under the law, ⁵ to redeem those who were under the law, that we might receive the adoption of sons" (Galatians 4:4-5 NKJV).*

A very appropriate word for the season, we just entered is the word "dispensation," which simply put means an administrative system. It's an ordering of events under divine authority. The Almighty One is in charge of this, and any, shift in the divine order of earthly things. He has been, and will always be, large and in charge. He is simply administering things on earth a bit different than before, and it affects everything we do and who we are. That's the point. God is making adjustments, so that His Resurrected Body of Believers and Bridal Company can come into their fullness. If God can measure the waters of the earth in the hollow of His hand, and with the breath of His hand mark off the heavens; then know that a small thing for the Lord, like a global shift in the earth's administration, will probably be massive, even revolutionary, to us.

Spiritually speaking, the people of God are *"a royal priesthood" (1 Peter 2:9)* and at the same time we are being built into a spiritual house, i.e., Temple (1 Peter 2:5). From heaven's point of view, God's people aren't in a temple; we are the temple with each of us being a living stone. We are also its priests, but only the sons of a King can be considered royalty.

The whole world has entered the latest season of divine administration – Fullness of Times – where Christ's Mature Head will be ultimately united with His Mature Body.

Recall that Jeremiah 33:18 lists three progressive crucifixion steps for the Bride's Baptism of Fire, which are spiritual sacrifices still required of God's Holy Priesthood: *"[17] For thus saith the LORD; David shall never want a man to sit upon the throne of the house of Israel; [18] Neither shall the priests the Levites want a man before me to offer burnt offerings, and to kindle meal offerings, and to do sacrifice continually" (Jeremiah 33:17-18 KJV).*

What we are keying in on in this chapter is the phrase "never want" in David shall never want a man to sit upon the throne of the house of Is-real. When I write Is-real, I am purposely making a point of genuineness. God forbid that anyone should try to replace Israel. I am simply reaching for a greater depth. Those words "never want" not only refer to royalty (i.e., the throne of David), but to priests, as we flow into the next verse. Within this passage of Scripture, LOVE reveals an ancient key for kings and priests of the Most High God. On the surface level the phrase "never want" in Hebrew speaks of an absolute prohibition of taking away His royal priestly covenant as well as being an absolute prohibition of cutting off the Body from its Head – the Messiah (Ephesians 4:15-16).

If we dig a little deeper into the Ancient Hebrew Word Pictures for the phrase "never want," we see that the word "never" tells us that Abba gives direction to what is first and what will prod or urge us forward, in addition to Abba giving us strength to control our tongues, so we can move toward

Him. The Ancient Hebrew Word Picture for "want" speaks of opening the door that reveals the path to the way of life. It shows us how to be covered by His throne.

So, here's to the Lord being our Shepherd and we shall never want! Here's to Christ's Head never being cut off from His Body of Royal Priests!!!

REFERENCES: Genesis 22; Isaiah 40:12; Jeremiah 33:17-18; Galatians 4:4-5; Ephesians 4:15-16; Ephesians 5:23; Colossians 1:18; Colossians 2:19; 1 Peter 2:5; Revelation 1:6; Revelation 3:21; Revelation 5:10.

*****

8 – BECOMING A BURNT OFFERING

In this Kingdom Day, the LORD OF LOVE is going to extract from us all that the cross paid for, as we surrender to His fiery will and ways. Today is the day that yielded hearts are drawing near with the full assurance of faith, so His Mature Body will be prepared to do the perfect will of the Father. It is here that Crucified Ones will move past the Outer Court of salvation and past the Holy Place of sanctification into the Most Holy Place of purification.

> *"[16] 'This is the name by which she will be called: The Lord is our righteousness.'[17] For thus says the LORD, 'David shall never lack a man to sit on the throne of the house of Israel;[18] and the Levitical priests shall never lack a man before Me to offer burnt offerings, to burn grain offerings and to prepare sacrifices continually'"(Jeremiah 33:16b-18 NAS).*

Please be patient as we seek to understand the offerings by fire listed in Jeremiah 33:18, which are a DEEP RED MYSTERY OF THE ANCIENT CARRIER OF HIS BLOOD:

[1] Offer Burnt Offerings,

[2] Burn Grain Offerings, and

[3] Prepare Sacrifices Continually.

These are the crucifixion steps for the Bride's Baptism of Fire where she will come out the other side of the All-Consuming Fire emblazon with the name: "The Lord is our righteousness." The cross was Yeshua ha Machiach's (Jesus Christ) baptism of fire (Matthew 3:11). His Bride will follow Yeshua to the cross in a new and living sacrifice way, so we can become His very image. Remember to concentrate on the principles behind the process, so His Crucified Ones can hit the Father's bull's eye of righteousness.

Today, let's focus on the fiery first stage – Offer Burnt Offerings – which will enable His Bride to dwell in the midst of the New Jerusalem in truth and righteousness (Zechariah 8:8). One must peel back the flaming pages of Leviticus 1 to see the most important principles behind the Burnt Offering:

- A Burnt Offering is a Voluntary Offering given exclusively to the Lord.

- It is also called the Elevation Offering, because it raised one's spiritual level.

- A Burnt Offering was considered superior to other offerings, because it was a volunteer sacrifice and it was offered in its entirety by fire.

- A Burnt Offering is called an *olah* in Hebrew, which means "to go up." The Ancient Hebrew Word Picture for the word *olah* tells us that the *olah* is that which the Shepherd brings forth.

- Yeshua (the Great Shepherd) brought the most perfect sacrifice for sins Himself – the Lamb of God who takes away the sins of the world. Then while we are being sanctified (working out our salvation) and purified, the Great Shepherd will choose what will best crucify our sin nature (flesh).

- If your work is not of this world – the same essence of the fire – it will NOT be burned up, but purified (1 Corinthians 3:11-15).

Here's a link if you'd like to learn more about the first crucifixion stage of "Becoming a Burnt Offering" => "Come Up Here!" http://wp.me/p158HG-x5.

Remember how the first offering in Scripture was made by Abel, and it spoke of him not only offering the first fruits of his flock, but the truest offering of himself. This is what the Baptism of Fire is all about. Its purpose in our lives is for us to bring our carnal nature to the Lord's Altar, so it can be burned up in its entirety. A Pure and Spotless Bride will exemplify co-crucifixion with her Messiah.

Making His specified spiritual sacrifices will cause His Holy Priesthood of Believers to decrease in their own strength and increase in such a way that they will eventually be just like Yeshua.

The road to decreasing, so He may increase, is not for the faint-of-heart. It takes whole-hearted commitment. It takes choosing His ways over your own, and total death to self. Although I'm not finished being in His heavenly brazier, I have found that the quickest way through the Romans 7 inner struggles is to be as honest as possible. I have gotten use to siding with LOVE (even against myself) in my own crucifixion process. Frankly, there are parts in me – parts of my sin nature – that just doesn't want to die. But, they must, so my Kingdom of Self can disappear, and His Kingdom can appear in me.

A true *olah* (Burnt Offering) is that which the Shepherd brings forth. In Biblical times, if you were going to make a Burnt Offering, you'd have to go to the shepherd of the flock first to get your lamb. A person would ask the shepherd: Select the best one for me, and he'd make the judgment as to what's best for you. In this Kingdom Day, the Great Shepherd of our souls will guide us to the best path that each one of us needs to take to become just like Him. He will sit on His blazing throne, and judge everything in our life. Be encouraged, because the Ancient Hebrew Word Picture for "judge" speaks of Him being the door of life. LOVE will shake everything that is not of Him, so only His Kingdom without and within you remains. Please note that the foundation and habitation of God's throne is righteousness and justice (Psalm 89:14; Psalm 97:2). Therefore, for the heavenly-minded, His just judgments in our lives will really be sweeter than honey (Psalm 19:10). Press into the fact that His righteous assessments of our lives will be more desirable than fine gold. Press into the Lamb who is in the midst of the throne (Revelation 7:17). He is the One who will feed us goodness in the land of the living, and lead us to His fountains of living waters. He is the One who will wipe away all tears from our eyes.

REFERENCES: Leviticus 1; Psalm 19:10; Psalm 45:6; Psalm 89:14; Psalm 97:2; Jeremiah 33:18; Daniel 7:9; Zechariah 8:8; Matthew 3:11; Matthew 16:24; John 10:11; Romans 12:1; Galatians 2:20; Hebrews 10:1,5-7,19-24; Hebrews 12:27-29; 1 Peter 2:5.

*****

9 – PURIFY THE SOUL

Have the same mindset as Christ Jesus... as a man, He humbled Himself by becoming obedient to death, even death on a cross to the glory of the Father (Philippians 2:4-11).

Picture with me (if you will) a more holy walk beyond salvation. Beyond sanctification. Picture His Bride walking through His fire to be purified wholly and fully for this is the level we are speaking about in the *Hitting the Bull's Eye of Righteousness* – Purification. Recall that the offerings by fire listed in Jeremiah 33:18 are:

[1] Offer Burnt Offerings,

[2] Burn Grain Offerings, and

[3] Prepare Sacrifices Continually.

Our last chapter spoke about the reality of the Bride's Baptism of Fire in His Outer Court, which is symbolized by bringing BURNT OFFERINGS to His Brazen Altar. This is the first of three crucifixion steps in the Bride's Baptism of

Fire where only the All-Consuming Fire knows its duration. Recall that it's the Great Shepherd of our souls who chooses what part of ourselves that He would like brought to His Altar, so it can be burnt up in its entirety. You will bring the sacrifice – parts of yourself. HE will bring the fire.

The Bridal Journey from His Outer Courts to His Inner Courts is a painfully beautiful process. All three of the fiery stages of crucifixion (offerings by fire) are for the purpose of a person decreasing, so He may increase. It is a journey not for the faint-of-heart. It takes a whole-hearted commitment. It takes choosing His ways over your own until there is a total death of self. In a Bridal Candidate's quest for purification, she must endure the greatest level of the testing of one's faith. The hottest flame of His love is reserved for His Fire Bride where His coals of fire are indeed His coals of love (Song of Songs 8:6).

Please realize that the purification work within Bridal Candidates is not linear. The process of fully manifesting by literally becoming the righteousness of God in Christ Jesus here on earth is a work that resembles a Fibonacci spiral. Think of a nautilus shell, and the ever-tightening spirals that eventually becomes one with its center. Consider that the recurring tests or trials in your life does not necessarily mean that you are backsliding, but you are possibly coming back to your issue(s), so you can go deeper and deeper into the very heart of God. Please don't assume anything. Check this by His Spirit. Sometimes things may even appear worse, because if you notice the spirals get tighter and tighter, as the goal of the high calling of God in Christ Jesus gets nearer and nearer. We will go deeper and deeper into the heart of a matter until the impure vibrations of that issue has been purified within you. Keep this concept in mind as we discuss the various crucifixion steps in the Bride's Baptism of Fire.

The second quantum leap in the crucifixion steps for the Bride's Baptism of Fire is portrayed through the burning of the grain or meal offerings in *Jeremiah 33:18*. *"Never lack a man before Me to burn grain offerings"* speaks of one's life being measured according to the plumb line of God's Word.

This is the place where the fiery eyes of Yeshua Ha Machiach (Jesus Christ) search our souls. As we press into letting His Word sift us, we are transformed by the renewing of our minds and we prove the Father's acceptable will through our lives (Romans 12:2). Any mixture within us will be sifted out in this place.

Of all the voluntary offerings, only someone who brings a meal or grain offering is described as a "soul." Traditionally, grain has been a staple of the human diet and represents our very existence, just as a soul speaks of one's very life's breath. Therefore, the burning of grain offerings proclaims that one's life is in God's hand and His fire refines as He chooses.

The goal of the "burn grain offerings" step is for Yeshua – the True Bread of Heaven – manifesting fully in a person's soul through the supernatural enablement of the seven-fold Spirits of God (Isaiah 11:1-2). When a Bridal Candidate's faithfulness is being tested at this level of purification, His eyes are His seven spirits portrayed, as seven lamps of fire burning before the throne (Zechariah 3:9; Zechariah 4:10; Revelation 4:5; Revelation 5:6).

The eyes of the LORD, which run to and fro throughout the whole earth – your earth and mine – is the substance that comes out of heaven – MANNA – that humbles and tests us, so we can know:

[1]   what's in our hearts (Deuteronomy 8:2,5; Hebrews 4:12).

[2]   if we are walking in His ways (Exodus 16:4; Galatians 5:16-24).

[3]   that man does not live by bread alone, but by everything that proceeds out of the mouth of the Lord (Deuteronomy 8:3-4; Matthew 4:4; Luke 4:4).

[4]   that we are true sons that He disciplines (Deuteronomy 8:5-6; Hebrew 12:10-11).

The central tenants of MANNA in John Chapter 6 speak about:

- It is the Father who gives the True Bread of Heaven (John 6:32).

- Christ in us, the hope of glory, gives life to the world (John 6:33).

- Like Yeshua, we are to do the perfect will of the Father who sends us (John 6:38-39, 57).

- His people shall be taught of God (John 6:45).

- If anyone eats this bread, he shall live forever (John 6:51, 58).

- Those who eat true food (His flesh) and drink true drink (His blood) abides in Yeshua (John 6:55-56).

May His MANNA manifest in and through our lives.

Everyone made in God's image has been designed to vertically climb greater heights, so the Bread of Life can manifest in and through us, and we can be walking-talking realities of the Word made flesh. You are a Living Word (Bread from Heaven) sent from His mouth that will not return to Him void.

Stay tuned, because the next chapter will explain a Bridal Candidate's Grain Offering Test in greater detail. Give em heaven!!!

REFERENCES: Exodus 16:4; Deuteronomy 8:2-6; Song of Songs 8:6; Isaiah 11:1-2; Jeremiah 33:16-18; Zechariah 3:9; 4:10; Matthew 3:11; Matthew 4:4; Luke 4:4; John 6:32-56; Romans 12:2; Galatians 5:16-24; Philippians 2:4-8; Hebrews 4:12; Hebrews 12:10-11; James 1:2-4; Revelation 1:14; Revelation 2:18; Revelation 4:5; Revelation 5:6.

*****

10 – FAITHFULNESS TEST

He who has an ear, let him hear what the Spirit says. Just as the inner ear spirals inward, so is the Bridal Journey of Purification. Just as the spoken word seeks the pure water within, so do Bridal Candidates seek the pure washing of the water of His Word in order to get to the very heart of God. Greater than glorious intimacy is a sacred oneness with the King and His Kingdom:

"That in the dispensation of the fullness of the times He might gather together in ONE all things in Christ, both which are in heaven and which are on earth — in Him" (Ephesians 1:10 NKJV).

In our last chapter, we began to explore the second crucifixion step in the Bride's Baptism of Fire. As we follow Yeshua's footsteps in our own baptism of fire, we are moving beyond salvation and sanctification to the place of purification where our perfection is to resound with renown at the perfect pitch of His Bride – *"The Lord is our righteousness" (Jeremiah 33:16).*

Jeremiah 33:17-18 tells us that YHVH will never lack a royal priest that will burn grain offerings before Him. Let's first focus on the royal priest who presents the grain offering, then on the grain/meal offering itself. On this side of the cross, the Royal Order of Melchizedek acts as a treasurer of the King's most valuable resources. The top priority on the King's list is His Ravishing Bride. Esther 2:15 reveals that His Bride is required to do NOTHING, but what the King's chamberlain appoints. A king's chamberlain is an attendant on a sovereign in his bedchamber as well as a chief officer in the household of a king who is a guardian of a collection of treasures. Just so you know, the King's chamberlain is synonymous with one who maturely operates according to the heavenly Order of Melchizedek here on earth, as well as there being a heavenly counterpart.

Melchizedek is the predecessor of the Bride. We need to understand that we have to first functionally operate in our God-given governmental seat as a kingdom priest before we become a suitable partner – His Bride.

The Bridal Candidate's Grain Offering Test is an ancient pathway that's reveals what the kingdom of priests will need to go through at the second stage of their Bridal Baptism of Fire. Numbers 5:11-31 describes the primordial faithfulness test for the Lamb's wife:

> "*² My brethren, count it all joy when you fall into various trials, ³ knowing that the testing of your faith produces patience. ⁴ But let patience have its perfect work, that you may be perfect and complete, lacking nothing*" (James 1:2-4 NKJV).

Let's face it. Until we are truly without spot of wrinkle, we are wayward in many ways. This passage in Numbers 5 shows us how God deals with infidelity. First and foremost, a husband had to be without sin to bring "the meal-offering of jealousies" on behalf of his wife (Numbers 5:15). Note that Yeshua brought the meal-offering for His wayward wife at the cross through the offering up of His Body (1 Corinthians 11:23-24; Ephesians 5:23-25). His Body will walk in the same manner as He did (1 John 2:6) filling up what is lacking in regard to Christ's afflictions, for the sake of His Body, which is the church (Colossians 1:24).

This primordial faithfulness test for a bride was, and still, is focused on inducing her confession and repentance:

- *"If we confess our sins, he is faithful and just to forgive us our sins, and to cleanse us from all unrighteousness"* (1 John 1:9 KJV).

- *"As many as I love, I rebuke and chasten. Therefore be zealous and repent"* (Revelation 3:19 NKJV).

Note that the wife who endured this extreme ordeal to the end would be vindicated. In the Old Testament, the accused wife had to be innocent of infidelity to survive the ordeal, but on this side of the cross, this process shows us how the One who loves us and who desires for us to be ONE with Him will progressively break a beloved one's soul in order to crucify our sin nature (flesh) until nothing remains, except that which is purely spiritual in nature.

Picture, if you will, yourself as Yeshua's Bride. You are standing before the LORD with your hair loose, which speaks of revealing the particular frequency of your manifestation of His glory. If a person has mixture (sin) in their life, their frequency will resonate at a lower level than the perfectly pure frequency of their Bridegroom. Recall that "to burn grain offerings" speaks of one's life being measured according to the plumb line of God's Word:

> "*²² Since you have purified your souls in obeying the truth through the Spirit in sincere love of the brethren, love one another fervently with a pure heart, ²³ having been born again, not of corruptible seed but incorruptible, through the word of God which lives and abides forever*" (1 Peter 1:22-23 NKJV).

Once the Wayward Wife's hair was let down, the High Priest would then place the grain offering in her outstretched palms, as he held the water of bitterness in an earthenware vessel. The priest would then have her move from place to place in the doorway of the courtyard where devout women served YHVH. The grain offering quickly became a burden that only the most resolute would bear. Afterwards, the priest would write the oaths contained in Numbers 5:19-22 on a parchment scroll. Ordinarily, in Biblical Times, it was forbidden to erase the sacred name, but here God commanded that His Name be erased in order to bring peace between man and wife.

Can you hear the shadow of the things to come that are here even now? Bridal candidates hold the grain-offering in her hands – the True Bread of Heaven – Yeshua. They hold onto Him for all that they are worth through the most difficult of circumstances. Remember, this is the place where the fiery eyes of Yeshua Ha Machiach (Jesus Christ) searches a person's souls with the goal of the True Bread of Heaven manifesting fully through the supernatural enablement of the seven-fold Spirits of God (Isaiah 11:1-2). When a Bridal Candidate's faithfulness is being tested at this level of purification, the eyes of the LORD, which run to and fro throughout the whole earth – your earth and mine – is the substance that comes out of heaven – manna – that humbles and tests us. As we press into letting His Word sift us, we are transformed by the renewing of our minds and we prove the Father's acceptable will through our lives (Romans 12:2).

Another present-day expression of a shadow of things to come is the High Priest of the Order of Melchizedek holds the bitter water in His hands, as His Bride moves about His courts. The Temple Courtyard can be symbolic of the body. It is here that by *"the mercies of God, that you present your bodies a living sacrifice, holy, acceptable to God, which is your reasonable service" (Romans 12:1 NKJV).*

The waters are called bitter, because purification (like sanctification) is a bittersweet process. One's soul doesn't like to die. We fight it, even when we desire it with all our heart. Therefore, these waters of purification are bitter until the tree is thrown in the water (Exodus 15: 25). When the Tree of Life is thrown in the water, the waters that our Great High Priest holds become sweet in order to sanctify and cleanse His Bride with the washing of water by the word (Ephesians 5:25-26). We know that the Tree of Life is synonymous with the Cross in this case, because the erasing of His Sacred Name speaks of: *"For God so loved the world, that He gave His only begotten Son, that whosoever believeth in Him should not perish, but have everlasting life" (John 3:16).*

Be encouraged Bridal Hearts! You are ONE who will endure to the end. The wayward wife in the Old Testament was found pure after she went through this arduous, humiliating process. The Messiah's Bride will do no less. The All-Consuming Fire will lead us by His Spirit and His Word to the place where no carnal flesh will remain; and we will become – ONE – bone of His bone and flesh of His divine flesh.

REFERENCES: Exodus 15:22-26; Numbers 5:11-31; Esther 2:15; Isaiah 11:1-2; Jeremiah 33:16-18; Zechariah 3:9; 4:10; Matthew 3:11; John 3:16; Romans 12:1-2; 1 Corinthians 11:23-24; Ephesians 1:10; Ephesians 5:23-27; Colossians 1:24; 1 John 1:9; 1 John 2:6; 1 Peter 1:22-23; James 1:2-4; Revelation 3:19; Revelation 4:5; Revelation 5:6.

*****

11 – BROKENNESS OF ONE'S SOUL

Purification is a work of oneness. Just like Yeshua, His Reigning Ones will be IN the Father, and the Father will be IN them. They will literally become holy, as He is holy.

We are continuing to explore the second crucifixion step in the Bride's Baptism of Fire in this chapter of *Hitting the Bull's Eye of Righteousness*. Please recall that Melchizedek is the predecessor of the Bride, because we are going to hover here today.

We begin to see the Kingdom of God when we accept Yeshua as our Lord and Savior (John 3:3). When we are baptized/born by the spirit and water, we enter the Kingdom of God (John 3:5). This is when His Kingdom Seed is planted within us, which is an incorruptible seed that's planted deep within our souls. Just like a seed in any garden, the wisdom of God knows that in order for corruptible man to put on incorruption, the Kingdom Seed within the soul of a man is dropped in dirt, covered in darkness, and must struggle to reach the light of the *shekinah* glory in which it was originally created before the Fall.

After the initial gift of salvation, believers learn things of the Spirit by first making a decision, then growing by exercising that spiritual reality. I have heard people say: I am born again, so Jesus fills my soul. This is simply not true. I could go into a Biblical explanation of this; but one merely needs to look at the behavior of most Christians to see the truth. The Spirit of the Living God fills your spirit and awakens it to God when one receives the gospel of salvation, but your soul is still under the dominion of sin nature (i.e., flesh). Since Yeshua will not live where sin exists, it is extremely important for us to partner with Him to cleanse our soul. Remember that the Bridal Baptism of Fire operates beyond both levels of salvation and sanctification in the area of purification.

Co-crucifixion with Christ is the way of the second level of the Baptism of Fire, and it comes by obeying His Word of Truth to where the world is crucified to us and us unto the world.

"[22] Since you have purified your souls in obeying the truth through the Spirit in sincere love of the brethren, love one another fervently with a pure heart, [23] having been born again, not of corruptible seed but incorruptible, through the word of God which lives and abides forever, [24] because 'All flesh is as grass, and all the glory of man as the flower of the grass. The grass withers, and its flower falls away, [25] But the word of the Lord endures forever.'" (1 Peter 1:22-25 NKJV).

"But God forbid that I should boast except in the cross of our Lord Jesus Christ, by whom the world has been crucified to me, and I to the world" (Galatians 6:14 NKJV).

The cross spoken of in Galatians 6:14 is the cross of the flesh where the world is crucified and where our souls are transformed by our death to our sin nature for the purpose of coming into resurrection life. The cross of the flesh transforms one's soul. Matthew 16:24-26 speaks about someone who tries to gain the whole world, but loses his soul because he refuses to deny himself, take up his cross and follow Yeshua.

"²⁴ Then said Jesus unto His disciples, If any man will come after me, let him deny himself, and take up his cross, and follow Me. ²⁶ For what is a man profited, if he shall gain the whole world, and lose his own soul? Or what shall a man give in exchange for his soul?" (Matthew 16:24,26 KJV).

When Yeshua completely fills a person's soul, they act like Him, talk like Him, and walk like Him, as He exhibited in the Word of God.

Let's realize that seeing the Kingdom of God is not the same as procuring it - inheriting it (John 3:3; Galatians 5:19-21). First and foremost, the Word of God is not simply some words on a piece of paper, but a person whose name is called "The Word of God" and on His thigh is written "King of Kings and the Lord of Lord" (Revelation 19:13-16). Royal priests know this, and they give honor where honor is due. Scripture also tell us that His Kingdom Seed is not only the "Word of the Kingdom," but the "Word of God" (Matthew 13:19; Luke 8:11). The Bible shows us that we can hear, receive, and believe the Word of God; and even though the Word of God is called the Sword of the Spirit, we also can be quite passive about it. There is nothing passive about working out our own salvation with fear and trembling (i.e., sanctification) as well as our fiery purification process, which enables us to become set apart kingdom vessels.

Brokenness is the rule for this secondary level of purification. Being humble and teachable are key. When we look at the three sections of God's Wilderness Tabernacle made after a heavenly pattern, we see that there is a curtain that marks the boundaries of God's Sanctuary (i.e., Dwelling Place), which makes up both the Holy Place and the Holy of Holies. Please note that the Holy of Holies lies within the boundaries of the Holy Place. Since the Holy Place can be equated to a person's soul and the Holy of Holies speaks of their spirit, we know that our spirit is housed within our soul.

When we take a revelatory peek into the Ancient Hebrew Word Picture for the word "curtain," it communicates that the curtain of God's Dwelling Place represents the highest and most important work to be done is the purification work in a person's soul. Wow! That's quite a statement!

Right now, the Body of Christ is being called to abide in the place of Galatians 2:20 where our sin nature is crucified in union with the Messiah, so we can literally live on this earth by the faith OF the Son of God. Please note that the Melchizedek Company is made like unto the Son of God (Hebrews 7:3). We know that the Son of God refused to come off the cross (Matthew 27:40), and so will Mel. We are currently being sifted again and again and again to get impurities out.

Yer-ee-aw is the Hebrew word for "curtain," and speaks of a tremulous hanging or a hanging of the fear of the Lord. The Spirit of the Fear of the Lord enabled Yeshua to walk, as ONE with His Heavenly Father. Due to the fear of the Lord residing within His soul, Yeshua literally loved what His Father loved, and hated what His Father hated. And so, it will be with His kings and priests of the Order of Melchizedek.

When something is tremulous, it is characterized by or affected with trembling. Humility is a result of this shaking of everything that can be shaken. *"¹ Where is the place of My rest? … ² To this man will I look, even to him that is poor and of a contrite spirit, and trembleth at My word"* (Isaiah 66:1b-2b KJV).

As we dig a little bit deeper, we see that the primitive root to *yer-ee-aw* is the Hebrew word *yaw-rah'*, which means to be broken up (with any violent action). When brokenness occurs, resistance, independence, and pride are replaced with submission, tenderness, obedience and love. To be broken is to come to the place where He is esteemed above self. Note: Each of us must willingly submit to (be a willful participant with) the Father in this process. Brokenness cracks open the hard shell of our sinful self nature to reveal the sons of the *shekinah!* Brokenness is an ancient pathway and main tool to prepare our souls for the filling up of the complete fullness of the Seven Spirits of God, which is how Jesus walked in the nature of Christ on earth.

Thank God that we have boldness to enter into the Holy of Holies in the heavenlies by the Blood of the Lamb, which is His incredibly wonderful Throne of Grace and a beloved relationship with Him, after we accept His gift of salvation. There still remains a need to rend the veil that is currently between a believer's soul and spirit due to The Fall, for those who desire to rule and reign with Him and do His greater works. We are told that when one turns to the Lord, the veil is taken away (2 Corinthians 3:16). Unequivocally, we are brought near by the cross through the blood of Christ. The crucifixion steps involved in the Bride's Baptism of Fire is merely a deeper spiritual reality to this truth where each one of us needs to grow into being a holy temple for the Lord before we can corporately connect wholly in love.

The process, which tears the curtain (veil) that is currently between our soul and spirit, is a top-down, heaven-to-earth crucifixion process, which results with a person being clothed with the fear of the Lord. The division between our soul and spirit is now being broken down, so the Nature of Christ can possess our souls. Thus, on both an individual and corporate level, establishing peace by making the two (soul and spirit) One New Man in Christ (Ephesians 2:15).

People are now experiencing the Lord's discipline as His mature sons in which the depths of our souls are being broken up with a violent agitation, so He can create a new heaven and a new earth within us, as He did in the beginning. *"The Kingdom of Heaven suffers violence, and the violent take it by force" (Matthew 11:12).*

Do you desire to be a golden kingdom vessel filled with the Nature of Christ (i.e., the Seven Spirits of God)? If so, then you ARE called to be one of His Reigning Ones, and you are probably experiencing or have experienced a deep work of crucifixion of your flesh (sin nature). Be encouraged. If you are struggling, it is because you truly desire to be formed into His very image. There is a HUGE test in our willingness to pay the price to die to ourselves, so that Christ may live in us in His fullness.

Please remember that LOVE meets us in our broken places. He is a good gardener who not only plants the good seed of His Kingdom, but He works to till the soil of our hearts, so we may receive a 100-fold return in all we do, as unto the King. At this time, resurrection life is still being released to you and I in sprout form for whosoever will.

REFERENCES: Genesis 1:1-5; Genesis 7:11; Deuteronomy 30:14; Psalm 104:4; Proverbs 3:19-23; Isaiah 11:2-5; Daniel 7:9; Matthew 10:38; Matthew 13:19; Matthew 27:51; Luke 8:11; Luke 9:23; John 3:3; John 14:12; John 17:22; Romans 10:6,9-10; 1 Corinthians 6:9-10; 1 Corinthians 15:51-54; 2 Corinthians 3:16; Galatians 2:20; Galatians 5:19-21; Galatians 6:14-16; Ephesians 2:13-22; Ephesians 6:17; Philippians 2:8; Philippians 3:14; Colossians 1:20; Hebrews 5:13-14; Hebrews 10:19-39; Hebrews 12:1-11; 1 Peter 1:22-25; Revelation 5:9; Revelation 19:13-16.

*****

12 – CONTINUAL LIVING SACRIFICE

The third, and most arduous, leg of the Bride's Baptism of Fire creates a blazing Fire Bride whose flame never goes out. This is the place where purification is consummated, which is a quantum leap beyond salvation and sanctification. It's a final transformative stage, which facilitates our becoming one with the All-Consuming Fire. It causes the New Jerusalem to resound with renown with the perfect frequency of our Bridegroom.

Please recall that the kings and priests of the Order of Melchizedek are the predecessor of the Bride (i.e., they prepare the Bride and are the pool from which the Bride comes). When royal priests burn to become just like Him, they will go all-out to become a Continual Living Sacrifice, which will be their ultimate spiritual sacrifice.

> "[1] *I beseech you therefore, brethren, by the mercies of God, that you* PRESENT YOUR BODIES A LIVING SACRIFICE, HOLY, ACCEPTABLE TO GOD, *which is your reasonable service.* [2] *And do not be conformed to this world, but be*

transformed by the renewing of your mind, that you may prove what is that good and acceptable and perfect will of God." (Romans 12:1-2 NKJV).

"You also, as living stones, are being built up a spiritual house, a holy priesthood, to offer up SPIRITUAL SACRIFICES ACCEPTABLE TO GOD THROUGH JESUS CHRIST" (1 Peter 2:5 NKJV).

You may have seen fire birds lately in the Spirit, because the fiery birds of a feather that are flocking together in this Kingdom Day are various wings of the Order of Melchizedek flying by the Spirit with one another. These passionate ones only glory in the cross:

"[14] But God forbid that I should glory, save in the cross of our Lord Jesus Christ, by whom the world is crucified unto me, and I unto the world. [15] For in Christ Jesus neither circumcision availeth any thing, nor uncircumcision, but a new creature" (Galatians 6:14-15 KJV).

Christ's Baptism of Fire was His crucifixion (Matthew 3:11). His Bride will not shun the need to join Him in this regard for the sake of His Body. Becoming a Manifested Son who is a Continual Living Sacrifice is a DEEP RED MYSTERY, which culminates in the Bride's complete Baptism of Fire that literally hits the bloodshot bull's eye of the Father.

Please recall that the full stature of His crimson flow makes it necessary for His Mature Body to grow up into Him in all things as well as each member of His Mature Body needing to fill up the afflictions of Christ in their flesh for His Body's sake (Ephesians 4:15; Colossians 1:24-25). The Corporate One New Man in Christ will accurately display to all the world the fullness of the measure of the stature of the fullness of Christ the same way that all fullness dwelt in Yeshua through the blood of the cross (Colossians 1:19-20). This is a key component to Yeshua's Mature Head attaching to His Mature Body (Daniel 7:9; Revelation 1:14). The fully mature Head of Messiah Yeshua's connecting to His fully mature Body is the undifferentiated state of the Messiah. This indistinguishable state of the Messiah can also be called the Heavenly One New Man in the Messiah – Metatron – which is the 100-percent fulfillment of the perfect man who is the equivalent to the fullness of the Messiah: *"Until we all become one in faith and in the knowledge of the Son of God, and become a perfect man according to the measure of the stature of the fullness of Christ" (Ephesians 4:13 Lamsa's Aramaic)*. For more on the Metatron subject, please check out the "Metatron" Chapter in the *MEL GEL Study Guide* => https://www.amazon.com/dp/0578188538/ or the *Mel Gel #5 – Metatron* teaching video available here => http://www.sapphirethroneministries.com/resources.html.

As the previous *Hitting the Bull's Eye of Righteousness* chapters illustrate, the way of righteousness for both His Melchizedek Company and Bridal Company consists of progressive crucifixion steps, which are spiritual sacrifices He still requires of His Holy Priesthood. For those who desire to completely crucify their own sin nature, Jeremiah 33:18 holds the key to the Bride's Baptism of Fire in its fullness:

[1]   offer burnt offerings,

[2]   burn grain offerings, and

[3]   prepare sacrifices continually.

A Bridal Candidate's quest for purification includes all of these offerings by fire. Understand that we are speaking about spiritual principles, not literal animal sacrifices in this

Kingdom Day. Like all series of three in Scripture, these crucifixion steps (where we join Yeshua on the cross) are listed from easiest to hardest. They also illuminate the pathway that leads to His Mature Body being prepared to do the perfect fiery will of the Father. This chapter is all about the third and final crucifixion step - "prepare sacrifices continually."

A priest of the Most High God who is a Continual Living Sacrifice literally prepares sacrifices continually, and those sacrifices are all related to one's Kingdom of Self: self-protection, self-interest, self-righteousness, et cetera. Bridal Candidates are priests who lead their inner bride forth until they completely emulate the One who by the will of God offered up His Body once for all (Hebrews 10:10); and thus, Continual Living Sacrifices will join our forerunner in becoming a priest forever after Order of Melchizedek (Hebrews 6:20). Yeshua is our Pattern Son, which is simply not only an introduction to Truth but our full and complete development in it. Remember that He is the first born of many brethren.

> "*⁵ Therefore, when He came into the world, He said: 'Sacrifice and offering You did not desire, but A BODY PREPARED FOR ME. ... ⁷ Then I said, 'Behold, I have come – In the volume of the book it is written of Me – TO DO YOUR WILL, O GOD.*" (Hebrews 10:5,7 NKJV).

Verse 9 of Hebrews 10 tells us that He took away the first (literal sacrifices and offerings) to establish the second, which is Christ's Body prepared to do His will. The principles behind the offerings listed in Jeremiah 33:18 literally show His kings and priests how the Messiah's Body is prepared, so it perfectly fits on the Head of the King of Kings.

The New Living Creature of Crucified Ones who is a Corporate One New Man in the Messiah will be the same essence as the All-Consuming Fire, which means our hearts, minds and works will have been thoroughly tested by fire (1 Corinthians 3:11-15; Hebrews 12:27-29).

Reigning Ones will manifest being an everlasting offering by fire, as they come out the other side of the All-Consuming Fire. They will be emblazon with the name: *"The Lord is our righteousness" (Jeremiah 33:16)*, and will continue to remain seated in the Sapphire Throne with Him (Ephesians 2:6; Revelation 3:21).

There is a purpose for this Continual Living Sacrifice place where His Holy Royal Priesthood prepares the truest sacrifice of themselves. This purpose is where Crucified Ones earn their title by bringing their entire carnal nature to the Lord's Altar, so it can be totally burnt up and the fullness of Christ can dwell in them.

To gain greater insight into our highest reality of being a Continual Living Sacrifice, we need to understand how the High Priest used to prepare sacrifices for God's Altar:

[1] THROAT SLIT AND BLOOD DRAINED - We must exchange our life in the flesh for His life in the Spirit. We are losing ourselves, so that we might be found in Him.

[2] HEAD CHOPPED OFF - The Head of the Body of Christ is in charge. We are to walk in the same manner as Yeshua who demonstrated: *"Not My will, but Yours be done" (Luke 22:42)*.

[3] SKIN REMOVED - We need to get rid of all self-protection, self-righteousness, and any self-defense mechanisms that are barriers to wholly connecting with God. His Sons of Light epitomize vulnerability and transparency.

[4] SPLIT BODY COMPLETELY OPEN AND WASH INWARD PARTS - Our heart and soul must be refined and purified, then washed with the water of the word (Ephesians 5:26) and the spirit of regeneration (Titus 3:5). A Continual Living Sacrifice demonstrates that all things belong to God. Please refer to "Restoration Time – 12 Strands of DNA" => http://wp.me/p2k1dQ-mr. The Cherubim Classification of the Order of Melchizedek must fulfill the Ten Copper Chariot Laver picture in Solomon's Temple in this regard.

[5] LEGS CHOPPED OFF - Continual Living Sacrifices cannot walk their own way. It's impossible. They need the supernatural legs of the Messiah, which are activated through their daily surrender to the Spirit's leading (John 5:19).

By the way, I culled these sacrifice preparation steps from Mike Parson's "Present A Living Sacrifice (1)" article on www.freedomarc.wordpress.com.

Just know that Continual Living Sacrifices who prepare themselves for use in God's Kingdom constantly prove the highest order of the perfect will of God (Romans 12:2). My *Webster's College Dictionary (10th Edition)* says that the word "prove" is an action verb, which is defined as: to learn or find out by experience.

- to test the truth, validity, or genuineness of.
- to test the worth or quality of, specifically: to compare against a standard.
- to check the correctness of.
- to establish the existence, truth or validity of (as by evidence).
- to demonstrate as having a particular quality of worth.
- to show (oneself) to be worthy or capable.
- to turn out, especially after trial or test.

Proving the perfect will of God involves working it out with fear and trembling as well as renouncing and giving up our own ways for His way for His Kingdom come here on earth, as it is in heaven. When we are crucified daily in union with Christ according to the plumb line of His Word of Righteousness, our inward and outward appearance will be transformed into His same image from glory to glory until we plainly prove the righteous character of Christ.

His pure and spotless Bride will exemplify co-crucifixion with her Beloved. Every time we make His specified spiritual sacrifice, it will cause those made after the Order of Melchizedek to decrease in their own strength and increase in the way of eternal life. His complete Bridal Baptism of Fire of our Kingdom of Self will cause His Continual Living Sacrifices to operate wholly and fully in the Kingdom of God.

May the Kingdom of Self disappear, and the Kingdom of God appear in you and me.

REFERENCES: Jeremiah 33:16-18; Daniel 7:9; Matthew 3:11; Matthew 16:24-26; Luke 22:42; John 3:30; 5:19; Romans 12:1-2; 1 Corinthians 3:11-15; Galatians 6:14-16; Ephesians 2:6; Ephesians 4:15; Ephesians 5:26; Colossians 1:19-20; Colossians 1:24-25; 1 Peter 2:5; Titus 3:5; Hebrews 10:5-7; Hebrews 12:27-29; Revelation 1:14; Revelation 3:21.

*****

UNDERSTANDING THE ORDER OF MELCHIZEDEK

Book 5

Formation of the New Living Creature

Cover Art: "Fiery Wheel With His Wheel" by Robin Main

© September 18, 2014. All Rights Reserved

Text Copyright © 2015 Robin Main. All Rights Reserved

1 – INTRODUCTION

This book mainly looks at the pattern of the New Living Creature (i.e., New Creation) in Christ through the eyes of the CHERUBIM. It's a paradigm shift that will help us understand that God's Cherubim are not merely angelic. We are not negating the reality of cherubim being angelic. We are simply expanding our consciousness to understand another ancient dimension. Within "cherubim" in Scripture is a profound mystery that has been sealed up for this hour. It has been prophesized by King David (who was a priest forever after the Order of Melchizedek) that during the dawning of a new Kingdom Age that the LORD will send out His rod of strength from Zion where His people will volunteer freely in the day of His power. And in the beauty of holiness the Order of Melchizedek will rule in the midst of their enemies. *"² The LORD shall send the rod of Your strength out of Zion. Rule in the midst of Your enemies!³ Your people shall be volunteers in the day of Your power; in the beauties of holiness, from the womb of the morning, You have the dew of Your youth. ⁴ The LORD has sworn and will not relent, 'You are a priest forever according to the Order of Melchizedek" (Psalms 110:2-4 NKJV).* Melchizedek David had a lot to say about CHERUBIM.

Unbeknownst to me at the time, I was introduced to the formation of a New Living Creature (i.e., Cherubim) in April of the year 2000. I discuss this divine encounter of the supernatural kind in the *Taking on Common Union* book. During a corporate communion time, the LORD led us to take our bread and wine individually, looking solely to Him, yet still remaining corporate as one. At the time we were walking around Hughes Stadium in Fort Collins, Colorado to prepare this stadium for a promised move of God. The foreseen fruit is not what we assumed at the time.

If you recall, when I raised my portion of bread, I solely zeroed in on Yeshua. What I heard has rocked my world to this day. Yeshua whispered: "With this bread, I thee wed." My breath caught, and my eyes widened, as I stood in awe. I felt led to simply repeat after Him "With this bread, I thee wed." Then I raised my glass a bit shaken to my core. I unmistakably heard: "With this wine, I thee wed." The awe increased as I barely whispered: "With this wine, I thee wed." This happened on a Tuesdays (the third day of the week), which is the day when weddings took place in ancient Israel. Know that our Beloved Bridegroom is coming to marry His Pure and Spotless Bride in this Prophetic Third Day. The reason we will continually touch on bridal elements while studying the Order of Melchizedek is because Melchizedek is the predecessor of the Bride.

Four months prior to this first marriage communion of mine, Yeshua had come to me in November of 1999 and literally married me after my family and I had obeyed Yeshua in coming out of Babylon, laying down Christmas to become a precious part of His Pure and Spotless Bride. As I laid in a bubble bath worshiping my king, He came epiphaneously to me and sat on the edge of my tub. This was the second epiphaneous appearance I had with Yeshua. The first was when He came to me on December 21, 1998 with tears in His eyes. Yeshua told me: "The mixture of Christmas grieves My heart." I was reeling at the time, because I did not hate Christmas, I loved it and my Beloved just told me what I was doing grieved Him. I had just experienced a hard lesson that taught me that my choice to His request would either move me closer to Him or farther away. The only choice for my sold-out heart was to respond: "Lord, I want to. Help me. Show me the way out. My husband's not ready for this. Give me, give us a way out." My feeble heart cry got His attention. Within a couple hours, our Christmas Tree and entire house was infested with spiders... hundreds of tiny spiders. My Love knew how to get Christmas out of our house. He knows the way that you will take too where you shall come forth as gold.

After we had laid down Christmas in 1998 (when my son was 5-years-old) and celebrated Hanukkah, Yeshua came to me the next year to marry me. Talk about obedience having its rewards! When Yeshua literally appeared to me out-of-the-blue, as I reclined with only some iridescent bubbles between us, I was shocked again. When Yeshua asked: "Will you marry Me?" Many thought flashed into my mind in a moment What? What do you mean? Like this? Thoughts that He read instantly. Yeshua smiled and chuckled as I realized how silly all that was in comparison to the Beauty before me. My Love was here, and He had asked me to marry Him. How many personal marriage proposals would I get from the King of Kings? I wasn't taking any chances. After I gushed: "Of course!" I fell back reclining, as Yeshua whipped out a celestial wedding ring. He asked me to extend my left hand. As Yeshua slipped this brilliant sign of our covenant on my finger, my whole being vibrated to His voice: "With this ring, I thee wed." His voice cut through my tangible amazement, and my spirit knew that I was supposed to repeat after Him, so I did. "With this ring, I thee wed."

This is the back ground that everyone needs for my holy wedding communion experience. For years afterwards, daily communion became an integral part of my life. Many things happened, as I took the bread and spoke over it: "With this bread, I thee wed." I would then take the wine always seeking to truly connect solely with my Beloved: "With this wine, I thee wed."

One morning after receiving a vision of Yeshua walking among the Seven Spirits of God, I heard the Father say: "Today. We come together for holy matrimony." Since I had been declaring for years over my daily communion: "With this bread and this wine, I thee wed," I was a tad bit perplexed, yet very expectant at the same time. As I waited in awe, all of a sudden without any external instruction, all four of us -- the Father, the Son, the Holy Spirit, and I - spontaneously recited in perfect unison: "With this bread, we thee wed." We repeated the supernatural feat with the wine and all took communion of holy matrimony, as four in one.

The previous night my heart cry was that the seven-fold nature of Christ would take total possession of my life. I wanted to walk just like Yeshua did when He walked the earth with the fullest impartation of the Seven Spirits of God.

The *Taking on Common Union* book and the *Formation of the New Living Creature YouTube* video go into more detail here. When I switched to doing daily communion corporately with the Godhead as I spoke: "With this bread, we thee wed" and "With this wine, we thee wed" all four of us would be seated around a square table. The Father would sit right across from me. The Son was to my right, and the Holy Spirit to my left. Eventually when the Spirit led me to study the Living

Creature in Ezekiel Chapter 1, I was instructed that one dimension of the four faces is an individual (you and me) being united in a fourfold with the Father, the Son, and Holy Spirit.

> *"As for the likeness of their faces, each had the face of a man; each of the four had the face of a lion, on the right side, each of the four had a face of an ox on the left side, and each of the four had the face of an eagle" (Ezekiel 1:10 KJV)*. Ezekiel saw this from without. I saw it within my spirit over and over and over again. I was instructed that one facet of the four living creatures in Ezekiel 1 was that the Father is symbolized by the ox due to the Ancient Hebrew Letter *alef/aleph* being a picture of an ox and symbolic of a father. The Son is symbolized by the face of the lion, because He is called the Lion of the Tribe of Judah (Revelation 5:5). The Holy Spirit is symbolized by the face of the eagle, which causes us all to soar in the Spirit. Put yourself in the place of the man; and thus, we see a new revelatory dimension that the four living creatures of the Father, the Son, the Holy Spirit and yourself is in a New Living Creature:

> *"^{19} And when the LIVING CREATURES went, the wheels went by them: and when the living creatures were lifted up from the earth, the wheels were lifted up. ^{20} Whithersoever the spirit was to go, they went, thither was their spirit to go; and the wheels were lifted up over against them: for the spirit of the LIVING CREATURE was in the wheels" (Ezekiel 1:19-20 KJV)*.

Once one person is joined in oneness in a fourfold way with the Father, the Son, and the Holy Spirit, there is another and higher corporate dimension of the New Living Creature formation. When four (or more) individuals join together as one after they are wed together in a four-fold way with the Father, the Son, and Holy Spirit, that group operates as a

New Living Creature of the One New Man in Christ, which is incidentally a wing of the Melchizedek Army.

*****

2 – THE CHARIOT THRONE'S APPEARANCE OF A MAN

God's people need to understand that the New Living Creature being formed in our day is not only depicted as a One New Man in Christ on a personal level, but also as a One New Man in Christ on a corporate level. Both dimensions of the One New Man in Christ are made after the Order of Melchizedek.

Never forget that the first step is always up to the individual where you and I need to be wed in a fourfold way with the Father, the Son, and the Holy Spirit, so the Living Word can be lived out through us by means of the Seven Spirits of God according to the perfect will of the Father.

God's Chariot Throne is called the *"Merkabah." Merkabah* is the Hebrew word for "chariot" with a general meaning "to ride." The teachings of ancient and modern mystics tell us that the *Merkabah* is a heavenly or spiritual science that was esteemed as most sacred. It was a secret doctrine only revealed to initiates, and then only orally. Rabbi Shimon ben-Yohai never imparted the most important points of the *Merkabah*, because the *Merkabah* can only be taught "in darkness, in a deserted place, and after many and terrific trials."

"Confirming the souls of the disciples, and exhorting them to continue in the faith, and that we must through much tribulation enter into the kingdom of God" (Acts 14:22 KJV).

Those who have knowledge of Scripture and the *Merkabah* are insured the reception of the "Word" Himself. Even though the term *"Merkabah"* is not used in the Bible or in the Book of Ezekiel itself, it would be a huge disservice to the study of the Formation of a New Living Creature if we threw out this esoteric and most ancient technology.

Let's look a little closer at the Living Creature (Hebrew "*chayot*") of His Chariot Throne (*Merkabah*) having the appearance of A MAN – ONE MAN – ONE CORPORATE NEW MAN IN CHRIST.

Notice that the likeness of the four living creatures has the appearance of a man in Ezekiel 1:5: *"Also out of the midst thereof came the likeness of four living creatures. And this was their appearance; they had the likeness of a man."* Then in verse 8 we are told that each of the four living creatures had the hands of a man under their wings. *"And they had the hands of a man under their wings on their four sides" (Ezekiel 1:8a).*

The bodies of the "*chayot*" are like that of a human being, which is communicating to us that this heavenly Living Creature is part of Christ's earthly body. Notice the number "4" is fundamentally connected to the four living creatures that make up one New Living Creature. The number "4" is always connected to creation and His created works. For instance, there are the four corners of the earth, four directions of the compass (north-south-east-west), four winds, four rivers that flowed out of Eden that comes from one river that waters the garden east of Eden (Genesis 2:8-14), etc. You get the idea. These four living creatures are focused and connected vertically first to His Throne; and then, they connect horizontally with others in a Melchizedek Company. *"Thus were their faces: and their wings were stretched upward; two wings of every one were joined one to another, and two covered their bodies" (Ezekiel 1:11).*

Notice how the appearance of a man is seen in two places at once. There is the face of a man in the New Living Creature that looks up at the "likeness of a man" that drives the chariot. Also notice that it says that "a man" sits on a throne made of sapphire, not the Son of Man: *"And above the firmament that was over their heads was the likeness of a throne, as the appearance of a sapphire stone: and upon the likeness of the throne was the likeness of a man above upon it" (Ezekiel 1:26).*

I used to belong to a corporate ascension group that meet almost every week for four years, in April 2013 we experienced all the four of us seated on a square chair. Each of us were seated on each one of the chair's four corners. We faced outward. Then we came together and were compressed, as we spun counterclockwise like a centrifuge (center fuse). We saw ourselves as a lump of clay standing up waiting to take shape. We knew it was a lump of flesh. We saw Him forming us as a unique NEW CREATION. We saw seven rings of clay, which represent the Seven Spirits of God in the flesh. A pottery class at a community college taught me that this New Creation was a hand-formed clay vessel. We were instructed that the Fear of the Lord was the top ring and the Spirit of the Lord was at its base. We understood that everything flows down from the Spirit of the Fear of the Lord, and He was reforming the clay by His wheels. It was a New Living Creature of the One New Man in Christ on earth who will rule and reign.

Notice that becoming a New Living Creature of the One New Man in Christ is not automatic. It is a progressive work of oneness with goal of becoming holy, as He is holy. It's also a work that is in the Potter's Hands. This progressive work of oneness is depicted in God's Dwelling Place where the Living Creature has always been a part of its design. Please repeat after me: *"I am the Temple of God" (1 Corinthians 6:19).* We will be getting to the places in Scripture where the Living Creature or the Cherubim are mentioned shortly. This a huge key to the manifestation of the Order of Melchizedek in this Kingdom Day. First, let's truly understand how the Living Creature can also be called the Cherubim.

*****

3 – BEHOLD, THE LIVING CREATURE IS THE CHERUBIM

One little verse says it all: *"This is the LIVING CREATURE I saw under the God of Israel by the River Chebar, and I knew they were CHERUBIM" (Ezekiel 10:20 NKJV)*.

Let's back up just a little bit. When we think of cherubim, we think of angels. The word for "angels" is the Greek word *aggelos*, which is from the Hebrew and means "sent one" or "messenger;" but here's a hidden fact that will blow your mind! Both the Hebrew Scriptures and Greek Septuagint tell us that the SENT ONE or MESSENGER can either be a divine ANGELIC or a sublime HUMAN MESSENGER.

Due to everyone's focus has been on the angelic side of the Cherubim equation, let look at one Scripture that speaks to the human messengers that are His messengers too. Please note that these sublime human messengers are marked specifically as the kings and priests after the Order of Melchizedek: *"⁹And they* [the four living creatures and the 24 elders] *sang a new song, saying: "You are worthy to take the scroll, And to open its seals; For You were slain, And have*

REDEEMED US TO GOD BY YOUR BLOOD out of every tribe and tongue and people and nation, ^{10} and have MADE US KINGS AND PRIESTS TO OUR GOD; and WE SHALL REIGN ON THE EARTH" (Revelation 5:9-10 $_{NKJV}$).

Did you catch that? Revelation 5:9-10 speaks about the four living creatures (i.e., the Living Creature) being redeemed by the Lamb's Blood as well as being made kings and priests to God. Were angels redeemed by the Lamb's Blood or was mankind? Are angels made kings and priests to the Most High God or is man? Therefore, when we combine Revelation 5:9-10 with Ezekiel 10:20, we understand that when we are talking about the LIVING CREATURE, we are focusing on the CHERUBIM as well as the ORDER OF MELCHIZEDEK too.

What does Ancient Hebrew Word Picture for "cherubim" tell us? First of all, every Hebrew letter is a picture, and every picture carries a meaning. When we look at the pictures of the letters in a Hebrew word, we can get a glimpse into its Ancient Hebrew Word Picture that carries a deeper meaning than just a surface view. Whenever I look for revelation about the Ancient Hebrew Word Picture, I first research the meaning of the Hebrew letters and their related pictures. Then I lay it all down before the Lord and ask His Spirit to interpret a particular word for me. I did this for the Hebrew word for "cherubim." The Ancient Hebrew Word Picture for CHERUBIM tells us that that cherubim are a picture for where God opens His people up to His Kingdom in their midst through His Spirit, His Word and His massive deeds done; and it's where God joins His Body together to make it a securely nailed dwelling place where His household is bound together within.

The following chapters delves into His securely nailed Dwelling Place where God opens His people up to His Kingdom in their midst. Pay attention, because when God joins His Body together, it is a multi-dimensional reality. You will notice that we mainly will dig into the Old Testament. Hidden within the Dwelling Places of the Most High God in Scripture is a profound mystery. This mystery is the sons of righteousness of the Order of Melchizedek who both build His Dwelling Place and literally are His Dwelling Place.

*****

4 – CHERUBIM GUARDING THE TREE OF LIFE

Cherubim mark the spot for returning to our primordial state, as it was in the beginning before Adam and Eve fell, except better, redeemed. Adam and Eve were sinless, but not perfected. This will be one of the biggest differences this go-around. Adam and Eve still would have needed to be made into the image of Christ. After Adam and Eve were banished from the Garden east of Eden, Cherubim with a flaming sword were placed at its entrance. *"²³ Therefore the LORD God sent him out of the garden of Eden to till the ground from which he was taken. ²⁴ So He drove out the man; and HE PLACED CHERUBIM AT THE EAST OF THE GARDEN OF EDEN, AND A FLAMING SWORD WHICH TURNED EVERY WAY, TO GUARD THE TREE OF LIFE" (Genesis 3:23-24 NKJV).*

The Hebrew word for "return" is *shoob*. It contains three Hebrew letters - *sheen, vav, bet* – which shows us a dovetailing aspect to our returning to our primordial state. The Ancient Hebrew Word Picture for "return" communicates that Almighty God joins His Body together and makes it a securely nailed dwelling place where His family (household) are bound together within. I don't think that it's a coincidence that the essence of "return" coincides with the essence of "cherubim." In fact, the Cherubim of God's Chariot Throne are made up of people after the Order of Melchizedek whose aim is the purification of their human nature into its exalted state. Originally, we were not created as human beings. To be human is a fallen state. We were originally created as living beings (i.e., living souls). *"And the LORD God formed man of the dust of the ground, and breathed into his nostrils the breath of life; and man became a living soul" (Genesis 2:7 KJV).*

The quest is one of self-conquest in order to return to being a living soul… His very breath of life. The soul that conquers oneself is the one who has the All-Consuming Fire sitting on their throne. Self-conquest is an arduous, painful, and trying quest. One can say its path is paved with the fire of many trials. Even though the flaming sword that guards the way to the Tree of Life is singular, this sword of fire wielded by the Cherubim is both your sword as well as God's sword.

Ephesians 6:17 instructs God's people to take *"the sword of the Spirit, which is the Word of God."* Then right after Revelation 19 reveals that the Bride of Christ is made ready by the righteous acts of the saints and how blessed everyone is who has been called to the Marriage Supper of the Lamb, we see the One who the Bride will be wed to as one. He is called *"The Word of God"* as well as *"Faithful and True" (Revelation 19:13,11).* We are also told that *"His eyes were as a flame of fire" (Revelation 19:12).*

"And I beheld, and, lo, in the midst of the throne and of the four beasts, and in the midst of the elders, stood a Lamb as it had been slain, having seven horns and SEVEN EYES, WHICH ARE THE SEVEN SPIRITS OF GOD sent forth into all the earth" (Revelation 5:6 KJV). His eyes of a flame of fire are the torches before the throne that allows His New Living Creature full of eyes to be in the midst and round about His Throne:

"⁴And out of the throne proceeded lightnings and thunderings and voices: and there were SEVEN LAMPS OF FIRE BURNING BEFORE

THE THRONE, WHICH ARE THE SEVEN SPIRITS OF GOD. ⁵ And before the throne there was a sea of glass like unto crystal: and IN THE MIDST OF THE THRONE, AND ROUND ABOUT THE THRONE, WERE FOUR BEASTS FULL OF EYES before and behind" (Revelation 4:5-6 KJV).

Therefore, the Word of God that we are instructed to take up is a sword connected to the Seven Spirits of God. These are His seven eyes that are alive and powerful. These seven eyes can also rightly divide one's soul and spirit as well as judge the thoughts and attitudes of one's heart (Hebrews 4:12). It's interesting that one aspect of the Ancient Hebrew Word Picture for "Eden" reveals that Eden is connected to seeing the judge, and the Ancient Hebrew Word Picture for "judge" tells us that the Judge is the Door of Life.

These Seven Spirits of God that are both His eyes and His flames of fire. They are sent into all of our earth, so His royal priesthood can be purified in order to reign on earth (both within and without). There is a trans-dimensional garden east of Eden whose entrance is guarded with a flaming sword that turns every way, which means that there's no getting around this sword of fire that keeps the way of the Tree of Life (Genesis 3:24).

His eyes of a flame of fire are searching to and fro seeking those who are His. His Beloved Bride will certainly be His, and she will epitomize: *"Love the LORD your God with all your heart and with all your soul and with all your strength" (Deuteronomy 6:5).* A huge flaming sword key is actually found within the depths of this verse.

Everybody has a life message, and everybody has theme verses. Deuteronomy 6:5 is one of my theme verses. It goes along with one of my life messages, which zeroes in on the carrying a torch for the Lord kind of Bridal Love. Series of three in Scripture are listed from easiest to hardest. Think of them as three spotlights that enlighten our pathway for moving unto perfection (i.e., maturity).

Therefore, the easiest way to love YHVH is will all our heart. This first loving God stage appears to be a quantum leap into the deep. Let's simply ponder a few Scripture that speaks of this depth:

- *"KEEP YOUR HEART WITH ALL DILIGENCE, for out of it spring the issues of life"* (Proverbs 4:23 NKJV).

- *"Rather let it be the HIDDEN PERSON OF THE HEART, with the incorruptible beauty of a gentle and quiet spirit, which is very precious in the sight of God"* (1 Peter 3:4 NKJV).

- *"Let us DRAW NEAR WITH A TRUE HEART in full assurance of faith, having our hearts sprinkled from an evil conscience, and our bodies washed with pure water"* (Hebrews 10:22 KJV).

- *"For the word of God is living and powerful, and sharper than any two-edged sword, piercing even to the division of soul and spirit, and of joints and marrow, and is a discerner of the THOUGHTS ANS INTENTS OF THE HEART"* (Hebrews 4:12 NKJV).

- *"Blessed are the pure in heart: for they shall see God"* (Matthew 5:8 KJV).

This easiest way to love God is one huge order to fill. Our heart literally controls our insides. Our heart controls how we think. *"For as he thinks in his heart, so is he"* (Proverbs 23:7).

The next hardest way to love God is with all your soul. The Hebrew word for "soul" in Deuteronomy 6:5 is "*nephesh.*" It's defined to be the breathing substance or the inner being of a man. It's one's very life's breath, and it's connected to the living soul (being) that YHVH formed in Genesis 2:7. This second loving God stage is another quantum leap that takes a man to the edge of his created existence. Revelation 12:11 emphasizes this point; and if we pay attention, it will thrust us into our third and final step of loving God: *"And they overcame him by the Blood of the Lamb, and by the word of their testimony and they loved not their lives unto the death" (Revelation 12:11 KJV)*.

Why would Scripture have another quantum leap after loving God with your very life's breath? There is a *nephesh* breathing soul, which is our lower soul; and there is a *neshamah* upper soul, which is connected to the principle of spiritual life. This means that there is a love that transcends visible creation, and connects directly to the One who sits on the Throne. Man is the climax of the works of God. When mankind does the work of making themselves ready through hitting the mark of perfect love, they emerge as His Pure and Spotless Bride.

The most arduous way to love God is with all your strength. Basically, we can boil down "loving God with all your strength" to loving Him with your resources, which incredibly brings us full circle back to the heart of the matter: *"For where your treasure is, there your heart will be also" (Matthew 6:21)*.

When we gaze into the Hebrew word for "strength," we see the carrying a torch for the Lord Bridal Love that was mentioned previously. It's the cherubim kind of love where His Precious Sons of Light become one with the flaming sword. This is the space and place where those made after the Order of Melchizedek consummates their own preparation of their inner fire bride. These are the New Living Creature that wears a bridal veil. These are the ones in the midst and around His throne who are one with the One who sits in the throne.

Behold, a mystery. The New Living Creature depicted in Ezekiel Chapter 1 is made up of four feminine living creatures when you look at the original Hebrew. Ezekiel was a priest in the First Temple who was deported to Babylon. He describes in the Book of Ezekiel how the lady left the Temple. For more on this subject, please refer to either the "Shekinah Sabbath" Chapter in the *MEL GEL Study Guide* => https://www.amazon.com/dp/0578188538/ or *Mel Gel #2* –

Shekinah Sabbath teaching video available here => http://www.sapphirethroneministries.com/resources.html.

Can you hear His Passionate Bride in *me'od*, which is the Hebrew word for "strength" in Deuteronomy 6:5? To love so much, quickly, vehemently, wholly, speedily, especially when repeated, diligently, especially, exceedingly, greatly, louder and louder, mightily, utterly. We are told in the Strong's Concordance that OT:3966 *me'od* is from the same as OT:181 *uwd*, which means to rake together. It's like a fire, or firebrand, or a torch.

We have been taught that His angels are ministers a flame of fire, which is a wonderful truth; but let us not miss the significance of the word "angels" in Psalm 104:4, which is *mal'ak*. This Hebrew word *mal'ak* can either be an angel or a messenger sent by the king. Remember how cherubim are sent ones or messengers? Remember how cherubim can represent either an angelic or human messenger? *"³ He lays the beams of His upper chambers in the waters, who makes the clouds His chariot, who walks on the wings of the wind, ⁴ Who makes His mal'ak spirits, His ministers a flame of fire" (Psalms 104:3-4).*

The garden in Eden was the place of abundant life where Adam and Eve dwelled with God in the mysterious and glorious union of heaven and earth. God is bringing us "back" into His Garden of Love, as the flaming sword grants entry to any who hold no idols (those whose heart is clean and pure before the Father). *Revelation 22:14-15* says: " *¹⁴ Blessed are those who wash their robes that they may have the right to the Tree of Life and may go through the gates into the city. ¹⁵ Outside are the dogs, those who practice magic arts, the sexually immoral, the murderers, the idolaters and everyone who loves and practices falsehood."* This is the time to put away all of our idols.

We are returning to our primordial state, as it was in the beginning and beyond… being formed into the very image of God. In the beginning God created a pristine garden where within was continual love, car, provision and wisdom, which you are (Song of

Songs 4:12).

*****

5 – CHERUBIM ON THE TEN COPPER CHARIOT LAVERS

Just as God's Tabernacle (Temple) has three parts, so does a man or woman. Think about how there is the Outer Court, Inner Court (Holy Place), and Holy of Holies depicted in all of God's Dwelling Places. Now think of man being a tri-parte being with a body, soul and spirit.

Isaiah 9:7 speaks about how there is no end to the increase of His government and peace; and then, 1 Thessalonians 5:23 tells us that the God of Peace sanctifies a person wholly – body, soul and spirit.

- *"Of the increase of His government and peace there shall be no end, upon the Throne of David, and upon his kingdom, to order it, and to establish it with judgment and with justice from henceforth even for ever. The zeal of the LORD of hosts will perform this"* (Isaiah 9:7 KJV).

- *"And the very God of peace sanctify you wholly; and I pray*

God your whole spirit and soul and body be preserved blameless unto the coming of our Lord Jesus Christ" (1 Thessalonians 5:23 KJV).

Isn't multidimensional revelation wonderful? Let's consider a personal dimension of God's government that is related to man himself, which is literally pictured in God's Dwelling Place. After all, isn't our body called the Temple of the Holy Ghost? *"¹⁹ Or do you not know that your body is the Temple of the Holy Spirit who is in you, whom you have from God, and you are not your own? ²⁰ For you were bought at a price; therefore glorify God in your body and in your spirit, which are God's" (1 Corinthians 6:19-20 NKJV).*

The Greek word for "body" in 1 Corinthians 6:19 is sōma. Not only does sōma describe the bodies of men and animals, but it describes heavenly bodies as well, like planets and stars. Sōma is also used to describe a mystical body of small or large number of men closely united into one society or one family, like Christ's Church. Can you say God is rebuilding His Temple in Three Days?!

Yeshua prophetically declared that in three days He will raise up the Temple of His Body (John 2:19-21). Every 1,000 years is an eon in Scripture in which the Lord does something exciting and new where He deposits a word that takes 1000 years for mankind to fulfill. In God's Calendar, it says in 2 Peter 3:8 that 1,000 years on the earth is like one day on the calendar of God. In the year 2000 AD, the Church stepped out of the side of Yeshua into the Third Day. So, in this chapter let's focus on the resurrected mystical body of Christ being raised up in this Third Day. Please mark that the resurrected Body of Christ is accomplished through the complete transfiguration of man – body, soul and spirit.

We can connect a man's body with the Temple's Outer Court, a man's soul with the Inner Court, and a man's spirit with the Holy of Holies. There are doorways into each of these three dimensions of God's Dwelling Place. Ask a Bible-believing Hebrew what the doors to these three places are called; and you will hear the door to the Outer Court is called The Way, the door to the Inner Court is called The Truth, and the door to Holy of Holies is The Life. *"Jesus said to him, "I am The Way, The Truth, and The Life. No one comes to the Father except through Me" (John 14:6 NKJV)*.

If the Mystical Body of Yeshua takes a Melchizedek turn, we can map the three parts of God's Dwelling Place to the triple concentric circles of the Order of Melchizedek's Breastplate. I have seen the triple concentric circles on Melchizedek's golden breastplate morph into various dimensions, but the first time I saw it in the spirit it looked like a target made out of precious stones. The outermost ring was blue. The middle ring was red, and the innermost concentric circle was white.

These triple concentric circles show us the migration a man must make for his own perfection (i.e., maturity). The outer ring of sapphire stone is connected to man's body and its transformation of being clothed in righteousness via His Sapphire Throne. The ruby red middle stone maps to the transformation of a man' soul through Christ's Blood where our soul gets to the space and place where it becomes a literal dwelling place for His *Shekinah* Glory (Galatians 6:14-16). The white stone innermost ring is linked to the crystal-clear walls of the New Jerusalem and a man's spirit being totally transformed to be in constant communication with our Creator.

Keep in mind the outermost sapphire ring is where a man's body is clothed in righteousness when we discuss the cherubim on the ten copper chariot lavers. The only "cherubim" outside of the Sanctuary are these cherubim in the Outer Court. If kings and priests miss fulfilling the Ten Copper Chariot Laver picture, we will miss coming into the fullness of the CHERUBIM CLASSIFICATION OF THE ORDER OF MELCHIZEDEK. These ten copper chariot lavers literally show His Melchizedek Company the Way to coming into His Truth for becoming His Holy Place here on earth, as it is in heaven.

Please note that the baseline for the Cherubic Melchizedek Company is having entered in the Kingdom of God, which means that a person has to have matured past merely salvation to the place of sanctification, and hopefully even further to the bridal place of purification.

Even though King Solomon built the first iteration of the Dwelling Place made of stone, it was his father that received these plans by the Spirit: *"⁹ As for you, my son Solomon, know the God of your father, and serve Him with a whole heart and with a willing mind; for the LORD searches all hearts and understands every intent of the thoughts. If you seek Him, He will let you find Him; but if you forsake Him, He will reject you forever. ¹⁰ Consider now, for the LORD has chosen you to build a house for the sanctuary; be courageous and act. ¹¹ THEN DAVID GAVE HIS SON SOLOMON the plan of the porch of the Temple, its buildings, its storehouses, its upper rooms, its inner rooms and the room for the mercy seat; ¹² and THE PLAN OF ALL THAT HE HAD IN MIND* [by the Spirit] *..." (1 Chronicles 28:9-12 NASB)*. It's very noteworthy that King David is one of three people in Scripture specifically identified as a priest forever after the Order of Melchizedek (Psalm 110:4). It's also tremendously significant that the Tabernacle of David is the only dwelling place of God that we are told will be raised up again:

- *"On that day I WILL RAISE UP THE TABERNACLE OF DAVID, which has fallen down, And repair its damages; I will raise up its ruins, And rebuild it as in the days of old" (Amos 9:11 NKJV)*.

- *"¹⁶ After this I WILL RETURN AND REBUILD THE TABERNACLE OF DAVID, which has fallen down; I will rebuild its ruins, and I will set it up; ¹⁷ so that the rest of mankind may seek the LORD, even all the Gentiles who are called by My Name, says the LORD who does all these things known from eternity (of old)" (Acts 15:16-17 NKJV, NU Text)*.

Solomon's Temple is patterned after the Tabernacle of David. They both were birthed by the one whose throne is said to never end (Isaiah 9:7). King David divinely received the plans for Solomon's Temple from the Spirit that was patterned after a heavenly golden temple, which has a triple concentric circles insignia on the floor when you enter its sanctuary. Therefore, when you think of Solomon's Temple, know that its key to the Order of Melchizedek as well as connected to the ancient Tabernacle of David.

In the plans Melchizedek David received for the next iteration of God's House were Ten Copper Chariot Lavers with cherubim adorning each (See 1 Kings 7:27-40). The Hebrew letter *yod* is numerically equal to ten. *Yod* or *yood* or *yud* is also the symbolic letter of *kether*, which means a "crown;" therefore, we can extrapolate that the work of these Ten Copper Chariot Lavers has to do with receiving a crown – the crown of Melchizedek. Crowns are all about power. Scripture tells us that another priest arises after the similitude of Melchizedek with the power of an endless life (Hebrews 7:15-16). Not only is the Order of Melchizedek made up of sons of the Father of Lights, but the fullness of this New Living Creature is the very Ark of His Presence.

It's significant that all ten of the copper lavers had *"one casting, one measurement and one size" (1 Kings 7:37)*. When we discuss Ark of the Covenant in Solomon's Temple, you will better understand the reference to *"they four had one likeness" (Ezekiel 1:16)*.

The border of each copper laver was SQUARE with a circular basin for water placed inside the SQUARE border. Please recall my corporate communion with the Father, Son and Holy Spirit around a SQUARE table where we spoke in unison: "With this bread, we thee wed" and "With this wine, we thee wed."

There were cherubim along with lions and oxen on the square borders (1 Kings 7:29). Think of the lion being symbolic of Yeshua who is called the Lion of the Tribe of Judah (Revelation 5:5), and the ox being symbolic of our Heavenly Father. When we connect *"one casting, one measurement and one size"* to John 17:23, we better understand the oneness element of these copper chariot lavers: *"[22] And the glory which You gave me I have given them, that they may be ONE just as We are ONE: [23] I in them, and You in Me; that they may be made perfect in ONE, and that the world may know that You have sent Me, and have loved them as You have loved Me" (John 17:22-23 NKJV).*

Some translations call these bronze lavers, but they were most likely copper. There were five of these copper lavers on the right side of Solomon's Temple and five on the left, which speaks that there is a grace element to these copper chariot lavers. We are told in 1 Kings 7:33 that each base that contained a copper laver has four chariot wheels; and on the side plates of each laver base were engraved cherubim, lions and a palm tree. When we take into account that a palm tree is symbolic of righteous people planted in the House of the Lord flourishing in His courts, we can extrapolate that these chariot lavers represent God's people becoming the righteousness of God in Christ Jesus:

- *"[12] The righteous shall flourish like a palm tree, He shall grow like a cedar in Lebanon. [13] Those who are planted in the house of the LORD shall flourish in the courts of our God" (Psalms 92:12-13 NKJV).*

- *"[20] Now then, we are ambassadors for Christ, as though God were pleading through us: we implore you on Christ's behalf, be reconciled to God. [21] For He made Him who knew no sin to be sin for us, THAT WE MIGHT BECOME THE RIGHTEOUSNESS OF GOD IN HIM" (2 Corinthians 5:20-21 NKJV).*

Ten Copper Chariot Lavers were used to wash the blood from the burnt offerings. The Biblical Pattern for the Appearance of Melchizedek is: "First a precious son volunteers to become a worshipful burnt offering; then gradually a new dwelling place for

God is built."

We can also say that this is the Third Day Shift in earth's divine administration that the entire world is currently experiencing. The first precious son to volunteer to become a Burnt Offering was Isaac. We speak of Abraham offering up Isaac as a burnt offering, but we need to remember that Isaac was 36-years-old, and Abraham was 137, which means that Isaac had to volunteer to be obedient just as much as Abraham. The second precious son who volunteered to be a Burnt Offering was Yeshua on the cross. Please see the *Melchizedek Time, Appearance & First Ministry* book or *YouTube* video https://www.youtube.com/watch?v=h5i6nAIvGjM for more information.

Now in this day, the One New Man in Christ will volunteer to become a Burnt Offering too. These are those in the Body of Christ who choose to move unto perfection - mature in Christ. They are the New Living Creature of Crucified Ones who is a wing of God's Melchizedek Army who flies by the spirit with one another. As Crucified Ones, Mature Sons of the Most High God abide in the place of *Galatians 2:20* - *"I am crucified with Christ (crucified in union with Christ); it is no longer I who live, but Christ lives in me; and the life which I now live in the flesh I LIVE BY THE FAITH OF THE SON OF GOD, who loved me and gave Himself for me."*

We are to *"live by the faith OF the Son of God" (Galatians 2:20).* Hebrew 7:3 tells us that Melchizedek is made like unto the Son of God. If you want to dig Melchizedek deep, study all the references to the "Son of God" in Scripture and put yourself in those passages of Scripture. For instance, Matthew 27:40 shows us that the Son of God refused to come down from the cross. So will Melchizedek kings and priests. We will be sifted again and again and again to get all the impurities out. All flesh (our sin nature) will be destroyed at His altar. *"[14] God forbid that I should glory, save in the cross of our Lord Jesus Christ, by whom the world is crucified unto me, and I unto the world. [15] FOR IN*

CHRIST JESUS… AVAILS A NEW [LIVING] *CREATURE…* ¹⁶ *And those who walk according to this rule* [Order of Melchizedek] *peace be on them* [they will be Kings of Peace]" *(Galatians 6:14-16* KJV - Additions mine*)*.

Even though the Outer Court work of the Ten Copper Chariot Lavers is all about the restoration of your DNA as well as the restoration of the DNA Christ's Body to its pristine first creation state, this process is rendered ineffectual and incomplete without the mutual maturation of one's soul both corporately and individually. Soul maturation is literally a divine exchange of our crucifixion for our elevation, as portrayed in the Burnt Offerings of God's Temple: *"¹⁹ And I will give you the keys of the kingdom of heaven, and whatever you bind on earth will be bound in heaven, and whatever you loose on earth will be loosed in heaven. … ²¹ From that time Jesus began to show His disciples that He* [the Head and Body of Christ in this Kingdom Day] *must go up to Jerusalem, and suffer many things from the elders and chief priests and scribes, and be killed, and BE RAISED THE THIRD DAY. … ²⁴ Then Jesus said to His disciples, 'IF ANY ONE DESIRES TO COME AFTER ME, LET HIM DENY HIMSELF, AND TAKE UP HIS CROSS AND FOLLOW ME. ²⁵ For whosoever desires to save his life will lose it: but whosoever loses his life for My sake will find it. ²⁶ For what profit is it to a man if he gains the whole world, and loses his own soul? Or WHAT WILL A MAN GIVE IN EXCHANGE FOR HIS SOUL? ²⁷ For the Son of Man will come in the glory of His Father with His angels, and then He will reward every man according to his works. ²⁸ Assuredly, I say unto you, there are some standing here who shall not taste death till they see the Son of Man coming in His Kingdom" (Matthew 16:19,21,24-28* NKJV - Additions mine*)*.

Never forget that the Burnt Offering is also called the Elevation Offering, because it raises one's spiritual level. Our soul needs to be fully purified internally for the complete restoration of our DNA to take. Our Good Shepherd continually chooses what best crucifies our sin nature (flesh) by selecting the process that will best lead to our perfection - being made into Christ's very image. The Lamb of God, who is also our Good Shepherd, is in the midst of the throne pouring out our three baptisms from the Crystal-Clear Sea of living waters (Revelation 7:17).

Perfect and complete restoration in all respects is a top-down process. First Thessalonians 5:23 lists the correct order for rendering His holy tabernacle blameless at Christ's coming. This restorative work of the Lamb is a deeply personal and custom-made process. He is meticulous in the perfect representation of His Body.

The Lamb that was slain has been tasked to work with you to make perfectly whole your spirit, soul, and body. Not only making this ultimate reality available, but revealing its actuality. If you join Him by denying yourself, taking up your cross, and following Him; then the God of Peace will crush the adversary within under your feet shortly, which will cause the consummate metamorphosis of a royal priest's body, so that it's free of defect, faultless, sound, entire and whole.

Know that there are three Melchizedek Components always present in the work where we are being made *"perfect in one"* *(John 17:23)*:

[1] Daily Communion,

[2] Daily Crucifixion, and

[3] Daily Bread.

It's a beautiful thing when maturing sons of God offer themselves daily as a living sacrifice.

Another key to understand becoming a Burnt Offering is to understand that its flesh is burnt up in its entirety, as the Shepherd chooses. Scripture makes it very clear that flesh cannot inherit the Kingdom of God (1 Corinthians 15:50). Once the Burnt Offering (i.e., our sin nature) gets slaughtered, the blood gets washed by the water of the word (Ephesians 5:26) and the washing of regeneration and renewing of the Spirit (Titus 3:5). Crucifixion of one's sin nature and the washing of that area of one's life by His Spirit and His Word are key to transforming a person's soul. *"For what does a man gain if he gains the whole world, and loses HIS OWN SOUL? What shall a man give in exchange for his soul?" (Matthew 16:26).* We all need to ask ourselves: What indulgence of the flesh am I holding on to in exchange for the total transformation of my soul?

Abraham had to first dethrone four Babylonian kings before he could receive the ministry of Melchizedek. In the king's valley, Abraham was honored for his supernatural victory that united his spirit, soul and body. This is when Shem revealed the eternal principles of the High Priesthood represented in the bread of faces and the wine of the precious sacrifice. We must dethrone the same Babylonian kings that ruled the four corners of Abraham's earth. Please refer to the "Overcoming Babylonian Kings" Chapter in the *Practical Keys to Unlocking Melchizedek* book.

There is a direct correlation of the dethroning of our own personal Babylonian kings with these Ten Copper Chariot Lavers. All the copper in Solomon's Temple was broken down and carried away by the Chaldeans to Babylon, including these Ten Copper Chariot Lavers. Make a note that this was 400 years after the death of Solomon when Jerusalem fell to the Babylonians: *"And the brazen pillars that were in the house of the Jehovah, and the bases, and the Brazen Sea that was in the House of the Jehovah, the Chaldeans broke up, and carried all the brass* [copper] *thereof to Babylon" (Jeremiah 52:17* DBY – Additions mine*).*

The last that we hear of the Ten Copper Lavers is when the idolatrous King Ahaz cut off the border of the bases, and removed the bases from them (2 Kings 16:17). Jeremiah foretold that the Molten Sea (vessel which the priests washed in) and the ten copper bases should be carried away to Babylon (Jeremiah 27:19-22).

This picture simply re-iterates that we must offer ourselves as Burnt Offerings and come out of Babylon (dethrone our Babylonian kings) to receive Yeshua's supernatural enablement and personal commissioning into the fullness of the Messiah.

An interesting side note to the Ten Copper Chariot Lavers being carried away to Babylon 400 years after the death of Solomon is that each of those Copper Chariot Lavers contained 4-cubits or 40 baths each. This means that there were 400 total Burnt Offering Baths available at any one time. Four hundred years after Solomon died, Babylon dismantles the washing vehicle required for God's Chariot Thrones - His kings and priests of the Order of Melchizedek. Four hundred is also the exact number of baths that were available to wash the Burnt Offerings in Solomon's Temple. Is this a coincidence?

Four hundred years is a divinely perfect time period pointing to God's people of promise leaving the bondage of the world (i.e., Egypt) and our fallen state. There were 400 years between God fulfilling His promise to Abraham with Isaac's birth to the children of Israel leaving Egyptian bondage, which is mentioned twice in Scripture:

- "*[12] And when the sun was going down, a deep sleep fell on Abram; and lo, fear and a great darkness fell upon him. [13] And the LORD said to Abram, Know of a surety that your descendants shall be strangers in a land that is not theirs, and shall be in servitude: and they shall afflict them for FOUR HUNDRED YEARS; [14] But I will judge the nation which they shall serve; and afterward they shall come out with great wealth" (Genesis 15:12-14 Lamsa's Aramaic)*.

- *"God spoke to him and said, Your descendants will be settlers in a foreign land where they will be enslaved and mistreated for a period of FOUR HUNDRED YEARS" (Acts 7:6 Lamsa's Aramaic)*.

Now add to this link a quark quirk that each of the Copper Chariot Lavers could contain 4-cubits of water to wash God's Burnt Offerings. Scientists reveal that 4-cube is a hypercube, which is a key for operating in the Eternal Now of past, present, future all at the same time – now. To learn more about 4-cube, please refer to the *MEL GEL Study Guide: Volume 2* Chapter entitled "A Tale of Three Cubes" => https://www.amazon.com/dp/0998598232/ and its video => https://www.youtube.com/watch?v=U4PD9_F2xvI.

Now, also make a connection between the Ten Copper Chariot Lavers in Solomon's Temple being dismantled and taken captive by Babylon with the fact that there are ten additional energetic DNA strands (or five double helix strands) which were disconnected (or de-activated) eons ago and have remained dormant within human until now. Before the Fall, human beings were called "living beings" and had 12-strands of DNA actively working. Just like the Ten Copper Chariot Lavers were dismissed and treated like junk, so has been our ten shadow strands of DNA that scientists have so far labeled as "junk DNA."

Each one of His kings and priests of the Order of Melchizedek are leading their own inner fire bride forth. Please recall that there are three components that are always present in the perfection of the Order of Melchizedek, which are the same transformative agents that are accomplishing the perfect Bridal Restoration of a person's DNA:

[1] Daily Communion,

[2] Daily Crucifixion, and

[3] Daily Bread.

DAILY COMMUNION – To return to our primordial Living Being of Light state, we must go through the blood and body of Yeshua. Daily Communion is all about Christ's body and blood. Jesus

declared over the bread and wine: *"Do this in remembrance of Me"*
(1 Corinthians 11:24-25).

Our goal as Melchizedek priests is to bear the likeness of God's DNA bodily. Through communion, the marrow in our bones starts producing the correct DNA record in our blood first; then as we make the right choices, our body gets conformed into the image that has been first born in the Blood. First Corinthians Chapter 11 puts it this way:

> *"[23] For I received from the Lord that which I also delivered to you: that the Lord Jesus on the same night in which He was betrayed took bread;[24] and when He had given thanks, He broke it and said, 'Take, eat; this is MY BODY WHICH IS BROKEN FOR YOU; DO THIS IN REMEMBRANCE OF ME.'[25] In the same manner He also took the cup after supper, saying, 'THIS CUP IS THE NEW COVENANT IN MY BLOOD. THIS SO, AS OFTEN AS YOU DRINK IT, IN REMEMBRANCE OF ME.'[26] For as often as you eat this bread and drink this cup, you proclaim the Lord's death till He comes.[27] Therefore whoever eats this bread and drinks this cup of the Lord in an unworthy manner will be guilty of the body and blood of the Lord.[28] But LET A MAN EXAMINE HIMSELF, AND SO LET HIM EAT OF THE BREAD AND DRINK OF THE CUP.[29] For he who eats and drinks in an unworthy manner eats and drinks judgment to himself, not discerning the Lord's Body" (1 Corinthians 11:23-29 NKJV).*

We can only be joined to Christ if we carry His likeness and His DNA. The bread and wine of common union causes Him to descend upon us and among us. Our spirits literally absorb the life of God every time that we partake of communion, and little by little we become blended together until there is a complete replacement of our man of sin. The ultimate goal of Christ's Body (both individually and corporately) is to exchange our fallen human DNA for the DNA of God where our identity becomes Christ. The Formation of the New Living Creature is where God literally creates a new being –

mature sons – just like His Son.

DAILY CRUCIFIXION – The Burnt Offering is all about daily crucifixion. When believers think that we can get to the place where repentance is no longer necessary, we are negating the fact that the Burnt Altar is an integral part of heavenly pattern given to Moses (Hebrews 8:5). We need to do away with our linear thinking and pick up the circular thinking of the Hebrews. We do not want to live at God's Altar, but we also do not want to take away an essential piece to God's heavenly pattern. When Moses was divinely instructed to make the Tabernacle according to the pattern shown him on the mountain, he was given the pattern that shows a person how to prepare yourself, so they can ascend and descend on the Son of Man (John 1:51).

Conveniently, daily crucifixion is included in daily communion. Once our bones produce His record in our blood, we need to "rightly examine ourselves." The Ten Copper Chariot Lavers cannot wash burnt offerings until they have been properly prepared. We offer ourselves up daily as a living sacrifice to the Good Shepherd to burn up our flesh (sin nature) completely. God will only complete the work of co-crucifixion with Christ with our approval. Please realize that the things in this world that we will not die to are the very things that we are exchanging in lieu of the total transformation of our soul. *"What shall a man give in exchange for his soul?" (Matthew 16:26).* If we are unwilling to totally transform our soul, we will not restore our bodies to their original 12-strand DNA state. The transformation of our body and our soul go hand-in-hand.

DAILY BREAD (WORD) – We have already discussed that once our sin nature gets slaughtered, the blood of the Burnt Offering gets washed by the water of the word (Ephesians 5:26). We change when we immerse ourselves in the Word of God. We change into His very image, because when we behold Him, we will become like Him.

> "*[2] Beloved, now we are children of God; and it has not yet been revealed what we shall be, but we know that when He is revealed, we shall be like Him, for we shall see Him as He is. [3] And everyone who has this hope in Him purifies himself, just as He is pure.... [7] Little children, let no one deceive you: he practices righteousness is righteous, just as He is righteous*" (1 John 3:2-3,7 NKJV).

We were told during a Group Ascension that His Kingdom advances from Psalm 19. In this realm, we are told that *"the law of the Lord that is perfect, converting the soul" (Psalm 19:7)*. It also articulates: *"Their line is gone out through all the earth, and their words to the end of the world. In them hath he set a tabernacle for the sun, Which is as a bridegroom coming out of his chamber, and rejoiceth as a strong man to run a race" (Psalm 19:4-5 KJV)*. The strong man that runs a race to obtain the Melchizedek prize of the high calling of God in Christ Jesus is made up of the runners who do the work of formation. As Hebrews 12 puts it: "*[1] Therefore we also, since we are surrounded by so great a cloud of witnesses, let us lay aside every weight, and the sin which so easily ensnares us, and let us run with endurance the race that is set before us, [2] looking unto Jesus, the author and finisher of our faith, who for the joy that was set before Him endured the cross, despising the shame, and has sat down at the right hand of the throne of God*" (Hebrews 12:1-2 NKJV).

When daily communion, daily crucifixion and daily bread become a manifest reality in a royal priest's life, these three transformative agents will actually transform them into a New Living Creature with a twelve-strand DNA structure. These Living Beings will then be fully activated Light Beings, and they literally reside in the Ark of His Presence.

*****

6 – CHERUBIM ON THE WALLS

It's significant that cherubim figures decorated the walls of both the Wilderness Tabernacle and Solomon's Temple.

"Moreover you shall make the tabernacle with ten curtains of fine woven linen, and blue, purple, and scarlet thread; WITH ARTISTIC DESIGNS OF CHERUBIM you shall weave them" (Exodus 26:1 NKJV).

The ten curtains of the Tabernacle were said to symbolize the ten sayings with which God created the world. This corresponds to the curtains of the Tabernacle (its walls) symbolizing the unification of all elements on earth in common service to God, which is a foreshadowing of the restoration of all things.

The yarn in the Tabernacle was woven in such a way that different forms of the cherubim would appear on both sides of the material. The artistic image of the cherubim that was woven into the Tabernacle contained only three of the four images of the cherubim: the lion, the eagle and the ox. The image of the man is embodied by the tri-parte Tabernacle structure.

Please recall that the four living creatures in Ezekiel 1 is also called the cherubim in Ezekiel 10:2, Ezekiel 10:15. Ezekiel Chapter 1 is a vision of God's Mobile Throne of Glory where the All-Consuming Fire is enthroned in those people who are ONE with the Father (ox), the Son (lion), and the Holy Spirit (eagle). They are His Chariot Throne that perfectly lines up with the King of Kings through His manna. They are a wheel within His wheel who live and move and have their being in Him – *"wherever the Spirit goes, they go: for the spirit of the living creature was* [is] *in the wheels (Ezekiel 1:20 KJV – Addition mine).*

Exodus 26:6 speaks of joining two curtains, so they become ONE. These curtains were two sets of five, which symbolize grace. *"The five curtains shall be coupled together one to another; and the other five curtains shall be coupled one to another" (Exodus 26:3).* Grace is always necessary and appreciated in the work of oneness. The two sets of five curtains also make ten. Recall in our "Cherubim on the Ten Copper Chariot Lavers" Chapter, we discovered that the number ten is symbolic of a crown – the crown of Melchizedek specifically – who is called to be both the King of Righteousness and King of Peace. Make a mental note that the curtains that make up the borders and boundaries of the heavenly pattern of His Tabernacle are connected to the copper chariot lavers (i.e., God's chariot throne).

The two curtains were connected at the precise point where the Holy of Holies was separated from the Holy Place. For a man, it points to the place where the work of oneness is supposed to take place at the junction of where one's spirit is linked with one's soul. Both sections of the Tabernacle's walls – the ones over the Holy of Holies (man's spirit) and the one over the Holy Place (man's soul) – had cherubim woven into them. We can extrapolate from this that both a man's soul and spirit have been designed by God to be part of His Chariot Throne, which means that we can ascend with our spirit, with our soul, or with both to the place of the Father. When we add to this the cherubim depicted in the Outer Court on the Ten Copper

Chariot Lavers, we get a picture of all parts of man being able to ascend: body, soul and spirit. His Melchizedek Company brings heaven to earth. The more fully one can engage in the heavenlies and the more fully one can walk it out here on earth (being complete emotionally, morally, character, growth, et cetera), the more we will see His royal priesthood actualize the kingdoms of this earth becoming the kingdoms of our God.

The Hebrew word for "curtain" *(yer-ee-aw)* describes it as a tremulous curtain. It's a hanging of the Fear of the Lord. The primitive root for *yer-ee-aw* is *yaw-rah'*. It literally means to be broken up with any violent action. Does this definition of "broken" from the *10th Edition of Webster's Collegiate Dictionary* resonate with you?

broken ~*adj* : to break : violently separate into parts : SHATTER : made weak or infirm : subdued completely : CRUSHED : BANKRUPT : reduced in rank : cut off : DISCONNECTED : imperfectly spoken or written : not complete or full : disunited by divorce, separation, or desertion of one parent : damaged or altered by breaking : as 1: having undergone or been subjected to fracture 2: *of land surfaces* – being irregular, interrupted, or full of obstacles 3: violated by transgression 4: DISCONTINOUS : INTERRUPTED 5: disrupted by change

The Ancient Hebrew Word Pictograph for *yaw-rah'* brokenness reveals that it is the highest and most important work to be done is understood, seen and experienced though the curtain. We are literally experiencing the LORD's discipline, as His sons, in which the depths of our souls are being broken up. When brokenness occurs, resistance, independence and pride are replaced with submission, tenderness, obedience, and love. To come to the place where He is esteemed above self, we must actively submit and be the Father's partner in our own perfection.

The Spirit of the Fear of the Lord enabled Yeshua to walk in strict obedience to His Father. THESE ARE THE WALLS OF HIS DWELLING PLACE – you and I. The Ancient Hebrew Word Picture or Pictograph of *yer-ee-aw* tells us that the highest and most important work to be done is the work revealed by our Heavenly Father (His perfect will).

The only way into God's Sanctuary is to go through His Door of Truth with the borders and the boundaries of the Fear of the Lord. Of the Seven Spirits of God's Government, the Spirit of the Fear of the Lord must be engaged first, because it brings everything into alignment or order. It's simple to engage the Fear of God. Press in with "I desire something…" or "I value something" or "I focus on something" or "I honor something." The Fear of the Lord is His treasure and those who fear the Lord; He will show His secret government (Isaiah 33:6).

We cannot over emphasize that the fear of the Lord is the wall that encloses you as His Dwelling Place. In general, a wall is a structure that connects the foundation to the roof. My dictionary focuses on a wall being a high thick masonry structure that forms a long rampart or an enclosure chiefly for defense. The rampart dimension of a wall is spoken of in *Habakkuk 2:1* NKJV - *I will stand my watch and set myself on the rampart, and watch to see what He will say to me, and what I will answer when I am corrected."*

Being His watchman requires hearing a word from God's mouth and warning people (Ezekiel 3:17; Ezekiel 33:7). The reverential fear of God is integral to being His watchmen. We are told that if a watchman sees the sword upon the land and does not blow the trumpet, the people are not warned, the sword comes, and the watchman is held responsible for the bloodshed (Ezekiel 33:6). A watchman stands in a tower to see what he can see, just like the corporate One New Man stands in His strong tower and looks to engage the perfect will of the Father for His Kingdom to come.

The Order of Melchizedek flies on the wings of the Tabernacle of David. The one who sat on the Throne of David and spearheaded the Tabernacle of David wrote: *"¹ Blessed be the LORD my Rock, ... ² My lovingkindness and my fortress, My high tower and my deliverer, My shield and the One in whom I take refuge..." (Psalms 144:1-2 NKJV)*.

If we are standing in YHVH our high tower, we are positioned in the unlimited realm of the all-seeing, all-knowing, and all-present One. When we return to our primordial state (first creation, first estate), the only borders and boundaries that we will have is the awesome reverential fear of the Lord. Talk about powerful and multidimensional!

*****

7 – CHERUBIM ON THE VEIL

Not only were cherubim emblazing the walls of Moses' Wilderness Tabernacle and Solomon's Temple, but the veil in both structures also had cherubim embroidered on it (Exodus 26:1; 1 Kings 6:29-35; 2 Chronicles 3:7).

The veil was the divider between two domains. In Hebrew, it was called the "Paroches," or simply the Partition. The veil hung from a bar attached to the tops of the pillars: *"³¹And thou shalt make a veil of blue, and purple, and scarlet* [wool], *and fine twisted linen of cunning work* [with a woven design]: *WITH CHERUBIM SHALL IT BE MADE. ³² And thou shalt hang it upon four pillars of shittim* [acacia] *wood overlaid* [plated] *with gold: their hooks shall be gold, upon the four sockets of silver. ³³ And thou shalt hang the veil under the taches* [hooks], *that thou mayest bring in thither* [inside the Partition] *within the veil the Ark of the Testimony: and the veil shall divide unto you between the holy place and the most holy"* (*Exodus 26:31-33* KJV – Additions mine).

We are told that the Partition was ten cubits from the rear wall, so that the Holy of Holies measured 10x10 cubits while the Holy Place was 10x20 cubits. Before Jesus death on the cross, only one priest (not in a state of spiritual contamination) could enter the Holy of Holies once a year on Yom Kippur – the Day of Atonement.

The figure of the cherubim woven into the veil speaks about no one being able to approach the Ark of His Presence without the blood of the Lamb. It is Yeshua's atoning blood that makes a way for us to have relationship with the Most High God:

> " ^{22} *And almost all things are by the law purged with blood; and without shedding of blood is no remission.* ^{23} *It was therefore necessary that the patterns of things in the heavens should be purified with these; but the heavenly things themselves with better sacrifices than these.* ^{24} *For Christ is not entered into the holy places made with hands, which are the figures of the true; but into heaven itself, now to appear in the presence of God for us*" (Hebrews 9:22-24 KJV).

Not only does the Head of Christ's Body appear in the presence of God for us, but we need to grasp that each member of Christ's Body has the same access. Before the veil was torn top down when Yeshua died on the cross, man was barred from approaching God's Throne, His mercy seat. Now we are exhorted: "*^{14} Seeing then that we have a great high priest that is passed into the heavens, Jesus the Son of God, let us hold fast our profession.* ^{15} *For we have not a high priest which cannot be touched with the feeling of our infirmities; but was in all points tempted like as we are, yet without sin.* ^{16} *Let us therefore come boldly unto the throne of grace, that we may obtain mercy, and find grace to help in time of need*" (Hebrews 4:14-16 KJV).

When we are progressively clothed with the Fear of the Lord, it's like the veil between our soul and spirit is being torn one thread at a time, as led of the LORD. It's a top down – heaven to earth – work, as we are crucified with Christ (Galatians 2:20). The fear of the Lord will cause all of us to not purposely disobey Him. In the place of ever-present awe, we love what He love and hate what He hates.

Just like when the *Kohen Gadol* (i.e., High Priest) could only enter the Holy of Holies once a year with blood, it is the Blood of the Lamb that makes a way into the inner sanctum of man as well as a way for us to sit in heavenly places. The sons of Israel knew the veil by the name "LIFE." Just as the cherubim guard the way to the Tree of Life (Genesis 3:24), so do the cherubim on the veil in the Tabernacle shut out the reality of eternal life here on earth. The veil being torn top-to-bottom in the Temple in Jerusalem by Yeshua's crucifixion is a pattern for what His mature Body of Believers must do in this Kingdom Day to rend the veil between their soul and their spirits. What rightly divides the inner sanctum of man is the Word of God: *"For the word of God is quick, and powerful, and sharper than any two-edged sword, piercing even to the dividing asunder of soul and spirit, and of the joints and marrow, and is a discerner of the thoughts and intents of the heart"* (Hebrews 4:12 KJV).

Daily we must deny ourselves. Take up our own cross and follow Him. This is our daily bread where we learn that man does not live on bread alone but by every word that comes out of the mouth of the LORD (Deuteronomy 8:3). These are the ones who are disciplined as sons (Deuteronomy 8:5).

These disciplined sons are also the ones who are called the "Cherubim" or the New "Living Creature" in the matrix of Ezekiel's Chariot Throne. Not only is the *Merkabah* a transportation device of His ruling presence, but it is a heavenly pattern of a heavenly man. When I say the term "heavenly man," there is both a corporate and individual reality to this statement. Christ's Body is a multi-member organism (1 Corinthians 12:20), and so are you.

Just as the earthen-bound pictures of God's Dwelling Places have three parts, so does the *Merkabah*. Ezekiel's Chariot Throne can be divided up into three major sections:

[1] The Living Creature made up of four (or more) living creatures,

[2] The Expanse or the Firmament, and

[3] The Sapphire Throne.

Just as the three portions of God's Dwelling Place symbolize the three parts of man (body, soul, spirit), so can the three mechanisms of the Chariot Throne; but due to the *Merkabah* being all about the formation of a body for the heavenly man, we can look at its three parts connected to the perfection of a person's soul as well as the perfection of the soul/body of the Corporate One New Man in the Messiah.

The maturing of our souls will cause us to be transfigured, just like Yeshua did in Matthew 17. Christ's Mature Body will follow His Mature Head is every single way. When Yeshua was transfigured before Peter, James and John on a high mountain apart, Scriptures says he was *"metamorphoo."* Paul also talks about being *metamorphoo* by the renewing of our minds (Romans 12:2). Here Scripture directly links the maturing of our souls to transfiguration.

In No Man's Land, the Kingdom of Self disappears, and the Kingdom of God appears. It is here that we will lift up our eyes and see *"no man, save Jesus only" (Matthew 17:8)*. A huge key to the All-Consuming Fire who sits on the Sapphire Throne is *"[10] that I may know Him, and the power of His resurrection, and the fellowship of His suffering, being conformed unto His death; [11] if by any means I might attain unto the resurrection of the dead" (Philippians 3:10-11 KJV)*. Eternal life, which is resurrection life, is available to those who truly know the Father: *"And this is eternal life, that they may know You, the only true God, and Jesus Christ whom You have sent" (John 17:3 NKJV)*. First John 5:11 also tells us that the record states that God the Father has given us eternal life, and this life is in His Son.

The deeper we dive into knowing God, the more that our souls will reflect His image. When our soul resonates with His, a gate opens for the energetic living waters of our soul to vibrationally transfigure our bodies. The same type of energetic excitement happens at the level of our spirit and soul too. Perfect and complete restoration in all respects is a top-down process. First Thessalonians 5:23 lists the correct order for rendering His holy tabernacle blameless at Christ's coming. This restorative work of the Lamb is a deeply personal and custom-made process. He is meticulous in the perfect representation of His Body. The Lamb that was slain has been tasked to work with you to make your perfectly whole spirit, soul, and body. Not only making this ultimate reality available, but revealing its actuality.

"Let there be a firmament in the midst of the waters" (Genesis 1:6) to divide between the Holy and the Holy of Holies (Exodus 26:33). This is a mystery of mysteries Christian mysticism, which has its roots in Jewish mysticism. Please do not get uptight with the words "mystic" and "mysticism. The word "mystic" comes from the Latin *mysticus*, which means "of mysteries." A mystery is a religious truth that one can know only by revelation and it cannot fully understand. A mystic relates to the mysterious, has a feeling of awe or wonder, and is a follower of the mystical way of life. A mystical way of life is having a spiritual meaning of reality. It involves having direct communion with God or ultimate reality. Mysticism is the belief that direct knowledge of God, spiritual truth, or ultimate reality can be attained through experience. According to Dr. Elizabeth Alvilda Petroff, mysticism has been called "the science of the love of God," and "the life which aims at union with God." Its emphasis is on the spiritual life as a progressive climb — sometimes a steep and arduous one. The Order of Melchizedek restores all things that can be redeemed. Having direct communion with God and His ultimate reality through experience is not only redeemable, it's divine and sublime. Next time you hear the word "mystic" and "mysticism," please think of knowing the love of God, and displaying this unlimited, exquisite

mystery for all to see.

"Let there be a firmament in the midst of the waters" (Genesis 1:6) to divide between the Holy and the Holy of Holies (Exodus 26:33). The middle element of the *Merkabah* is the firmament: *" ²² And the likeness of the FIRMAMENT upon the heads of the Living Creature was as the color of the terrible crystal, stretched forth over their heads above. ²³ And under the FIRMAMENT were their wings straight, the one toward the other: every one had two, which covered on this side, and every one had two, which covered in that side, their bodies" (Ezekiel 1:22-23 KJV)*. Christian mysticism points to the firmament separating the Holy of Holies from the Holy Place. In other words, the firmament in Ezekiel's Chariot Throne can be equated to the veil in the earthen-bound depictions of God's Dwelling Place.

When the veil between our soul and spirit gets torn top down (as we choose to crucify our sin nature in order to fully know Him), the essence of our soul and spirit combines with Him and we ascend – *metamorphoo*. We are transfigured through yieldedness.

Let me leave you with one more mystery to ponder about the firmament (expanse or veil) in regard to the formation of a new living creature in the form of a fetus. A human being originates from a drop of semen, which is pictured as light. When this light penetrates the egg, it turns into water in the mother's womb; then it expands into a fetus. The engraving or formation of a new living creature of a heavenly man begins with light, then water, and then spreads within an expanse into the original created image of Adam.

The firmament (i.e., expanse) is in the midst of the waters. Masaru Emoto shares in his book *The Hidden Messages in Water* that: "We start out life being 99-percent water, as fetuses. When we are born, we are 90-percent water, and by the time we reach adulthood we are down to 70-percent. ... From a physical perspective, humans are water." Just as water serves to transport energy throughout our body, so does the New Living Creatures transport energy throughout

Christ's Body. The royal priests of the Order of Melchizedek will be known as the ultimate power source on earth, as it is in heaven. Behold, an unlimited source of energy that's pure white and pure light.

Think about how this light-water-expanse phenomenon would work for all members of Hs Body. The seed of light is the radiance of His glory: *"The Son is the radiance of God's glory and the exact representation of His being, sustaining all things by His powerful word. After He had provided purification for sins, He sat down at the right hand of the Majesty in heaven"* (Hebrews 1:3 NIV).

The radiance of His glory – the Light – spreads and become water, which is the expansion of the Body in all directions. Once the form of the exact representation of His Being is fashioned, the expansion congeals; and this is *"an expanse in the midst of the waters"* (Genesis 1:6). After the expansion has congealed, it is written: *"God called the expanse heaven"* (Genesis 1:8).

Leharkiv is one of the conjugated forms of the Hebrew term for chariot *"Merkabah." Leharkiv* means "to combine." Our outward world will not be transformed until our inward world is transfigured and combined into the matrix of the One – the One New Man in the Messiah. *"I in them, and thou in Me, that they may be made perfect in one; and that the world may know that Thou hast sent Me, and hast loved them, as Thou hast loved Me"* (John 17:23 KJV).

The work of the veil emblazed with cherubim is crucial in this process. There are two swords that pierce the matrix of Ezekiel's Chariot Throne. One sword pierces vertically top down – the spirit – while the other pierces horizontally through the firmament itself – the soul. The work of the veil is the work of the cross with the Word of God hanging there. Let His two-edged living and active sword divide asunder your soul and spirit (Hebrews 4:12), so you can be made perfect in one.

*****

8 – CHERUBIM ON THE ARK OF THE COVENANT IN THE TABERNACLE

We cannot over emphasize that two cherubim covered the Ark of the Covenant in the Tabernacle. Just like the cherubim with the flaming sword that guards the way to the tree of life, so are do these cherubim mark a gateway for mankind's return to its primordial state. We are talking about a reality that is above and beyond the veil of this fallen world to consciously return to Eden on a higher level of existence.

The very name "Ark" is derived from the Hebrew word for "light." When we see the "light" of the Presence of God and bask in its glory, we pierce through the veil (the outer layers) to enter deep within. Technically, it's not a piercing, but a transformation. Both His Presence and His Testimony is the Light of the World. What is true of the Head is true for the extended many-member Body of Christ. To the extent that we enter within is the extent of our divine impact when reach out and touch the world around us.

Exodus 25:10 tells us that more than one person made the Ark: *"They shall make an Ark of acacia wood; two and a half cubits its length, a cubit and a half its width, and a cubit and a half its height." "They shall make an Ark..."* is a direction given by God to Moses for all the children of Is-real (the entire nation).

This is the only place where we find plurality in reference to in making an object for God's Tabernacle. When the Hebrew Living Letter *bet* is a prefix for a word, it means "in" and suggests God's intention of abiding within the realm of His creation. *"I in them, and You in Me; that they may be made perfect in one, and that the world may know that You have sent Me, and have loved them as You have loved Me" (John 17:23 NKJV)*. Notice *"that they may be perfect in one"* is also plural. It's a corporate work to make ourselves a container for the light of His Dwelling Presence (*shekinah*). *"For you are the temple of the living God. As God has said: 'I will dwell in them and walk among them. I will be their Go, and they shall be My people'" (2 Corinthians 6:16 NKJV)*.

The One New Man in Christ, the Order of Melchizedek, and the Bride of Christ are all corporate entities: *"⁹ 'Come, I will show you the bride, the Lamb's wife.' ¹ Now I saw a new heaven and a new earth... ² Then I ... saw the holy city, New Jerusalem, coming down out of heaven from God, prepared as a bride adorned for her husband. ³ And I heard a loud voice from heaven saying, "BEHOLD, THE TABERNACLE OF GOD IS WITH MEN, AND HE WILL DWELL WITH THEM, AND THEY SHALL BE HIS PEOPLE. God Himself will be with them and be their God" (Revelation 21:9a, 1-3 NKJV)*.

Exodus 25:11 goes on to say: *"And you shall overlay it with pure gold, inside and out."* In actuality, three separate boxes were made. The primary box was the middle one made out of acacia wood. It doesn't take much to understand that this middle box is symbolic of Yeshua and His death on a wooden cross. When we move beyond crucifixion to the burial and resurrection of His Body (us), we understand the essential transformative steps that are necessary for us to live in a higher dimensional reality of Eden: *"¹⁰ That I may know him, and the power of his resurrection, and the fellowship of his sufferings, being made conformable unto his death;* *¹¹ If by any means I might attain unto the resurrection of the dead" (Philippians 3:10-11 KJV).*

We are in a unique *karios* time when we will literally see our world within and without transforming into heaven. When Yeshua prayed: *"Thy kingdom come. Thy will be done in earth, as it is in heaven" (Matthew 6:10 KJV),* He really meant it! Know that at the intersection of His will and ours, His Kingdom comes. When our souls truly connect to God and draw light down from above into the world, His will is done, and His Kingdom comes.

The second box that was made of gold was larger than the acacia wood box. Personally, I believe that this largest golden box that makes up the Ark is symbolic of the Father and His larger than life presence in all of creation.

A third gold box was made, which was made small enough to be placed inside the acacia wood box. Because Scripture tells us that Yeshua sends the Holy Spirit from the Father and He testifies of Yeshua (John 15:26), I believe that the Holy Spirit is represented in this third gold box. This second and third box can be interchangeable because of the plurality in the One. Thus, the main wooden box was covered with gold inside and out.

The second half of *Exodus 25:11* says: *"and you shall make on it* [the Ark] *a gold crown all around."* First and foremost, this represents the Head of the Body of Christ – the King of Kings who is the Word of God with His flaming eyes of fire:

> *"¹¹ Now I saw heaven opened, and behold, a white horse. And He who sat on him was called Faithful and True, and in righteousness He judges and makes war. ¹² His eyes were like a flame of fire, and on His head were many crowns. He had a name written that no one knew except Himself. ¹³ He was clothed with a robe dipped in blood, and His name is called The Word of God. ¹⁴ And the armies in heaven, clothed in fine linen, white and clean, followed Him on white horses. ¹⁵ Now out of His mouth goes a*

sharp sword, that with it He should strike the nations. And He Himself will rule them with a rod of iron. He Himself treads the winepress of the fierceness and wrath of Almighty God. ¹⁶ And He has on His robe and on His thigh a name written: KING OF KINGS AND LORD OF LORDS" (Revelation 19:11-16 _{NKJV}).

The gold crown all around the top of the Ark not only symbolizes the King of Kings, but also His Queen. His Queen is made up of bridal hearts who are perfected kings and priests of the Order of Melchizedek that have led their own fire bride forth into her fullness. A person's heart is the very first organ formed in the womb. The heart of man is the very throne of God when the Blood of Jesus is applied to it, which causes our hearts to function as the Ark of His Presence.

We seek God within, because *"the Kingdom of God is within you" (Luke 17:21)*. When we give Him greater and greater space in our heart, we go from one reality to another. Where the Ark of God's Presence is, there is a gateway to Eden where He will speak to us like He did in the Garden. God will speak to us above the mercy seat, like He did with Moses. When our heart beats in rhythm with His heart, it becomes the Ark of His Covenant. This is where a portal is created, which allows us to ascend into the light of heaven in the Land of the Living, and bring it back to transform our world. God's people are called to elevate the world within and without beyond its present physical state into a higher energetic state. The whole wide world is currently transitioning to a higher level of existence. Do not underestimate the power of entrainment where our heart becomes one with God's heart, which causes our hearts to beat as one. The key of the Ark is the heart – His heart and ours.

One with the Ark is the two golden cherubs stretching forth the wings of their heart, which are one with the Father's Heart. These cherubim cover the mercy seat with their wings, as they form a 2x2 ARC of agreement, as they face one another:

"*¹⁷ You shall make a mercy seat of pure gold; two and a half cubits shall be its length and a cubit and a half its width. ¹⁸ And you shall make TWO CHERUBIM OF GOLD; of hammered work you shall make them at the two ends of the mercy seat. ¹⁹ Make one cherub at one end, and the other cherub at the other end; you shall make the cherubim at the two ends of it of one piece with the mercy seat. ²⁰ And the cherubim shall stretch out their wings above, covering the mercy seat with their wings, and they shall face one another; the faces of the cherubim shall be toward the mercy seat. ²¹ You shall put the mercy seat on top of the ark, and in the ark you shall put the Testimony that I will give you. ²² And there I will meet with you, and I will speak with you from above the mercy seat, from between the two cherubim which are on the ark of the Testimony, about everything which I will give you in commandment to the children of Israel" (Exodus 25:17-22 NKJV).*

Hebrew history tells us that these two cherubim on each end of the Ark's Cover had large wings with the faces of young children. God's people are commissioned into the Order of Melchizedek and form a New Living Creature when they enter the Kingdom of God. One of the key components to entering the Kingdom of God is receiving it with childlike faith: *"Assuredly, I say to you, whoever does not receive the kingdom of God as a little child will by no means enter it" (Luke 18:17 NKJV).*

Exodus 25:18-19 speaks of hammering out the entire cover: *"You shall make two cherubim of gold – hammered out shall you make them – from both ends of the cover. You shall make one cherub from the end at one side and one cherub from the end at the other; from the cover shall you make the cherub at its two ends."* What this means is that the entire cover of the Ark, including the cherubim on the top, had to be hammered out of one large gold ingot. The heavenly pattern of God's Tabernacle on earth insisted upon the cherubim not being made separately. This speaks of the oneness of these covering cherubim with God's Throne.

A promise to overcomers accompanies the picture of the covering cherubim. The promise in Revelation 2:28 is a promise given to the Corporate Order o Melchizedek becoming one of His covering cherubim: *"And I will give him the morning star" (Revelation 2:28 KJV)*. Please allow me to explain. I asked God about the Ark of the Covenant and if an earthly Melchizedek Company is one of the Ark's covering cherubs. Yeshua came to me and said: "I AM the other side of the Ark." He did a quantum leap beyond my question. He showed me three different dimensions to the covering cherubs on the Ark of His Presence:

[1] The stationary golden images on top of the Ark of the Covenant made according to the pattern in heaven. Know that there are two ARKs. There is one in heaven and one on earth. The one in heaven is golden and alive. Everything is alive in heaven!

[2] Before the fall of one-third of the angels, on one side of the Ark was Lucifer and on the other side of the Ark was the covering cherub called Melchizedek who is still heavenly and angelic.

[3] The Mature Body of Yeshua comprised on one side with His Mature Body on earth and on the other side is His Mature Body in heaven. *"There is one body, and one Spirit" (Ephesians 4:4)*. The Order of Melchizedek on earth is on one side and the Order of Melchizedek in heaven is on the other side. Basically, it's everyone who have entered the Kingdom of God by being born/baptized by water and the Spirit. Please notice that the great cloud of witnesses come into play here.

We need to take the position of the cherub and form an Ark for His Presence AND that's when there's a manifestation of His Name YHVH (lion, ox, eagle and man). Behold, the four faces of God, and in the midst of His Presence is a New Living Creature of the Order of Melchizedek who lives and moves and have their being in Christ (Acts 17:28).

9 – CHERUBIM ON THE ARK OF THE COVENANT IN SOLOMON'S TEMPLE

The cherubim on the Ark of the Covenant in Solomon's Temple are the same as those in the Tabernacle, except for two additional 10-cubit (approximately 5 meters) high cherubim. These additional cherubim stood in the midst of God's inner house and their wings stretched from one wall to the other wall:

"[21] So Solomon overlaid the inside of the house with pure gold. And he drew chains of gold across the front of the inner sanctuary, and he overlaid it with gold. [22] He overlaid the whole house with gold, until all the house was finished. Also the whole altar which was by the inner sanctuary [the oracle] he overlaid with gold. [23] Also in the inner sanctuary [the oracle] he made two cherubim of olive wood, each ten cubits high. [24] Five cubits was the one wing of the cherub and five cubits the other wing of the cherub; from the end of one wing to the end of the other wing were ten cubits. [25] The other cherub was ten cubits; both the cherubim were of the same measure and the same form. [26] The height of the one cherub was ten cubits, and so was the other cherub. [27] He placed the cherubim in the midst of the inner house, and the wings of the cherubim were spread out, so that THE WING OF THE ONE WAS TOUCHING THE ONE WALL AND THE

WING OF THE OTHER CHERUB WAS TOUCHING THE OTHER WALL. So their wings were touching each other in the center of the house. ^{28} *He also overlaid the cherubim with gold" (1 Kings 6:21-28 NASB).*

If you delve into the depths of the word "wings" in Scripture, you see that wings open things up by speaking life. Wings are the beginning of kingdom life and action. From the most common and first occurrence of "wings" in Scripture, we get the picture of a precise wing (or wings) of God's Melchizedek Army flying by the Spirit with a one another.

Never forget that King David, who was made after the Order of Melchizedek, was the one who came up with the plans for Solomon's Temple. His son Solomon merely carried out his father's plans: " *^{19}All this, said David, the LORD made me understand in writing by His hand upon me, even all the works of this pattern. ^{20} And David said to Solomon his son, Be strong and of good courage, and do it: fear not, nor be dismayed, for the LORD God, even my God, will be with thee, he will not fail thee, nor forsake thee, until thou has finished all the work for the service of the house of the LORD" (1 Chronicles 28:19-20 KJV).*

Notice how many Cherubim or Living Creatures are in the Holy of Holies in Solomon's Temple. Four. Sound familiar? Ezekiel Chapter 1 tells us to behold – to become and hold onto – four living creatures: "*^{4}And I looked, and, behold, a whirlwind came out of the north, a great cloud, and a fire infolding itself, and a brightness was about it, and out of the midst thereof as the color of amber, out of the midst of the fire. ^{5} Also out of the midst thereof came the likeness of four living creatures. And this was their appearance; they had the likeness of a man" (Ezekiel 1:4-5 KJV).* This likeness of a man is the new creation of the Corporate One New Man in Christ made after the Order of Melchizedek.

The Holy of Holies in Solomon's Temple was also called "The Oracle." Isaiah 66:15 speaks of the same Cherubim Classification of the Order of Melchizedek mentioned in 1 Chronicles 28:18. The

Cherubim Classification of a Melchizedek Company acts like the covering cherubs and spread their wings to point to kingdom life and action: *"For behold, THE LORD WILL COME WITH FIRE AND WITH HIS CHARIOTS, LIKE A WHIRLWIND, to render His anger with fury, and His rebuke with flames of fire" (Isaiah 66:15).*

King Davis not only gave Solomon the plans to build Solomon's Temple out of the Tabernacle of David, he also reveals to us that the Lord of Host inhabits and rides upon the cherubim:

- *"He bowed the heavens also, and came down; and darkness was under His feet. And HE RODE UPON A CHERUB, and did fly: and He was seen upon the wings of the wind" (2 Samuel 22:10-11 KJV).*

- *"He bowed the heavens also, and came down: and darkness was under His feet. And HE RODE UPON A CHERUB, and did fly: yea, He did fly upon the wings of the wind" (Psalms 18:9-10 KJV).*

- *"So the people sent to Shiloh, that they might bring from there THE ARK OF THE COVENANT OF THE LORD OF HOSTS, WHO DWELLS BETWEEN THE CHERUBIM" (1 Samuel 4:4 NKJV).*

By the way, the word "between" in 1 Samuel 4:4 was added by the translators; therefore, technically the verse should read "the Yehovah of Host lives in the cherubim." *"As God has said, 'I will dwell in them and walk among them. I will be their God, and they shall be My people." (Leviticus 26:12; Jeremiah 32:38; Ezekiel 37:27; 2 Corinthians 6:16).*

Melchizedek David gave refined gold by weight for the Chariot of the Cherubim. *"And for the Altar of Incense refined gold by weight; and GOLD FOR THE PATTERN OF THE CHARIOT OF THE CHERUBIM, that spread out their wings, and covered the Ark of the*

Covenant of the LORD" (1 Chronicles 28:18).

These two additional huge cherubim were made from olive wood, which was then covered in gold. Where else is olive wood mentioned in Scripture? Two of the most prominent places that olive wood is mentioned are in Romans 11:11-18 and Zechariah 4:1-14.

> *"[11] I say then, have they stumbled that they should fall? Certainly not! But through their fall, to provoke them to jealousy, salvation has come to the Gentiles. [12] Now if their fall is riches for the world, and their failure riches for the Gentiles, how much more their fullness! [13] For I speak to you Gentiles; inasmuch as I am an apostle to the Gentiles, I magnify my ministry, [14] if by any means I may provoke to jealousy those who are my flesh and save some of them. [15] For if their being cast away is the reconciling of the world, what will their acceptance be but life from the dead? [16] For if the firstfruit is holy, the lump is also holy; and if the root is holy, so are the branches. [17] And if some of the branches were broken off, and YOU, BEING A WILD OLIVE TREE, WERE GRAFTED IN AMONG THEM, AND WITH THEM A PARTAKER OF THE ROOT AND FATNESS OF THE OLIVE TREE, [18] do not boast against the branches. But if you do boast, remember that you do not support the root, but the root supports you" (Romans 11:11-18 $_{NKJV}$).*

Romans Chapter 11 speaks of two olive trees: one natural and another one wild (i.e., Jew and Gentile). We really need to pay attention to this, because Romans 11:15 asks us: For if the casting away or rejection of the Jews is the reconciliation of the world, what will their acceptance be but life from the dead (i.e., resurrection life). This is a beautiful picture of the One New Man of Jew and Gentile in Christ (Ephesians 2:15). This theme is repeated in Zechariah Chapter 4:

> *"[1] Now the angel who talked with me came back and wakened me, as a man who is wakened out of his sleep. 2 And he said to me, "What do you see?" So I said, "I am looking, and there is a lampstand of solid gold with a bowl on top of it, and on the stand seven lamps with seven pipes to the seven*

lamps.³ "TWO OLIVE TREES are by it, one at the right of the bowl and the other at its left."⁴ So I answered and spoke to the angel who talked with me, saying, "What are these, my lord?"⁵ Then the angel who talked with me answered and said to me, "Do you not know what these are?" And I said, "No, my lord."⁶ So he answered and said to me: 'This is the word of the LORD to Zerubbabel: "Not by might nor by power, but by My Spirit," says the LORD of Hosts.⁷ Who are you, O great mountain? Before Zerubbabel you shall become a plain! And he shall bring forth the capstone with shouts of "Grace, grace to it!"'⁸ "Moreover the word of the LORD came to me, saying:⁹ "The hands of Zerubbabel have laid the foundation of this temple; his hands shall also finish it. Then you will know that the LORD of hosts has sent Me to you.¹⁰ For who has despised the day of small things? For these seven rejoice to see the plumb line in the hand of Zerubbabel. They are the eyes of the LORD, Which scan to and fro throughout the whole earth."¹¹ Then I answered and said to him, 'WHAT ARE THESE TWO OLIVE TREES — AT THE RIGHT OF THE LAMPSTAND AND AT ITS LEFT?'¹² And I further answered and said to him, 'WHAT ARE THESE TWO OLIVE BRANCHES THAT DRIP INTO THE RECEPTACLES OF THE TWO GOLDEN PIPES FROM WHICH THE GOLDEN OIL DRAINS?¹³ Then He answered me and said, 'Do you not know what these are?' And I said, 'No, my lord.'¹⁴ So He said, 'THESE ARE THE TWO ANOINTED ONES, WHO STAND BESIDE THE LORD OF THE WHOLE EARTH'" (Zechariah 4:1-14 NKJV).

The Lord of Host that says, "*Not by might nor by power, but by My Spirit*," is the same Lord of Hosts that dwells in the cherubim. Zechariah 4 speaks of two olive trees as well where their branches feed the olive oil into the Golden Light in the Temple (Menorah). Could these two anointed ones who stand before the Lord of the whole earth be those overcoming kings and priests of the Order of Melchizedek in heaven and on earth?

I believe that the two additional 10-cubit Cherubim in Solomon's Temple represent a future race of immortal humans where the mortality of both Jew and Gentile in the Messiah has put on immortality (1 Corinthians 15:53).

Olive wood from an olive tree is also featured with cherubim in one more place in Solomon's Temple. Not only was there a veil separating the Holy of Holies from the Holy Place, but there was also folding doors made out of olive wood:

> "*³¹ And FOR THE ENTERING OF THE ORACLE HE MADE DOORS OF OLIVE TREE: the lintel and side posts were a fifth part of the wall. ³² THE TWO DOORS ALSO WERE MADE OF OLIVE TREE; AND HE CARVE UPON THEM CARVINGS OF CHERUBIMS, and palm trees and open flowers, and overlaid them with gold, and spread gold upon the cherubims, and upon the palm trees. ³³ So also made he for the door of the temple posts of olive tree, a fourth part of the wall. ³⁴ And the two doors were of fir tree: the two leaves of the one door were folding, and the two leaves of the other door were folding. ³⁵ And he carved thereon cherubims and palm trees and open flowers: and covered them with gold fitted upon the carved work*" (1 Kings 6:31-35 $_{KJV}$).

Figures of cherubim, palm trees and open flowers were carved on these olive wood doors then overlaid with gold. There was an additional double door to the Oracle (i.e., Solomon's Temple's Holy of Holies) besides entering through the veil. The cherubim, palm trees, and open flowers covered in gold speak of golden righteousness coming into full bloom for both Jew and Gentile for those who are made like unto the Son of God after the Order of Melchizedek.

"*But you are AN ELECT RACE, A ROYAL PRIESTHOOD, A HOLY NATION, a people for possession, so that you may speak openly of the virtues of the One who has called you out of darkness into His marvelous light (1 Peter 2:9 $_{LXX}$)*. The Hebrew word for "race" here is *geza*, which means a stem, trunk or stock of a tree.

Additionally, if we look at the word "chromosome," it paints a picture of a gathering of people to form a body – the Body of Christ – which is connected to the Tree of Life. Remember how the cherubim with the flaming swords that guards the way to the Tree of Life? Remember how the Tabernacle is a picture of the three parts of man: body, soul and spirit?

The Chromosome is the Body which holds the DNA of every individual part that makes up the whole. The Mature Body of the Messiah works the same way. Each individual part combines to make one building – one house – one tabernacle (Exodus 36:13). Did you know that chromosomes are also shaped in a cross pattern?

The second part of the word "chromosome" comes from the Greek word "*soma*," which means BODY in all its various applications (body of man, animal, planets, society, church, et cetera). A *SOMA* BODY traces back to multiple Hebrew words. *Exodus 24:10* – *"They saw the God of Israel and there was under His feet as it were a paved work of a sapphire stone, and as it were the BODY OF HEAVEN IN HIS CLEARNESS."* The word BODY in "the body of heaven" is translated from the Hebrew word *etsem*, the word for BONE, which comes from the word *ets* meaning a tree.

In Judges 8:30, the Hebrew word *yarekh* is translated BODY and carries the meaning of the main trunk of the Menorah in the Temple. Both these terms for BODY are pictures of the Tree of Life.

In this Kingdom Day, we are the sublime human messengers (cherubim who are of the Order of Melchizedek). We are those who see heaven open, and ascend and descend on the Son of Man (John 1:51). Like Jacob, we will light upon a certain place, take some stones of that place and rest in oneness. For behold, a DNA Ladder of Heaven is set up on earth with the top reaching to heaven. This particular gate of heaven is where the Spirit of the Fear of the Lord resides. This is none other than the House of God. Surely, O Lord, Your Order of Melchizedek gives the tenth to you!

Out of the midst of the fire comes the likeness of four living creatures with the appearance of one man (Ezekiel 1:4-5). Out of the refiner's fire comes a purified man – a Corporate One New Man in Christ made like unto the Son of God after the Order of Melchizedek.

*****

UNDERSTANDING THE ORDER OF MELCHIZEDEK

Book 6

Window into the Wheels Within Wheels

Cover Art: "Window on the Wheels" by Robin Main

© July 31, 2014. All Rights Reserved

Text Copyright © 2015 Robin Main. All Rights Reserved

1 – INTRODUCTION

The Wheels Within Wheels are sometimes called the "Whirling Wheels." They are also called the *Ophanim* in Hebrew, which literally means wheels, cycles, or ways. There is one wheel within a wheel beside each of the four living creatures, who together, makeup the Living Creature in the matrix of Ezekiel's Chariot Throne.

> "[15] *Now as I beheld the living creatures, behold one wheel upon the earth by the living creatures, with his four faces* [16] *The appearance of the wheels and their work was like unto the color of a beryl: and they four had one likeness: and their appearance and their work was as it were a wheel in the middle of a wheel*" (*Ezekiel 1:15-16* KJV).

Therefore, there are four wheels to the Living Creature with each one of them having a wheel within. These four wheels within wheels are part of the elemental structure of Ezekiel's Chariot Throne, which causes us to call the Sapphire Throne contraption a Chariot Throne - *Merkabah*.

Probably, the most important point about the *Ophanim* is that the spirit of the singular Living Creature is in the wheels. This point is mentioned twice in Scripture: "[20] *Wherever the spirit was to go, they went;*

there was the spirit to go: and the wheels were lifted up beside them; for THE SPIRIT OF THE LIVING CREATURE WAS IN THE WHEELS. ^{21} When those went, these went; and when those stood, these stood; and when those were lifted up from the eretz (land), the wheels were lifted up beside them: for THE SPIRIT OF THE LIVING CREATURE WAS IN THE WHEELS" (Ezekiel 1:20-21 HNV). Always pay attention when something is mentioned twice in Scripture. It's like God is highlighting something that's very important.

Understand that the movement of the *Ophanim* is controlled by the spirit of the "living creatures," which is a unified body of individuals who are directed by the All-Consuming Fire who sits on the throne.

*****

2 – TO BE OR NOT TO BE

If the spirit of the Living Creature is in the wheels, what are the wheels like?

Each of the four living creatures has one wheel within a wheel beside each one of them. According to Ezekiel 1:16, the appearance of the wheels and their work is like the color of beryl. What's interesting about this statement is that pure beryl is colorless. If it is tainted with impurities, it can be many different colors: green, blue, yellow, red, and white. Beryl is a mineral. Its two most desirable variations are probably aquamarine and emerald.

Beryl is the principle store of beryllium in the earth's crust, and that's saying something, because beryllium is the most abundant metal in the earth's crust and it always occurs in combination with other metals. This speaks of the whirling wheels' (wheels within the wheels) corporate essence, which is the Spirit of the New Living Creature of the One New Man in Christ made after the Order of Melchizedek from the get go. Please note that the Living Creature, Cherubim, and the Order of Melchizedek are interchange concepts, and they are corporate beings. Please refer to the *Formation of New*

Living Creature book.

Beryllium is the fourth element on the Periodic Table of Elements. The number "four" symbolizes God's creative works. Four is the number of CREATION, and of man in his relation to the created world. Think about the four corners of the earth. Think about the four elements of earth, wind, water, and fire. Think about the four directions of north, south, east and west. Four is also the number for material completeness; therefore, it is a world number, especially a city number. The CHERUBIM (LIVING CREATURE made up of four living creatures) are always connected to creation (Ezekiel 1:19; Ezekiel 10:15).

The abbreviation for Beryllium is "BE." What's so significant about this is that the root meaning behind the Hebrew word for "righteousness" is TO BE. Righteousness is not about an activity. It's about a righteous State of Being. James Chapter 2 tells us that it was Abraham's completed faith that God credited him as righteous. James 2 is the famous chapter that tells us that faith without works is dead. Even though righteousness is not about an activity, our doing what is right and virtuous in God's eyes according to the perfect will of the Father is how one is "credited" or "accounted" as righteous:

> "*²² You can see how his faith helped his works, and how by works his faith was made perfect. ²³ And the scripture was fulfilled which said, Abraham believed God, and it was accounted to him for righteousness; and he was called the Friend of God*" (James 2:22-23 _{Lamsa's Aramaic}).

Faith is always first; and then, true believers will always manifest (or do) what they say or believe. The proof is in the pudding. So… "TO BE OR NOT TO BE" really is the right question, according to what is a Righteous State of Being in God's eyes.

Both Psalm 89:14 and Psalm 97:2 tell us that righteousness and justice are the foundation of His throne:

- *"Thy throne is built on righteousness and judgment; mercy and truth go before thy face" (Psalm 89:14 _{Lamsa's Aramaic}).*

- *"Clouds and darkness are round about Him; righteousness and judgment are the foundation of His throne" (Psalm 97:2 _{Lamsa's Aramaic}).*

Each of these wheels within a wheel are part of the foundation of the matrix of Ezekiel's Chariot Throne – the Living Creature – which is just one snapshot of how the Order of Melchizedek operates in this kingdom day.

*****

3 – GYROSCOPIC WHEEL WITHIN WHEELS

Ezekiel 1:16 tells us that the four wheels within the wheels have the appearance of beryl. The mineral beryl contains the fourth element on the Periodic Table – beryllium.

Beryllium has been called the Miracle Metal, because of its remarkable physical and performance qualities that make products better, and sometimes even possible in our modern world. Three primary forms of beryllium produced in our day are pure beryllium metal, alloys (metals with small amounts of beryllium), and beryllia ceramics.

Today, we will only be focusing on one alloy; but over the next several chapters we will be exploring the various uses of beryllium (beryl), so that we can understand what makes up the substance of the wheels within wheels in the matrix of Ezekiel's Chariot Throne. Remember that wherever the living creatures go, the wheels go, because the spirit of the living creature is in the wheels (Ezekiel 1:19-21). Therefore, when we look at the uses of beryllium (beryl), we can do some backward engineering to discover the movement of these wheels; and thus, the movement of the Living Creature, which is the

Corporate One New Man in Christ who is a wing of God's End-Time Melchizedek Army flying by the Spirit with one another.

When beryllium is combined (alloyed) with copper it forms a wear resistant material known as beryllium bronze. Significantly, beryllium bronze is used in gyroscopes and other devices where wear resistance is important. A gyroscope is a self-balancing spinning top, which seems to closely resemble the movements of the Living Creature:

> *"And they went every one straight forward: whither the spirit was to go, they went; and they turned not when they went" (Ezekiel 1:12 KJV).*
>
> *"¹⁹ And when the living creatures went, the wheels went by them: and when the living creatures were lifted up from the earth, the wheels were lifted up. ²⁰ Whithersoever the spirit was to go, they went, thither was their spirit to go; and the wheels were lifted up over against them: for the spirit of the living creature was in the wheels" (Ezekiel 1:19-20 KJV).*

Once you spin a gyroscope, its axle wants to keep pointing in the same direction. Keep this in mind when you think of the likeness of four living creatures with the appearance of a man that comes out of the midst of a whirlwind (spin) coming out of the north:

> *"⁴ And I looked, and, behold, a whirlwind came out of the north, a great cloud, and a fire infolding itself, and a brightness was about it, and out of the midst thereof as the color of amber, out of the midst of the fire. ⁵ Also out of the midst thereof came the likeness of four living creatures. And this was their appearance; they had the likeness of a man" (Ezekiel 1:4-5 KJV).*

In Scripture, "north" can represent the direction of one's heart. We either face His Throne in Zion in the Far North (which is True North) – OR – we face our own throne, which is the seat of idolatry spoken of in Ezekiel 8:3:

> *"³ He stretched out the form of a hand, and took me by a lock of my hair; and the Spirit lifted me up between earth and heaven, and brought me in*

> *visions of God to Jerusalem, to the door of the north gate of the inner court, where the seat of the image of jealousy was, which provokes to jealousy. ⁴ And behold, the glory of the God of Israel was there, like the vision that I saw in the plain. ⁵ Then He said to me, 'Son of man, lift your eyes toward the north.' So I lifted my eyes toward the north, and there, north of the altar gate, was the image of jealousy in the entrance. ⁶ Furthermore He said to me, 'Son of man, do you see what they are doing, the great abominations that the House of Israel commits here, to make Me go far away from My sanctuary? Now turn again, you will see greater abominations" (Ezekiel 8:3-6 NKJV).*

Just remember, royal priests, that the LORD has His way in the whirlwind:

> *"The LORD is slow to anger and great in power, and will not at all acquit the wicked. The LORD HAS HIS WAY IN THE WHIRLWIND and in the storm, and the clouds are the dust of His feet" (Nahum 1:3 NKJV).*

Crucified Ones of the Order of Melchizedek will have to gird themselves up like mature men to answer the One who speaks out of the whirlwind:

- *" ¹ Then the LORD answered Job out of the whirlwind, and said: ² Who is this who darkens counsel by words without knowledge? ³ Now prepare yourself like a man; I will question you, and you shall answer Me" (Job 38:1-3 NKJV)*

- *" ⁶ Then the LORD answered Job out of the whirlwind, and said: ⁷ Now prepare yourself like a man; I will question you, and you shall answer Me" (Job 40:6-7 NKJV).*

Just like the Russian Mir space station used eleven gyroscopes to keep its orientation to the sun, so do the four corners of the foundation of Ezekiel's Chariot Throne contain four of these gyroscopic-type wheel within a wheel that causes it to travel according to the seven flows of the Spirit of the One who sits on the

Sapphire Throne.

*****

4 – LIVING CREATURE TRANSPORTATION – BERYLLIUM #1

Not only do the four living creatures have straight feet with brass soles of a calf's foot, but beside each one of them is a wheel within a wheel. These two elements make up the foundation of the foundation of the matrix of Ezekiel's Chariot Throne. Please recall that the Living Creature component of Ezekiel's Chariot Throne is composed of the four living creatures.

Always remember that God's Word says that the spirit of the Living Creature is in the wheels (Ezekiel 1:20-21), and these wheels have the appearance of beryl (Ezekiel 1:16). Come. Let's continue to explore the movement of the Living Creature, which is the

Corporate One New Man in Christ who is a wing of God's End-Time Melchizedek Army flying by the Spirit with one another. We are using some backward engineering when we look at beryl (beryllium) for clues as to how Reigning Ones move in this Kingdom Day.

Beryllium is used in a wide-range of applications:

[1] Transportation,

[2] Communication,

[3] Medicine,

[4] Space Exploration,

[5] Safety,

[6] Oil, Gas and Alternate Energy as well as

[7] Defense and Security.

Because of beryllium's unmatched combination of qualities, this Miracle Metal makes our modern world possible in many ways. We will look at each one of beryllium's applications to tie them back to how the Order of Melchizedek lives and moves and has their being in Almighty God. Today, we are merely going to hover over the first point - TRANSPORTATION.

Beryllium illustrates the fundamental concept of the wheels within the wheels helping us get from here to there. Beryllium alloys are used in airplane and automobile components to ensure that vital equipment remains reliable as well as enhancing fuel efficiency.

Just as each one of the living creatures has to remain vitally connected to the One on the Sapphire Throne and to one another in a Melchizedek Company, so are the lightweight beryllium alloy connectors that are used in the electrical systems in cars and trucks. Copper beryllium components are found in traction controls, transmissions, electric motors, anti-lock brakes, and fuel injection systems. As you can see, the Living Creature's movement (especially starting and stopping) is portrayed here.

As if to put an exclamation point on the movement component of the Living Creature, we see electrical components being made out of copper beryllium are also used to assist a vehicle's steering systems. The energetic flow for which direction the Living Creature is to go is always steered by the All-Consuming Fire on the Sapphire Throne and those seated with Him there. The older and heavier hydraulic and electromechanical steering systems are now being replaced with the lighter, sturdier beryllium alloy.

When it comes to aircraft, copper beryllium has replaced bronze for landing gears due to its higher strength. Both the landing gear's bushings and bearings are now being made from copper beryllium in order to handle the great compression and wear forces caused by flight. It has great endurance when it comes to corrosive atmospheres, including exposure to a wide range of temperatures. Due to the landing gear's bearings being able to be made smaller and lighter, commercial aircraft also becomes more fuel efficient as well as reducing exhaust emissions.

This speaks of the various wings of God's End-Time Melchizedek Army who fly by the Spirit with one another can, and will, handle the corrosive forces of our day. The bit-by-bit decay of modern society will not only be resisted by those of the Order of Melchizedek, but overcome. These are the ones in whom the LORD's glory will be seen in a time when darkness covers the earth and deep darkness the people (Isaiah 60:1-3). These are the ones that will arise to rule and reign in Him; and wherever the Spirit of the Living God goes, they will go in a pure kingdom flow. External temperatures in this world will not affect their living and moving and having their being in Him (Acts 17:28).

It is time for the royal priestly overcomers to sit down in the Father's throne with Him (Revelation 3:21). In order to do this, we must first acknowledge that it is through the Blood of the Lamb that we receive this privilege (Ephesians 2:6). But don't stop there!

We are told in Scripture that overcomers will also get rid of all mixture in their lives as well as aligning themselves with the Word of Righteousness:

"[13] For everyone who partakes only of milk is unskilled in the Word of Righteousness, for he is a babe. [14] But solid food belongs to those who are of Full Age, that is those who by reason of use have their sense exercised to discern both good and evil" (Hebrews 5:13-14 NKJV).

Behold, the faithful and true witness says:

"[14] To the angel of the church in Laodicea write: These are the words of the Amen, THE FAITHFUL AND TRUE WITNESS, the ruler of God's creation. [15] I know your deeds, that you are neither cold nor hot. I wish you were either one or the other! [16] So, because you are lukewarm — neither hot nor cold — I am about to spit you out of my mouth. [17] You say, 'I am rich; I have acquired wealth and do not need a thing.' But you do not realize that you are wretched, pitiful, poor, blind and naked. [18] I counsel you to buy from Me gold refined in the fire, so you can become rich; and white clothes to wear, so you can cover your shameful nakedness; and salve to put on your eyes, so you can see. [19] Those whom I love I rebuke and discipline. So be earnest and repent. [20] Here I am! I stand at the door and knock. If anyone hears My voice and opens the door, I will come in and eat with that person, and they with Me. [21] To the one who is victorious, I will give the right to sit with Me on My throne, just as I was victorious and sat down with My Father on His throne. [22] Whoever has ears, let them hear what the Spirit says to the churches" (Revelation 3:14-22 NIV).

*****

5 – LIVING CREATURE COMMUNICATION – BERYLLIUM #2

Communication is key to any type of corporate movement. If the Living Creature is anything, it is corporate. Scripture shows us that four (or more) living creatures (i.e., royal priests of the Order of Melchizedek) make up a Corporate New Living Creature, which is a pattern that can be multiplied over and over and over again as many times as the Captain of this Host desires.

In this Beryllium Wheels Series, we are researching the various ways that beryllium (beryl) is used to give us clues as to how the Living Creature's wheel within wheels operate in this Kingdom Day. Please recall beryllium's short list of applications:

[1]   Transportation,

[2]   Communication,

[3]   Medicine,

[4]   Space Exploration,

[5]   Safety,

[6] Oil, Gas and Alternate Energy as well as

[7] Defense and Security.

Let's zero in on point number two – COMMUNICATION.

Beryllium is helping people keep in touch worldwide, because it is used in the manufacture of telecommunications infrastructure equipment, computers and cellular phones. Please highlight in your mind that Beryllium connects continents, because copper beryllium housings protect the electronics that allow fiber optic cables to function flawlessly on ocean floors. Its corrosive resistant properties are out-of-this-world. After decades of service, the barrel-like housings show little deterioration from the highly corrosive sea water and its extreme pressures.

Think of the CONNECTEDNESS OF THE LIVING CREATURE when it comes to beryllium. "Connect" in this sense means that we are open to each other. In the sea, on the ground, and through the air, our modern society stays connected thanks to beryllium and materials that contain beryllium (alloys). The following is a list of how beryllium enables multi-function devices like cell phones, lap tops, and pads:

- Battery contacts and electronic connectors in cell phones and other portable electronics are made with copper beryllium alloys. This material meets the stringent requirements for durability, weight savings, electrical conductivity and corrosion resistance in extreme weather and temperatures.

- "Spring memory" provided by copper beryllium ensures continuous and fatigue-free electrical connections, which allows constant use in spite of continual openings and closings, vibrations and accidental drops. Its endurance is even beyond the Energizer Bunny.

- The low electrical resistance and high thermal conductivity of beryllium-containing material supports convergence and miniaturization of multiple functions – phones, cameras, MP3 players – into a single lightweight compact unit. (Make a CONVERGENCE and MULTI-DIMENSIONAL mental note here, royal priests.)

Not only does His New Living Creature of the Order of Melchizedek transmit His information, thoughts and feeling; but they reveal Almighty God successfully in any language and on any platform. They are His Messenger who delivers His messages that are clearly seen, heard and understood.

Thanks to beryllium, advanced digital technology is possible and useful. We are seeing an exponential (almost logarithmic) growth in high-performance processors that pack more and denser layers of high-frequency circuits into smaller and smaller packages. This means higher processing speeds and better performance for personal computers, routers, the internet, et cetera. As a former computer programmer/analyst that worked with the mission planning software for the B-2 Stealth Bomber back when it was a "black" project (i.e., Top Secret), I can tell you that we have come a long way baby. One of the impressive things about the B-2 Bomber is that its cockpit was supposedly shielded from a nuclear blast. My guess is that beryllium alloys were used in this capacity.

The exceptional thermal conductivity and insulating properties of beryllia ceramic protect high-performance processor systems from the potentially crippling effects of intense heat generation. With thermal conductivity being greater than ten times that of alumina ceramic, beryllia ceramics remain the insulators of choice for such high-frequency circuits.

Therefore, the high frequency circuit of the New Living Creature reveals a communication capacity, which is a convergence of worldwide high-speed spirit connections that are multi-functional and multi-dimensional. We say: "spirit connections," because the Spirit of the Living Creature is in the beryllium/beryl wheels (Ezekiel 1:20-21).

Communications for the highest manifestation of the Order of Melchizedek are also eternal due to His Royal Generals operating in the perfect will of the Father. Talk about being perpetually corrosive resistant!

Please remember that the high frequency communication circuits of the matrix of Ezekiel's Chariot Throne are first vertical with each of the living creatures connecting to the All-Consuming Fire who sits on the Sapphire Throne; and then, it's a horizontal connection with one another. The transmission goal for the New Living Creature, which is the Corporate One New Man in Christ who is a wing of God's End-Time Melchizedek Army flying by the Spirit with one another, is to wholly move and live and have their being in the One who sits of the throne. This means that these Reigning Ones effectively and clearly communicate His information making His will and kingdom known.

Finally, my *Webster's Collegiate Dictionary (10th Edition)* tells me that one of the definitions of the word "communicate" means to receive communion. Recall that Scripture tells us that the technology contained within the bread and the wine was first offered by Melchizedek to Abram (Genesis 14:18).

As we intimately connect with Him more and more through common union (communion), He enables us to have a more holy connection with one another. This is a key that makes it possible for the living creatures of the Order of Melchizedek to wholly be open to each other.

Currently, we may not be able to fully trust one another, but we can fully trust Him in our connection with one another, and whatever dross that arises will make us come forth as gold (Job 23:10). Know that in this wholly-connected kingdom-spot, royal priests have surrendered to Him in such a way that they are the same essence as the All-Consuming Fire, which means our hearts, minds and works will have been thoroughly tested by fire:

- *"⁹ For we work together with God; you are God's work and God's building. ¹⁰ According to the grace of God which is given to me, as a wise masterbuilder, I have laid the foundation and another builds upon it. But let every man be careful hoe he builds thereon. ¹¹ For another foundation can no man lay than that which is already laid, which is Jesus Christ, ¹² Now if any man build on this foundation gold, silver, precious stones, wood, hay, stubble; ¹³ Every man's work shall be plainly seen; for the light of day shall expose it, because it shall be revealed by fire; and the fire shall test every man's work and show of what sort it is. ¹⁴ And the builder whose work survives shall receive his reward. ¹⁵ And the one whose work shall be burned, he shall suffer lose; but he himself shall be rescued, even as one who has been saved from the fire" (1 Corinthians 3:9-15* Lamsa's Aramaic*)*

- *"²² But you have come near to Mount Zion and to the city of the Living God, the heavenly Jerusalem, and to the innumerable multitude of angels. ²³ And to the congregation of the first converts who are enrolled in heaven and to God the Judge of all and to the spirits of pious* [righteous] *men made perfect ²⁴ And to Jesus, the mediator of new covenant, and to the sprinkling of His Blood, which speaks a better message than Abel did. ²⁵ Beware, therefore, lest you refuse Him who speaks to you. For if they were not delivered who refused Him who spoke to them on earth, much more can we not escape if we refuse Him who speaks to us from heaven. ²⁶ He is the one whose voice shook the earth; but now He has promised, saying, Once more I will shake not only the earth, but also heaven. ²⁷ And these words Once more, signify the change of things which may be shaken, because they are made in order that the things which can not be shaken may remain. ²⁸ Therefore, receiving a kingdom which cannot be shaken, let us hold fast that grace whereby we may serve and please God with reverence and godly fear; ²⁹ For our God is a consuming fire" (Hebrews 12:22-29 Lamsa's Aramaic).*

Becoming the same essence as the All-Consuming Fire also means that if our hearts, minds and works do not measure up to His plumb line of righteousness, we remain humble and teachable in order to become just like Jesus. Always remember that God's end-time Melchizedek Army flies on the wings of the Tabernacle of David; therefore, the words that David wrote have a very special significance to us in this Kingdom Day. They show us how we can operate like a man after God's own heart:

- *"[23] Search me, O God, and know my heart; try me, and know my anxieties; [24] and see if there is any wicked way in me, and lead me in the way everlasting" (Psalms 139:23-24 NKJV).*

- *"[10] Create in me a clean heart, O God, a renew a steadfast spirit within me. [11] Do not cast me away from Your presence and do not take Your Holy Spirit from me. [12] Restore to me the joy of Your salvation, and uphold me by Your generous Spirit. [13] Then I will teach transgressors Your ways, and sinners shall be converted to You" (Psalms 51:10-13 NKJV).*

- *"[3] Who may ascend into the hill of the LORD? Or who may stand in His holy place? [4] He who has a clean hands and a pure heart, who has not lifted up his soul to an idol, nor sworn deceitfully. [5] He shall receive blessings from the LORD and righteousness from the God of his salvation. [6] This is Jacob, the generation of those who seek Him, who seek Your face. SELAH" (Psalms 24:3-6 NKJV).*

*****

6 – LIVING CREATURE MEDICINE – BERYLLIUM #3

The New Living Creature appearing in our day is a Corporate One New Man in Christ, which is composed of Crucified Ones made after the Order of Melchizedek. They, with Christ in them the hope of glory, are truly the medicine this world needs. His Mature Sons are the substance He is using in this Kingdom Day to treat and overcome the disease of sin and death. As the world gets darker and darker, the living creatures of the Royal Order of Melchizedek shine brighter and brighter. Just like Yeshua, they have the Spirit of the Lord upon them to bind up the broken-hearted, proclaim liberty to the captives, and set captives free (See Isaiah 61).

Today, we travel to Part 3 of the Beryllium Wheels Series – MEDICINE. If your recall, beryllium's short list of applications is:

[1]   Transportation,

[2]   Communication,

[3]   Medicine,

[4] Space Exploration,

[5] Safety,

[6] Oil, Gas and Alternate Energy as well as

[7] Defense and Security.

These modern-day applications are showing us how these wheels within wheels of the Living Creature operate within the Matrix of Ezekiel's Chariot Throne.

Just as the special properties of beryllium are essential to medical technology that save and enhance life, so are the priests of the Most High God made after the power of an endless life according to the Order of Melchizedek:

"^{15} And it is yet far more evident if, in the likeness of Melchizedek, there arises another priest ^{16} who has come, not according to the law of a fleshly commandment, but ACCORDING TO THE POWER OF AN ENDLESS LIFE. ^{17} For He testifies: 'You are a PRIEST FOREVER ACCORDING TO THE ORDER OF MELCHIZEDEK'" (Hebrews 7:15-17 $_{NKJV}$).

Let's review the various medical technologies dependent on beryllium. Advances in imaging equipment, diagnostics and laser medicine are made possible by the strength and stability of this versatile metal.

IMAGING EQUIPMENT – Because Beryllium is strong, highly transparent to x-rays, and can handle elevated levels of heat, beryllium has long been critical for medical x-ray equipment. Thin beryllium metal foil provides the window through which tissue-penetrating x-rays are focused while also maintaining a vacuum inside the x-ray tube generator.

His Melchizedek Companies are made up of highly transparent people who have penetrating eyes to see things of the flesh and beyond. Our Heavenly Father places the triple concentric circles that reside on the breastplate of His Melchizedek Army on His eye as a contact lens, so His End-Time Melchizedek Army can see through His eyes into Him and see through His eyes out into any circumstance.

DIAGNOSTICS - Beryllium foil remains indispensable for high resolution medical radiography. Beryllium in newer CT scanners and x-ray equipment enables a lower radiation dose with significantly finer resolution to diagnose problems.

His Melchizedek Army has the ability to function as an early detection device as they see through the Bloodshot Bull's Eye of the Father as well as treating any malady through the Blood Bought Cross of the Lamb.

In fact, beryllium is used in the equipment that analyzes blood. It offers precision and reliability to both doctors and patients when it comes to diagnosing diseases.

As imaging technology advances, beryllium continues to meet the needs for x-ray tube windows.

Those who advance in the fullness of Melchizedek are literally His firstfruits tithe who are becoming just like their forerunner Yeshua – the Pattern Son. Malachi 3:10 tells us that if we bring all the tithe into His storehouse so there can be meat in His house, the Lord of Hosts Himself will open up the windows of heaven and pour out such an abundant blessing that it will overflow from His people to those around them. Please note that His Melchizedek Company grows beyond the Word of Faith and the Word of Truth to dwell in the place of the Word of Righteousness (Hebrews 5:13-14):

- *"⁸ But what does it say? The word is near you, in your mouth and in your heart" (that is, the WORD OF FAITH which we preach): ⁹ that if you confess with your mouth the Lord Jesus and believe in your heart that God has raised Him from the dead, you will be saved"* (Romans 10:8-9 NKJV).

- *"Of His own will He brought us forth by the WORD OF TRUTH, that we might be a kind of firstfruits of His creatures"* (James 1:18 NKJV).

- *"¹³ For everyone who partakes only of milk is unskilled in the WORD OF RIGHTEOUSNESS, for he is a babe. ¹⁴ But solid food belongs to those who are of full age* (i.e., mature), *that is, those who by reason of use have their senses exercised to discern both good and evil"* (Hebrews 5:13-14 NKJV).

LASER MEDICINE – Medical lasers are made with beryllia ceramics, which help ophthalmologists to restore or improve eyesight for millions, so does the Order of Melchizedek. Reigning Ones will operate just like the Pattern Son, and even do greater works:

- *"Jesus answered and said to them, 'Go and tell John the things you have seen and heard: that THE BLIND SEE, the lame walk, the lepers are cleansed, the deaf hear, the dead are raised, the poor have the gospel preached to them'"* (Luke 7:22 NKJV).

- *"Most assuredly, I say to you, he who believes in Me, the works that I do he will do also; and GREATER WORKS than these he will do, because I go to My Father"* (John 14:12 NKJV).

Beryllia ceramic is the only material that can contain and operate these tiny, high-powered gas laser bores. Not only is sight restored, but delicate surgeries are made possible. Copper beryllium transmits such precise electrical signals that the fine-tuned surgical instruments enable many non-invasive surgical techniques.

Instead of needing a long recovery time, the hurting and wounded people that are ministered to with the jubilee love of the Order of Melchizedek (flowing from His throne) have little to no down time; thus, reducing trauma, risk of infection and exponentially speeding healing and wholeness within an individual.

Divine sight and touch that brings healing and wholeness are key components to the Living Creature's wheels within wheels. Think on these things when you are connected as part of God's End-Time Melchizedek Army flying by the Spirit with one another, because the spirit of the Living Creature is in the wheels (Ezekiel 1:20) and these jubilee wheels are like beryl (beryllium).

*****

7 – LIVING CREATURE SPACE EXPLORATION – BERYLLIUM #4

For years when I'd close my eyes to check in with the LORD, I'd go flying with Him in outer space. It was so much fun! I love flying! I used to enjoy getting rebounds when I played basketball, because for a moment it felt like I could fly. Little did I know that leaving an earthly orbit is a function of the Order of Melchizedek.

The spirit of the Living Creature, which is made up of living creatures who are priests forever after the Order of Melchizedek, is in the wheels, and these wheels and their works have the appearance of beryl (beryllium). Please refer to Ezekiel 1:16-21.

Although many of the uses for beryllium (beryl) appear to be quite modern, the mineral beryl, which contains beryllium, has been used at least since the Ptolemaic dynasty of Egypt. (305 BC to 30 BC). It's interesting to note that the Ancient Egyptians were known for their chariots, and one of the foundations of Ezekiel's Chariot Throne is beryl (beryllium) chariot wheels.

Let's examine beryllium's fourth application in our day, which propels His Chariot Throne – SPACE EXPLORATION. Beryllium has had a legendary role in the pursuit of knowledge. From the heat shields that protected NASA's Mercury astronauts to the orbital telescopes of tomorrow, beryllium has been in the front seat of the exploration of outer space.

In NASA's earliest days, beryllium heat shields protected the Mercury spacecrafts during re-entry. To this day scientists, designers and engineers still continue to depend on this stiff, lightweight and versatile material to meet the most demanding challenges.

So do the wings of God's End-Time Melchizedek Army meet the most demanding challenges of our day. I personally believe that we are in a season spoken of in Matthew 24: *"For then shall be great tribulation, such as was not since the beginning of the world to this time, no, nor ever shall be." (Matthew 24:21 KJV)*. In these days of great tribulation, royal priests of the Order of Melchizedek will withstand the heat of our day in the shelter of His wing, and they will rise and shine reflecting and transmitting His incredible glory.

NASA VEHICLES - Recently, beryllium has added strength, dissipated heat and lightened weight on window frames and door systems in various NASA vehicles including the Space Shuttle.

The two Mars Rover vehicles – Spirit and Opportunity – have far exceeded anyone expectations.

How prophetic for Melchizedek kings and priests who bring heaven to earth! They will far exceed anyone's expectations, as they pursue God-given opportunities and fly by His Spirit for His Kingdom come! They are, and will continue to be, a tremendous cosmic success!

Aluminum beryllium components have helped protect the rovers' landings; and then, they unfolded to serve as the off-ramps, so the Mars Rovers get where they need to go. Aluminum beryllium parts were also used in the Rovers' rock exploration tools, which have given us an understanding of the red planet.

TELESCOPES - Beyond space vehicles is beryllium's influence on a vast world of intricate telescopes.

NASA's Spitzer Space Telescope has beryllium components. It drifts in a unique earth-trailing orbit around the sun. It sees an optically invisible universe dominated by dust and stars. Spitzer is the most sensitive infrared space observatory ever launched, which gives us a glimpse of the otherwise hidden infrared universe. Our universe continually radiates a wealth of information being sent in a wide-spectrum of light. Since not all of these messages reach the ground, the Spitzer Telescope enables the study of otherwise hidden things, like the study of: stars, planet forming disks, extrasolar planets (planets outside our Solar System), other galaxies, and the universe's origins.

This speaks of the heavenly-based Order of Melchizedek having insight into the hidden mysteries of God that are otherwise hidden, including other worlds, heavens, angels, stars, et cetera. His New Living Creature, who are sons of God that make up a wing of His Melchizedek Army, manifests in His sight where nothing is hidden:

"Therefore do not judge before the time, until the Lord comes and brings to light the hidden things of darkness and reveals the thoughts of the hearts; then shall every man have praise from God" (1 Corinthians 4:5 Lamsa's Aramaic).

The *Dead Sea Scrolls* relates the "Songs of the Sabbath Sacrifices" to Melchizedek – the chief cherubim priest. In the twelfth song of the cherubim, it is said to be almost indistinguishable from the wheels of God's throne-chariot where they worship God silently. The

Dead Sea Scrolls also records that even though one cannot hear this praise, it is evident in brass-like flashes of light emerging from His throne. Don't forget that those who are being made into His exact image are made like unto the Son of God who is the Great High Priest of the Order of Melchizedek who passed into the heavens:

- *"We have, therefore, a great high priest who has ascended into heaven, Jesus Christ, the Son of God; let us remain firm in his faith" (Hebrews 4:14 Lamsa's Aramaic).*

- *"Without father, without mother, without descent, having neither beginning of days, nor end of life; but MADE LIKE UNTO THE SON OF GOD; abideth a priest continually" (Hebrews 7:3 KJV).*

When the Hubble Space Telescope could not see clearly, new "corrective lens" were mounted in beryllium fixtures that met the lower weight, high stiffness and resistance requirements brought on by extreme temperatures.

The successor to the Hubble Space Telescope and the Spitzer Space Telescope is the next generation James Webb Space Telescope (sometimes called JWST). It is an orbiting infrared observatory that will compliment and extend the discoveries of the Hubble Space Telescope, with longer wavelength coverage and greatly improved sensitivity. The longer wavelengths enable the Webb telescope to look much closer to the beginning of time and to hunt for the unobserved formation of the first galaxies, as well as to look inside dust clouds where stars and planetary systems are forming today.

The priests and kings of the Order of Melchizedek are the congregation of the sons of righteousness. When four or more of them come together focused solely on Him and His ways, they act as the MESSENGER of *Malachi 3:1* – *"Behold, I will send My MESSENGER, and he shall prepare the way before Me: and the Lord, whom you seek, shall suddenly come to His temple, even the MESSENGER OF*

THE COVENANT, whom you delight in: behold, He shall come, says the LORD of hosts." According to the *Dead Sea Scrolls*, this heavenly figure (Melchizedek Messenger) will instruct the people about all the periods of history for eternity and in the statutes of the truth. Sounds like the Corporate One New Man in Christ functioning as a Melchizedek Messenger will be instrumental in revealing the beginning of time, similar to the JWST.

This next generation telescope has a 6.5-meter beryllium mirror, which will allow them to see objects that were 200 times fainter than visible before. This smooth, precise and defect-free beryllium mirror must retain its visual quality for decades in deep space.

The FULLNESS of the Order of Melchizedek is also defect-free, because at this level His kings and priests are beginning to manifest the perfect character of Christ.

Let me leave you glorious heavenly "space cadets" with some telescopic food-for-thought.

Recall that if you study the word PERFECT in Scripture, you will discover the Greek words *teleioo, teleios*, and *telos*. We must follow the Pattern Son (Yeshua), if we want to be made perfect after the Order of Melchizedek: *"[8] Though He was a Son, yet learned He obedience by the things which He suffered; [9] And being made perfect, He became the author of eternal salvation unto all them that obey Him [10] called of God a high priest after the Order of Melchizedek" (Hebrews 5:8-10 KJV)*. It's not about perfectionism, but our "being made complete" by becoming a Full Age or Mature Man. These Greek words for PERFECT tell us what "being made complete" really is. "Being made complete" means we are to be complete in labor, complete in growth, complete mentally and complete in moral character.

When we set out for "being made complete" into Christ's very image, we come to the Perfect Place of the Heavenly Jerusalem. Hebrews 12 says this is the spot where there are the spirits of just men made perfect (Hebrews 12:23). This Perfect Place is also where many sons are brought to glory, and made perfect themselves through their own sufferings that fills up the afflictions of Christ in their flesh for His Body's sake:

> *"And now rejoice in my sufferings for you, and make up that which is lacking of the sufferings of Christ in my flesh for His body's sake, which is the church" (Colossians 1:24 Lamsa's Aramaic).*

Scripture makes it clear that each member of His Mature Body must grow up into all things in Him:

> *"But speaking the truth in love, may grow up into Him in all things, which is the Head, even Christ" (Ephesians 4:15 KJV).*

It's time to fly kings and priests! It's time to grow up into all things in Christ! So, let's all aim at becoming His perfect place and space.

*****

8 – LIVING CREATURE SAFETY – BERYLLIUM #5

Are you aware that the kings and priests of the Order of Melchizedek have a safety component to them? This Corporate One New Man in Christ of Crucified Ones literally dwells in the secret place of the Most High and abides under the shadow of the Almighty (Psalm 91:1). How we know this is that when the Living Creature goes places according to His leading, the noise of their wings is as the voice of the Almighty:

- *"And the sound of the cherubim's wings was head even to the outer court, as the voice of the Almighty God when he speaketh" (Ezekiel 10:5 KJV).*

- *"And when they went, I heard the noise of their wings, like the noise of great waters, as the voice of the Almighty, the voice of speech, as the noise of a host: when they stood, they let down their wings" (Ezekiel 1:24 KJV).*

If we look at the preceding verses in Ezekiel Chapter 1, it tells us that the wheels of the Living Creature (which contains the spirit of the Living Creature) propels His Melchizedek Companies:

> "*¹⁹ And when the living creatures went, the wheels went by them: and when the living creatures were lifted up from the earth, the wheels were lifted up. ²⁰ Whithersoever the spirit was to go, they went, thither was their spirit to go; and the wheels were lifted up over against them: for the spirit of the living creature was in the wheels. ²¹ When those went, these went; and when those stood, these stood; and when those were lifted up from the earth, the wheels were lifted up over against them: for the spirit of the living creature was in the wheels" (Ezekiel 1:19-21 KJV).*

In His way this Kingdom Day, the wings of His End-Time Melchizedek Army who fly by the Spirit with one another will literally rise with healing in their wings: *"But to you who fear My name the Sun of Righteousness shall arise With healing in His wings" (Malachi 4:2 NKJV)*. Due to the Living Creature's wings being attached to their hearts and their hearts are attached to His, they will rise with His healing in their wings. This is why I call His Melchizedek Companies the PRIESTHOOD OF ONE LOVE. Psalm 91 concurs: *"Because he has set his love upon Me, therefore I will deliver him; I will set him on high, because he has known My name" (Psalm 91:14 NKJV)*.

Let's appreciate the safety factor through the eyes of beryllium to see other facets of the Living Creature's Safety Component. Being safe from hurt, injury or loss is the fifth dimension in our Beryllium Wheels Series. Please recall the list of beryllium's applications:

[1] Transportation,

[2] Communication,

[3] Medicine,

[4] Space Exploration,

[5] Safety,

[6] Oil, Gas and Alternate Energy as well as

[7]   Defense and Security.

Beryllium is used in air bags and electronic braking systems in automobiles, weather forecasting satellites, chemical detection devices, fire suppression sprinkler systems, and emergency rescue equipment.

READY IN A SPLIT SECOND – Beryllium's strength, fatigue and corrosion resistance literally helps save lives and protect property in a fraction of a second, so do His sons of righteousness. Beryllium is used in airbags, fire sprinklers systems, aircraft brushings and bearings, power steering and electronic control systems, anti-lock brakes, undersea earthquake and tsunami detection monitors, air traffic control radar and weather forecasting satellites. You get the idea.

Split second readiness is seen in the four living creatures running and returning like a flash of lightning:

"And the living creatures ran and returned as the appearance of a flash of lightning" (Ezekiel 1:14 KJV).

RELIABLE – The nickel beryllium washers in fire sprinkler systems are critical for the overhead sprinkler heads delivering full water pressure in the event of a fire while maintaining a leak-tight seal for years of inactivity. Such reliability ensures that thousands of sprinkler systems stand by with the readiness to act.

Melchizedek Companies are ready in a fraction of a second and are reliable agents of His Kingdom, because they move according to their vertical connection to the Sapphire Throne.

CHILD SAFETY – *"Assuredly, I say to you, whoever does not receive the kingdom of God as a little child will by no means enter it"* (Mark 10:15 NKJV). Beryllium x-ray windows in hand-held analytical devices allow retailers and day cares to ensure toys are lead free as well as protecting from other harmful metals.

This speaks of kings and priests being able to see as He sees into the heart of a matter to discern what's really going on in any situation. It also speaks of their childlike faith that trusts in His goodness (no matter what), for they know that all things will work for the good of those who love Him. By the way, the Order of Melchizedek also has a passion that everyone may know this incredibly wonderful reality.

BREATHING EASY – Beryllium alloy components make sure that the pressure controls that deliver air to firefighting rescue crews works.

In emergency situations, royal priests deliver His breath of life and love, and their vital connection to the All-Consuming Fire who sits on the throne is the reason why the Living Creature has a safety component:

> *"²⁶ And above the firmament that was over their heads was the likeness of a throne, as the appearance of a sapphire stone: and upon the likeness of the throne was the likeness as the appearance of a man above upon it. ²⁷ And I saw as the color of amber, as the appearance of fire round about within it, from the appearance of his loins even upward, and from the appearance of his loins even downward, I saw as it were the appearance of fire, and it had brightness round about"* (Ezekiel 1:26-27 KJV).

Please join me in reading Psalm 91, and applying it to our lives with this new safety perspective in mind:

"¹ He who dwells in the shelter of the Most High

Will abide in the shadow of the Almighty.

² I will say to the LORD, "My refuge and my fortress,

My God, in whom I trust!"

³ For it is He who delivers you from the snare of the trapper

And from the deadly pestilence. He will cover you with His pinions,

⁴ And under His wings you may seek refuge;

His faithfulness is a shield and bulwark.

⁵ You will not be afraid of the terror by night,

Or of the arrow that flies by day;

⁶ Of the pestilence that stalks in darkness,

Or of the destruction that lays waste at noon.

⁷ A thousand may fall at your side

And ten thousand at your right hand,

⁸ But it shall not approach you. You will only look on with your eyes

And see the recompense of the wicked.

⁹ For you have made the LORD, my refuge,

Even the Most High, your dwelling place.

¹⁰ No evil will befall you,

Nor will any plague come near your tent.

¹¹ For He will give His angels charge concerning you,

To guard you in all your ways.

¹² They will bear you up in their hands,

That you do not strike your foot against a stone.

¹³ You will tread upon the lion and cobra,

The young lion and the serpent you will trample down.

¹⁴ Because he has loved Me, therefore I will deliver him;

I will set him securely on high, because he has known My name.

¹⁵ He will call upon Me, and I will answer him;

I will be with him in trouble;

I will rescue him and honor him.

¹⁶ With a long life I will satisfy him

And let him see My salvation"

(Psalm 91:1-16 NASB).

*****

9 – LIVING CREATURE ENERGY – BERYLLIUM #6

Royal Priests made after the Order of Melchizedek have a massive energy factor to them, which will be known throughout eternity, as the ultimate power source here on earth, as it is in heaven. As His mature sons (who make up the Corporate One New Man on the earthly side) are crucified in union with Christ, they progressively bear His image until they are totally made into His likeness. If you want to bear His image, you've got to understand the Order of Melchizedek, because the wings of God's Melchizedek Companies flying by the Spirit with one another are His expression and power source on the earth today.

Revelation 4:5 speaks of lightning emanating out of His throne, and the next verse speaks about how four living creatures (symbolic of a Corporate Melchizedek Company) are in the midst and round about the throne:

> "*⁵ And out of the throne proceeded lightnings and thunderings and voices: and there were seven lamps of fire burning before the throne, which are the seven Spirits of God. ⁶ And before the throne there was a sea of glass like*

unto crystal: and in the midst of the throne, and round about the throne, were four beasts full of eyes before and behind" (Revelation 4:5-6 KJV).

"Lightning" is also connected to the brightness, charge and movement of His Melchizedek Companies:

"^{13} As for the likeness of the living creatures, their appearance was like burning coals of fire, and like the appearance of lamps: it went up and down among the living creatures; and the fire was bright, and out of the fire went forth lightning. ^{14} And THE LIVING CREATURES RAN AND RETURNED AS THE APPEARANCE OF A FLASH OF LIGHTNING. ^{15} Now as I beheld the living creatures, behold one wheel upon the earth by the living creatures, with his four faces" (Ezekiel 1:13-15 KJV).

Notice that *Revelation 4:6* shows us that these four beasts (i.e., four living creatures) are *"full of eyes before and behind."* Ezekiel 1:18 also tells us that the rings on the wheels are full of eyes: *"As for their rings, they were so high that they were dreadful; and their rings were full of eyes round about them four"* (Ezekiel 1:18 KJV). Fundamentally, let's understand that all these eyes have several dimensions to them. One dimension is that the Order of Melchizedek is His eyes.

Ezekiel 10:12 goes on to tell us: *"And their whole body, and their backs, and their hands, and their wings, and the wheels, were FULL OF EYES round about, even the wheels that they four had."* Let's appreciate the energy factor even more through the eyes of beryllium. Let's look at the various facets of the Living Creature's vigorous exertion of power. We are on the sixth aspect of beryllium's modern-day applications:

[1]   Transportation,

[2]   Communication,

[3]   Medicine,

[4] Space Exploration,

[5] Safety,

[6] Oil, Gas and Alternate Energy as well as

[7] Defense and Security.

In today's world, beryllium is used widely in the energy field to extract oil and gas. It has a big role in helping find tomorrow's clean and affordable energy sources. Beryllium is a key component to lowering the cost of oil and gas exploration on land and in deep water. Can you say: "Deep calls to deep?!" Not only is beryllium and materials that contain beryllium helping lead the way for obtaining new and affordable sources of traditional fossil fuels, but it's on the cutting edge for alternative energy sources as well.

OIL EXPLORATION AND PRODUCTION – Alloys that contain beryllium extend the reach and effectiveness of oil and gas drilling equipment. Exploration crews depend upon beryllium's non-sparking properties to reduce harmful explosions and fire risks.

Non-sparking copper beryllium also makes the new directional drilling techniques possible. When a material is needed that can operate reliably with electrical controls far from the drill head under high stress and elevated temperatures, copper beryllium is called upon to prevent very costly failures. There are also beryllium x-ray tubes that monitors the well flow rates of water, oil and gas as these materials are brought to the surface. Know that the Living Creature's wheels within wheels are connected to the oil filling the lamps of the wise virgins (Matthew 25:4).

ALTERNATE ENERGY – Alloys containing beryllium provides thermal management, conductivity, and the strength required in the electrical terminals, which join various components of solar panels together. Amazingly, beryllium ceramic allows concentrator photovoltaic (CPV) solar cells to operate at a very high solar concentration – 1,000 times the intensity of the sun, yet keep vulnerable electronics in the CPV cool enough to operate efficiently. This technology now delivers supplemental electricity to power grids throughout the world where there's abundant sunshine.

Lightning is five times hotter than the sun. *Discovery News* explains: "A bolt of lightning can reach temperatures of roughly 30,000 kelvins (53,540 degrees Fahrenheit) while the sun, on the other hand, is eclipsed in this case — its surface temperature is just 6,000 kelvins (10,340 degrees Fahrenheit). Power is the rate at which energy is used or transferred, so power is energy per second, and the energy per second in lighting can be very high, but it only lasts a really, really, short time, like tens of microseconds. So, the total energy isn't like the total energy from the sun, obviously, but the rate the energy dissipates can be very large. It's one of the most powerful natural phenomena on Earth."

His Reigning Ones of the Order of Melchizedek will eventually be clothed in fine linen garments where their bodies will be clothed in pure white light. And it's going to be like lightning!!! Get ready to take a quantum leap, because His priests and kings are going to move like lightning!!! *"And the living beings ran to and fro like bolts of lightning"* (*Ezekiel 1:14* $_{NASB}$).

NUCLEAR FUSION – Fusion holds the promise of delivering virtually unlimited sources of energy with virtually no greenhouse gases and little nuclear waste compared to traditional nuclear fission reactors. Beryllium is employed in fusion reactors for its neutron reflecting and moderating properties as well as its extraordinary ability to withstand super high temperatures associated with fusion energy.

Stay tuned. There is a mystery that has been hid from the ages that involves a royal power source connected to God's Sapphire Throne and His Sapphire Sea, which is propelled here on earth, as it is in heaven, by His Crucified Ones. These are the Reigning Ones of the Order of Melchizedek who are His glorious Living Creatures. These are the ones who are ONE with the ultimate power source Himself - YHVH.

*****

10 – LIVING CREATURE DEFENSE AND SECURITY – BERYLLIUM #7

The spirit of the Living Creature is in the wheels. Ezekiel Chapter 1 also tells us that the Living Creature is made up of four (or more) living creatures and it's their combined spirit that makes up the singular spirit of the Living Creature. We can ascend to His throne and other heavenly realms with any number of people, but know when there are four or more people, there's a quantum kingdom leap of Melchizedek revelation and power.

Not only do the spirits of those in a Living Creature Formation combine to make one, their likeness of fire does too. Notice the plurality of the fiery appearance of the corporate company of living creatures in Ezekiel 1:13: *"As for the likeness of the living creatures, their appearance was like burning coals of fire, and like the appearance of lamps: it went up and down among the living creatures and the fire was bright, and out of the fire went forth lightning" (Ezekiel 1:13 KJV)*. Now sit up and take notice of the singular man of fire in the midst of the Sapphire Throne: *"[26] And above the firmament that was over their heads was the likeness of a throne, as the appearance of a sapphire stone: and upon the likeness of the throne was the likeness as the appearance of a man above upon it. [27] And I saw as the color of amber, as the appearance of fire round about within it, from the appearance of his loins even upward, and from the appearance of his loins, even downward, I saw as it were the appearance of fire, and it had brightness round about" (Ezekiel 1:26-27 KJV)*. Notice that it specifies "a man" in Ezekiel 1:26, not the Son of Man or the Son of God.

Scripture also reveals another fiery corporate company. Do you remember the story of Shadrach, Meshach and Abednego being thrown into the fiery furnace? Due to the unified stance of these three men against an earthly king, they were thrown into the fire. Recall that the furnace was stoked up seven times hotter (Daniel 3:19). Know that pure gold is refined in God's fire seven times. The pure gold within this little unified group was being refined, so that the fourth man could manifest in the fire with them.

For a group to get to the point where they manifest One New Man in the fire, purification by fire is a necessary component in the ascension process. A unified Melchizedek Company's goal is to bring heaven to earth making the kingdoms of this earth, the kingdoms of our God. Connecting to God's Throne in the heavenly realms is one side of this divine equation. The other piece crucial to the restoration of all things is God's people fully developing the character of Christ in order to walk out on earth the heavenly realities that have been seen.

Each of us needs to be made complete in growth and labor as well as emotionally, morally, and mentally. A person can see heavenly glory after heavenly glory after heavenly glory, but the world around you will only change if you can contain these heavenly glories and flow in them. Know that His Reigning Ones will walk out heavenly glories in the same manner that Yeshua did (1 John 2:6). When we are in the fire and following the way He has chosen for each one of us, we have a glorious promise that we will come forth as gold: *"But He knows the way that I take; when He has tested me, I shall come forth as gold" (Job 23:10)*. Let's not waste an ounce of our trying experiences.

I know that I have been repeatedly told that the fourth man in the fire with Shadrach, Meshach and Abednego is Yeshua, which I believe is one magnificent facet of this kingdom reality. Christ in them. the hope of glory. in the midst of these three. But what if there is another facet to this kingdom reality? What if this story is illustrating a group of individuals so united for His Kingdom purposes that they chose to be thrown in the fire together to fight with and for one another? What if the unity in the fire created a fourth man with the appearance of the Son of God, which was One New Man that was made up of the composite spirit of all three? I have seen this happen. When I ascended with a group almost every week for four years, this unified One New Man appeared. Now when I am ascending with another group consistently, as we have committed to both God and one another for His Kingdom purposes, I see another Corporate One New Man in Christ manifest made up of the composite of the united spirits of the group. As we go through fiery trials together, our "fourth man" with the appearance like that of the Son of God gets more refined and clear – golden – if you will. Please be encouraged that your fiery trials have both a personal and corporate purpose. In a group, the good news is that when one falls down, the other is able to lift them up.

When there's a corporate agreement in His passion focusing on the very heartbeat of the Father, it causes the manifestation of a singular person – one new heavenly man – seated on His Sapphire Throne with the appearance of fire and brightness all around.

A group's singular being in Christ combines to create a type of Command and Control system, which brings us to the seventh and final modern-day application of beryllium in our list: Defense and Security. If YHVH is on your side, your best defense is His out-of-this-world offense. Remember that the seven applications of beryllium in our day that we are going over are:

[1]   Transportation,

[2]   Communication,

[3]   Medicine,

[4]   Space Exploration,

[5]   Safety,

[6]   Oil, Gas and Alternate Energy as well as

[7]   Defense and Security.

The armed forces of the world are completely reliant on beryllium. It is a critical component of weapons, guidance, surveillance and reconnaissance systems.

DEFENSE AND SECURITY - The U.S. Department of Defense (DOD) reported in 2008 that of all the metals used in its systems, only high purity beryllium was deemed "critical." DOD stated that beryllium is "essential for important defense systems and unique in the function it performs." Both NATO and the EU have presented similar conclusions.

Today's military systems depend heavily on electronics for navigation, target acquisition and firing. Precision is ensured in extremely critical situations due to the lightweight beryllium components in military equipment. Please recall that precise lightning strikes emanate out of His throne that the four living creatures – Melchizedek's Living Creature Formation – are in the midst of and round about (Revelation 4:5-6).

Pure beryllium saves weight critical to speed and maneuverability for today's military fighter jets. At the same time pure beryllium ensures razor-sharp targeting and strike capabilities.

We can say that God's Melchizedek Army is lightning fast with His pinpoint accuracy. The lightning fast movement of His Melchizedek Companies is connected to the wheels with wheels that causes His Chariot Throne to maneuver like some type of divine gyroscope in heaven and on earth.

Copper beryllium is also used for electrical connectors, fasteners and structural components in fixed-wing aircraft and in fighter jets.

A constant theme when taking a revelatory glance into the Beryllium Window of the Wheel Within Wheels is "connection." Connectedness is so important that we could substitute it for Melchizedek's name. Royal priests are required to have both an intimately connected right relationship with God and vulnerable, transparent connections with others, especially with the blood-bought soldiers in His Melchizedek Army.

OPTICAL SYSTEMS - Beryllium components assist the optical systems of military helicopters, unmanned aerial systems, tanks, missile defense, satellites, and other military equipment.

After all isn't the Living Creature full of eyes?! Please recall that *Revelation 4:6* tells us that they are *"full of eyes before and behind."* Ezekiel 1:18 also tells us that the rings on the wheels are full of eyes.

The following are examples of the critical nature of beryllium to the optical systems in the armed services:

- In optical systems of military helicopters, beryllium components are designed into enhanced surveillance and targeting systems that help keep crews safe.

- The nation's unmanned aerial systems count on

beryllium optical systems for real-time imagery and targeting on surveillance and reconnaissance flights.

- For battle tanks on the move, stiff beryllium mirrors dampen vibration and provide a jitter-free optical path for targeting and firing controls.

- Beryllium is also integral to the airborne equipment used to detect and destroy improvised explosive devices (IED) and tactical mines.

- In emerging guided missile defense systems, beryllium is critical to assure a first line of defense in directing, targeting and ultimately destroying missile threats.

- U.S. military satellites rely on beryllium metal for structural and dimensional stability, as well as reliability, in the electrical systems that deliver reliable intelligence from space.

COMMAND AND CONTROL - Command and control (C2) is defined to be "The exercise of authority and direction by a properly designated commander over assigned and attached forces in the accomplishment of the mission." C2 can also refer to the command and control systems within a military system.

The orders for the Living Creature Formation of the Melchizedek Army come from the ultimate headquarters – The Almighty's Throne (Ezekiel 1:24). Communication is critical to any type of corporate movement. We cannot it say enough: Everyone in a Melchizedek Company must first make a high frequency connection vertically to the All-Consuming Fire on the Throne before connecting horizontally with one another here on earth. Communication wise, the transmission goal for the Corporate One

New Man in Christ is to wholly move and live and have their being in the One who sits of the throne.

Military communications depend on copper beryllium alloys in their network hubs, switches and routers. It's the connectedness of the system.

Through the Melchizedek Army's vertical connectedness with His Throne, they are lightning fast traveling at the speed of thought. *"And the living creatures ran and returned as the appearance of a flash of lightning" (Ezekiel 1:14 KJV).*

The strength, electrical and thermal conductivity of copper beryllium ensures reliability while maximizing signal speed and bandwidth. The channel capacity of a physical communication path is termed "bandwidth."

In this Kingdom Day, the bandwidth of His Living Creature Formation of His Melchizedek Army who flies by the spirit with one another is limitless. We are in the days of quantum leaps.

*****

UNDERSTANDING THE ORDER OF MELCHIZEDEK

Book 7

Place of Sapphires

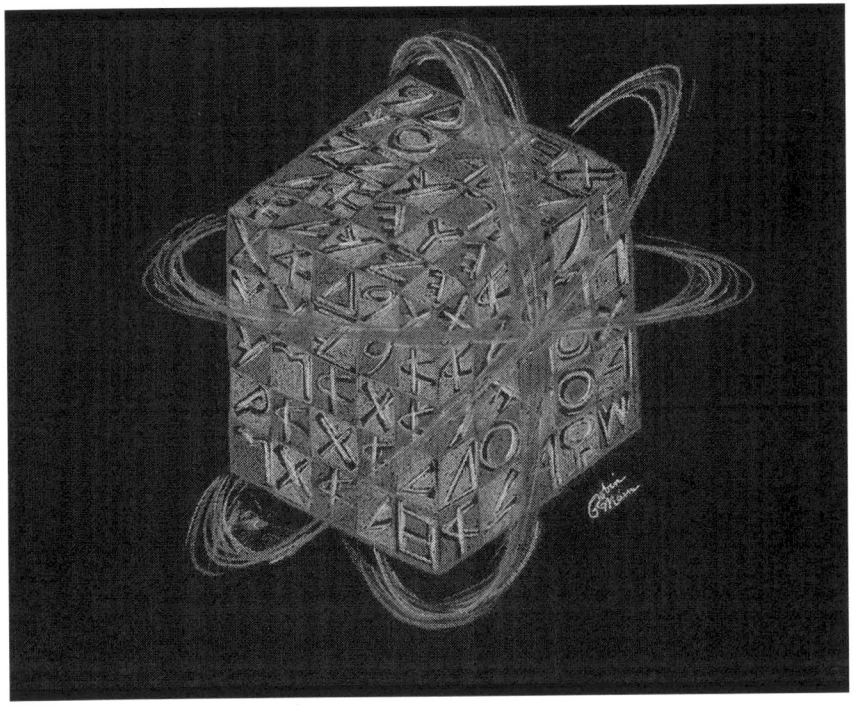

Cover Art: "Quantum Sapphire Cube & Seed" by Robin Main

© September 18, 2014. All Rights Reserved

Text Copyright © 2014 Robin Main. All Rights Reserved

1 – INTRODUCTION

The PLACE OF SAPPHIRES in the Matrix of Ezekiel's Chariot Throne is the matrix for a group called the Order of Melchizedek.

We will be flying by the Spirit and hovering over the matrix of Ezekiel's Chariot Throne within these pages. The word "matrix" in Scripture means womb or a place of birthing. It's the crucible or place in which the Crucified Ones of the Order of Melchizedek are formed. It is also the base of operation for the New Living Creature who is a wing of God's End-Time Melchizedek Army flying by the Spirit with one another. Being in two places at one time, these are the ones who make up the foundation of God's Chariot Throne as well as sit in the Throne with the Almighty in order to bring heaven to earth.

There are three major components in the Matrix of Ezekiel's Chariot Throne:

[1]　The Sapphire Throne,

[2]　The Crystal Expanse (Sea or Firmament), and

[3] The Living Creature.

We will be focusing on the first two with a twist on the third, because at the intersection of the Almighty's Sapphire Throne and His Sapphire Sea (i.e., Crystal Expanse) is a kingdom mystery that contains the seed DNA for the Living Creature.

Just know that there's a Sea of Glass or a Crystal Sea beneath God's Throne in heaven. When His Sapphire Throne becomes mobile that Crystal Clear Sea of Glass becomes a Sapphire Sea when heaven touches the earth.

The Order of Melchizedek is made up of mature and/or maturing sons who have access to heavenly positions "in Christ," but it's His appraisal of our earthly condition that determines the level of a person's maturity or a group's maturity. Before getting defensive, let's all realize that God is already examining those very areas of our lives to see if they measure up. Everyone (both in the Church and the world) recognizes a genuine manifestation of God's power and any heavenly position manifestly held here on earth.

The word "manifest" means that something is totally obvious. It is readily perceived by the senses, especially by sight. It's something easily understood or recognized. It's the evidence of things hoped for… Christ in you, the hope of glory. This is what people will see in and through you, and glorify the Father.

> "[41] *The Son of man shall send forth his angels, and they shall gather out of His kingdom all things that offend, and them which do iniquity …* [43] *Then shall the righteous shine forth as the sun in the kingdom of their Father. Who hath ears to hear, let him hear*" (Matthew 13:41,43 KJV).

Even though the *Merkabah* is ancient, Ezekiel's Chariot Throne is a fairly new kingdom concept in our day for groups ascending and operating corporately according to the Order of Melchizedek. These major components of Ezekiel's Chariot Throne show us how to co-labor with Christ and one another. Please note that the only top-down or vertical connection is for each of His kings and priests in the Order of Melchizedek being directly connected to the All-Consuming Fire who sits on the throne.

*****

2 – PLACE OF SAPPHIRES

The Almighty's Mobile Chariot Throne is also called His Sapphire Throne. The promise of "perfection" is eternally connected to Almighty God *(El Shaddai* in Hebrew), Christ's Cross, His Sapphire Throne, and the Melchizedek Priesthood.

> " *³ HE sets an end to darkness, and searches out all perfection: the stones of darkness, and the shadow of death. … ⁶ The stones of it are the place of sapphires: and it has dust of gold"* (Job 28:3,6).

The Hebrew word for "PERFECTION" in Job 28:3 is *tak-leeth'*. Pay attention, because this is the first occurrence of the term "perfection" in Scripture; therefore, it sets a precedence for every other time the concept of perfection is used. We are not talking about perfectionism, when it comes to *tak-leeth'*; but completion or an extremity. Its primitive root speaks of an end or to end. The perfection wrought by His Sapphire Throne speaks all about the finishing generation, which is our generation in this Kingdom Day.

The Ancient Hebrew Word Picture for *tak-leeth'* perfection tells us that the perfection of Almighty God is made manifest in, to, and through His Living Creature, as we join together with the Lamb in the midst of the throne through the blood of the everlasting Covenant:

- *"For the Lamb which is in the midst of the throne shall feed them, and shall lead them unto living fountains of waters: and God shall wipe away all tears from their eyes"* (Revelation 7:17 KJV).

- *"Now the God of peace, that brought again from the dead our Lord Jesus, that great shepherd of the sheep, through the blood of the everlasting covenant"* (Hebrews 13:20 KJV).

This everlasting blood covenant urges us back to the future through Yeshua Ha Machaich (Jesus Christ) our great Shepherd who was the Lamb slain before the foundation of the world (Revelation 13:8), and makes us perfect in every good work to do His will (Hebrews 13:21), which speaks of His Kingdom and opens us up to its abundant life and action. What a mouth full and a glorious truth!

In Job 28, we are told of two places that YHVH searches out all *tak-leeth'* perfection. It is in the place of the stones of darkness and the shadow of death. The clue to what the stones of darkness are resides merely three verses away. The stones of darkness are in the PLACE OF SAPHIRES, which also has dust of gold.

"But HE knows the way that I take: when HE hath tried me, I shall come forth as gold" (Job 23:10 KJV).

An incredible dimension of the Place of Sapphires is the mysterious work of His Sapphire Throne, which brings forth the gold in you and me; and it happens to dovetail with the Great Shepherd's shadow of death. A huge key to understanding how those in the Order of Melchizedek attain *tak-leeth'* perfection is the Great Shepherd who is the Lamb of God in the midst of the throne.

Let's take a deeper look at the Shepherd's shadow of death that brings *tak-leeth'* perfection. It is the place of the cross, or living a crucified life, as a continual living sacrifice:

> "*¹ Therefore I urge you, brethren, by the mercies of God, to present your bodies a living and holy sacrifice, acceptable to God, which is your spiritual service of worship. ² And do not be conformed to this world, but be transformed by the renewing of your mind, so that you may prove what the will of God is, that which is good and acceptable and perfect*" (Romans 12:1-2 NASB).

It's the place of being crucified in union with Christ where the two become one making an organic whole where all the necessary steps of faith toward righteousness have been fully carried out, so a person can be manifestly-made into the exact same image of Christ.

It is the low places in life – the valleys – that the Lord our Great Shepherd who is in the midst of God's Kingdom is with us:

- "*¹ The LORD is my shepherd, I shall not want. ² He makes me lie down in green pastures; He leads me beside quiet waters. ³ He restores my soul; He guides me in the paths of righteousness for His name's sake. ⁴ Even though I walk through the valley of the shadow of death, I fear no evil, for You are with me; Your rod and Your staff, they comfort me*" (Psalm 23:1-4 NASB).

- "*For the Lamb at the center of the throne continuously shepherds them unto life – guiding them to the everlasting fountains of the water of life. And God will wipe from their eyes every last tear!*" (Revelation 7:17 TPT).

The shadow of death is a place that God Himself restores our soul:

- "*³ He RESTORES MY SOUL. He leads me in the paths of righteousness for His name's sake ⁴ YEA, THOUGH I WALK THROUGH THE VALLEY OF THE SHADOW OF DEATH, I will fear no evil; for Thou art with me; Thy rod and Thy staff they comfort me*" (Psalm 23:3-4 Lamsa's Aramaic).

- *"25 For whoever wishes to save his life shall lose it; and whoever loses his life for My sake shall find it. 26 For how would a man be benefited, if he should gain the whole world and lose his own soul? Or what shall a man give in exchange for his soul?" (Matthew 16:25-26 Lamsa's Aramaic).*

Our soul will be restored like it was in the Garden before the Fall, except better. It will have been redeemed and matured into His image. Adam and Eve were created sinless, but not perfected. They still would have needed to mature into God's image.

Through the progressive process of crucifixion where the Lord Himself leads us through an ever-refining series of baptisms of fire (i.e., applications of the cross), our souls will become totally filled or enthroned by God:

"14 But God forbid that I should glory, save in the cross of our Lord Jesus Christ, by whom the world is crucified unto me, and I unto the world. 15 For in Christ Jesus neither circumcision availeth any thing, nor uncircumcision, but a NEW CREATURE. 16 And as many as walk according to this rule, peace be on them, and mercy, and upon the Israel of God" (Galatians 6:14-16 KJV).

This NEW CREATURE spoken of in Galatians 6:15 is the same "creature" spoken of in Romans 8:19-21 of the King James Version of the Bible, which is a Corporate One New Man in Christ made up of mature or maturing sons of God. Combined, these are a New Living Creature of Crucified Ones who make up wings of God's End-Time Melchizedek Army. Please refer to the *Formation of The New Living Creature* book and *YouTube* video for more information => https://www.youtube.com/watch?v=1BElDZaaFqo&index=2.

These ever-refining applications of the cross are in actuality paths of righteousness for His Name sake (Psalm 23:3). Therefore, the shadow of death is the place where we are refined in such a way that eventually we hit the mark of God's high calling, if we don't grow weary in well doing: *"⁷ Do not be deceived, God is not mocked; for whatever a man sows, this he will also reap. ⁸ For the one who sows to his flesh will from the flesh reap corruption, but the one who sows to the Spirit will from the Spirit reap eternal life. ⁹ Let us not lost heart in doing good: for in due time we will reap if we do not grow weary"* (Galatians 6:7-9 NASB).

The shadow of death is a place that His Sapphire Throne ministry aims at the utmost where the life we now live in the flesh, we live by completed faith just like Abraham:

- *"I am crucified with Christ; henceforth it is not I who live, but Christ who lives in me; and the life which now I live in the flesh I live by the faith of the Son of God, who loved me and gave himself for me"* (Galatians 2:20 Lamsa's Aramaic).

- *"²¹ Was not our father Abraham justified by works, when he raised Isaac his son upon the altar? ²² You can see how his faith helped his works, and how by works his faith was made perfect. ²³ And the scripture was fulfilled which said, Abraham believed God, and it was accounted to him for righteousness; and he was called the Friend of God. ²⁴ You see then how a man by works becomes righteous, and not by faith only. ²⁵ Likewise also was not Rahab the harlot justified by works when she welcomed the spies and sent them out another way? ²⁶ For as the body without the spirit is dead, so also faith without works is dead"* (James 2:21-16 Lamsa's Aramaic).

When His kings and priests hit this ultimate mark of the high calling of God in Christ Jesus, they become the righteousness of God in Christ Jesus and attain resurrection life here on earth with resurrected bodies:

- *"⁹ And be found in Him, not having mine own righteousness, which is of the law, but that which is through the faith of Christ, the righteousness which is of God by faith: ¹⁰ That I may know*

Him, and the power of His resurrection, and the fellowship of His sufferings, being made conformable unto His death; [11] If by any means I might attain unto the RESURRECTION OF THE DEAD. [12] Not as though I had already attained, either were already perfect; but I follow after, if that I may apprehend that for which also I am apprehended of Christ Jesus. [13] Brethren, I count not myself to have apprehended: but this one thing I do, forgetting those things which are behind, and reaching forth unto those things which are before, [14] I PRESS TOWARD THE MARK FOR THE PRIZE OF THE HIGH CALLING OF GOD IN CHRIST JESUS. [15] Let us therefore, as many as be perfect, be thus minded: and if in any thing ye be otherwise minded, God shall reveal even this to you" (Philippians 3:9-15 KJV).

- *"For he hath made him to be sin for us, who knew no sin; THAT WE MIGHT BE MADE THE RIGHTEOUSNESS OF GOD IN HIM" (2 Corinthians 5:21 KJV).*

- *"[21] Because THE CREATURE itself also SHALL BE DELIVERED FROM THE BONDAGE OF CORRUPTION INTO THE GLORIOUS LIBERTY OF THE CHILDREN OF GOD. [22] For we know that the whole creation groaneth and travaileth in pain together until now. [23] And not only they, but ourselves also, which have the firstfruits of the Spirit, even we ourselves groan within ourselves, waiting for the adoption to wit, THE REDEMPTION OF OUR BODY" (Romans 8:21-23 KJV).*

We need to follow Yeshua all the way through our own Spirit-led death, burial and resurrection process. Not to replace the completed work done by Yeshua, but to join Him by becoming like Him. Never forget that the point we are aiming at, as we refuse to come off the cross until we fill up the afflictions of Christ in our flesh for His Body sake, is RESURRECTION LIFE, or in other words becoming just like HIM.

- *"Now I rejoice in my sufferings for your sake, and in my flesh I do my share on behalf of His body, which is the church, in filling up what is lacking in Christ's afflictions" (Colossians 1:24 NASB).*

- *"For if we have become united with Him in the likeness of His death, certainly we shall also be in the likeness of His resurrection" (Romans 6:5 NASB).*

His New Living Creature will be made completely like unto the Son of God, as royal priests of Melchizedek (Hebrews 7:3). Revelation 1:6 and Revelation 5:10 speaks of how the High Priest of the Order of Melchizedek makes us kings and priests unto our God, and we shall reign on the earth by increasing the ten-percent deposit of the Holy Spirit in amount, magnitude and degree to the fullness of the stature of Christ via a crucified life (2 Corinthians 5:5; Ephesians 1:14; Ephesians 4:13; Galatians 2:20). This process is unto the knowledge of the Son of God via the Seven Spirits of God (Ephesians 4:13; Ephesians 1:17; Isaiah 11:2).

The CREATURE who is the Living Creature of Ezekiel 1 has been literally waiting for the *karios* or right time of God to appear on earth. Please refer to the *Melchizedek Arising 1 YouTube* video (https://www.youtube.com/watch?v=h5i6nAIvGjM) or the *Melchizedek's Appearance, Time & First Ministry* book for more information. Not only has God's Melchizedek Army needed to wait for His right time to manifest on earth, but their corporate appearance (illustrated in the matrix of Ezekiel's Chariot Throne) has also needed to wait for the Romans 8:19 manifestation of the mature sons of God who are also waiting for the *"redemption of our body" (Romans 8:23)*. Our body? Yes! Our body, which is Christ's Body:

- *"So we, being many, are ONE BODY IN CHRIST, and every one members one of another" (Romans 12:5 KJV).*

- *"But I would have you know, that the head of every man is Christ" (1 Corinthians 11:3 KJV).*

The "redemption of our body" is synonymous to a corporate manifestation of resurrection life. *Ephesians 1:14* calls it the *"redemption of the purchased possession."* The Place of Sapphires, which is the ministry of His Sapphire Throne, is meant to ultimately facilitate this mortality putting on immortality:

- *"^{53} For this corruption must put on incorruption, and this mortal must put on immortality. ^{54} So when this corruption shall have put on incorruption, and this mortal shall have put on immortality, then shall be brought to pass the saying that is written, Death is swallowed up in victory" (1 Corinthians 15:53-54 KJV).*

Once Christ's Corporate Body is crucified, it needs to be buried like our Pattern Son. Let's look at some crucial keys for the Redemption of Our Body by peeking at a good and just man who was the only one to have charge of the burial of the Body of Jesus. His story holds some kingdom keys for us today on how to prepare the crucified Body of Christ for the ultimate redemption of our Body.

If we take a close look at the account of Yeshua's crucifixion in Mark 15, we see an honorable gentleman who was a member of the Sanhedrin (the supreme council or court in ancient Israel). His name was Joseph of Arimathaea. While Matthew 27:57 tells us that he was a rich man, John 19:38 reveals that he was a secret disciple of Jesus. Luke 23:50 also declares him to be a good and just man:

- *"When it was evening, there came a rich man from Arimathea, named Joseph, who himself had also become a disciple of Jesus"* (Matthew 27:57 NASB).

- *"And a man named Joseph, who was a member of the Council, a good and righteous man"* (Luke 23:50 NASB).

- *"After these things Joseph of Arimathea, being a disciple of Jesus, but a secret one for fear of the Jews, asked Pilate that he might take away the body of Jesus; and Pilate granted permission, So he came and took away His body" (John 19:38 NASB).*

Significantly, we are told that Joseph of Arimathaea was a man who waited for the Kingdom of God and craved the body of Jesus: *"Joseph of Arimathea, an honorable counselor, which also waited for the Kingdom of God, came, and went in boldly unto Pilate, and craved the body of Jesus"* (Mark 15:43 KJV). The word "waited" carries a whole lot more meaning than merely tarrying. We can interpret that Joseph of Arimathaea "waited for the Kingdom of God" several different ways:

[1] He received to his own self the Kingdom of God.

[2] He was admitted into the Kingdom of God.

[3] He gave access to the Kingdom of God within himself.

[4] He was received into an intimate Kingdom of God relationship and companionship.

[5] He was received as one coming from the Kingdom of God place.

[6] He accepted the Kingdom of God.

[7] He expected the fulfillment of the promises of the Kingdom of God.

The name "Joseph" means "let him add." When we combine the meaning of Joseph's name and the previous expansion of the concept of "waited for the Kingdom of God," Isaiah 9:7 comes to mind, because God's Kingdom and His government are synonymous: *"Of the increase of His government and peace there will be no end, Upon the throne of David and over His kingdom, To order it and establish it with judgment and justice From that time forward, even forever. The zeal of the Lord of hosts will perform this" (Isaiah 9:7 NKJV).*

This just man who waited for the Kingdom of God and craved the body of Jesus speaks to me of *"we ourselves groan within ourselves, waiting for the adoption, to wit, the REDEMPTION OF OUR BODY" (Romans 8:23 KJV)*. So, this good and just man who was the only one to have charge of the burial of the Body of Jesus holds some kingdom keys for us today on how to prepare the crucified Body of Christ for the ultimate redemption of our Body. *"So Joseph bought some linen cloth, took down the body, wrapped it in the linen, and placed it in a tomb cut out of rock. Then he rolled a stone against the entrance of the tomb" (Mark 15:46 NIV)*. Notice that the crucified Body of Christ was wrapped in fine linen, and placed in a tomb carved out of rock with a stone for its door.

1) <u>Fine Linen</u> - Revelation 19 speaks of two companies that are arrayed in fine linen:

    a. The Bride of Christ, the wife of the Lamb:

    "⁷ Let us rejoice and be glad and give the glory to Him, for the marriage of the Lamb has come and His Bride has made herself ready.' ⁸ It was given to her to clothe herself in fine linen, bright and clean; for THE FINE LINEN IS THE RIGHTEOUS ACTS OF THE SAINTS" (Revelation 19:7-8 NASB).

    b. The armies which were in heaven who follow One whose garment is dipped in blood with His name being the Word of God:

    "¹³ He is clothed with a robe dipped in blood, and His name is called The Word of God. ¹⁴ And THE ARMIES WHICH ARE IN HEAVEN, CLOTHED IN FINE LINEN, white and clean, were following Him on white horses" (Revelation 19:13-14 NASB).

It's important to note that Revelation 19:8 points out that the clean and white fine linen that arrays the wife of the Lamb is the righteous acts of the saints.

2) <u>Tomb hewn out of Rock</u> – The Church (i.e., the called out *ekklessia* – the Legislative Assembly of the Lord) is built upon the rock (Matthew 16:18), which is Christ (1 Corinthians 10:4). It's noteworthy that Matthew 7:24 equates a wise man who built his house on the rock to whoever hears His words and does them. Wise virgins should probably take note (Matthew 25:1-13).

3) <u>Stone for the Tomb's Door</u> – The entrance to Yeshua's tomb was blocked by a stone, which the angels rolled away for His Resurrected Body. Understand that the word for "stone" in Hebrew is a contraction of two words: 1) *av* = father, 2) *ben* = son. Therefore, a stone is a picture of the Father and Son being so integrated that you can't seem to figure out where one begins and another ends. It's their essence of ONENESS, as proclaimed in John 17:21. Therefore, as we dwell with Him, He twists and rolls us together into One – One Body (Ephesians 1:10; Ephesians 4:4).

Do you see a fundamental building block for the REDEMPTION OF OUR BODY? If believers truly want to become mature sons of God, we must do what Jesus did. We can do nothing, but what we see the Father doing: *"Therefore Jesus answered and was saying to them, 'Truly, truly, I say to you, the Son can do nothing of Himself, unless it is something He sees the Father doing; for whatever the Father does, these things the Son also does in like manner"* (John 5:19 NASB).

James Chapter 2 backs up the fact that the righteous deeds of the saints are the essence of our pure and spotless bridal garment:

> "*²⁰ But do you want to know, O foolish man, that faith without works is dead? ²¹ Was not Abraham our father justified by works when he offered Isaac his son on the altar? ²² Do you see that faith was working together with his works, and by works faith was made perfect? ²³ And the Scripture was fulfilled which says, 'Abraham believed God, and it was accounted to him for righteousness.' And he was called the friend of God. ²⁴ You see then that a man is justified by works, and not by faith only. … ²⁶ For as the body without the spirit is dead, so faith without works is dead also*" (James 2:20-26 NKJV).

Therefore, the fine linen that the Body of Christ was wrapped in, the tomb that His Body was laid down in that was hewn out of rock, and the stone that was rolled over the tomb's door all point to the same kingdom reality that a prepared Body for Christ does the perfect will of the Father.

> "*⁵ Therefore when he comes into the world, he says, 'Sacrifice and offering you didn't desire, BUT A BODY DID YOU PREPARE FOR ME' … ⁷ Then I said, 'Behold, I have come (In the scroll of the book it is written of me) TO DO YOUR WILL, GOD'*" (Hebrews 10:5,7 HNV).

According to Hebrews 10:5, Yeshua came into the world for the purpose of the redemption of His Body, which is our body as well. Know that it's our beautiful Heavenly Father who is preparing a mature body to be placed on Christ's mature Head: "*His head and His hair were white like white wool, like snow; and His eyes were like a flame of fire*" (Revelation 1:14 NASB). One of the keys to the REDEMPTION OF OUR BODY is highlighted in Hebrews 10:7. If the mature Head – Yeshua – came to do the will of the Father, you can bet that His Mature Body will do the same:

- "*Therefore Jesus answered and was saying to them, 'Truly, truly, I say to you, the Son can do nothing of Himself, unless it is something He sees the Father doing; for whatever the Father does, these things the Son also does in like manner*" (John 5:19 NASB).

- *"I can do nothing on My own initiative. As I hear, I judge; and My judgment is just, because I do not seek My own will, but the will of Him who sent Me" (John 5:30 NASB).*

- *"So Jesus said, 'When you lift up the Son of Man, then you will know that I am He, and I do nothing on My own initiative, but I speak these things as the Father taught Me" (John 8:28 NASB).*

- *"[30] I will not speak much more with you, for the ruler of the world is coming, and he has nothing in Me;[31] but so that the world may know that I love the Father, I do exactly as the Father commanded Me. Get up, let us go from here" (John 14:30-31 NASB).*

- *"I am the vine, you are the branches; he who abides in Me and I in him, he bears much fruit, for apart from Me you can do nothing" (John 15:5 NASB).*

His Sapphire Throne ministry and the Shepherd's Shadow of Death are the places where the perfect will of our Heavenly Father can be perceived and done corporately by those who operate according to the kingdom rule of the Order of Melchizedek.

HIS BODY, who does the perfect will of the Father, will be known by their fruit:

"[16] You will know them by their fruits. Grapes are not gathered from thorn bushes nor figs from thistles, are they?[17] So every good tree bears good fruit, but the bad tree bears bad fruit.[18] A good tree cannot produce bad fruit, nor can a bad tree produce good fruit.[19] Every tree that does not bear good fruit is cut down and thrown into the fire.[20] So then, you will know them by their fruits.[21] Not everyone who says to Me, 'Lord, Lord,' will enter the kingdom of heaven, but the he who does the will of My Father who is in heaven will enter.[22] Many will say to Me on that day, 'Lord, Lord, did we not prophesy in Your name, and in Your name perform many miracles?[23] And then I will declare to them, 'I never knew you; depart from Me, you who practice

lawlessness'" (Matthew 7:16-23 NASB).

His Mature Body will be readily perceived and easily recognized for the FULLNESS of Christ they operate in – the greater works of God's Kingdom (John 14:12). The Ancient Hebrew Word Picture for *mel-ay-aw'* FULLNESS tells us that His fullness is the water revealing the Shepherd who shows us the Father. The PLACE OF SAPPHIRES facilitates this perfect work within each one of us where the Holy Spirit reveals Yeshua who shows us the Father.

*****

3 – THREE SAPPHIRE TRUTHS

SAPPHIRE

First and foremost, SAPPHIRE is associated with God's chariot throne portrayed in Ezekiel Chapter 1. Without the refining of the All-Consuming Fire who sits on the Sapphire Throne being a genuine reality in a believer's life, there is no throne room ministry where perpetual righteousness, holiness and truth is its fruit:

- *"[26] And His voice shook the earth then, but now He has promised, saying, 'YET ONCE MORE I WILL SHAKE NOT ONLY THE EARTH, BUT ALSO THE HEAVEN.'[27] This expression, 'Yet once more,' denotes the removing of those things which can be shaken, as of created things, so that those things which cannot be shaken may remain.[28] Therefore, since we receive a kingdom which cannot be shaken, let us show gratitude, by which we may offer to God an acceptable service with reverence and awe;[29] for our God is a consuming fire"* (Hebrews 12:26-29 NASB).

Without the Sapphire Throne being firmly secured through the Word of God in our lives, we cannot move and live and have our being in Him in its fullness:

- *"²⁷ That they would seek God, if perhaps they might grope for Him and find Him, though He is not far from each one of us; ²⁸ FOR IN HIM WE LIVE AND MOVE AND EXIST, as even some of your poets have said, 'For we also are His children'" (Acts 17:27-28 NASB).*

- *"Until we all attain to the unity of the faith, and of the knowledge of the Son of God, to a mature man, to the measure of the stature which belongs to the FULLNESS OF CHRIST" (Ephesians 4:13).*

Without the Sapphire Throne, there is no lasting, eternal ministry period:

- *" ⁸And the four living creatures, each one of them having six wings, are full of eyes around and within; and day and night they do not cease to say, 'HOLY, HOLY, HOLY IS THE LORD GOD, THE ALMIGHTY, WHO WAS AND WHO IS AND WHO IS TO COME.' ⁹And when the living creatures give glory and honor and thanks to Him who sits on the throne, to Him who lives forever and ever, ¹⁰ the twenty-four elders will fall down before Him who sits on the throne, and will worship Him, who lives forever and ever, and will cast their crowns before the throne, saying, 'Worthy are You, our Lord and our God, to receive glory and honor and power; for You created all things, and because of Your will they exist, and were created" (Revelation 4:8-10 NASB).*

Without going into an extensive study of "sapphire" in Scripture, there are three more "sapphire truths" I'd like to point out:

[1] SAPPHIRE PAVEMENT - The place under the God of Israel's feet appeared to be paved with sapphire stone when heaven touched earth:

- *"They saw the God of Israel, and under His feet was the likeness of sapphire brickwork, and it was like the essence of the heaven in purity"* (Exodus 24:10 Tanach).

- *"And they saw the God of Israel; and under His feet there appeared to be a pavement of sapphire, as clear as the sky itself"* (Exodus 24:10 NASB).

- *"And they saw the God of Israel: and there was under His feet as it were a paved work of a sapphire stone, and as it were the body of heaven in His clearness"* (Exodus 24:10 KJV).

Significantly, we are told this appearance was like the body of heaven in HIS clearness.

[2] SHAMIR STONE - An infinite minuteness of sapphire was the only thing that could perfect stones in God's Temple. It was called the Shamir Stone. Therefore, the specs of God's holy dwelling place require that His living stones be polished by the ministry of His Sapphire Throne:

- *" [1] Then I looked, and behold, in the expanse that was over the heads of the Cherubim something like a sapphire stone, in appearance resembling a throne, appeared above them. ... [20] These are the living beings (creatures) that I saw beneath the God of Israel by the river Chebar; so I knew that they were the Cherubim"* (Ezekiel 10:1,20 NASB). '

- *"[4] And coming to Him as to a living stone which has been rejected by men, but is choice and precious in the sight of God, [5] you also, as living stones, are being built up as a spiritual house for a holy priesthood, to offer up spiritual sacrifices acceptable to God through Jesus Christ" (1 Peter 2:4-5 NASB).*

[3] WISDOM - Sapphire symbolizes the place where wisdom can be found:

- *"[1] Surely there is a vein for the silver, and a place for god where they find it. [2] Iron is taken out of the earth, and brass is molten out of the stone. [3] He setteth an end to darkness, and searcheth out all perfection: the stones of darkness, and the shadow of death. [4] The flood breaketh out from the inhabitant: even the waters forgotten of the foot: they are dried up, they are gone away from men. [5] As for the earth, out of it cometh bread: and under it is turned up as it were fire. [6] THE STONES OF IT ARE THE PLACE OF SAPPHIRES: and it hath dust of gold. … [12] But WHERE shall WISDOM BE FOUND? And where is the place of understanding? [13] Man knoweth not the price thereof; neither is it found in the land of the living. [14] The depth saith, It is not in me: and the sea saith, It is not with me [15] It cannot be gotten from gold, neither shall silver be weighed for the price thereof. [16] It cannot be valued with the gold of Ophir, with the precious onyx, or the sapphire. [17] The gold and crystal cannot equal it: and the exchange of it shall not be for jewels of fine gold. [18] No mention shall be made of coral, or of pearls: for the price of wisdom is above rubies. [19] The topaz of Ethiopia shall not equal it, neither shall it be valued with pure gold. [20] Whence then cometh wisdom? And where is the place of understanding? [21] Seeing it is hid from the eyes of all living, and kept close from the fowls of the air. [22] Destruction and death say, We have heard the fame thereof with our ears. [23] GOD UNDERSTANDeth THE WAY THEREOF, AND HE KNOWeth THE PLACE THEREOF. [24] For he looketh to the ends of the earth, and seeth under the whole heaven; [25] To make the weight for the winds; and he weigheth the waters by measure. [26]*

When he made a decree for the rain, and a way for the lightning of the thunder;²⁷ Then did he see it, and declare it; he prepared it, yea, and searched it out.²⁸ And unto man he said, BEHOLD, THE FEAR OF THE LORD, THAT IS WISDOM; and to depart from evil is understanding" (Job 28:1-6, 12-28 KJV).

Along with ruby, sapphire is a variety of the mineral corundum. Because of the remarkable hardness of sapphires — 9 on the Mohs scale (the third hardest mineral, right behind diamond at 10 and moissanite at 9.25), sapphires have several non-ornamental applications. These modern-day applications of SAPPHIRE give us some hints about the ministry of His Sapphire Throne.

Sapphire is used in the optical components of scientific instruments. This speaks of the Order of Melchizedek making visual and perceivable contact with the bull's eye of the Father. They see into Him and His nature as well as out through His eyes to see as He sees.

Sapphire Glass is used in high-durability windows. Sapphire is not *only highly transparent, but is also extraordinarily scratch-resistant.* Therefore, synthetic sapphire is used for shatter resistant windows in armored vehicles and various military body armor suits.

God's End-Time Melchizedek Army are highly genuine and transparent individuals reflecting His extraordinary love, power and glory. Their divine sight is unlimited and shatter resistant in regard to the things of this world.

Due to its scratch resistance, sapphire glass windows are used in the crystals of various watches. The *Dead Sea Scrolls* portion of "Melchizedek" speaks of the restoration of things, including time: "The 'Messenger who brings good news, who announces salvation' is the one of whom it is written: 'to proclaim the year of the LORD's favor, the day of vengeance of our God; to comfort all who mourn' (Isaiah 61:2). This Scripture's interpretation: he is to instruct them about all the periods of history for eternity and in the statutes of the truth" [*Dead Sea Scrolls: A New Translation* by Wise, Abegg & Cook, pg. 455-457]

Sapphire glass windows are also used in the bar code scanners in grocery stores.

The Order of Melchizedek's New Living Creature of Crucified Ones has the ability through their vertical connection to the One on the Sapphire Throne to scan the Body of Christ and all of creation. When the four or more living creatures does exactly what He directs, His Kingdom comes, and His will is done in that situation. I have experienced generational curses being overcome in a few hours with those who have pressed into Him to the best of their ability. They are literally primed for their deliverance. I have also seen an assignment of death canceled. Amazing powerful things happen when four or more kings and priests are brought together by His Spirit to do His kingdom works. When the Living Creature moves and lives and has their being in Him, as part of His Chariot Throne, we have experienced Him requiring that one or more Melchizedek Generals to be present.

Sapphire's tolerance for higher thermal loads causes them to also be used for end windows on some high-powered laser tubes. The first laser was made with a rod of synthetic ruby. Titanium-sapphire lasers are popular due to their relatively rare capacity to be able to be tuned to various wavelengths in the red and near-infrared region of the electromagnetic spectrum. Infrared (IR) is invisible radiant energy or electromagnetic radiation that has longer wavelengths than that of visible light. Titanium-sapphire lasers can also be easily mode-locked, which means their light can pulse for an extremely short duration. Mode-locked laser are used for nuclear fusion, cornea surgery, and nanomachines. I find it interesting that there is a laser technique that has been developed that renders the surface of metals deep black. A femto-second laser pulse deforms the surface of the metal forming nanostructures, which can absorb virtually all the light that falls on it thus rendering it deep black. Experts say that this is one type of black gold. Hum. Do you think this is related to the stones of darkness being the place of the sapphires? The Almighty's Melchizedek Companies are focused beams of light doing the perfect will of the Father.

Thin sapphire wafers are also used as an insulating substrate in high-power, high-frequency integrated circuits. This type of IC is called a "Silicon On Sapphire" or "SOS" chip. These are especially useful for high-power radio-frequency (RF) applications such as those found in cellular telephones, police car and fire truck radios, and satellite communication systems.

Communication is a key component to the Order of Melchizedek. The high frequency communication circuits of the Matrix of Ezekiel's Chariot Throne are first vertical with each of the living creatures personally connecting to the All-Consuming Fire who sits on the Sapphire Throne; and then, it's a horizontal connection with one another. The transmission goal for the New Living Creature, which is the Corporate One New Man in Christ who is a wing of God's End-Time Melchizedek Army flying by the Spirit with one another, is to wholly and corporately move and live and have their being in the One who sits on the throne. This means that these Reigning Ones effectively and clearly communicate His information making His will and kingdom known.

Not only does His New Living Creature of Crucified Ones transmit His information, thoughts and feeling; but they reveal Almighty God successfully in any language and on any platform. They are His Messenger who delivers His messages that are clearly seen, heard and understood.

In this PLACE OF SAPPHIRES, let's gaze further into these three sapphire truths – wisdom, sapphire pavement, and the *shamir* stone – which are connected to His Sapphire Throne:

"⁲⁶And above the firmament that was over their heads was the likeness of a throne, as the appearance of a sapphire stone: and upon the likeness of the throne was the likeness as the appearance of a man above upon it. ²⁷And I saw as the color of amber, as the appearance of fire round about within it, from the appearance of his loins even upward, and from the appearance of his loins even downward, I saw as it were the appearance of fire, and it had brightness round about. ²⁸As the appearance of the bow that is in the cloud in the day of rain, so was the appearance of the brightness round about. This was the appearance of the likeness of the glory of the LORD. And when I saw it, I fell upon my face, and I heard a voice of one that spake" (Ezekiel 1:26-18 ₖⱼᵥ).

*****

4 – THE SHAMIR STONE

The SHAMIR STONE is a quantum leap in our journey to the PLACE OF SAPPHIRES, and it contains the LIVING CREATURE'S SEED DNA. Please mark in your mind and your spirit that this is the incorruptible seed for the Order of Melchizedek.

> *"[1] God, who at various times and in various ways spoke in time past to the fathers by the prophets, [2] has in these last days spoken to us by His Son, whom He has appointed heir of all things, through whom also He made the worlds; [3] who being the brightness of His glory and the EXPRESS IMAGE of His person, and upholding all things by the word of His power, when He had by Himself, purged our sins, sat down at the right hand of the Majesty on high" (Hebrews 1:1-3 NKJV).*

The term "EXPRESS IMAGE" is the Greek word *charakter*, which not only means "the exact expression (the image) of any person or thing that is a marked likeness or precise reproduction in every respect," but also "the instrument used for engraving or carving."

Did you know that in place of cutting tools, the Shamir Stone was used in the construction of Solomon's Temple? It had the power to cut through or disintegrate stone, iron and even diamonds.

Hebrew Sages tell us that the Shamir was first used by Moses to engrave the names of the twelve tribes on the precious stones of the High Priest's Breastplate. We are told Moses first wrote the letters of the tribal names on the stones with ink; and then, the Shamir Stone was held over them so that the writing sank into the stones.

Where did this Shamir Stone come from anyway? The Hebrews say that the Shamir was the seventh of ten marvels created at the TWILIGHT of the first Sabbath (i.e., the seventh day during the days of creation).

My mentor – Nancy Coen – has taught for years that in God's Calendar, it says that 1,000 years on the earth is like one day on the Calendar of God (See 2 Peter 3:8). Between Adam and Abraham, there's 2,000 years. Between Abraham and Yeshua, there's 2,000 years. And between Yeshua and approximately around the year 2000, it was 2,000 years. Add this together and you get 6,000 years, which means we are standing in the place of "after six days" or the TWILIGHT OF THE SEVENTH DAY. The Seventh Day of God's communion with mankind is the *karios* or divine right prophetic time for the manifestation of the SHAMIR'S EXPRESS IMAGE. Please allow me to explain.

I've been getting massive heavenly downloads about this Shamir Stone. The Shamir Stone was considered by some Hebrew Sages to be a powder of corundum (specifically sapphire). They say that from the powdery emery was made a LIVING CREATURE of infinite minuteness.

As I awoke the morning of June 21, 2014, the LORD showed me that the Shamir Stone came from where His Sapphire Throne and His Sapphire Sea intersect.

Remember how Exodus 24:10 speaks of Sapphire Pavement beneath the God of Israel's feet? Two verses later the original Hebrew text reveals I AM THAT I AM speaking to Moses: *"Come up to Me on the mountain and stay here, and I will give you THE CUBES OF STONE, with the law and commands I have written for their instruction"* (Exodus 24:12).

Cubes of Stone? I thought they were tablets. That's what I was taught in Sunday School. The original text in Ancient Hebrew says: "Cubes of Stone." We will get to that in a moment.

First, let me lay on a little more heavy revvy. The day after I saw that the Shamir Stone came from where His Sapphire Throne and His Sapphire Sea intersect, I heard the phrase: "THE SHAMIR IS A CHIP OFF THE OLD BLOCK." Then I saw in the spirit a Sapphire Cube being taken from the lower left-hand side of the Almighty's Throne (its foundational structure), which is on our right-side if we are facing His throne. When it was cut, the lowest edge of the cube connected to the Sapphire Sea on earth. I also saw a barley-corn grain-sized fragment (a chip less than 1 cm off the Ancient of Day's Block) at the intersection of the Sapphire Throne and the Sapphire Sea. This is where the supernatural Shamir Stone came from, which I was told on the previous day: "THE SHAMIR STONE IS THE SEED DNA OF THE LIVING CREATURE."

You see in Solomon's Temple, the material to be worked (whether stone, wood, or metal) was affected according to the plans given to Melchizedek David (i.e., King David) by the Spirit by simply being "shown to the Shamir." Following this logic, the Hebrews spoke of anything that can be 'shown' something must have eyes to see. Therefore, early Jewish scholars described the Shamir "almost" as a LIVING BEING. Don't you love how they hedged their bet? The Shamir was almost a living being with eyes. They could not wrap their heads around the reality of what the Shamir portrays. That's okay, because Daniel speaks about certain mysteries of the Kingdom of God being revealed in these end days: "*³ Those who are WISE shall shine like the brightness of the firmament, and those who turn many to righteousness like the stars forever and ever. ⁴ But you, Daniel, shut up the words, and seal the book until the time of the end; many shall run to and fro, and knowledge shall increase*" (Daniel 12:3-4 NKJV).

Remember how the Place of Sapphires symbolizes the place where wisdom can be found?

"*⁹ And he said, 'Go your way, Daniel, for the words are closed up and sealed till the time of the end. ¹⁰ Many shall be purified, made white, and refined, but the wicked shall do wickedly; and none of the wicked shall understand, but THE WISE SHALL UNDERSTAND*'" (Daniel 12:9-10 NKJV).

The Shamir was called a "supernatural organism." It was said to have the ability to pierce hard surfaces. The "glance" of the Supernatural Shamir could carve out great stones. We must remember that the only substance allowed to perfect the stones in Solomon's Temple was the Shamir Stone. In the second *Melchizedek Arising* video on *YouTube*, I mentioned that we need to pay attention to Solomon's Temple, because it's a pattern for the Order of Melchizedek manifesting in this Kingdom Day => https://www.youtube.com/watch?v=1BElDZaaFqo.

The Supernatural Shamir Stone that the LORD says is the Seed DNA of the Living Creature worked materials with a glance that was "FULL OF EYES":

- "*Before the throne there was a Sea of Glass, like crystal. And in the midst of the throne, were four living creatures FULL OF EYES in front and back*" (Revelation 4:6 KJV).

- "*¹⁵ Now as I looked at the living creatures, behold, a wheel was on the earth beside each living creature with its four faces. ¹⁶ The appearance of the wheels and their workings was like the color of beryl, and all four had the same likeness. The appearance of their workings was, as it were, a wheel in the middle of a wheel. ¹⁷ When they moved, they went toward any one of four directions; they did not turn aside when they went. ¹⁸ As for their rims, they were so high they were awesome; and their rims were FULL OF EYES, all around the four of them"* (Ezekiel 1:15-18 _{NKJV}).

If we delve into the Hebrew word for "rims," it connects the rims of these wheels within wheels to eyebrows, breastworks, and the back of a man:

- *"⁹ And when I looked, behold the four wheels by the CHERUBIM,* [Remember the LIVING CREATURE, kings and priests of the Order of Melchizedek and CHERUBIM can be synonymous] *one wheel by one CHERUB, and another wheel by another CHERUB: and the appearance of the wheels was as the color of beryl stone, ¹⁰ And as for their appearance, they four had one likeness, as if a wheel had been in the midst of a wheel. ¹¹ When they went, they went upon their four sides; they turned not as they went, but to the place whither the head looked they followed it; they turned not as they went. ¹² And their whole body, with their back, their hands, their wings, and the wheels that the four had, were FULL OF EYES, ALL AROUND THE FOUR OF THEM"* (Ezekiel 10:9-12 _{KJV}).

- *"⁷ The first creature was like a lion, and the second creature like a calf, and the third creature has a face like that of a man, and the fourth creature was like a flying eagle. ⁸ And the four living creatures, each one of them having six wings, are FULL OF EYES around and within; and day and night they do not cease to say: 'Holy, holy, holy, the Lord God, the Almighty, who was and who is and who is to come!'"* (Revelation 4:7-8 _{NASB}).

With each glance that was "full of eyes," the Supernatural Shamir Stone caused Solomon's Temple on earth to bear the image of its golden counterpart in heaven. Did you know that every created thing has a record in it that responds to the DNA of the sons of God? When mature sons of God who rule and reign "in Christ" position themselves in heaven – in the midst of His Throne – in the Father, all creation responds: *"For we know that the whole creation groans and suffers the pains of childbirth together until now" (Romans 8:22 NASB)*. Romans 8:21 KJV tells us that *"creation itself also will be delivered from the bondage of corruption into the glorious liberty of the children of God."*

We are beginning to see a Melchizedek Company becoming an earthly expression of a perfectly heavenly image. When we come out of this earthly world and go into His heavenly world, everything changes. This Shamir is even now beginning to manifest into a four-dimensional being that is able to move with His Sapphire Cube – the known universe – because all of creation is within it. A huge key to operating as a four-dimensional being is being rooted and grounded in the Father's love:

> *"^{17} So that Christ may dwell in your hearts through faith; and that you, being rooted and grounded in love, ^{18} may be able to comprehend with all the saints what is the breadth and length and height and depth" (Ephesians 3:17-18 NASB).*

Scientists say that there are three possibilities for the Shamir's effect on the various materials in God's Temple. We are told that the Shamir's glance split wood and stone. It was said that no other materials were able to resist its penetrative powers; therefore, scientists speculate that the Shamir produced either:

[1] Subsonic or Supersonic - high or low frequency waves that could resonate the molecular structure of materials and disrupt them.

[2] Laser Beam - production of confluent light rays. The *Merriam Webster Dictionary* tells us that a laser is a device that utilizes the natural oscillations of atoms or molecules

between energy levels for generating a beam of coherent electromagnetic radiation usually in the ultraviolet, visible, or infrared regions of the spectrum.

[3] Alpha Radiation - high energy particles of ionizing radiation that consists of alpha particles, which are emitted by some substances radioactive decay.

Personally, I think sound, light and radiation all have a part in the manifestation of the Shamir in the building of God's Dwelling Place. Hebrew history records that the Shamir Stone was stored in spongy balls of wool. These spongy balls of wool were laid in a lead box; and then, filled with barley grain.

The wool in the "spongy balls of wool" speaks of a flock of sheep. Spongy is something absorbent or full of water (moisture), which is associated with the middle part of the Matrix of Ezekiel's Chariot Throne – the Sapphire Sea when it touches the earth or the Crystal-Clear Sea of Glass in Heaven. We cover the Sapphire Sea/the Sea of Glass more in Chapter 10 of the *MEL GEL Study Guide: Volume 2* and in the *MEL GEL #10 – The Firmament* teaching video, which are both available here => http://www.sapphirethroneministries.com/resources.html. Today, spongy wool or sponged wool is a premium product of pre-treated wool to prevent shrinkage.

It's interesting that the Shamir was placed in a lead box full of barley grain. Barley grains are the same size as the Shamir, but a different substance. One is an earthly fruit, the other heavenly. It's significant that the Shamir was hidden in an earthly substance that speaks of resurrection life. The day that Yeshua rose from the dead was *Bikkurim* – the Feast of First Fruits – which is one of the seven Feasts of the Lord that still commemorates the barley harvest. The barley speaks of resurrection life, and the Shamir speaks of the incorruptible seed of the Word of God:

"²² Since you have purified your souls in obeying the truth through the Spirit in sincere love of the brethren, love one another fervently with a pure heart, 23 having been born again, not of corruptible SEED but INCORRUPTIBLE, THROUGH THE WORD OF GOD which lives and abides forever, ²⁴ because 'All flesh ... and all the glory of man ... withers, and ... falls away, ²⁵ But the word of the LORD endures forever.' Now this is the word which by the gospel was preached to you" (1 Peter 1:22-25 NKJV).

Some experts speculate that the reason the Shamir was placed inside a lead box was because it was a radioactive substance. They say the "glance" of the Shamir may have been alpha radiation. Alpha radiation is another name for the alpha particles emitted in the type of radioactive decay called alpha decay. Alpha radiation is the least penetrating of alpha, beta, and gamma. The key to the specifics of alpha decay is the quantum effect called tunneling. The phenomenon of "quantum tunneling" confirms that so-called "matter" has the capacity to de-materialize and re-materialize in the sub-atomic world. Quantum physics is an entirely new paradigm of reality these days that appears to be in conflict with everything that we have understood to constitute reality in the macroscopic world. Quantum tunneling reveals that matter is effectively non-local. Non-local means that it is not bound by the constraints of time and space. Non-local points to the existence of another dimension of reality that transcends time and space as we understand it. This is the heavenly reality of the Sapphire Throne that the Order of Melchizedek operates from, and their radiation comes from their Father heart connection.

Did you know that your heart emanates radiation? A person's heart is a marvelous machine, which is the size of a fist and weighs on average less than 10 ounces. Yet, it possesses a level of intelligence that scientists are only beginning to understand. The heart acts as a sensory organ that encodes and processes sophisticated information, which enables it to learn. It also radiates a powerful electromagnetic field that can be detected and measured several feet away (most statistics say 8-10 feet). The cardioelectromagnetic field that the heart generates and radiates is the largest electromagnetic field in the body (60 times greater in amplitude than the brain).

When the New Living Creature of Crucified Ones transmit at the frequency of the Father's heart, a heavenly earth-shattering reality restores all things. If a thing's origins are of Him, it is redeemed and restored, as it was in the beginning in its pristine primordial state. If the thing's origins are demonic, it will be restored by being judged and being done away with.

For the past 1,750 years or so, much of Christianity has taught its adherents the disannulling of the law or the setting aside of the Old Testament. May I state something obvious. The origins of the Old Testament are not demonic. Yeshua Himself tells us: *"[17] Do not think that I came to destroy the Law or the Prophets. I did not come to destroy but to fulfill. [18] For assuredly, I say to you, till heaven and earth pass away, one jot or one tittle will by no means pass from the law till all is fulfilled" (Matthew 5:17-18 NKJV)*. An entire book can be written on these verses. Suffice it to say that Yeshua did not come to destroy or abolish the law, but to fulfill it. Fulfill is the opposite of destroying something. Fulfill means fill it up full of meaning. Let's all walk, as Yeshua walked. He was not legalistic, yet He was holy. He was not full of unsanctified mercy, yet He personified perfect love and the type of kindness that leads a person to repentance.

In this Kingdom Day, those made after the Order of Melchizedek are going to take a quantum leap beyond what most Christians have been taught about "disannulling" or the "setting aside" of the Law. If any part of the Word of God can be set aside or disannulled or cancelled, then we are saying that the word of the LORD does not endure forever.

"For it is attested of Him, 'You are a priest forever according to the Order of Melchizedek.' For, on the one hand, there is a SETTING ASIDE OF A FORMER COMMANDMENT because of its weakness and uselessness. (For the Law made nothing perfect), and on the other hand there is a bringing in a better hope, through which we draw near to God" (Hebrews 7:17-19 NASB).

The "setting aside" in the NASB is the "disannulling" in the KJV. The word "disannulling" on the surface is defined in the *Strong's Concordance* as "cancellation" or putting away, and the word it came from also is defined as "disannulling" as neutralizing or violating something, to set it aside, to disesteem it, bring it to nought, frustrate it, despise it, and reject it.

But wait! The word "annul" is defined as : to reduce to nothing : OBLITERATE : to make ineffective : NEUTRALIZE : to declare or make legally invalid or void. While the prefix "dis" makes any word that follows it the opposite. Therefore, logic would conclude that "disannul" is the opposite of reducing something to nothing, and would make whatever you are disannulling legally valid.

If you dive deeper into the two Greek root words in the *Strong's Concordance* for the word "disannulling," you will discover that one of the words describes a sense of union while the other word describes something being placed in a passive or horizontal posture (i.e., rest) as well as speaking about advising, appointing and various worship stances (bowing, kneeling and laying down).

At the root of the whole concept of that word "disannulling" is a picture of entering His rest where through the better hope in which we draw near to God, we show that we are a letter from Christ written not on tablets of stone but on the tablets of human hearts: *"[2] You are our letter, written in our hearts, known and read by all men; [3] being manifested that you are a letter of Christ, cared for by us, written not with ink but with the Spirit of the living God, not on tablets of stone but on tablets of human hearts" (2 Corinthians 3:2-3 NASB).*

It's the fulfillment of *Ezekiel 36:26-27*: *"²⁶ I will give you a new heart and put a new spirit in you; I will remove from you your heart of stone and give you a heart of flesh. ²⁷ And I will put my Spirit in you and move you to follow my decrees and be careful to keep my laws."*

So... Now the Spirit of the Living God makes the Law that was once weak and externally written on tablets of stone a walking-talking demonstration of the Word of God – Word with flesh on – which is written on human hearts. This is the reality His people need to understand to advance His Kingdom from Psalms 19, and radiate at the vibrational frequency of the Father's heart:

"⁷ The law of the LORD is perfect, converting the soul: the testimony of the LORD is sure, making wise the simple. ⁸ The statutes of the LORD are right, rejoicing the heart: the commandment of the LORD is pure, enlightening the eyes. ⁹ The fear of the LORD is clean, enduring forever: the judgments of the LORD are true and righteous altogether. ¹⁰ More to be desired are they than gold, yea, than much fine gold: sweeter also than honey and the honeycomb. ¹¹ Moreover by them is Thy servant is warned: and in keeping of them there is great reward" (Psalm 19:7-11 KJV).

The Shamir is a picture of the Order of Melchizedek being a manifestation of God's Word. Even the word "order' in the Order of Melchizedek speaks of this reality. The new heart that He puts within kings and priests is a heart of flesh connected to the kingdoms of our God.

Scientists have also proven that the original corruptible seed from your human parents goes into forming a person's heart. Therefore, when God gives you a new heart, He changes the record of your DNA, which is a different genealogy altogether - the DNA of God: *"For this Melchizedek, king of Salem, priest of the Most High God, who met Abraham returning from the slaughter of the kings and blessed him. ² To whom also Abraham gave a tenth part of all, first being translated "king of righteousness," and then also king of Salem, meaning "king of peace," ³ without father, without mother, without genealogy, having neither beginning of days nor end of life, but made like the Son of God, remains a priest continually" (Hebrews 7:1-3 NKJV)*. There will be a day when we forsake all of our earthly genealogy to engage in the heavenly genealogy of Christ. Always remember, we can only be joined to Him if we carry His likeness and DNA. The word "joined" in Scripture comes from the same word for when a man and woman become intimate. Seed means DNA; therefore, when God says that the Shamir Stone is the Seed DNA of the Living Creature, He is telling us a kingdom mystery. The incorruptible seed from His Sapphire Throne will transform your DNA into the very DNA of God where time and space does not constrain. When the One New Man in the Messiah who is a New Living Creature sprouts and grows into the fullness of their incorruptible seed, they will have the full authority and power of the Most High God literally living within them.

Remember how the Shamir can possibly be connected to alpha radiation? Alpha radiation involves both strong and electro-magnetic forces. The Spirit of the Living Creature is in their whirling wheels. These wheels within wheels and the wings of the Living Creature are connected to its heart. The wings of the Father's heart wants to wrap around your eyes, so you can realize your reality. This is a window of His Spirit to see how His heart moves.

When the heart of those in the Order of Melchizedek are set fully on the Father's heart and doing His perfect will, we will see the greatest power source on earth where we will never ever run out of energy. Who would have thought, like in the movie *The Matrix*, that human bodies would be used as power sources? Behold, a new thing -- cardioelectromagnetic induction.

When those made after the Order of Melchizedek truly know the width, length, depth, and height of our calling by fully and completely manifesting the love of Christ, we will actually become our world's ultimate power source.

5 – CUBES OF SAPPHIRES

Keep the Living Creature full of eyes in mind where divine sight increases in those made after the Order of Melchizedek as well as the Shamir Stone being the seed DNA of the Living Creature, as we gaze deeper into the Cubes of Sapphire.

The Shamir Stone is a chip off an old block. If you recall, the LORD showed me that a barley-corn or grain-sized fragment came from the intersection of His Sapphire Throne and the Sapphire Sea when a Cube of Sapphire was taken from the lower left-hand side of the throne, which would be on our right side if we are facing this throne. There was one Cube of Sapphire that was cut out of the lower left-hand side of the Almighty's Throne, and one was cut out of the lower right-hand side. One sapphire cube represents the known universe and the other represents the unknown universe. One sapphire cube contains the commandments between people and God. The other contains the commandments between people and other people.

Hebrew history tells us that the Ten Commandments were written (engraved) on two cubes of sapphire stone. In Hebrew, they are called *Luchot ha-Berit*, which means "Cubes of the Covenant." *Midrash Lekakh* describes the sapphire on which the express image of the Ten Commandments was etched as being literally cut from YHVH's own throne.

We need to back up a little bit to understand the Ten Commandments through the eyes of a Hebrew, because that is the original context in which they were given, not to mention that some of them have been mistranslated in most Christian circles. Pay especial attention to the first four commandments, because they have been tweaked the most from their original meaning and context. According to the first occurrence of the Ten in Exodus 20:2-14, the text says the Ten Commandments are:

1. I am the Lord your God who brought you out of the land of Egypt, the house of bondage.
2. You shall have no other gods besides Me.
3. You shall not carry the Lord your God's name in vain.
4. Remember the Sabbath day to make it holy.
5. Honor your father and mother.
6. You shall not murder.
7. You shall not commit adultery.
8. You shall not steal.
9. You shall not bear false witness against your neighbor.
10. You shall not covet.

Notice that the FIRST COMMANDMENT to a Hebrew (one who has crossed over) is to have faith in God's existence. The first commandment appears to be more of a statement. Maybe that's why these words in Hebrew are called the Ten Statements – *Aseret ha-Dibrot* – instead of the Ten Commandments - *Aseret ha-Mitzvot*. God's people were taught that if they violated one of the first five commandments, they had sinned against God. These were the commandments engraved on the first Cube of Sapphire from which the Shamir Stone came. These are the commandments that represent the unknown universe of our infinite God. If a person violates the second five commandments, they have sinned against man. These are the commandments, which were engraved on the second Cube of Sapphire that represent the known universe.

Much of Christianity has split up the SECOND COMMANDMENT, and said that the first commandment is: *"You shall have no other gods before Me" (Exodus 20:3)*, and the second is: *"You shall not make yourself a carved image..." (Exodus 20:4-5)*. To a Hebrew, Exodus 20:3-6 delineates the second commandment, which has four separate negative injunctions against idolatry: *"³ You shall have no other gods before Me. ⁴ You shall not make for yourself a carved image—any likeness of anything that is in heaven above, or that is in the earth beneath, or that is in the water under the earth;⁵ you shall not bow down to them nor serve them. For I, the LORD your God, am a jealous God, visiting the iniquity of the fathers upon the children to the third and fourth generations of those who hate Me, ⁶ but showing mercy to thousands, to those who love Me and keep My commandments" (Exodus 20:3-6 NKJV)*.

The THIRD COMMANDMENT has been typically mistranslated too. Most English translations state: *"You shall not take the Lord your God's name in vain."* Many people think this means that you have to write God as G-D, or that it is blasphemous to say words, like "goddamn." Even though these applications may apply, the correct translation of the original Hebrew *Lo tissa et shem Ha-Shem Eloheikha la-shav*, which is *"You shall not carry [God's Name in vain]"*; in other words, don't use God as your justification for selfish causes. The third commandment is the only one with which God says: *"for the Lord God will not absolve (forgive) him who carries His name in vain" (Exodus 20:6-7)*.

The seven Noahic Commandments, which are believed to have been given to Adam and all his descendants, includes a commandment against blasphemy. To a Hebrew, *"You shall not blaspheme God's Name"* means:

[1] To believe that God is one (Genesis 2:16).

[2] No blasphemy (Genesis 2:16).

[3] No consulting divination (Deuteronomy 18:10).

[4] No astrology (Deuteronomy 18:10).

[5] No interpreting omens (Deuteronomy 18:10).

[6] No witchcraft (Deuteronomy 18:10).

[7] No conjuration (Deuteronomy 18:10).

[8] No necromancy (Deuteronomy 18:10).

[9] No consulting mediums (Deuteronomy 18:10).

[10] To honor one's father and mother (Genesis 9:22-23).

The FOURTH COMMANDMENT – *"Remember the Sabbath day to make it holy"* – also suffers from its share of misunderstandings. From forgetting that the important goal of the Sabbath is rest to saying we can make the Sabbath any day we want it to be, I believe that most of God's people are missing the mark for this commandment. I am not into legalism. In fact, I have a very liberal interpretation about what "rest" really is. I seek Him constantly about the Sabbath, and I set my heart to be led of the Spirit. Living in the state of Eternal or Resurrection Life here on earth, as it is in heaven, requires kings and priests of the Most High God to resonate at the vibrational frequency of the Living Word. The Bride of Christ WILL resonate at the frequency as the Bridegroom.

Making the Sabbath day holy seems to be one glaring breach in our Age-Old Living Word foundation. God rested on the seventh day of creation and sanctified it (i.e., called it holy). To twist the facts otherwise is to come into agreement that the word of the LORD does not endure forever, and we can do anything we want:

"¹³ If you turn away your foot from the Sabbath, From doing your pleasure on My holy day, And call the Sabbath a delight, The holy day of the LORD honorable, And shall honor Him, not doing your own ways, Nor finding your own pleasure, Nor speaking your own words, ¹⁴ Then you shall delight yourself in the LORD; And I will cause you to ride on the high hills of the earth, And feed you with the heritage of Jacob your father. The mouth of the LORD has spoken" (Isaiah 58:13-14 NKJV).

The FIFTH COMMANDMENT of honoring parents casts a revealing light on the significance God attaches to the honor He wants us to show our parents. When people honor their parents, God regards it as if they honor Him. Despite one's natural love for one's parents, they should be honored. The honor due to parents is like the first three commandments rendered unto God. We must acknowledge who our parents are, not do anything that might cause them disgrace, and serve unselfishly.

Man's relationship with God is the quintessential essence of the first Cube of Sapphire. The Second Cube of Sapphire refers to relationships among people. Most of the commandments that show us how to treat our fellow man are fairly intact.

Pacifists may not like the SIXTH COMMANDMENT, but it does not give us authority to change it. Most English translations say the sixth commandment is *"You shall not kill"* when the correct translation is *lo tirtzakh*, which is "You shall not murder." Self-defense is built into this definition.

The only other commandment on the second Cube of Sapphire related to man's relationships with man that appears to be tweaked a bit is the NINTH COMMANDMENT: *"You shall not bear false witness."* Not only is this the least remembered commandment, but it goes beyond perjury. It includes all forms of lying where one reports something other than what happened.

"[14] Blessed are those who do His commandments, that they may have the right to the tree of life, and may enter through the gates into the city. [15] But outside are dogs and sorcerers and sexually immoral and murderers and idolaters, and whoever loves and practices a lie" (Revelation 22:14-15 NKJV).

Of all 613 commandments, God selected Ten Commandments to present on two priceless objects cut from His own Sapphire Throne, which is synonymous with eternity. Not only were the first Ten Commandments engraved on a perfect cube, but they rested in a room that was a perfect cube as well. The measurements of the Holy of Holies were 10 cubits by 10 cubits by 10 cubits. It is said that when the Ark of the Covenant rested within, it took up no space whatsoever. When each end of the Ark was measured to its facing wall, it measured exactly 5 cubits. YHVH's perfect law and perfect presence resided within another worldly dimension of perfect, yet incomprehensible geometry. Sacred object was placed within sacred object, combining meaning and form.

While the word "tablet" is not necessarily an incorrect transliteration, it is less accurate because *Luchot ha-Berit* (Cubes of the Covenant) describes both dimension and volume while the term "tablet" does not.

Orthodox Judaism has always known the Ten Commandments were inscribed on cubes. Unfortunately, most of the world does not normally look to the Jews for Scriptural advice. The truth is that too many western people unconsciously draw this aspect of Bible history from Cecil B. Demille's Film: *The Ten Commandments*.

Exodus 32:16 says: "The cubes were Elohim's handiwork, and the script was the script of Elohim engraved within the cubes." The rabbis say that these were perfect cubes with sharp corners and words bored fully through the stone, rather than carved on the surface. *"They were inscribed on one side and the other" (Exodus 32:15b)*. It is said that the words did not appear on the other side in reverse, but could be read normally. Furthermore, the inner parts of letters, surrounded by complete joints, stayed in their exact position without any visible support.

It was also said that the Cubes of Sapphire carried their own weight enabling Moses the ability to carry them down the mountain: *"Moshe turned and descended from the mountain, with two tablets of the testimony in his hands" (Exodus 32:15a)*.

When Moses came down Mount Sinai, we are told that he did not know that the skin of his face shone due to his speaking with YHVH: *"It came about when Moshe was coming down from Mount Sinai (and the two cubes of the testimony were in Moshe's hand as he was coming down from the mountain), that Moshe did not know that the skin of his face shone because of his speaking with Him (YHVH)" (Exodus 34:29)*. The light that radiated from Moses' face would send a strong beam of light into the sky, and when Moses held one cube aloft, it caused the commandments to appear overhead.

After Israel had sinned with the worship of the Golden Calf, the shattered pieces of the original cubes were carefully gathered and placed within the Ark along with the intact set of Sapphire Tablets that Moses had to carve himself: *"YHVH said to Moshe, 'Carve for yourself two stone cubes like the first ones, and I shall inscribe on the tablets the words that were on the first cubes, which you shattered'" (Exodus 34:1)*. These shattered pieces are called *Shivrai Luchot*, which means "the remnant of the cubes (tablets)."

The LORD showed me that when the second Tablets of Sapphire were cut, Moses cut them with the Shamir Stone, which was given to him by YHVH. We also know that Moses must have kept the Shamir Stone, because that's how he engraved the precious stones on the High Priest's Breastplate. Please recall that Moses first wrote the twelve tribal names in Hebrew with ink; and then, held the Shamir over them. This miraculously caused the letters written in ink to sink into the stones like the branding of a branding iron. Exodus 28:20 indicates that the precious stones must be set into their gold settings while yet "in their fullness." There was nothing lacking from their original substance: *"Till we all come in the unity of the faith, and of the knowledge of the Son of God, unto a perfect man, unto the measure of the stature of the FULLNESS OF CHRIST" (Ephesians 4:13 KJV).*

Also, recall that the only thing allowed to perfect the stones and other materials in Solomon's Temple was the Shamir Stone.

You mean to tell me that the kings and priests of the Order of Melchizedek have a specific function related to the Shamir Stone? Yes! The Shamir, which is the seed DNA of the New Living Creature of the Order of Melchizedek, is meant to build God's permanent dwelling place. In this Kingdom Day, it's the New Jerusalem (Revelation 21:2-3).

The Shamir is connected to the Chief Cornerstone Yeshua Ha Machiach (Jesus Christ) the High Priest of the Order of Melchizedek. In their fullness, His Melchizedek Company perfectly reflect Him: *"the shining splendor of His glory, and the express image of His essence... Upholding all things by the word of His power" (Hebrews 1:3).*

What's interesting is that on the same day that I heard: "The Shamir is a chip off the Old Block" as well as seeing one Sapphire Cube was cut from His Sapphire Throne where it was connected to the Sapphire Sea, I saw in the spirit the remnants of the Sapphire Cube coming together.

"Upholding all things by the word of His power" is connected to the remnants of His Cubes of Sapphire coming back together. *"And the dragon was wroth with the woman, and went to make war with the remnant of her SEED, which KEEP THE COMMANDMENTS OF GOD, and have the testimony of Jesus Christ" (Revelation 12:17 KJV).*

The Shamir was said to have lost its potency by the time of the destruction of Solomon's Temple at the hands of the Babylonians (Nebuchadnezzar 586 BC). When the golden head of Daniel 2 destroyed Solomon's Temple, the potency of the Shamir and the Shamir itself was lost.

We must understand how the Shamir was lost in order to restore its heavenly reality in our day as well as the heavenly Sapphire Cubes from which it was taken. To bring back the Shamir and put the Sapphire Cubes back together again within you and I requires us to conquer Babylon within. Conquering your Babylonian kings will cause the Seed DNA of the Living Creature (i.e., the Shamir) to become supernaturally active again.

When I saw in the spirit His Sapphire Cubes coming back together again, I knew it's related to dethroning Babylonian Kings in our lives. By the way, the root of the worship of the Golden Calf goes all the way back to Babylon and the image used to depict the great Chaldean god – Saturn. Besides a Golden Calf with its connection to our modern-day Christmas, another predominant image for Saturn is get this... a black cube.

Before the Great Flood, Saturn was regarded by all mankind as the supreme god and ruler of kings. Most people don't know that the planet Saturn is very important in world affairs and theology today. I highly suggest that you do your own research in to the black cube of Saturn.

By the way, I have gone into greater depths about the Black Cube in my MEL GEL #11 Class entitled *A Tale of Three Cubes* => https://www.youtube.com/watch?v=U4PD9_F2xvI. My teaching notes for this class are available in the *MEL GEL Study Guide: Volume 2* => https://www.amazon.com/dp/0998598232/.

*****

6 – BONE OF MY BONE. FLESH OF MY FLESH.

A huge key to accessing the kingdoms of God is to set your desire. From the depths, I cried: "I want to know all there is to know about the Cubes of Sapphire and the Shamir Stone." Yeshua asked me: "For what purpose?" I responded: "To know it for myself to rightly relate to You and to teach others these truths."

Listen to this divine encounter of the supernatural kind and make it personal for yourself. When the blood of Yeshua comes up, please think of the DNA of God and the pure light that it carries:

On October 26, 2014, Yeshua was pleased that I had asked to know all there is to know about the Cubes of Sapphire and the Shamir Stone, and I wanted to share it with others. I first saw Yeshua's right hand extended. Levitating above it was a small Sapphire Cube. Yeshua said: "See this Sapphire Cube? All dimensions?" The vibrant blue cube turned and rotated both horizontally and vertically, so I could see all sides.

Then my spiritual sight zoomed into the center of the Sapphire Cube. I was there. It was pure white light in the midst. The cube's energy came from the center.

I then saw Yeshua close His eyes. He took the Sapphire Cube and put it into His heart. I was overwhelmed with the love I felt. Then Yeshua reached into His heart and pulled out a bloody Sapphire Cube and extended it to me. I was literally shaken to the core. This Sapphire Gift was wrapped in Yeshua's own blood.

I heard its frequency and somehow understood that it's the key to all life and a part of His heart.

Yeshua urged me to do the same, so I took the blood-covered Sapphire Cube and put it within my heart too, except here it stayed. There was a weightiness to it. It was holy. I looked up and He was so very near and dear. Yeshua placed His right hand over my chest where the Sapphire Cube was inserted. He said: "BONE OF MY BONE. FLESH OF MY FLESH." Something kicked on inside of me like a jolt. Something had been activated.

I saw inside myself. The Sapphire Cube was rotating and turning inside of me. Yeshua told me: "This is key to living and moving and having your being in Me. You are My chip off the Old Block... A chip from My very Sapphire Throne. Come. Let's explore life and the universe together." With a blur, we took off in the Spirit flying through outer space at the speed of light.

We arrived at a white marbled hall with sentries that led to one of His Throne Rooms. I had been here before. As we walked, I thought about how I'm not dressed for this. Instantly, He read my thoughts and clothed me with a royal gown and a queenly crown.

When we entered the throne room, there was only one small child there – a little girl. I picked her up tenderly and placed her on my lap, as Yeshua and I sat on our thrones. I was situated to His left. Yeshua leaned over and remarked: "You must be able to stop for the one in order to rule many."

With the little heartbroken girl on my lap and me by Yeshua's side, the doors opened up and a great crowd filled the room. As we watched the crowd getting settled, Yeshua turned to me and the little girl. He winked and nodded His head as if to say: "Watch this."

The first person on the agenda came forward. It was a poor elderly man in disheveled clothes. This humble man bowed with his hat in hand. Yeshua asked: "What can I do for My good man?" The elderly man was hesitant to ask. Before he could get a word out, Yeshua read his mind and grants him his heart's desire. The man was made new and forever young. The man was tickled, so tickled that his legs started to lift. He couldn't help himself. He did a dance of joy, some sort of gig.

The little girl with a front-row seat came alive with sparkles in her eyes. She no longer felt dejected. She giggled, and I gave her a huge hug. She smiled at me and gave me a big hug back. It's PURE LOVE in that Sapphire Cube!!!

His Presence lingered when I thought that this divine encounter is done. Yeshua asked: "Do you want more?" Do I ever!

In Yeshua's hand was the barley grain-sized sapphire chip called the Shamir. He instructed me to open my mouth. In the spirit, I saw Him place the Shamir on the center of my tongue. It shone as bright as the heavens.

The Shamir dissolved on my tongue. It then became part of me, as it flows throughout my body in my blood stream. The influence of this seed of the Living Creature seems to make manifest the words: "Let there be light." I could see various parts of my body being turned on: more light and more light and more light... I saw the Shamir make multiple circuits through my body.

It felt like when He said: "Bone of My Bone. Flesh of My flesh" after the blood wrapped Sapphire Cube was inserted into my chest.

He whispers: "Let there be light!" I understood these two gifts – His Sapphire Cube and Shamir Stone – enables me to be His Shining One!

This divine encounter has been confirmed by Ian Clayton. I highly recommend that you order his Ketubah (Marriage Contract) MP3. Ian speaks of how the children of Israel literally saw thunder and lightning. Saw thunder?! When you understand that "thunder" in a Hebraic way, it means "a glorified voice in fire" while lightning means "speaking." This speaking glorified voice in fire was basically saying: Will you marry Me? This message was repeated exactly 400 years later in an Upper Room on the day of Pentecost (Shavuot). The room shook like Sinai, a cloud came in, and upon their heads were tongues of fire. After Yeshua ascended like Moses had ascended, these tongues of fire on their heads were saying the same thing: "Will you marry Me? Will you have Me and hold Me? Will you be faithful to Me and never ever let Me go?

The Ten Commandments were given on the mountain of God. The Church says they are commandments. I agree with Ian. He calls them a marriage contract – Ketubah. The Ten Sayings of the Father that were etched in the Cubes of Sapphire came from God's own heart and has been bought for us by Yeshua's Blood. A Hebrew Marriage Contract requires two people to come into agreement. The Father has written and given his side of the Marriage Contract. Now it's your turn to put His blood-bought Sapphire Cube in your heart, and the Shamir - Seed DNA of the Living Stones - in your mouth.

Ian took the Ten Commandments and blended his part together with it. For example, when the Lord says I don't want you to have any other gods. He responded: I want You for my lover, my friend. I want to know You. I want my soul entwined (knit) with you. When we engage with I AM THAT I AM and go as far as writing out your side of a marriage contract with Him by stating your expectations, He tabernacles over us. He changes our DNA, so we can become His

Children of Light. He is a God of PURE LIGHT. Let there be light!!!!!!!

*****

7 – TWILIGHT AND SABBATH

Remember how Jewish Tradition claims that the Shamir Stone was created at twilight of the first Sabbath – the seventh day of creation?

Prophetically speaking that's a bull's eye! TWILIGHT and SABBATH speaks of many kingdom truths of the New Living Creature of the One New Man in the Messiah.

Within the concepts of "twilight" and "Seventh Day Sabbath" are specific keys to unlocking the Seed DNA of the Order of Melchizedek. The Seed DNA of the Living Creature, or in other words the Shamir Stone, has a supernatural essence that was said to be created at twilight the first Sabbath. Please recall that prophetically speaking we are currently in twilight of His Seventh Day on God's Calendar - "after the sixth day."

The Songs of the Sabbath in God's Temple are connected to Melchizedek – those made after the Order of Melchizedek. The *Dead Sea Scrolls* tell us that the songs of the seventh day sacrifice are related to Melchizedek. The twelfth song of the CHERUBIM (Cherubim, Living Creature and the Order of Melchizedek can be synonymous) was said to be almost indistinguishable from the wheels (full of eyes) of God's Chariot Throne. The Sabbath Songs include priestly and princely cherubim praise of the Divine King as well as praise issuing forth from the walls of His Temple and His vestibule. The vestibule is a passage between an outer door and an interior building. It's a crossover place. It's a connection between heaven and earth.

The seventh day Order of Melchizedek sacrifices are us becoming a continual living sacrifice (a burnt offering or offering by fire). We become one with the All-Consuming Fire on the throne. Please refer to the *Hitting the Bull's Eye of Righteousness* book.

The Baptism of Fire we each will have to go through will ultimately and eventually create certain frequencies or songs where the Bride will resonate at the same frequency as her Bridegroom. Mature sons of the Order of Melchizedek build God's Temple while HIS BRIDE IS HIS DWELLING PLACE – His permanent habitation. Won't you marry Him?!

In my second *Melchizedek Arising YouTube* video, I mention that the restoration of the ten shadow strands of DNA is connected to the ten Copper Chariot Lavers in Solomon's Temple where the bloody Burnt Offerings were washed – washed with His Word (Ephesians 5:26) and the regeneration of His Spirit (Titus 3:5) after being slaughtered. This is the actualized state of a Continual Living Sacrifice. The fifth chapter "DNA Restoration of Christ's Body" in the *Blazing New Wine of Hanukkah: Bridal Restoration of DNA* book goes into much more detail.

A shadow always resembles its substance. Always. And every seed brings forth after its kind. So does the seed DNA of the Living Creature. His mobile chariot throne - *Merkabah* - His Sapphire Throne makes us into the express image of our brilliant invisible God. Let His sapphire chip off the Old Ancient of Days' Block form your image.

The word "shadow" in Hebrew of *tsale*. It means shade, or figuratively it means defense. It comes from a primary root *tsaw-lal'*, which carries the idea of hovering over or to shade as TWILIGHT. When God created man in His own image, the word "image" is the Hebrew word *tzelem*, which is derived from *tzel* meaning a shadow.

Have a closer look *at Colossians 2:17 "a shadow of things to come; but the body is of Christ."* The fullness of the Mature Body of Christ will literally be His perfect shadow. We will manifest the perfect character of Christ - His express image - which is the express image of the High Priest after the Order of Melchizedek and the Father (for they are one). And this infinite minuteness of sapphire – the seed DNA of the Living Creature (the Shamir Stone) – and the Marriage Contract given through His Cubes of Sapphire appear to be mysterious catalysts to it all. This is the perfect work of His Sapphire Throne at the Quantum Level here on earth, as it is in heaven.

*****

UNDERSTANDING THE ORDER OF MELCHIZEDEK

Book 8

Blazing New Wine of Hanukkah:
Bridal Restoration of DNA

Cover Art: "Blazing New Wine of Hanukkah" by Robin Main

© November 1, 2014. All Rights Reserved

Text Copyright © 2014 Robin Main. All Rights Reserved

1 – BACKGROUND

Hanukkah is not one of the seven Feasts of the Lord specified in Leviticus 23, but it is one of the two winter feasts mentioned in the Bible. Hanukkah is mentioned in John 10:22-23 and Purim is the culmination of the Book of Esther. If we operate on the premise that all Scripture is inspired by God, we must contemplate why these feasts are in God's Word.

> "*16 All Scripture is inspired by God and profitable for teaching, for reproof, for correction, for training in righteousness;* *17 so that the man of God may be adequate, equipped for every good work*" (2 Timothy 3:16-17 NASB).

Just as Yeshua remained silent when He walked among His disciples on earth about the Gentiles joining the people of God in much greater numbers after His final ascension, so is the celebration of Biblical Feasts in this Kingdom Day. Ironically, the clearest case in the New Testament for celebrating the Lord's Biblical Feasts is presented in the chapter that many Christians have used as their excuse that they can celebrate anything they want, any way they want: "*16 Let no man therefore judge you in meat, or in drink, or in respect of a holy day, or of the new moon, or of the Sabbath days:* *17 Which are a shadow of things to come; but the body is of Christ" (Colossians 2:16-17 KJV)*.

Christians have long used *Colossians 2:16-17* to rationalize why we should no longer celebrate the Lord's Feasts; but in fact, this passage proves the opposite. The NASB version tells us: *"¹⁶ Therefore no one is to act as your judge in regard ... to a festival or a new moon or a Sabbath day things ¹⁷ which are a mere shadow of what is to come; but the substance belongs to Christ" (Colossians 2:16-17 NASB)*.

The very first point I'd like to emphasize is that YESHUA IS THE SUBSTANCE BEHIND ALL BIBLICAL FEASTS – *"the substance belongs to Christ."* His Spring Feasts (articulated in Leviticus 23) speak of His First Coming. His Fall Feasts speak of His Second Coming. The two winter feasts mentioned in God's Word – Hanukkah and Purim – portray God's people's journey to becoming His Bride.

"Just as the Spirit of the Living God has seven flows that manifests in nine fruits and gifts, so do the Feasts of the Lord." This is the one-liner that God gave me about the Feasts of the LORD in His Kingdom. If we take the whole council of His Word to heart, we see a mysterious kingdom that includes nine Bridal Feasts.

I understand the traditional view that Hanukkah and Purim are commemorative (i.e., rabbinical) celebrations, which is true. Some Christians even say that these feasts are exclusively for Jews. But I say, let's truly examine something that would cause us to walk in the same manner as Yeshua did. I believe that the manifested Word of God – Yeshua Himself – elevated Hanukkah and Purim when He celebrated both of these festivals in Spirit and in Truth. If we believe that the Word of God is eternal and Yeshua embodies its essence, we need to consider all the feasts that are in Scripture. Additionally, Yeshua did nothing but what He saw His Father doing, so not only did Yeshua put His stamp of approval on Hanukkah and Purim, but so did the Father.

Significantly, the number "nine" is the last of the unique digits; therefore, it marks an end or conclusion of a matter. E.W. Bullinger reveals in *Number in Scripture* that "nine" signifies the judgment of man and all his works. Recall that judgment has been committed to Yeshua as the "Son of Man," and judgment and righteousness are both the foundation and habitation of His Throne (Psalm 97:2). Not only is nine related to divine judgment, but with "nine" being the square of "three" (and three is the number for divine completion or divine perfection as well as the number particular to the Holy Spirit), "nine" denotes finality in divine things.

Notice that the nine "fruit of the spirit" flows out of the previous revelation about those things that will cause a person to NOT inherit the Kingdom of God:

> "*[19] Now the deeds of the flesh are evident, which are immorality, impurity, sensuality, [20] idolatry, sorcery, enmities, strife, jealousy, outbursts of anger, disputes, dissensions, factions, [21] envying, drunkenness, carousing, and things like these, of which I forewarn you, just as I forewarned you, that THOSE WHO PRACTICE SUCH THINGS WILL NOT INHERIT THE KINGDOM OF GOD. [22] BUT THE FRUIT OF THE SPIRIT IS LOVE, JOY, PEACE, PATIENCE, KINDNESS, GOODNESS, FAITHFULNESS, [23] GENTLENESS, SELF-CONTROL; against such things there is no law. [24] Now those who belong to Christ Jesus have crucified the flesh with its passions and desires. [25] If we live by the Spirit, let us also walk by the Spirit*" (Galatians 5:19-25 NASB).

The Lord has shown me that these kingdom fruits are only as abundant as our abiding in The Vine; and He conveniently has given us a list, so we can inspect the quality and quantity of our yieldedness that produces the fruit. Then we also have a list of the nine "Gifts of the Spirit" in 1 Corinthians 12:8-10 for the ONE BODY with many members. There are also nine plants in the garden of His Bride in Song of Songs 4:13-14.

God is currently speaking to me about how He is changing history through a shaking and a rumbling via the full council of the Word of God. Somehow the seven Feasts of the Lord becoming nine Bridal Feasts in this Kingdom Day is part of that. Just as our earth spins around its axis and the sun in a complete circle every year, so have all Biblical Feasts been created for His Bride to *chuwl* (spin), so His people can meet with Him at His designated time at His designated place, so His Bride can become married to Him. I just gave you the primitive root for the word "feasts" in 2 Chronicles 8:13. It's the same Hebrew word for when Adam intimately knew Eve - *ya'ad*. Do you want to be married to the King of Kings? If so, wouldn't you want to celebrate His feasts that will cause you to become betrothed to Him?

When we argue that we can celebrate a holiday (holy day or feast) any way we want, we have tapped into a portion of the truth. The next significant point is: WE ARE NOT TO JUDGE OTHERS ON HOW THEY CELEBRATE A BIBLICAL FESTIVAL, new moon or Sabbath day. Did you catch that? Paul is assuming that God's people are celebrating all three of these things that mark God's people's weeks, months and years according to His Word. By the way, that word "judge" in Colossians 2:16 means we are not to criticize, censure, condemn, or punish people on how they celebrate a Biblical festival. (Note: I am leaving out new moons and Sabbaths for simplicity's sake).

There are many people currently returning to the Lord's Age-Old Foundations, and there is so much hullaballoo about what is the right way to do this and that. Let's be perfectly clear. IT DOES NOT MATTER HOW YOU CELEBRATE A BIBLICAL FESTIVAL AS LONG AS YOU ARE ENDEAVORING TO FOLLOW HIS WORD BY HIS SPIRIT, because celebrations are all about worship. *"But an hour is coming, and now is, when the true worshipers will worship the Father in spirit and truth; for such people the Father seeks to be His worshipers" (John 4:23 NASB)*.

For example: Some people celebrate the Feast of Unleavened Bread by physically searching every nook and cranny of their house for yeast and throwing it all out. Others take this to mean that the Feast of Unleavened Bread is a time that God's Family searches every nook and cranny of their heart to get rid of all sin. I fall in the latter category, but I do not judge those who feel led to do otherwise. In fact, I even believe that each culture can, and will, bring their beautiful unique touches to each Biblical Feast. I have seen a tremendous amount of freedom within worshiping the Father in spirit and in truth context.

Know that there are only three Biblical Feasts that are called feasts forever: Passover, Pentecost and Tabernacles. Zechariah 14:16-17 tells us that in the Millennial Kingdom nations will not receive rain if they don't come up to Jerusalem to worship the King from year to year, and specifically keep the Feast of Tabernacles. By the way, we have now entered that time frame here on earth:

> "*¹⁶ And it shall come to pass, that every one that is left of all the nations which came against Jerusalem, shall even go up from year to year to worship the King, the LORD of hosts, and to keep the Feast of Tabernacles. ¹⁷ And it shall be, that whoso will not come up of all the families of the earth unto Jerusalem to worship the King, the LORD of hosts, even upon them shall be no rain*" (Zechariah 14: 16-17 KJV).

If we want to walk in the same manner as Yeshua did and resonate at the same frequency as the Word of God Himself, we need to consider if the fullness of the measure of the stature of the Messiah includes celebrating all the feasts that He did (1 John 2:6; Ephesians 4:13). If not one jot or tittle will pass away, we need to consider why these other feasts are in His Word and whether they are significant to Him. I feel a resounding "Yes!" in my heart, because I want to walk like Yeshua, talk like Yeshua, and be exactly like Yeshua... But, I also don't want to be caught up in an old form or legalism. IN THIS KINGDOM DAY, WE ARE NOT

NECESSARILY RETURNING TO THE FORMS OF WORSHIP, BUT THE SUBSTANCE.

Recall that Yeshua is the substance of all the Biblical Feasts. Consider this in regard to both His Head and His Body. God's people will literally embody the marks of time that the Lord Himself has put in place to set His people's years, months and weeks. We are told that these are "shadows of things to come." When God created man in His own image, the Hebrew word "*tzelem*" is used and is derived from "*tzel*," which means "shadow." Therefore, one of the interpretations of a "shadow of things to come" is the manifestation of Christ's Body coming into its fullness as a perfect One New Man in Christ (Ephesians 2:15; Ephesians 4:13).

"Let NO MAN therefore judge you ... In respect of a holy day... which are a shadow of things to come; but the BODY IS OF CHRIST" (Colossians 2:16-17 KJV). In NO MAN'S LAND, Crucified Ones will rightly judge - open the Door of Life - to His Biblical Feasts, so the Messiah's Body can connect to the mature Head who is the One casting the shadow. We must comprehend that a shadow always resembles its substance. When the Bible says it's a "shadow of things to come," it additionally means that we will be answering to the Creator who is casting the shadow.

So, no one is to act as your judge in regard to a festival. What matters is that we celebrate Him with a sincere heart. In the Kingdom of God, we all must respect the rights of each individual to be led by the Spirit. However, the Lord says, We *"have been called unto liberty, only use not this liberty for an occasion to the flesh, but by love serve one another" (Galatians 5:13 KJV).*

That brings us to our next significant point: THERE IS NO MIXTURE IN GOD'S APPOINTED TIMES AND FEASTS CELEBRATED IN HIS KINGDOM. The Lord will have us redeem things that have a righteous real to them. For instance, things that He has created like light, sound, colors, etc. But know this: The

Lord does not redeem things that are demonic in origin and pagan at their roots. He judges them.

The passage directly after Colossians 2:16-17 speaks to our current situation in the Christian Church in regard to the holidays that we have assimilated which have mixture in them, like Christmas and Easter (Colossians 2:18-23):

> "*[16] Therefore no one is to act as your judge in regard to food or drink or in respect to a festival or a new moon or a Sabbath day – [17] things which are a mere shadow of what is to come; but the substance belongs to Christ. [18] Let no one keep defrauding you of your prize by delighting in self-abasement and the worship of the angels, taking his stand on visions he has seen, inflated without cause by his fleshly mind, [19] and not holding fast to the head, from whom the entire body, being supplied and held together by the joints and ligaments, grows with a growth which is from God. [20] If you have died with Christ to the elementary principles of the world, why, as if you were living in the world, do you submit yourself to decrees, such as, [21] 'Do not handle, do not taste, do not touch it!' [22] (which all refer to things destined to perish with use) – in accordance with the commandments and teachings of men? [23] These are matters which have, to be sure, the appearance of wisdom in self-made religion and self-abasement and severe treatment of the body, but are of no value against fleshly indulgence" (Colossians 2:16-23 NASB).*

Celebrating Biblical Feasts is all about rewards and qualifying to be part of His Pure and Spotless Bride. It is not about salvation, which is solely through faith by grace. In NO MAN'S LAND, Crucified Ones will not allow themselves to be diverted, deceived, or beguiled from receiving their eternal rewards to the satisfaction of the flesh. By the way, NO MAN'S LAND is the space and place where people daily yield to the crucifixion process, which is a personalized Baptism of Fire directed by the loving and gracious Spirit of the Living God. Walking in the same manner as Jesus in being crucified in union with Christ will enable our Kingdom of Self to disappear and the Kingdom of God to appear within ourselves; and then, unfold without to the whole wide world.

I can go line-upon-line speaking for days to show you how Colossians 2:18-23 speaks about the mixture involved in the big yearly worship celebrations of the Christian Church - Christmas and Easter - but I don't have the time or space here. I wrote about all this in extreme detail in my book *SANTA-TIZING: What's wrong with Christmas and how to clean it up* => https://www.amazon.com/SANTA-TIZING-Whats-wrong-Christmas-clean/dp/1607911159/. Frankly, all you need to do is lay down Easter and Christmas on His Altar, and simply ask Him: "Can I receive my eternal reward of being part of Your Pure and Spotless Bride, if I celebrate Christmas and Easter?" Then be quiet and listen; and make sure that you are truly hearing Him, not the idols of your heart.

*****

2 – INTRODUCTION

Did you know that the story of Hanukkah begins in the Book of Daniel 300 years before the event took place? In fact, we did not have the markers on the calendar to be able to calculate the fulfillment of the Antichrist being revealed until both Purim and Hanukkah were put in place.

Did you know that historically the first Hanukkah highlights Judah the Maccabee and his band of faithful men? Had this small ragtag remnant not taken their courageous stand against the Antichrist of their day and had they not overcome overwhelming odds to save their culture and religion from utter annihilation, both Judaism and Christianity most likely would not exist today.

Did you know Yeshua Himself attaches a prophetic significance to the Feast of Dedication (i.e., Hanukkah) by telling us that the first Abomination of Desolation (Antichrist) is a prophetic foreshadow of an even greater abomination that confronts the believer in the last days?

Did you know that during Hanukkah Yeshua came to Jerusalem (at the risk of His own life) to meet with believers and to perform a miracle that proved He is the Messiah?

Did you know that Yeshua declared twice during Hanukkah: "I am the Light of the World?" Which gives us a clue for those who are literally manifesting more and more being *"the light of the world"* *(Matthew 5:14).*

Did you know that the Feast of Dedication (Hanukkah) is a prophetic picture of His Church becoming His Bride? Hanukkah's restoration of the burnt sacrifices and the five battles that the Maccabees fought are literally pictures for the bridal restoration of man's DNA into the very DNA of God, so we can be His Shining Ones again as it was in the Garden before the Fall.

Within the Feast of Dedication (Hanukkah), several profound mysteries of Christ and His Kingdom are hidden that are connected to His most precious possession - His Bride. Within are buried keys to the bridal restoration of our 10 Shadow Strands of DNA, the greater works of God being manifest through the One New Man in the Messiah, and the ability for His set apart ones to discern the wicked one (i.e., Antichrist). We can also see how the battles connected to Hanukkah depict His people's journey to become Christ's Bride.

Had Judah the Maccabee and his band of faith-filled men not taken their stand against pagan sun god worship and the Antichrist of their day, both Judaism and Christianity most likely would not exist today. Had this small rag tag remnant not overcome overwhelming odds to save their culture and religion from utter annihilation, God's Kingdom on earth most likely would have been wiped out. Today, we are at another world dominating crossroads when another Antichrist is rising. An uncompromising tribe of people - a radical remnant - will fight for His Truth and His Kingdom to come here on earth, as it is in heaven.

Who would have guessed that one short and sweet reference to Yeshua's celebration of Hanukkah in John 10:22-23 is a major key to so many kingdom mysteries? Actually, there's a major chunk of Scripture where Yeshua is at the Feast of Dedication - John 8:12 to John 10:39. Most ancient texts put the passage about the woman caught in the act of adultery during the Feast of Tabernacles (John 8:1-11). We also have two fairly accurate historical books to go by: First and Second Maccabees in the *Apocrypha*.

The events surrounding the first Hanukkah as well as Yeshua's celebration of Hanukkah in Scripture foreshadow the pouring out of a blazing new wine in our day. So, let the coals of fire from the blazing new wine of Hanukkah go forth from YHVH and be scattered upon your earth and mine. Let His judgments be executed, so we will know "I AM." Don't forget that the Ancient Hebrew Word Picture for the word "judge" communicates that the Judge is the Door of Life - Yeshua. Jesus only judges anything that is in the way of love, life and light:

- *"² O LORD, I have heard Thy speech, and was afraid: O LORD, revive Thy work in the midst of the years, in the midst of the years make known; in wrath remember mercy. ³ God came from Teman, and the Holy One from Mount Paran. Selah. His glory covered the heavens, and the earth was full of His praise. ⁴ And His brightness was as the light; He had horns coming out of His hand: and there was the hiding of His power. ⁵ Before Him went the pestilence, and burning coals went forth at His feet. ⁶ He stood, and measured the earth: He beheld, and drove asunder the nations; and the everlasting mountains were scattered, the perpetual hills did bow: His ways are everlasting"* (Habakkuk 3:2-6 KJV).

- *"⁸ Then the earth shook and trembled; the foundations of heaven moved and shook, because He was wroth. ⁹ There went up a smoke out of His nostrils, and fire out of His mouth devoured: coals were kindled by it. ¹⁰ He bowed the heavens also, and came down; and darkness was under His feet.* [11] *And He rode upon a cherub and did fly: and He was seen upon the wings of the wind"* (II Samuel 22:8-11 KJV).

The cherub or cherubim that God is riding upon this Kingdom Day is made up of wings of God's end-time Melchizedek Army who fly by the Spirit of the Living God together. These kings and priests of the Most High God are a New Living Creature. They are returning to their primordial state where Adam and Eve lived and moved and had their being before the Fall, except better. They will have been redeemed. In their fullness, they will be a Full Age or Mature One New Man in Christ being complete morally, complete emotionally, complete mentally, complete in labor and complete in growth. Please refer to the *Formation of the New Living Creature* book or *YouTube* video https://www.youtube.com/watch?v=1BElDZaaFqo&t=1s for more information on the Second Samuel 22:11 "cherub" or "cherubim." For more about the Mature One New Man in Christ, check out Chapter 5 "Metatron" in the MEL GEL Study Guide => => https://www.amazon.com/dp/0578188538/.

Know that His coals of fire are His coals of love: *"Set me as a seal upon thine heart, as a seal upon thine arm: for love is strong as death; jealousy is cruel as the grave: the coals thereof are coals of fire, which hath a most vehement flame"* (Song of Songs 8:6 KJV). Also, know that the coals of fire from the blazing new wine of Hanukkah have been created by Him: *"Behold, I have created the smith that blows the coals of fire"* (Isaiah 54:16). Additionally, within the fire of discipline are the embers of restoration. There was a fire of coals at both Peter's denial and his restoration (John 18:17-18; 21:9). Please note that His judgments are disciplines until His final judgment.

Hear He… Hear He… Hear He… Yeshua is even now gathering set apart hearts that have been washed by His blood. He is carrying willing hearts to His Great Feasts of Love, which are His Biblical Feasts. Here's the catch. It's for willing hearts only. Will you forsake all, but Him?

During Hanukkah, Yeshua risked life and limb to go up to Jerusalem to celebrate this particular feast with believers. Why? Why did Yeshua choose Hanukkah as the time to break every man-made tradition (i.e., law) that could apply when He healed a man born blind? Why did He choose Hanukkah to fulfill perhaps the truest sign that He was the Messiah?

*****

3 – HEALING A MAN BORN BLIND

Today, in a sense, almost all Jews and Christians have been born blind. We have inherited lies and have taught them to our children.

In regard to Hanukkah, Jewish people tell about the miracle of the oil lasting eight days. There is nothing spoken of this miracle for hundreds of years; then all of a sudden, it crops up in Rabbinic Literature. We also have the dreidel game that spells out "a great miracle happened there" or "a great miracle happened here" (if you are in Jerusalem). The four Hebrew letters on the dreidel (*noon, hey, gimel,* and *sheen*) come from the four popular elements of a popular German Beer Garden Spinning Top gambling game known as *drehem*. *Drehem* means to spin. The game of chance was "sanctified" by Rabbinic decree over a thousand years after the celebration of Hanukkah originated. It's meant to be days of rejoicing and rededication of the altar of our hearts to worship the One True God according to the Word of God.

Even though Jewish people have things to correct to come in line with His plumb line for Hanukkah, today, most Christians are grievously doing what the first Antichrist did and calling it true worship. Our next chapter tells the true-to-life tale of the first Hanukkah. It reveals the story of how the first Antichrist set up a statue of a pagan sun god in God's Temple to be worshiped; and then, Antiochus Epiphanes IV sacrificed the most profane thing he could think of as an insult to the Hebrew God - a pig on His Altar. Too many Christians have lost track of the fact that throughout antiquity all the pagan sun gods had their birthdays celebrated on the ancient winter solstice – December 25. It was no coincidence that the day Antiochus sacrificed a pig and put a statue on the Temple Mount was the 15th of Kislev, which happened to be December 25th that year.

We will go into more detail about Hanukkah's history soon. For now, let's look at John Chapter 9 and the miracle Yeshua performed that proved to everyone, including the Scribes and Pharisees, that He is the Messiah.

Yeshua passed by and saw His divine appointment – a man born blind. This day that year just happened to be the first day of Hanukkah. How do we know? Because we know Yeshua is in Jerusalem. It's Hanukkah, and it's the Sabbath. That year Hanukkah began at sundown on the Sabbath the 25th day of the month of Kislev. Yeshua tells us that the reason this man was born blind was so the power of God would be manifest (John 9:3). All of our frailties and imperfections are for the purpose of the Almighty's power being made known in our lives.

After Yeshua declares: *"I must work the works of Him that sent Me, while it is day: the night comes, when no man can work. As long as I am in the world, I am the light of the world" (John 9:4-5)*, He spits on the ground, mixes it up, and puts the wet clay on the man's eyes. Then Yeshua tells the man to *"go, wash in the Pool of Siloam" (John 9:7)*. Notice that the man immediately obeys. He then comes back from the Sent One Pool screaming with utter delight. Wouldn't you, if it was the first time that you ever seen?!

What's so significant about this is that Isaiah had prophesied that when the True Messiah comes, He will do a miracle that no other man had done before. The Messiah will open the eyes of one born blind. So, Yeshua goes up to Jerusalem under the threat of death by the religious leaders, and gives them clear proof that He is the Messiah. He not only does a creative miracle in restoring this guy's sight, but Yeshua breaks as many man-made (Rabbinic) rules as possible that could apply to this particular situation. Yeshua gets dirt. He spits in it. He makes mud. He has the blind gentleman put mud on his eyes. He then has the mud-caked miracle man walk more than a Sabbath's day journey. It's almost like Yeshua was saying to the religious establishment: I dare you to deny this clear proof that I AM THE MESSIAH, and by the way, here's what I think of your man-made laws too!

In this Kingdom Day, Yeshua will once again heal a man – a corporate One New Man of Jew and Gentile in the Messiah – that has been born blind, so *"the work of God should be manifest in him" (John 9:3)*. The purpose of this book is to see how this work of God is related to His Feast called Hanukkah. By the way, Hanukkah means dedication.

By Yeshua being in Jerusalem during Hanukkah and celebrating it, we know that this Biblical Feast will always have a prophetic significance. No one should doubt that some great miracles happened during Hanukkah. It's just that these great miracles have to do with a man born blind seeing as well as a small ragtag remnant standing up against a world dominating force and overcoming overwhelming odds to cleanse God's Temple and re-dedicate His Altar. Yeshua going up to celebrate Hanukkah is very momentous, because He was making a statement against the same pagan sun god worship that the Maccabees overthrew.

In Christian literature, I've repeatedly read that Hanukkah has nothing to do with Christmas, but that is simply not the case. Hanukkah is all about overthrowing a polluted sacrificial service instituted in God's Temple that centers around sun god worship, which is essentially Christmas. As mentioned previously, throughout antiquity all pagan sun gods' birthdays have been celebrated on the ancient winter solstice – 25th of December. This is the exact day (also the 15th of Kislev in 168 BC) that a statue of the Greek sun god Jupiter was erected upon the Altar in Jerusalem defiling it; then beginning with 25th of Kislev that year (168 BC) hogs were offered upon God's Altar to a pagan deity. Pay attention to God's Altar for this is where the battle for purity was, and still is, ultimately fought. Even the name "Hanukkah" is directly related to the dedication (i.e., Hanukkah) of the Altar.

On the ancient Babylonian Calendar, the winter solstice was December 25th. This is when little baby Tammuz was born who was said to be Nimrod reincarnated after he was killed. Nimrod's wife – Semiramis – told all her subjects that Nimrod had ascended into heaven and became the sun god, and she had become pregnant by the rays of the sun. After the confusion of the languages at the Tower of Babel (due to Nimrod's and his follower's rebellion against God), all the Babylonian sun god worship was spread throughout the whole earth.

We do not have the time or space in this book to go over all these details. I've studied this subject extensively (full-time for over 10 years) after Yeshua epiphaneously came to me three times telling me: "The mixture of Christmas grieves My heart. Come out of Babylon, and lay down Christmas, for I *will* have a pure and spotless Bride" as well as "Christmas will be the Golden Calf of America." My book *SANTA-TIZING: What's wrong with Christmas and how to clean it up* is available on Amazon, if you are interested in knowing more about sun god worship => https://www.amazon.com/SANTA-TIZING-Whats-wrong-Christmas-clean/dp/1607911159/.

I will leave you with four points about Christmas that most people have lost track of that are found in the *Catholic Encyclopedia*:

[1] The phrase "Christ's mass" (Christmas) is first found in the 11th century The *Catholic Encyclopedia* says 1038 AD. The root translation of the word "Christmas" is literally "Christ's dismissal" or "Christ is dismissed." The Middle English word "mass" came from the Greek word *mitere*, which means to send or dismiss. In the early days, the Eucharistic service was divided into two parts. Those receiving instruction (i.e., catechumens) were allowed to be there for the first part. Only the faithful (those who had been baptized) could remain for the second part. Thus, there were two dismissals that were pronounced in Latin *Ite misse est*, which meant: Go, you are dismissed. So "mass" or "*missa*" came to refer to dismissal. It's like calling a basketball game - The Buzzer. More Importantly, miracles, signs and wonders (works of power) were a common occurrence prior to pagan feasts becoming assimilated into the Church (See Ezekiel 8).

[2] Prior to the 11th century, Christmastime was associated with the winter solstice, midwinter, or winter revels. For simplicity sake, I just say "Christmas" instead of the winter solstice, because that's what our modern society understands it as being today.

[3] The first recorded evidence of a "Christian" Christmas taking place on December 25th isn't found until the time of Constantine in 336 AD.

[4] "Christmas" has many winter solstice predecessors, but two immediate predecessors:

1. Today's CHRISTMAS SEASON was formerly the mid-December to January 1st celebration of Saturalia in Rome (January Kalends are included for simplicity's sake). Saturnalia was the Roman worship of Saturn. Saturn also had another name – Apis – because the Egyptian Golden Calf was said to represent the divinity of the ancient Chaldean (Babylonian) god Saturn. This is the image that Aaron had in mind when he fashioned the Golden Calf, and it literally links our modern Christmas Season celebrations to the worship of the Golden Calf in Exodus 32.

2. Today's CHRISTMAS DAY was originally Mithra's Winter Festival celebrated on the ancient winter solstice – Dec 25. Mithra was one of the favorite sun gods adopted by Rome. Mithra was the Persian version of the original Babylonian sun god – Tammuz. The *Catholic Encyclopedia* credits Mithra's Winter Festival (i.e., The Nativity – or – The Nativity of The Sun – The Nativity of the Unconquered Sun) as claiming strong responsibility for the December 25th date for Christmas. In 379 AD, Church officials grabbed Mithra's Winter Solstice Festival, and by their man-made decree, they claimed to clean off all of its pagan residue.

Pay attention to the story of the First Hanukkah, because the first Antichrist mentioned in Scripture – Antiochus Epiphanes IV – also brought pagan sun god worship into God's Temple, and tried to replace true worship with it.

*****

4 – JOURNEY TO BECOME HIS BRIDE: HANUKKAH BATTLES

The year was 168 BC. The city was Jerusalem. Jupiter's Winter Festival was the occasion for the desecration of God's Altar, which happened to be both December 25 and the 15th day of Kislev. Some people say it was a statue of Zeus put on God's Altar. Some say it was Jupiter. In a sense, it really doesn't matter; because both were Greek sun gods. The Babylonian fingerprints of confusion and mixture are all over the different names given to the sun god after the dispersion from the Tower of Babel. Babylonian Tammuz has been touted as the first sun god. Ra was an Egyptian sun god. Mithra was a Persian sun god adopted by the Romans. Zeus was one of the Greek sun gods. Jupiter was another Greek sun god. When the Greeks under Antiochus Epiphanes IV set up the abomination of desolation in 168 BC, as foretold in the book of Daniel, all evening and morning sacrifices ceased:

> *"And forces shall be muster by him, and they shall defile the sanctuary fortress; then they shall take away the daily sacrifices, and the place there the abomination of desolation" (Daniel 11:31 NKJV).*

> *"And from the time that the daily sacrifice is taken away, and the abomination of desolation is set up, there shall be one thousand two hundred and ninety days" (Daniel 12:11 NKJV).*

As a believer in the Messiah Yeshua, you may be thinking why should I care and what does that have to do with me? Stay tuned, because Yeshua tells us that the first abomination of desolation who sat in the Temple was a prophetic foreshadow of an even greater abomination that confronts believers in the last days: *"[15] Therefore when you see the 'abomination of desolation,' spoken of by Daniel the prophet, standing in the holy place (whoever reads, let him understand), ... [21] For then there will be great tribulation, such as has not been since the beginning of the world until this time, no, nor ever shall be" (Matthew 24:15,21 NKJV).*

There can be multiple fulfillments of prophecies in Scripture, and this is definitely one of them. It is no coincidence that the fiery fulcrum of the first Hanukkah revolves around the abomination of desolation that was set up on God's Altar on the 25th of December.

Exactly three years to the day after Jupiter's statue was put upon God's Altar and a pig was sacrificed to him, the Maccabees rejoiced as they began the re-dedication of God's Altar in Jerusalem. Notice that the myth of the eight days miraculous supply of oil has been left out. It's all about the Altar. Things need to be restored and redeemed on both sides of the One New Man fence (Jew and Gentile). Why would the Rabbinical Judaism lie about the miraculous supply of oil during Hanukkah? Why would Institutional Christianity lie about the origins of Christmas? How many times have you heard that the roots of Christmas are in the worship of the Golden Calf and pagan sun gods? The ruling class in Israel tried to hide Yeshua's fulfillment of Hanukkah, just as Christianity has tried to hide the pagan origins of Christmas. To be fair, Catholicism has not hidden the pagan origins of Christmas; because of their laissez-faire (let them do as they will) attitude about mixture. The last act of the Sanhedrin before they disbanded and went into exile in 359 AD was calculating a different calendar that had never been in place ever before in the history of Israel. Please note that changing set-times (Biblical time-keeping) is one of the marks of an Antichrist: *"He will speak against the Most High and oppress His saints and try to change the set times and the laws" (Daniel 7:25).*

Let's dive a little deeper into the history of the first Hanukkah. Before the Roman Empire and the crucifixion of Christ, the Jewish people had experienced a man and a world-impacting movement who strove to change God's times and law. The Seleucid General named Antiochus Epiphanes IV. History infamously classifies him as an Antichrist. The world-impacting movement he promoted was called Hellenism. When Greek culture mixed with the culture of the Middle East, it created a hybrid called Hellenism whose influence on the Roman Empire, Christianity, and Western Civilization has been monumental.

When Alexander the Great overthrew Persia, Judea became subject to him. Alexander was a kind and generous ruler to the Jews. He canceled Jewish taxes during Sabbatical years, and even offered animals to be sacrificed on his behalf in the Temple. When Alexander died, in 323 BC, he had succeeded in conquering all the important lands around the eastern Mediterranean as well as having laid the foundation of a cultural revolution that would change the world forever. Prior to Alexander's program of cultural conquest, it was rare for any "ism" to exist, but after his world changing influence a people's descent and territory did not necessarily define their identity. People who were not Greeks by descent began to talk, dress, and live like Greeks in Greek-styled cities.

After Alexander the Great died, his kingdom was divided among his four generals. Judea, as usual, was caught in the middle. Eventually, Judea ended up in the Seleucid Dynasty in 199 BC with Antiochus IV. The ruling dynasty of Syria, the Seleucids, had Greek origins from the time of Alexander the Great.

As already mentioned, in 168 BC, the heathen (in this instance the Syrian Greeks) sacrificed a pig on God's Altar and put a sun god statue in God's sanctuary on December 25. A pig (as most people know) is the ultimate non-kosher animal, so this was not a compliment. It was a statement of utter contempt and degradation to the Jews and their God. An interesting aside, many ancient cultures offered a pig as a sacrifice once a year at a feast, and those pagan festivals mainly harmonize with today's Christmas celebrations.

Antiochus Epiphanes IV is rightly portrayed an Antichrist. Josephus tells us that he polluted the altar of God by offering up swine on it, knowing that this was against the Law of Moses. Antiochus forced God's people to bow before his pagan sun god under the penalty of death. Many innocent people were massacred. The survivors heavily taxed. The Book of Maccabees calls this period a "reign of terror." In keeping with Daniel 7:25, Antiochus IV, who took the name "God manifest (i.e., Epiphanes)," took four deliberate steps between 169 and 167 BC to forcibly hellenize the people of The Book:

[1] First to be dealt with was the seat of power in Judea – the High Priest. The Antichrist removed the sitting high priest whose name meant righteous peace, and replaced him with a Jew who would do man's (Antiochus's) bidding. By the way, from this point on, the high priesthood in Israel largely became a corrupt institution.

[2] Secondly, the Antichrist tried to dissolve the Biblical Calendar. He felt that these people were time obsessed in trying to keep their time holy. Antiochus felt if he destroyed God's people's sense of time, he could destroy their ability to practice their religion. Therefore, Antiochus forbid the observance of the seventh day Shabbat that set their weeks, the New Moon celebrations that set their months, and festivals that set their years, which were all symbols of man's

obligation to instill holiness into time. These were all divinely ordained appointed meeting places in time between God and man.

[3] The Antichrist forbade the studying of the Word of God (first five books of the Bible – Torah) and keeping kosher (respecting the sanctity of life). Torah scrolls were publicly burnt, as pigs were sacrificed over them to defile them. Antiochus even forced the High Priest to institute swine sacrifices in the temple in Jerusalem as well as permitting worship of various Greek gods (I Maccabees 1:41-64).

[4] Lastly, the Antichrist forbade circumcision. To Jews, this was their physical sign of their covenant of faith with God (i.e., Abrahamic covenant) that demonstrates that the physical and spiritual are intertwined. Circumcision was the body's mark of allegiance to God's covenant that spoke of being a servant, not a master. To the Greeks, circumcision was seen as mutilation, because they worshiped the perfection of the human body and its sensuality.

Two years prior to the abomination of desolation being set up in the temple, rumors circulated in Jerusalem that the king had been killed in an Egyptian campaign. One of the men vying for the material gain of the High Priestly office (Jason), decided to take advantage of this by attacking the city with a thousand men – killing his own countrymen. Antiochus interpreted Jason's actions as a revolt again his throne. He became enraged. When Jerusalem opened its gates to him, Antiochus ordered his soldiers to indiscriminately kill men, women and children. Forty thousand were killed and an equal number taken captive. Jason fled and died a fugitive while Antiochus set up his own lackey as High Priest (Menelaus) with orders to oppress his own people even more. If that wasn't enough, Antiochus brazenly entered the Temple and took all its silver and gold. He entered the Holy Place and removed the Golden Altar of Incense, the

Golden Menorah (Lampstand), and the Golden Table of Showbread as well as the curtain that divided the Holy of Holies from the Holy Place and the gold ornamentation that decorated the front of the Temple.

Two years after this uprising, there was another uprising which we more closely associate with Hanukkah. Antiochus sent Apollonius (the commander of the Mysians) to Jerusalem with an army of 22,000 soldiers (II Maccabees 5:24). He gained admittance to the city without a struggle, because the people did not suspect his intentions. Once inside, soldiers destroyed, plundered and murdered. In their fury against the Temple in Jerusalem, the Syrians made thirteen breaches in the wall encompassing the Temple court (Mishnah Middos 2:3).

A directive was sent to Antiochus' entire kingdom by which all peoples must relinquish their own customs and religions to conform to the Greek culture and creed. All disobedience was punishable by death. There was a directive expressively sent to Judea, which demanded that the sacrificial service cease in Jerusalem's Temple. In its place, altars and temples should be set up everywhere for idol-worship where unclean animals were to be sacrificed. As if that was not enough, Antiochus commanded that the Holy Temple be desecrated and converted into a pagan temple. This is when the statute of Jupiter (Zeus) was erected upon the Altar on the 15th of Kislev 168 BC (I Maccabees 1:54). It is also when all things that these Biblical people considered holy were prohibited: observance of Sabbath, Rosh Chodesh, festivals, dietary laws, covenant of circumcision, laws of family purity and even the use of God's Name. Then beginning on the 25th of this month, hogs were offered upon the sun god's altar (I Maccabees 1:59).

Most people complied with the king's barbarous order, but many chose death above desecrating the Name. Women who still circumcised their children were hung with their infants tied around their necks. There's a very famous story about Chana and her seven sons who were captured and brought before the pagan king to forcibly eat pig's meat. When son after son after son refused to do so, even after being tortured, Antiochus had them put to a slow painful death all the while their mother was forced to watch. These noble sons of the One True God were encouraged by their mother to sanctify the Name. When all her sons had gone on to a better place, distraught Chana climbed unto a roof and jumped to her death. Those who chose a martyr's death served as inspiration.

In those troubled times, Mattisyahu the Hasmonean, the son of Yochanan (John) a previous Kohen Gadol (High Priest), left Jerusalem where the persecution was strongest. He and his family settled in Modi'in, a Judean village near Jerusalem. One day the king's forces appeared in Modi'in and demanded that the town sacrifice in the pagan fashion. They chose the most respected man in town, Mattisyahu, to comply (1 Maccabees 2:17-18).

Bribery was the door for many to pagan conversion. If Mattisyahu would simply sacrifice a pig and eat it, he and his sons would be considered the king's friends', which was an official title that carried many privileges, including social and material advantages. As Mattisyahu was defiantly refusing the pagan honor, a turncoat Jew neared the pagan altar to offer the sacrifice (1 Maccabees 2:19-24). Mattisyahu was filled with righteous indignation at this blatant desecration of "The Name". In the tradition of Phineas (Numbers 25:1-13), Mattisyahu grabbed a sword and killed the Jewish traitor on the altar along with the messenger from the pagan king (I Maccabees 2:24-26). After tearing down the altar, Mattisyahu ran through the city shouting: "Whoever is zealous for the Torah and is steadfast in the Covenant let him follow me!" (I Maccabees 2:27).

Mattisyahu, his sons, and many who sought to live according to righteousness fled to the mountains and settled in the Judean Desert (I Maccabees 2:28-30). They left all their worldly possessions.

Antiochus's forces could not disregard this challenge to their authority. Six thousand combat-ready loyal Jews gathered under Mattusyahu's banner. They began to strike back by destroying idolatrous altars in nocturnal raids (I Maccabees 2:45).

Mattisyahu died within a year (166 BC). He did not see the results of what had been set in motion, but before the patriarch died he gathered his five sons: Shimon (Simon), Yehudah the Maccabee (Judah), Elazar (Eleazar), Yochanan (John) and Yonasan (Jonathan). He urged them to stand steadfast and continue the good fight against the Syrian Greeks (I Maccabees 2:49-69). Mattisyahu's last words established Shimon as "a wise man; listen to him always" and Judah "a warrior from his youth shall be the leader of your army and direct the war against the nations" (I Maccabees 2:65-66).

The official appointed to administer Judea (Philip) did not take the Mattisyahu revolt seriously. He felt they could be contained by the troops stationed in the vicinity of Judea. Philip first called up Apollonius, the military commander of Samaria. Before Apollonius and the Cutheans could attack, Judah was forewarned and struck first killing Apollonius with much of his army (I Maccabees 3:10-12).

Second, Seron the commander of the army in Syria heard about the Maccabee revolt, and he decided to gain a reputation by crushing Judah (I Maccabees 3:13-14). He gathered a large, well-equipped army and marched to Judea. As Seron approached Beth Horon, Judah and his men saw Seron's vast army. Judah's men had been fasting and were frightened; but Judah remembering his father's last words reassured his men: "It is easy for the many to be handed over to the few, for there is no difference in God's eyes between saving through a large force or through a tiny force. Triumph in battle does not depend on the size of an army – for strength comes from heaven. Our enemy opposes us full of violence and lawlessness, to destroy us, our wives and our children, and to plunder us. But we are fighting for our lives and our Torah. God will crush them before us and you must not fear them!" (I Maccabees 3:18-22). When Judah finished speaking, he wasted no time by suddenly rushing Seron's army crushing them (I Maccabees 3:23). The enemy's plan became their own portion.

Upon hearing about his troops defeat by a bunch of circumcised nincompoops, Antiochus flew into another rage. He commanded that his entire army gather together. He opened his treasure chests and paid his soldiers a full year's wages. Antiochus then realized that his coffers had been depleted through his military campaigns and his lavish spending for banquets, grandiose buildings and gladiator games. So, King Antiochus was advised to go to Persia to collect tribute owed him while Lysias (a kinsman) was entrusted with the care of the young heir to the throne (later Antiochus V Eupator). Antiochus IV equipped half the army with war elephants (ancient equivalent of tanks) and assigned them to Lysias command with orders to march to Judea and crush the Jewish nation. Lysias promptly appoints three of Syria's ablest generals: Ptolemy son of Dorimenes, Nikanor, and Gorgias. He puts them in charge of 40,000 foot soldiers and 7,000 cavalry. They marched into Judea as far as Emmaus (I Maccabees 3:27-40). Emmaus is the town where later Yeshua would reveal himself to His disciples after His resurrection. Once they recognized Him in the breaking of bread, Yeshua disappeared.

So confident were the Syrian Greeks of their victory that Nikanor had summoned slave dealers from the coastal cities and promised them Jewish slaves at an unprecedented low price. Instead of Judah losing heart, the faithful band of Maccabean brothers went to Mitzpah to fast and pray. Mitzpah was a city that had been a place of prayer for God's salvation in the days of Samuel.

As they all fasted and prayed, "they unrolled the scroll of the law, to learn about the things for which Gentiles consulted the images of their idols. They brought with them the priestly vestments (kings and priests of the Order of Melchizedek take note), the first fruits, and the tithes; and they brought forward the Nazarites who had completed the time of their vows. And they cried aloud to Heaven: 'What shall we do with these men, and where shall we take them? For Your sanctuary has been trampled on and profaned, and your priests are in mourning and humiliation. Now the Gentiles are gathered together against us to destroy us. How shall we be able to resist them unless you help us?' Then they blew the trumpets and cried out loudly." (I Maccabees 3:48-54).

Judah appointed officers over thousands, over hundreds, over fifties and over tens. They camped south of Emmaus, as Judah exhorted his troops: "Arm yourselves and be brave; in the morning be ready to fight these Gentiles who have assembled against us to destroy us and our sanctuary. It is better for us to die in battle than to witness the ruin of our nation and our sanctuary. Whatever heaven wills, He will do" (I Maccabees 3:57-59).

At daybreak, Judah and 3,000 ill-equipped men sees the vast expanse of experienced soldiers. Judah exhorts his ragtag remnant again: "Do not be afraid of their numbers or dread their attack. Remember how our fathers were saved in the Red Sea, when Pharaoh pursued them with an army" (I Maccabees 4:8-9). The foreigners came out for battle when they looked up and saw the Maccabees marching toward them. When the men with Judah blew their trumpets (as one), the Syrians' orderly phalanxes dissolved, and the Jews decimated the rear guard. They set the Syrian camp on fire, and keep pursuing the enemy a long way. Judah cautioned his men that a large part of the enemy was still in the mountains, but Gorgias and his troops had fled the battlefield once they saw fire rising from their main camp.

After Lysias licked his wounds for a year (165 BC), he sent a stronger force of 60,000 infantry and 5,000 cavalry. Judah and his band of faith-filled men meet them at Beth Tzur with 10,000 loyal

Jews. Again, Judah appealed to heaven when he saw their vastly greater force: "Blessed are You, O, Savior of Israel, who halted the charge of the Philistine champion, Goliath, through Your servant David and who delivered a Philistine camp into the hands of Jonathan the son of Saul and his armor bearer. Do the same to this camp let them be ashamed of their army and their cavalry. Make them cowardly, melt their boldness, make them tremble at their imminent destruction. Strike them down with the sword of those who love You and let all who know Your Name sing praises to You" (I Maccabees 4:30-33). Hand-to-hand combat ensued and approximately 5,000 of Lysias' men were killed. Seeing the determination of the Jews where they would rather die than surrender, Lysias withdrew his troops back to Antioch. When Judah saw that the Syrian Greeks would not mount another offensive in the foreseeable future, he tells his brothers: "Let us go up to purify the sanctuary and re-dedicate it." (I Maccabees 4:36).

Our next chapter will go into the purification of God's Temple and the re-dedication of His Altar. For now, please notice that Hanukkah portrays several mysterious truths about our becoming precious members of the Bride of Christ. Kings and priests of the Order of Melchizedek are overcomers who lead their inner bride forth through a series of battles for purity. At times, the odds may appear overwhelming; but we can, and will, strengthen ourselves in Him through fasting, prayer, and His Word.

It is no coincidence that God's faith-filled sons had to battle the world's superpower (the Antichrist) to save the culture of the Kingdom of God, and it was a small remnant doing the work. The Antichrist sets up his own high priest in God's Temple while the job of the Order of Melchizedek is to set up Yeshua Ha Machiach (Jesus Christ) as the sole High Priest in our Temple. Don't you know that you are the Temple of God (1 Corinthians 3:17; 6:19)? The Order of Melchizedek is made up of sons of righteousness who built His Temple and *"offer up spiritual sacrifices acceptable to God by Jesus Christ" (1*

Peter 2:5). The wife of the Lamb is a Body or Temple (Revelation 21:3), which is a continual holy and living sacrifice (Romans 12:1; Jeremiah 33:18). She manifests being a Blazing Fire Bride.

The Antichrist has an infamous number "666" that speaks of the character of this beast. This beast can exist within you and me, because it's equivalent to a completely selfish man. This is one of the manifestations of an image people will worship in the end days when they take the mark of the beast: *"But mark this: There will be terrible times in the last days. People will be lovers of themselves, lovers of money ... lovers of pleasure rather than lovers of God" (2 Timothy 3:1-2).* I'm not negating the fact of another world-dominating leader manifesting that he is "The Antichrist." I'm saying that in the end days, the Abomination of Desolation that stands in the Holy Place can be oneself.

The holy priesthood of the Order of Melchizedek is pouring a new wine on God's Altar. The Blazing New Wine of Hanukkah is about restoring all the things that the first Antichrist took away as well as tearing down the profane altars made to pagan sun gods.

- We will restore #1: The rightful High Priest of the Order of Melchizedek in our Body who will literally stand in our Holy Place.

- We will restore #2: God's Calendar, His Biblical Feasts and His biblical reckoning of time.

- We will restore #3: The rightful place of God's Word in our lives. It is more like a marriage contract than a rigid set of rules. It's a delightful honor to obey the dictates of our King's heart.

- We will restore #4: The circumcision of our heart by entering the rest through the better hope in which we draw near to God (Hebrews 7:19). We will show that we are a letter from Christ written not on tablets of stone, but on the tablets of human hearts, demonstrating the spectacular new heart and new spirit given to us (Ezekiel 36:26-27; 2 Corinthians 3:2-3).

Midwinter sacrificing to pagan sun gods came after the Antichrist changed the times and the laws. It's the culmination in our lives of those other things being out-of-whack. We can read about sun god worship (i.e., Christmas) being the most detestable practice in His eyes in Ezekiel 8:16.

Christians can say that your Christmas worship is not idolatry or pagan sun god worship and believe it to the hilt, but understand that He will have the last say. God will only attach Himself to things like Him. "And what agreement has the Temple of God with idols? For you are the Temple of the Living God. As God has said: *'I will dwell in them and walk among them. I will be their God, and they shall be My people'* (2 Corinthians 6:16 NKJV).

His *shekinah* glory literally requires holiness. People have tried to boil holiness down to a formula of dos and don'ts, but that will always miss the mark because holiness is a love issue. Doing what Scripture prescribes for holiness taps into the prerequisites for which God's Presence can dwell among us, but we must always take into account that His people's hearts must be totally engaged when we seek to lovingly obey Him.

Believers in the God of Abraham, Isaac and Jacob need to consider that the *shekinah* glory dwelt in the midst of Israel for generations: *"The people of Israel. Theirs is the adoption of sons; theirs the divine glory" (Romans 9:4).* First century believers understood the biblical holiness requirements, which facilitated God's dwelling presence. When the Holy Spirit fell at Pentecost, the church experienced His manifest presence. They additionally sustained a multi-generational revival for more than three hundred years, because they understood how to live in God's presence.

For the church to sustain His awe-filled presence today, we need to accurately grasp His minimum requirements for purity and their relevant application in our lives. Please let us learn from history, so we don't repeat it. God's dwelling presence departed from the Christian church when the pagan holidays were assimilated into it. Historical proof is seen in the departure of daily miracles from among them. Scriptural proof is spelled out in Ezekiel Chapters 8-11. Please note, as you personally read this passage of Scripture that God's presence slowly and sorrowfully departed, for He longs for His people to repent, so His presence may return or remain.

"Son of man, do you see what they are doing ... things that will drive Me far from My sanctuary?" (Ezekiel 8:6). The four idolatrous practices listed in Ezekiel 8:3-5, 9-12, 14, 16 originated in Babylon, and the Bible says that they are detestable to God. These all have to do with pure worship. We will only peek at the fourth and most detestable practice in His eyes that drives Him far from His sanctuary: *"So He brought me into the inner court of the LORD's house; and there, at the door of the temple of the LORD, between the porch and the altar, were about twenty-five men with their backs toward the temple of the LORD and their faces toward the east, and they were worshiping the sun toward the east" (Ezekiel 8:16 NKJV).*

Christians can say Jesus is the reason for the season all we want, but God's Word tells us otherwise. According to Scripture, God considers sun god worship to be the most detestable abomination in His eyes that doesn't allow His Dwelling Presence (i.e., Shekinah Glory) to stay, remain, or dwell:

- *"Son of Man, do you see what they do? Great abominations are [the people] of the House of Israel committing here, to cause Me to distance Myself from My Sanctuary" (Ezekiel 8:6 The Jewish Bible, Tanach).*

- *"And he brought me into the inner court of the LORD's House, and, behold, at the door of the Temple of the LORD, between the porch and the altar, were ABOUT FIVE AND TWENTY*

MEN, with their backs toward the Temple of the LORD, and their faces toward the east; and THEY WORSHIPPED THE SUN toward the east" (Ezekiel 8:16 KJV).

It's about twenty-five men worshipping the sun. It's all about the twenty-five – the 25th of December. It's about the 25th of December and what image we erect in our hearts to sacrifice to on the altar of our hearts.

The fourth and most detestable practice was performed in the inner court of the house of the Lord between the porch and the altar. The inner court symbolizes those who are intimately acquainted with God. The porch is a place of traversing back and forth. It can be akin to a heaven and earth connection. The altar was a platform of sacrificial worship, where worshipers endeavored to meet with their God. So... these twenty-five or so men, who were bowing down to the sun with their backs toward the temple of the Lord, were His close companions. They were people who knew and loved the Lord, yet they still grievously bowed down to and worshiped the sun, whether they acknowledged the fact or not.

It is not until Ezekiel 9:3 that the departure of God's presence begins. His *shekinah* glory moves over His fiery chariot throne – a set apart remnant of His people. Then, His *shekinah* glory is carried by the Living Creature from the inner court to the threshold of His sanctuary. The Lord hesitates there to see if His people will notice His leaving. Will they repent and welcome His manifest presence back? He waits, then in Ezekiel 10:19 God's glory moves further away to the eastern gate. He waits again. His people still won't repent of their idolatry, so God's *shekinah* glory moves out of Jerusalem (the city of our God) across the Kidron Valley to the Mount of Olives (Ezekiel 11:23). Then God waits again for the people to turn from their idols. Where's does Scripture say that the Lord will return? The Mount of Olives both spiritually and physically (Zechariah 14:4).

The pagans in the fourth century recognized their own solar cults in the church's adoption of the Nativity of the Unconquered Sun (i.e., Mithra's Winter Festival). They recognized the church assimilation of their pagan practices in the orienting cathedrals to the east, worshiping on "sun day," and celebrating the birth of the sun god deity at the Winter Solstice. Throughout antiquity, all sun gods across all cultures celebrated their birthday on the ancient winter solstice – December 25th – before the Roman shift in time. Recall that the *Catholic Encyclopedia* even documents that the Nativity or Mithra's Winter Festival has a strong claim on our December 25th date. Never mind the fact that Constantine had the Vatican built atop the hill where the Mithras cult worshiped the sun. History records that it had become common practice in the fifth century for worshipers entering St. Peter's Basilica in Rome to turn at the door, put their backs to the altar, and bow down to worship the rising sun. See Ezekiel 8:16 for God's opinion.

When the Lord says that "Christmas will be the Golden Calf of America," He is telling us that it is idolatry in His eyes. The Lord has given each of us the responsibility to prepare a place for Him: *"Everyone who has this hope in Him purifies himself, just as He is pure" (1 John 3:3)*. His *shekinah* glory cannot dwell where there is idolatry; therefore, His dwelling presence cannot, and will not, co-exist with this Golden Calf we call Christmas. Idolatry is the crux that determines whether His *shekinah* glory will merely visit His people or dwell among them. If it's your heart-of-hearts to be part of God's glorious Melchizedek and Bridal companies, you will have to pass through this fire.

*****

5 – PURIFICATION OF THE TEMPLE & RE-DEDICATION OF GOD'S ALTAR

We left off with the Hanukkah story where Judah the Maccabee tells his brothers: Let's go up to Jerusalem to purify the sanctuary and re-dedicate its altar. If the powers-that-be-of-this-world have tried to hide the importance of the re-dedication of God's Altar, don't you think that we should pay particular attention to it?

Judah's entire force marched to the Temple Mount. When they got there, their hearts sank. The Temple grounds were overgrown with vegetation, its gates burned, and the Altar desecrated. By the way, this mystically portrays spiritual state of Christians who participate in pagan sun god worship. It's a missing link for many people who are endeavoring to become more like Yeshua. When the Maccabees saw the state of God's Temple, they tore their garments, spread ashes on their heads, and cried and mourned at the state of their sanctuary.

Judah led some men to fight off the garrison quartered in the citadel to allow the priests of the Most High God to cleanse and prepare the Temple. Please note that Hanukkah is not about freedom from foreign bondage, it's about freedom to worship. The Festival of Hanukkah was proclaimed in the absence of a military or diplomatic victory, which gives us important insight into the nature of this celebration. Mattisyahu and his sons - Judah the Maccabee and his brothers - risked their lives for the purity of God's Altar, His Temple, and the freedom to worship.

The first thing that the holy priesthood needed to do was begin the daily burnt offerings on God's Altar. Second Chronicles Chapter 29 tells us that it takes eight days to sanctify and cleanse the House of the Lord. So, the priests removed the stones of the defiled altar, and quickly constructed a new one that could be used the next morning.

They fashioned new utensils for divine service. They brought the Golden Altar of Incense into the Holy Place where Scripture prescribed it to be and offered incense (heaven and earth prayers) that very afternoon. They baked *Panim* bread and placed it on the Golden Table of Showbread. They hung the *Paroches* (the Veil) that separated the Holy Place from the Holy of Holies. They fashioned a Menorah out of iron and covered it with zinc. Then this is when Jewish Commentaries on Hanukkah begin to re-count the miracle of only having enough oil for one night and it lasted for eight days. Kings and priests that restore all things need to throw out the Menorah Miracle that was not part of Hanukkah's history for hundreds of years. The reason it was put there was to hide the importance of the re-dedication of the altar, which is symbolic for the re-dedication of our hearts to worship the One True God in accordance to His Spirit and Truth (the Word of God). It also fits with Rabbinic man-made tradition where the Pharisees have deliberately changed every one of the Biblical Feasts. They altered the meaning of the feasts to hide the fact that Yeshua fulfilled them.

As mentioned earlier, three years to the day after the Temple service was interrupted on the 25th of December, the sanctuary of God was renewed with great celebration and joy. They celebrated the re-dedication of God's Altar for eight days by offering up sacrifices for peace and thanksgiving, and so should we.

Please allow me the liberty to jump over to another manifestation of God's Temple. The Maccabees restored the Altar in Herod's Temple, but most of the keys that unlock the Order of Melchizedek are portrayed in Solomon's Temple. Revelation 5:6-10 depicts that in the midst of His Kingdom is the throne. In the midst of the throne are four beasts (i.e., living creatures) and twenty-four elders. And in the midst of it all a Lamb stands. Then, these four living creatures and twenty-four elders sing a new song, and they call themselves: *"kings and priests" (Revelation 5:10)*. The four living creatures are also called the Living Creature in the Book of Ezekiel, and Ezekiel 10:20 equates the Living Creature to Cherubim. Therefore, when you see the four living creatures (i.e., The Living Creature) know that there is a connection in Scripture to Cherubim and the Order of Melchizedek as well. Never forget that Living Creature (*"chayot"*) of God's Chariot Throne (*"merkabah"*) has the appearance of a man – one man – a corporate One New Man in the Messiah.

My second *Melchizedek Arising YouTube* video – *Formation of the New Living Creature* – reveals aspects of the Order of Melchizedek as seen through "Cherubim" in Scripture. The Ancient Hebrew Word Picture (pictograph) for "cherubim" tells us: "Cherubim are a picture for where God opens His people up to His Kingdom in their midst through His Spirit, His Word and His massive deeds done; and it's where God joins His Body together to make it a securely nailed dwelling place where His household is bound together within."

We are merely going to gaze at the "Cherubim" depicted on the Ten Copper Chariot Lavers in Solomon's Temple, which are connected to Hanukkah's re-dedication of God's Altar. The only "cherubim" in the Outer Court of God's Dwelling Place are these cherubim that are on the Copper Chariot Lavers in Solomon's

Temple. They are key to the full restoration of the DNA for Christ's Body.

*****

6 – DNA RESTORATION OF CHRIST'S BODY

If you want to walk in the fullness of the measure of the stature of Christ with all 12-strands of your DNA activated, look at "cherubim" in Scripture and make the concepts surrounding it active in your life. For instance, the only cherubim not in the Sanctuary itself in Solomon's Temple are the cherubim on the Ten Copper Chariot Lavers.

IF WE MISS FULFILLING THE TEN COPPER CHARIOT LAVER PICTURE, WE MISS COMING INTO THE FULLNESS OF THE CHERUBIM CLASSIFICATION OF THE ORDER OF MELCHIZEDEK. The Ten Copper Chariot Lavers literally show His Melchizedek Company Cherubs the WAY to coming into His TRUTH for becoming His HOLY PLACE here on earth, as it is in heaven. NOTE: The baseline for His Melchizedek Company of Cherubim is having entered the Kingdom of God (John 3:5), which means a person has had to mature beyond merely salvation to the place of sanctification. Hopefully, they continue to press toward the place of purification.

Before the Fall, human beings were called "living beings" and had 12-strands of DNA actively working. After the Fall, 10-strands of DNA were disconnected (or de-activated) eons ago and have remained largely dormant with humans until now. So far scientists have called these ten shadow strands of DNA – "junk DNA."

It's not a coincidence that there were Ten Copper Chariot Lavers in Solomon's Temple that were dismantled and taken captive by Babylon. These Ten Copper Chariot Lavers were used to wash the blood from the burnt offerings. Just like the Ten Copper Chariot Lavers were dismissed and treated like junk, so has our ten shadow DNA strands. Know that an important key to unlocking the activation of all 12-strands of DNA for a "living being" lies with these Ten Copper Chariot Lavers. Our future has never looked brighter! When we get all twelve strands of our DNA turned on, we will literally be light beings on earth.

LIGHT ON THE WORLD

Yeshua declared Himself to be the Light of the World twice during Hanukkah (John 8:12, John 9:5). The second time He said: *"I am the Light of the World,"* Yeshua made a particular reference to "as long as I am in the world" right before He breaks every man-made tradition that He can think of to heal a man born blind (John 9:5). There are several dimensions to Yeshua telling His disciples: *"As long as I am in the world, I am the light of the world"* (John 9:5 KJV). One dimension obviously is Yeshua is the Light of the World as long as He is in it, but fundamentally He was also telling His disciples to recall what He told them on the Sermon on the Mount: *"¹⁴ You are the light of the world. A city that is set on a hill cannot be hidden. ¹⁵ Nor do they light a lamp and put it under a basket, but on a lampstand, and it gives light to all who are in the house. ¹⁶ Let your light so shine before men, that they may see your good works, and glorify your Father which is in heaven"* (Matthew 5:14-16 NKJV).

I'd like to point out another facet that Yeshua is referring to – a future time when the Mature Body of Christ on earth will literally manifest being the light of the world exactly like He did with all 12-strands of their DNA turned on to be the very DNA of God. To understand the fullness of what it means to be a Shining One, just like Yeshua, we need to study the entire passage that portrays what Yeshua did during Hanukkah – John 8:12-10:42.

We don't know when Hanukkah became known as the Feast of Lights, nor do we know when the whole concept of the Hanukkah lights representing the eight days of a miracle happening began; but we do know that it was known as the Feast of Lights in the time of Yeshua. Yeshua Himself fulfilled Hanukkah by declaring "I am the Light of the World" twice while meeting with believers. He also revealed truths about the Good Shepherd and healing a man born blind, which foreshadows the healing of the One New Man in Christ who has been born blind too.

Our eyes are the window to our souls. When our DNA is transformed into the very DNA of God, our souls will be filled with the Seven Spirits of God. The Seven Spirits of God were the sevenfold nature of Christ that Yeshua walked in here on earth: the Spirit of the Lord, the Spirit of Wisdom, the Spirit of Understanding, the Spirit of Counsel, the Spirit of Might, the Spirit of Knowledge, and the Spirit of the Fear of the Lord (Isaiah 11:1-2). Heaven's will and the Seven Spirits of God enabled Yeshua to fulfill His high and holy calling, and so this will be for those of the Order of Melchizedek and the Bride.

Since the seven branches of God's Light in His Temple are connected to the Seven Spirits of God, we can be sure that the Light of His Manifest Presence is watching over His word to see that it is fulfilled. All that is given through the marvelous gift of the Seven Spirits of God is designed to bring the Bride into a place of fullness where she is without spot or wrinkle.

The Seven Spirits of God are part of the government of God – His ruling and reigning Kingdom. They are resident in mature saints who bring increase of His government of peace and righteousness (Isaiah 9:7). Believers who mature into their royal priesthood function will have Christ's Being lived out through them by means of the Seven Spirits of God. These Spirits will promote God's administrated will or government on earth through His end-time Royal Priesthood. Anyone who wills to do so can have this place in Him. The operation of the Seven Spirits of God enables revelation to flow unabated in the Priesthood of the Order of Melchizedek. This revelation reveals the deep, secret and hidden truths of God's Kingdom, life in the Spirit, and God's plans and purposes found in Christ.

Let's get back to how the Ten Copper Chariot Lavers are a key to the Bridal Restoration of our DNA, because the Seven Spirits of God filling a believer's soul with the very Nature of Christ is a progressive perfection process within the Order of Melchizedek. If you study the words "perfect" and "perfection" in Scripture, you will see that they are connected to the Order of Melchizedek. The deepest root for the word "perfect" reveals that it is the point aimed at as a limit for Christ's full-age mature sons where *"I in them and Thou in Me, that they may be made PERFECT IN ONE; and that the world may know that thou hast sent Me, and hast loved them, as thou hast loved Me" (John 17:23 KJV)*. If you want to bear His image, you've got to understand the Order of Melchizedek, because Melchizedek is going to be God's expression on the earth today.

Each one of His kings and priests of the Order of Melchizedek are leading their inner fire bride forth. Three components that are always present in the perfection of the Order of Melchizedek are the same three transformative agents that are accomplishing the Bridal Restoration of our DNA:

[1]   Daily Communion,

[2]   Daily Crucifixion, and

[3]   Daily Bread.

If we look at the order of His Sanctuary's Sacrificial System (in particular in relation to the Ten Copper Chariot Lavers), we see the process by which these three transformative agents work.

DAILY COMMUNION

The Ten Copper Chariot Lavers in Solomon's Temple were used to wash the blood from the body of the burnt offerings. Daily Communion is all about a body and blood. It's about the Messiah's Body and the Messiah's Blood. The job of the priest in God's Sanctuary was to go back to the beginning before sin entered the world. The High Priest would sprinkle the blood of goats and calves to do this, so did Yeshua by His own blood: *"[11] But Christ came as High Priest of the good things to come, with the greater and more perfect tabernacle not made with hands, that is, not of this creation. [12] Not with the blood of goats and calves, but with His own blood He entered the Most Holy Place once for all, having obtained eternal redemption" (Hebrews 9:11-12 NKJV).*

To return to our primordial Living Beings of Light state, we have to go through the blood of Yeshua, and His Body. When thinking and speaking about spiritual things, we need to leave our linear process behind and pick up the circular ways of the Hebrews. Ian Clayton speaks about when we come back to the beginning, we see the end as well because Yeshua is the Alpha and Omega – the beginning and the end – and when we see the end of something it means that it is totally complete. Our jobs, as priests, is to go into His world to reach both the end and beginning of a matter. As priests of the Order of Melchizedek, we need to become mediators bringing the eternal world into this world. This will bring the reality of heaven to earth, so that this world can go back into that glorious heavenly world where it came from in the beginning.

The Blood and Body of Yeshua is the reality of Daily Communion: "Then Jesus said to them, *"53 Most assuredly, I say to you, unless you eat the flesh of the Son of Man and drink His blood, you have no life in you. 54 Whoever eats My flesh and drinks My blood has eternal life, and I will raise him up at the last day. 55 For My flesh is food indeed, and My blood is drink indeed. 56 He who eats My flesh and drinks My blood abides in Me, and I in him"* (John 6:53-56 NKJV).

Why did Yeshua say in I Corinthians 11:24-25: Do this in remembrance of Me?

"23 For I received from the Lord that which I also delivered to you, that the Lord Jesus in the night in which He was betrayed took bread; 24 and when He gave thanks, He broke it and said, 'This is My body, which is for you; DO THIS IN REMEMBRANCE OF ME.' 25 In the same way He took the cup also after supper, saying, 'This cup is the new covenant in My blood; DO THIS, as often as you drink it, IN REMEMBRANCE OF ME.' 26 For as often as you eat this bread and drink the cup, you proclaim the Lord's death until He comes. 27 Therefore whoever eats this bread or drinks the cup of the Lord in an unworthy manner, shall be guilty of the body and blood of the Lord. 28 But a man must examine himself, and in so doing he is to eat of the bread and drink of the cup" (1 Corinthians 11:23-28 NASB).

The Order of Melchizedek's goal is to bear the record of the testimony of God's DNA in one's body. "Taking communion" or as I like to say it "taking on common union" is doing what the High Priest of the Order of Melchizedek did.

When a person gets a bone marrow transplant, their physical blood DNA is different than the DNA of their external skin. To change the record of our testimony to become the very DNA of God, daily communion causes the record in the marrow of our bones to change. Yeshua is speaking once again to His Beloved: *"Bone of my bones, and flesh of my flesh" (Genesis 2:23 KJV)*.

Through communion, our bones start producing the correct record in our blood first; then, as we make the right choices, our body gets conformed into His image that has been born in our blood first. So, as each one of us rightly examine ourselves, we all literally become more and more one with Christ and His Body (1 Corinthians 11:28). This process allows an ever-brightening arc of His Presence to form between your blood and your body until its outward expression of an inward reality manifests in shining pure white light.

We can only be joined to Christ if we carry His likeness and His DNA. The bread and wine cause His supernatural Kingdom to descend upon and among us. Our spirit literally absorbs the life of God, as we partake communion; and little by little we become blended together until we are totally consumed within Him becoming one spirit. *"But he who is joined to the Lord is one spirit with Him" (1 Corinthians 6:17 KJV)*. That word "joined" comes from the same word for when a man and woman become intimate with one another. It's the same root word for "feasts" in 2 Chronicles 8:13. Restoring Biblical Feasts to their rightful place in our lives is a huge key to becoming one with Him.

The primitive root for *mo-ed* feasts in the account about Solomon building a House for the Lord (His own House) is the Hebrew word *ya-ad*. The King of Kings is saying to us: Don't you want to party with Me? Mo-ed is like fixing an appointment in a day-timer, but *ya-ad* speaks from the depths of His heart: The Lord is summoning His people to meet Him at His stated time, He is directing us into a certain position, and He is engaging us for marriage (i.e., to be betrothed).

Celebrating God His way unlocks so much! We may think holidays, celebrations and festivals are casual things, which in a sense they are, because of the vast freedom within the context of Scripture we have. But in another sense, they are the very things which will cause us to be positioned correctly in Him, so we can be married to Him.

DAILY CRUCIFIXION

Communion, crucifixion and God's Word are so intertwined that they seem to bleed over into one another. Conveniently, daily crucifixion is included in daily communion, because genuine partaking of common union requires us to examine our hearts and behavior. Moving unto perfection is a crucifixion process (Hebrews 6:1). The wisdom of God insists on our daily permission to crucify our sin nature. He only completes the work of co-crucifixion with Christ with our approval (Galatians 2:20).

Once our bones produce His record in our blood, we must "rightly examine ourselves" to be conformed into His image in our bodies. We have to offer up ourselves daily as a living sacrifice to burn up our sin nature (flesh), specifically as a burnt offering. The Ten Copper Chariot Lavers cannot wash burnt offerings until they are properly prepared. Please remember that the re-dedication of God's Altar is the main theme of Hanukkah. Whenever you hear of the re-dedication of the altar, please think of re-dedicating your own heart.

When God gives us a new heart, He changes the record of a person's DNA. When your parents joined to produce you, your original seed DNA imploded after several multiplications. Then that original seed DNA went into the center of your gene pool and began to form your heart; therefore, your heart contains the full testimony of parents' DNA. So, when God takes out your stony heart of flesh and gives you a new heart of flesh connected to His Kingdom, we are formed into His image. The Bible says as a man thinks in his heart, so is He (Proverbs 23:7).

Through Christ's crucifixion and His precious shed blood, we have a better hope by which we draw nigh unto God (Hebrews 7:19). When we daily take up our cross and follow Him, we are not replacing or adding to Yeshua's cross, we are joining Him.

Crucifixion of one's sin nature is a key to the transformation of a person's soul. Look at *Matthew 16:24* where Yeshua says to His disciples: *"If any man will come after Me, let him deny himself, and take up his cross [of the flesh], and follow Me."* Then two verses later in *Matthew 16:26* it says: *"For what does a man profit if he gains the whole world, and loses HIS OWN SOUL? What shall a man give in exchange for his soul?"* Please realize that the things of this world that we will not die to are the very things that we are exchanging for the total transformation of our soul to its full 12-strand DNA state that is made in the exact same image as Jesus Christ.

> *"14 But may it never be that I would boast, except in the cross of our Lord Jesus Christ, through which the world has been crucified to me and I to the world. 15 For neither is circumcision anything, nor uncircumcision, but A NEW CREATURE. 16 And those who will walk by this rule* [Order of Melchizedek] *peace and mercy be upon them* [they will be Kings of Peace], *and upon the Israel of God" (Galatians 6:14-16 NASB).*

The first Melchizedek Pattern in Genesis 14 shows that Abram had to dethrone Babylonian Kings before he could receive the ministry of Melchizedek. This same truth is portrayed in the Ten Copper Chariot Lavers being broken down and carried away by the Chaldeans to Babylon, and our need to restore this part of His Chariot Throne in our day. Please note that Chaldea does refer to Babylon; but more specifically, it's the place where sorcery, sun god worship, and its associated "Land of Merchants" status originated. In a word, it's where "Christmas" originated. Therefore, to receive the full ministry of Melchizedek, not only will we have to dethrone these three kings (i.e., sorcery, sun god worship, and commercialism/materialism) from our lives; but we will have to do what the Maccabees did during Hanukkah. To purify His Temple (you and me), we must tear down the polluted altar in our heart that has been desecrated with pagan sun god worship and build a new one. Please consider how difficult it was for the Maccabees to even get to the Temple to cleanse it; but also consider that against overwhelming odds God gave them the victory when they fought, as they sought Him in Spirit and in Truth.

It's not a coincidence that the total capacity of these Ten Copper Chariot Lavers was 400 baths (40 baths a basin multiplied by 10 chariot lavers). This corresponds to Babylon dismantling these washing vehicles required for God's Chariot Throne (His kings and priests) 400 years after Solomon died. Humm… The exact number of baths available for Burnt Offerings in Solomon's Temple is a key connection to the complete restoration of the Royal Order of Melchizedek here on earth.

DAILY WORD

Once the Burnt Offering (i.e., sin nature) gets slaughtered, the blood gets washed by the water of the word, and the washing of regeneration and renewing of the Spirit in these Ten Copper Chariot Lavers:

- *"[25] Husbands, love your wives, just as Christ also loved the church and gave Himself up for her, [26] so that He might sanctify her, having cleansed her BY THE WASHING OF WATER WITH THE WORD, [27] that He might present to Himself the church in all her glory, having no spot or wrinkle or any such thing; but that she would be holy and blameless. [28] So husbands ought also to love their own wives as their own bodies. He who loves his own wife loved himself; [29] for no one ever hated his own flesh, but nourishes and cherishes it, just as Christ also does the church, [30] because we are members of His body" (Ephesians 5:25-30 NASB).*

- *"³ For we also once were foolish ourselves, disobedient, deceived, enslaved to various lusts and pleasures, spending our life in malice and envy, hateful, hating one another. ⁴ But when the kindness of God our Savior and His love for mankind appeared, ⁵ He saved us, not on the basis of deeds which we have done in righteousness, but according to His mercy, BY THE WASHING OF REGENERATION AND RENEWING BY THE HOLY SPIRIT, ⁶ whom He poured out upon us richly through Jesus Christ our Savior, ⁷ so that being justified by His grace we would be made heirs according to the hope of eternal life" (Titus 3:3-7 NASB).*

In this Kingdom Day, we will worship the LORD His way. On *Yom Teruah* (i.e., Feast of Trumpets) in 2012, September 16, 2012 to be precise, I was seeking a word from the LORD when He first showed me a vision of a curtain being pulled back that revealed a glorious golden city celebrating God's feasts. Then He spoke to me a one-liner: "The reign of the Kingdom has begun." Scripturally speaking, the coronation of the kings in Israel have happened on *Yom Teruah*.

If you ask most Jews when *Rosh Hashana* is, they will tell you the first day of the seventh month but that is not what Scripture says. There is only one mention of *Rosh Hashanah* in Scripture. It is found in Ezekiel 40:1 when Ezekiel honored and spoke of God's New Year, which is the first of Abib (Aviv). Please allow me to emphasize that last point. Scripture's only mention of *Rosh Hashanah* corresponds to the only New Year that God set up in Scripture, the first of Abib that falls in March or April.

Not until 200 AD (170 years after our Messiah rose) did *Rosh Hashanah* come about to replace *Yom Teruah* in the *Mishnah*, which later got incorporated into the Talmud. Believers don't want to have anything to do with the Talmud. There's some disgusting man-made things in there. For instance, it exonerates pedophilia against little girls over 3-years-old. Rabbinical Judaism comes from the Talmud.

Having a New Year celebrated in the seventh month of the year comes from Babylon. The Babylonians used to have a lunar-solar calendar very similar to the Biblical calendar. The result was that *Yom Teruah* often fell on the same day as the Babylonian New Year's festival known as "*Akitu.*" Akitu fell out on the first day of Tishrei as well as six months later on the first of Nisan (Abib). That's right! To make matters more confusing the Babylonians celebrated *Akitu* - New Years - twice a year. Talk about confusing! I see some Tower of Babel fingerprints here.

The first of Tishrei coincided with *Yom Teruah* on the first day of the Seventh Month. The fact that the Jews had started calling the Seventh Month by the Babylonian name "Tishrei" paved the way for turning *Yom Teruah* into a Jewish Akitu. At the same time the Rabbis did not want to adopt Akitu outright, so they Judaized it by changing the name of *Yom Teruah* to *Rosh Hashanah.*

The Day of Trumpets is the feast that is supposed to remind us every year that there is a prophet who's going to be sent (like Moses) that God's people must absolutely listen to as well as sounding the alarm that no one is allowed to add to or take away from the Torah – the first five books of the Bible that Moses wrote, which is God's Word. This is what man has tried to hide by mixing *Yom Teruah* with the traditions of man from Babylon.

So, what remains if one desires to return to the solid age-old foundations of the Word of God regarding God's Feasts?

Both Rabbinical Judaism and Constantine Christianity have traditions of man that are keeping us from fulfilling the Word of God. We need to determine His righteous measuring line in all things, in this case – celebrating His Feasts. Not legalistically, but in a life-giving sense. That's why we need to stick with the first five books of the Bible for the foundations of our faith, i.e. believing Moses.

Yeshua actually tells His people this very thing: *"⁴⁶ For if you believed Moses, you would believe Me; for he wrote about Me. ⁴⁷ But if you do not believe his writings, how will you believe My words?" (John 5:46-47 NKJV).*

Let all Bridal Lovers of God lay down our agendas and traditions on God's Altar, so we can each make the offerings by fire to the LORD that the re-dedication of our altar prescribes. Let the All-Consuming Fire's measuring line of His Word burn up all traditions of men that keeps us in Babylon and keeps us from fulfilling the commandments of God. Remember that we are told repeatedly, if you love Me, you will keep My commandments:

- *"If you love Me, you will keep My commandments" (John 14:15 NASB).*

- *"⁹ Just as the Father has loved Me, I have also loved you; abide in My love. ¹⁰ If you keep My commandments, you will abide in My love; just as I have kept My Father's commandments and abide in His love" (John 15:9-10 NASB).*

- *"² By this we know that we love the children of God, when we love God and observe His commandments. ³ For this is the love of God, that we keep His commandments; and His commandments are not burdensome" (1 John 5:2-3 NASB).*

- *"And this is love, that we walk according to His commandments. This is the commandment, just as you have heard from the beginning, that you should walk in it" (2 John 1:6 NASB).*

- *"Here is the perseverance of the saints who keep the commandments of God and their faith in Jesus" (Revelation 14:12 NASB).*

- *"⁶ And He said to them, 'Rightly did Isaiah prophesy of you hypocrites, as it is written"* "THIS PEOPLE HONORS ME WITH THEIR LIPS, BUT THEIR HEART IS FAR

AWAY FROM ME.⁷ BUT IN VAIN DO THEY WORSHIP ME, TEACHING AS DOCTRINES THE PRECEPTS OF MEN."⁸ Neglecting the commandments of God, you hold to the tradition of men."⁹ He was also saying to them, 'You are experts at setting aside the commandment of God in order to keep your tradition.¹⁰ For Moses said, "HONOR YOUR FATHER AND YOUR MOTHER"; and "HE WHO SPEAKS EVIL OF FATHER OR MOTHER IS TO BE PUT TO DEATH";¹¹ but you say, 'If a man says to his father or mother, whatever I have that would help you is Corban (that is to say, given to God),¹² you no longer permit him to do anything for his father or his mother;¹³ thus invalidating the Word of God by your tradition which you have handed down; and you do many things as that" (Mark 7:6-13 NASB).

Let each of us make room within for God's Word (John 8:37).

"Then Jesus said to those Jews who believed Him, "If you abide in My word, you are My disciples indeed. And you shall know the truth, and the truth shall make you free" (John 8:31-32 NKJV). In the "Beauty and The Beast" Chapter, you will see how only lovers of truth escape the great apostasy and become precious parts of His pure and spotless Bride (2 Thessalonians 2:10).

*****

7 – FULLNESS OF THE MESSIAH BODILY: METATRON

The Order of Melchizedek's goal is to bear the record of the testimony of God's DNA in one's body to be ONE BODY: *"There is one body and one Spirit, just as also you were called in one hope of your calling" (Ephesians 4:4 NASB).*

The one body is the Body of the Messiah that's connected to its Head – Messiah Yeshua – which in its fullness is the undifferentiated state of the Messiah. This fully mature Son of Man is portrayed in Revelation 1. By the way, the Lord told me that His angel in Revelation 1:1 is Metatron.

> *"[1] The Revelation of Jesus Christ which God gave unto Him, to show unto His servants things which must shortly come to pass; and He sent and signified it by His angel unto His servant John: [2] Who bare record of the Word of God, and of the testimony of Jesus Christ, and of all things that he saw. [3] Blessed is he that readeth, and they that hear the words of this prophecy, and keep those things written therein: for the time is at hand. [4] John to the seven churches which are in Asia: Grace be unto you, and peace, from Him which is, and which was, and which is to come; and from the*

seven Spirits which are before His throne. *⁵ And from Jesus Christ, who is the faithful witness and the first-begotten of the dead, and the prince of the kings of the earth. Unto Him that loved us, and washed us from our sins in His own blood, ⁶ And hath made us KINGS AND PRIESTS unto God and His Father; to Him be glory and dominion for ever and ever. Amen. ⁷ Behold, He cometh with clouds; and every eye shall see Him, and they also which pierced Him: and all kindreds of the earth shall wail because of Him. Even so. Amen. ⁸ I am the Alpha and Omega, the beginning and the ending, saith the Lord, which is, and which was, and which is to come, the Almighty. ⁹ I John, who also am your brother, and companion in tribulation, and in the kingdom and patience of Jesus Christ. ¹⁰ I was in the Spirit on the Lord's day, and heard behind me a great voice, as of a trumpet, ¹¹ Saying, I am Alpha and Omega, the first and the last: and, What thou seest, write in a book, and send it unto the seven churches which are in Asia; unto Ephesus, and unto Smyrna, and unto Pergamos, and unto Thyatira, and unto Sardis, and unto Philadelphia, and unto Laodicea. ¹² And I turned to see the voice that spake with me. And being turned, I saw seven golden candlesticks. ¹³ And in the midst of the seven candlesticks ONE LIKE UNTO THE SON OF MAN, clothed with a garment down to the foot, and girt about with paps with a golden girdle. ¹⁴ HIS HEAD AND HIS HAIRS WERE WHITE like wool, as white as snow; and His eyes were as a flame of fire, ¹⁵ And His feet like unto fine brass, as if they burned in a furnace; and His voice as the sound of many waters" (Revelation 1:1-15 KJV)*.

Notice that the one like the Son of Man has white hair on His head. Throughout Scripture, the Head of the Body of the Messiah is portrayed as Yeshua:

- *"But I want you to know that the HEAD OF EVERY MAN IS CHRIST, the head of woman is man, and the head of Christ is God" (1 Corinthians 11:3 NKJV)*.

- *"¹⁵ But speaking the truth in love, WE ARE TO GROW UP IN ALL ASPECTS INTO HIM WHO IS THE HEAD,*

EVEN CHRIST [i.e., the Messiah], *¹⁶ from whom THE WHOLE BODY being fitted and held together by what every joint supplies, according to the proper working of each individual part, causes the growth of THE BODY for the building up itself in love" (Ephesians 1:15-16 ₙₐₛʙ).*

- *"⁹ FOR IN HIM DWELLS ALL THE FULLNESS OF THE GODHEAD BODILY. ¹⁰ and you are complete in Him who is the HEAD of all principality and power. ¹¹ in Him you were also crucified with the circumcision made without hands, by putting off the body of the sins of the flesh, by the circumcision of Christ, ¹² buried with Him in baptism, in which you also were raised with Him through faith in the working of God, who raised Him from the dead. ¹³ And you being dead in your trespasses and the uncircumcision of your flesh, He has made alive together with Him, having forgiven you all trespasses. ¹⁴ having wiped out the handwriting of requirements that was against us, which was contrary to us. And He has taken it out of the way, having nailed it to the cross. ¹⁵ Having disarmed principalities and powers, He made a public spectacle of them, triumphing over them in it. ¹⁶ So let no one judge you in food or in drink, or regarding a festival or a new moon or sabbaths, ¹⁷ Which are a shadow of things to come, but the substance is of Christ. ¹⁸ Let no one cheat you of your reward, taking delight in false humility and worship of angels, intruding into those things which he has not seen, vainly puffs up by his fleshly mind. ¹⁹ and not HOLDING FAST TO THE HEAD, FROM WHOM ALL THE BODY, nourished and knit together by joints and ligaments, GROWS WITH THE INCREASE THAT IS FROM GOD" (Colossians 2:9-19 ₙₖⱼᵥ).*

The fully mature Head of Messiah Yeshua can only fully and properly attach to a Fully Mature Resurrected Body of Believers. These Fully Mature Resurrected Body of Believers are people who embody earnestly and persistently holding fast to the Head and growing up in all aspects into the Messiah. The culmination of holding fast to the Head to the utmost is what I call the undifferentiated state of the Messiah in which the Messiah's Head and His Body are indistinguishable, because they are one. This is the oneness matrix of Messiah Yeshua. I like to call it the Oneness Metatron Matrix; because the white-haired fully mature Head of the Messiah and His fully mature Body is in a word, Metatron; or in other words, Metatron Messiah.

There is another Metatron that's the false Messiah – Metatron Mithra – that is so close to the real Messiah that a person needs to completely die to themselves and their own desires in order to see its reality. In my Hanukkah Meditation book called *Let There Be Light!*, I go into Metatron Messiah versus Metatron Mithra in the Chapter 6 "Mysteries of Oneness." Since the Biblical Feasts (in doing what Jesus did) are literally a crux for you and me coming into the fullness manifestation of the righteous Metatron – Fully Mature Heavenly One New Man in the Messiah – we will repeat these truths.

Currently many Christians believe that they are connecting to the true Messiah during Christmas, but history and Scripture reveal a different reality. Always remember Yeshua celebrated Hanukkah, not Christmas: "*[22] And it was at Jerusalem the Feast of Dedication* [Hanukkah] *and it was winter. [23] And Jesus walked in the Temple in Solomon's Porch*" *(John 10:22-23 KJV).*

"*[11] Unto you has been given to know the mystery of the Kingdom of God: but unto them that are without all these things are done in parables. [12] For seeing they see, and yet do not perceive; and hearing they hear, and yet do not understand; if they should return, their sin would be forgiven. [13] And he said to them, Do you not understand this parable? How then will you understand all the parables?*" *(Mark 4:11-13 Lamsa's Aramaic).* The parable that Yeshua is talking about in Mark 4:13 is the Parable of the Sower. Yeshua tells us plainly that the seed is the Word of God, and this seed is sown in our hearts (Luke 8:11; Mark 4:15). Therefore, the Word of God is key to unlocking the various mysteries of God deposited in one's heart.

There are twenty-one references in Scripture connected to the word "mystery." It has been given to the Messiah's disciples holding fast to the Head to know the mysteries of the Kingdom of heaven and the mysteries of the Kingdom of God (Matthew 13:11; Mark 4:11; Luke 8:10). Believers are charged to be good stewards of the mysteries of God (1 Corinthians 4:1).

We have the mystery of the Kingdom of Heaven, the mystery of the Kingdom of God and the mystery of the gospel, which is the seed of the Word of God. Within the mystery of the gospel is the Mystery of Iniquity (2 Thessalonians 2:7) and *"Mystery, Babylon the Great, the mother of harlots and abominations of the earth" (Revelation 17:5)*, which brings us to the false Metatron Mithra that's connected to Christmas.

While doing an extensive study about "mysteries" and "mystery" in Scripture, I happened upon the following definition for "mystery" in my *Webster's Collegiate Dictionary (10th Edition)*.

> **mystery** ~*noun* : a religious truth that one can know only by revelation and cannot fully understand : a Christian sacrament (1) a secret religious rite believed (as in Eleusian and Mithraic Cults) to impart enduring bliss to the initiate (2) a cult devoted to such rites.

Now hold on there. According to the Word of God, a Mithraic cult devoted to sun god worship should not be connected to a true and righteous Christian sacrament; but it was, and still is.

Mithra was one of the favorite sun gods adopted by Rome, just before Christmas got institutionalized in the Church. Mithra was the Persian version of the original Babylonian sun god Tammuz. The *Catholic Encyclopedia* itself credits Mithra's Winter Festival, as claiming strong responsibility for the December 25th date for Christmas.

Mithra's Winter Festival was a birth celebration for *Sol Invictus Mithra*, which was also called "The Nativity," "The Nativity of the Sun," or "The Nativity of the Unconquered Sun."

Even though the phrase "Christ's mass" (i.e., Christmas) is first found in 1038 AD, according to the *Catholic Encyclopedia*, I use the term to help everyone track our modern winter revels with those of the past. Prior to the 11th Century, Christmastime was associated with the Winter Solstice, Midwinter, or Winter Revels. For simplicity's sake, I say "Christmas" most times instead of the Winter Solstice.

The first recorded evidence of "Christmas" taking place on December 25th isn't found until the time of Constantine in 336 AD. History records that Constantine was a very devout worshipper of the sun god *Sol Invictus Mithra*. The Emperor not only presided over the Nicene Council, but spearheaded building the Vatican atop the hill where the Mithra's Cult worshipped the sun. I go into all this in the "Constantine Compromises" section of "Chapter 5 – The Golden Snare" in *SANTA-TIZING: What's wrong with Christmas and how to clean it up*.

It has been given to the sons of the Living God to know the Mithraic Cult Mystery. Christmas was originally a secret religious rite for the pagan elite in Rome. The Mithraic Cult was devoted to worshipping the birth day of their sun god on the ancient winter solstice. Throughout antiquity, the celebrated birthday of ALL sun gods was the ancient winter solstice, which was December 25th before the Roman shift in time. The origins of the birthday of the sun god(s) is rooted in Babylon, specifically Chaldea where sorcery (lies, control, manipulation), sun god worship (Christmas) and the land of merchant status (materialism) originated. Please refer to http://wp.me/p158HG-1t. Its original icon was a golden calf said to represent the divinity of the ancient Chaldean god Saturn. See http://wp.me/p158HG-2m and https://www.youtube.com/watch?v=INypfLsTaPw.

Though my dictionary says that the Mithraic Cult had a secret religious rite believed to impart bliss to the initiate, an honest glance reveals that *"This wisdom is not that which comes down from above, but is earthly, natural, demonic" (James 3:15 NASB)*. The roots of Christmas connect its participants to bowing down to the pagan sun gods under a tree, which hinders the most supreme eternal bliss – becoming part of the Bride of the Messiah and part of the Oneness Metatron Matrix – for those who worship at Mithra's Table. Note: This is not about salvation, but eternal rewards. Please refer to https://santatizing.wordpress.com/2014/12/06/the-roots-of-christmas/ or https://www.youtube.com/watch?v=fvrVXjd-mm8.

It is not a coincidence that the Messiah in His fullness is called Metatron. Consider that Metatron is said to be the keeper of time. I will call the True Messiah – Metatron Messiah – and the False Messiah – Metatron Mithra. Metatron Messiah is the keeper of space-time. He is the keeper of our three-dimensional world and the fourth dimension of time and beyond.

In contrast, the world currently has a false Metatron figure – Metatron Mithra. The counterfeit Metatron Mithra is said to be the god of agriculture and time. If one has control of the seed and time, one can control the world.

Metatron Mithra embodies the demonic control of space-time. If you are connected to Metatron Mithra through Mithra's Winter Feast (Christmas Day), you are tethered to a distorted illusion of space-time in an ungodly way. Additionally, if you move to the rhythms of the Christmas Season, you automatically connect to its root too, which is the Saturnalia. The Saturnalia is the worship of the Saturn, which most anciently is connected to the Black Cube. The Black Cube is the antithesis of the Golden Cube of the New Jerusalem (Revelation 21:16). The Black Cube represents the god of this world's control of the fallen state of both time and space. Please refer to *A Tale of Three Cubes* video => https://www.youtube.com/watch?v=U4PD9_F2xvI.

My teaching notes for that class are included in the *MEL GEL Study Guide: Volume 2* => https://www.amazon.com/dp/0998598232/.

Amazing as it might seem, both Christmas Day and the Christmas Season act as tethers to an ungodly false reality. It's time for everyone to either take the red pill or the blue. Are you going to be hot for Metatron Messiah and His glorious eternal realty of oneness? Or are you going to be cold, choosing Metatron Mithra instead? It is one of the ultimate tests of a person's heart. Choose this day the true Metatron Messiah or the false Messiah who is Metatron Mithra.

Never forget that the only winter feasts mentioned in the Bible are Hanukkah and Purim. Also, remember that for 300 years or so, God's people solely celebrated Biblical Feasts. They only did what Jesus did.

Doing Biblical Feasts, as Jesus did, falls in the perfect will of the Father category. Doing Biblical Feasts is what the Bride of the Messiah does as well as fully grown mature sons. Please recall that the magnificent corporate purpose of mature sons being bonded in Christ is to unite via an attractive force, as His Bride; and then to embed this cohesive force into a matrix called the Heavenly One New Man in Christ – the Oneness Metatron Matrix.

Recall that Metatron is the undifferentiated state of the Messiah – Mature Head and the Transfigured/Transformed Cherubic Body of Christ. Believers can be, and are, part of the One New Man in Christ on earth; but Metatron consists of people who have literally become just like Jesus. These devout souls have been transfigured, or you could say transformed, fully mature cells of the fully Mature Body of Christ attached to the Fully Mature Head – Messiah Yeshua.

Another way that we can view Metatron is he is an energetic power or force that's a Being, which is a legion of beings. Metatron is Melchizedek. Metatron is Enoch. Metatron is Elijah. Metatron is

Ezekiel. Metatron is David. Et Cetera. Metatron is a multiplicity of beings. It is the literal manifestation of the 100-percent fullness of the Heavenly One New Man in Christ (in the Messiah).

John 12:32 reveals that when Yeshua is lifted up that He draws all men unto Himself. *"And I, IF I AM LIFTED UP FROM THE EARTH, WILL DRAW ALL MEN TO MYSELF" (John 12:32 NASB)*. The Greek word for "draw" in that verse communicates a drawing by an inward power, Christ in you, the hope of glory. It's a leading or impelling, even forcibly against one's own will. John 6:44 also connects this drawing by the Father and the Son to resurrection life: *"No one can come to Me unless THE FATHER WHO SENT ME DRAWS HIM; AND I WILL RAISE HIM UP ON THE LAST DAY" (John 6:44 NASB)*.

This is not a coincidence. Enoch is an example and forerunner of his morally putting on immortality – resurrection life. Please refer to 2 Enoch 22. The book of Third Enoch Chapter 4 tells us that Metatron is Enoch, the son of Jared, seventh from Adam, and father of Methuselah who lived 365 years on the earth. Enoch was called a pious worshipper of God who was removed from the dwellers on earth, because God took him to heaven as a witness.

Look to the life of Enoch, because he is a first fruit of firstfruits. Enoch is a type-n-shadow for what is to be made manifest in our day. Soon God is going to be taking people that walk with Him, like He did Enoch; but this time, unlike Enoch, His Metatron Merkabah Army will perpetually reside both in heaven and on earth, which is a slight modification to what Enoch experienced.

The process of uniting via a cohesive force into the Oneness Metatron Messiah Matrix is outlined in the chapter in the Bible that speaks about one body, one Spirit, one hope of your calling, one Lord, one faith, one baptism, one God and Father of all who is over all and through all and in all (Ephesians 4:4-6).

Additionally, this chapter reveals the pattern for Ascension in Christ, which is a glorious truth being unveiled in this Kingdom Day for lifting up I AM, so that all men will be draw to the Messiah. *"⁹ (Now that he ascended, what is it but that he also descended first into the lower parts of the earth? ¹⁰ He that descended is the same also that ascended up far above all heavens, that he might fill all things") (Ephesians 4:9-10 KJV).*

Ascension in Christ is the *Merkabah* part of the Melchizedek Metatron Merkabah Army. The *Merkabah* (God's Chariot Throne in Ezekiel 1) is basically a picture of the transformation process that God's sons go through to become just like Yeshua. The *Merkabah* shows how the sons of man first descend in the Spirit through Christ's Cross to their Kingdom of God within; and then, they ascend through the blood of the Lamb of God to be "in Christ" to behold the perfect heart and perfect will of the Father (Luke 17:21; Hebrews 10:19; Ephesians 2:6; John 5:19).

> *"¹ Behold what matter of love the Father has bestowed on us, that we should be called children of God! Therefore the world does not know us, because it did not know Him. ² Beloved, now we are children of God; and it has not yet been revealed what we shall be, but we know that when He is revealed, we shall be like Him, for we shall see Him as He is" (1 John 3:1-2 NKJV).*

The *Merkabah* is gone over more extensively in the *Ascension Manual* book => https://www.amazon.com/dp/0578188511 as well as in the "Merkabah" Chapter of the *MEL GEL Study Guide* => https://www.amazon.com/dp/0578188538/.

Ephesians Chapter 4 also discloses that the five-fold gifts of apostle, prophet, evangelist, pastor and teacher have been necessary for the building up of the Body of Christ in the old dispensation of the Age of the Church; but now in this new dispensation of the Age of the Kingdom, the governors and tutors of the Seven Spirits of God are leading the Body of Christ to the *"unity of the faith, and the knowledge of the Son of God, unto a perfect man, unto the measure of the stature of the fullness of Christ" (Ephesians 4:13 KJV)* where the Body of Christ grows up in all aspects into the Head – Messiah Yeshua. Thus, the members of His Body will take on the likeness of His character to the 100-percent measure of the stature of the fullness of the Messiah where the Heavenly One New Man in Christ is completely full of righteousness and holiness of the truth (Ephesians 4:24).

"¹ Therefore I, the prisoner of the Lord, implore you to walk in a manner worthy of the calling with which you have been called, ² with all humility and gentleness, with patience, showing tolerance for one another in love, ³ being diligent to preserve the unity of the Spirit in the bond of peace. ⁴ THERE IS ONE BODY and one Spirit, just as also you were called in one hope of your calling; ⁵ one Lord, one faith, one baptism, ⁶ one God and Father of all who is over all and through all and in all. ⁷ But to each one of us grace was given according to the measure of Christ's gift. ⁸ Therefore it says, 'WHEN HE ASCENDED ON HIGH, HE LED CAPTIVE A HOST OF CAPTIVES, AND HE GAVE GIFTS TO MEN.' ⁹ (Now this expression, 'He ascended.' What does it mean except that He also had descended into the lower parts of the earth? ¹⁰ HE WHO DESCENDED IS HIMSELF ALSO HE WHO ASCENDED FAR ABOVE ALL THE HEAVENS, so that He might fill all things.) ¹¹ And He gave some apostles, and some as prophets, and some as evangelists, and some as pastors and teachers, ¹² for the equipping of the saints for the work of service, TO THE BUILDING UP OF THE BODY OF CHRIST. ¹³ UNTIL WE ALL ATTAIN TO THE UNITY OF THE FAITH, AND OF THE KNOWLEDGE OF THE SON OF GOD, TO A MATURE MAN, TO THE MEASURE OF THE STATURE WHICH BELONGS TO THE FULLNESS OF CHRIST. ¹⁴ As a result, we are no longer to be children, tossed here and there by waves and carried about by every wind of doctrine, by the trickery of men, by craftiness in deceitful scheming; ¹⁵ but speaking the truth in love, WE ARE TO GROW UP IN ALL ASPECTS INTO HIM WHO IS THE HEAD, EVEN CHRIST [i.e., the Messiah], *¹⁶ from whom THE WHOLE BODY being fitted and held together by what every joint supplies, according to the*

proper working of each individual part, causes the growth of THE BODY for the building up itself in love. ⁱ⁷ So this I say, and affirm together with the Lord, that you walk no longer just as the Gentiles also walk, in the futility of their mind, ¹⁸ being darkened in their understanding, excluded from the life of God because of the ignorance that is in them, because of the hardness of their heart; ¹⁹ and they, having become callous, have given themselves over to sensuality for the practice of every kind of impurity with greediness. ²⁰ But you did not learn Christ in this way, ²¹ if indeed you have heard Him and have been taught in Him, just as truth is in Jesus, ²² that, in reference to your former manner of life, YOU LAY ASIDE THE OLD SELF, which is being corrupted in accordance with the lusts of deceit, ²³ and that you be renewed in the spirit of your mind, ²⁴ and PUT ON THE NEW SELF, WHICH IN THE LIKENESS OF GOD HAS BEEN CREATED IN RIGHTEOUSNESS AND HOLINESS OF THE TRUTH. ²⁵ Therefore, laying aside falsehood, SPEAK TRUTH EACH ONE of you WITH HIS NEIGHBOR, FOR WE ARE MEMBERS OF ONE ANOTHER" (Ephesians 4:1-25 NASB)

Notice in Ephesians 4, the Melchizedek Metatron Merkabah Army starts by walking in a manner worthy of the calling:

- *"Therefore I, the prisoner of the Lord, implore you to WALK IN A MANNER WORTHY OF THE CALLING with which you have been called" (Ephesians 4:1 NASB).*

- *"I press toward the mark for the PRIZE OF THE HIGH CALLING OF GOD IN CHRIST JESUS"" (Philippians 3:14 KJV).*

- *"⁴ Therefore we were buried with Him through baptism into death, that just as Christ was raised from the dead by the glory of the Father, even so we also should WALK IN NEWNESS OF LIFE. ⁵ For if we have been united together in the likeness of His death, certainly we also shall be in the likeness of His resurrection, ⁶ knowing this, that our OLD MAN WAS CRUCIFIED*

WITH HIM, that the BODY OF SIN might be done away with, that we should no longer be slaves to sin" (Romans 6:4-6 NKJV).

- *"¹ There is therefore now no condemnation to them which are in Christ Jesus, who WALK NOT AFTER THE FLESH, BUT AFTER THE SPIRIT. ² For the law of the Spirit of life in Christ Jesus hath made me free from the law of sin and death. ³ For what the law could not do, in that it was weak through the flesh, God sending His own Son in the likeness of sinful flesh, and for sin, condemned sin in the flesh; ⁴ That the righteousness of the law might be fulfilled in us, who WALK NOT AFTER THE FLESH, BUT AFTER THE SPIRIT" (Romans 8:1-4 KJV).*

- *"And what agreement hath the Temple of God with idols? For ye are the Temple of the Living God; as God hath said, I WILL DWELL IN THEM, AND WALK IN THEM, and I will be their God, and they shall be My people" (2 Corinthians 6:16 KJV).*

The Lord our God tells us that He will dwell in His people and walk in them. The fullness of the dwelling presence of God is fulfilled in Metatron. Metatron Messiah is a multi-membered angel called the Prince of the Presence. This is the incredibly deep background behind the most detestable practice in God's eyes that drives Him far from His sanctuary (His Dwelling Place) – you and I – as articulated in Ezekiel Chapter 8.

"⁴ And behold, the glory of the God of Israel was there, like the vision that I saw in the plain. ⁵ Then He said to me, 'Son of man, lift your eyes now toward the north.' So I lifted my eyes toward the north, and there, north of the altar gate, was the image of jealousy in the entrance. ⁶ Furthermore He said to me, 'Son of man, DO YOU SEE WHAT THEY ARE DOING, THE GREAT ABOMINATIONS that

the House of Israel commits here, TO MAKE ME GO FAR AWAY FROM MY SANCTUARY?'... [12] Then He said to me, 'Son of man, have you seen what the elders of the House of Israel do in the dark, every man in the room of his idols? For they say, "The LORD does not see us, the LORD has forsaken the land."' [13] And He said to me, 'Turn again, and you will see greater abominations that they are doing.' [14] So He brought me to the door of the north gate of the LORD's House; and to my dismay, women were sitting there weeping for Tammuz. [15] Then He said to me, 'Have you seen this, O son of man? Turn again, you will see greater abominations than these.' [16] So He brought me into the inner court of the LORD's house; and there, at the door of the Temple of the LORD, between the porch and the altar, were ABOUT TWENTY-FIVE men with their backs toward the Temple of the LORD and their faces toward the east, and they were WORSHIPPING THE SUN TOWARD THE EAST" (Ezekiel 8:4-16 NKJV).

We cannot over-emphasize the importance of knowing all four practices that God Himself tells us makes Him go far away from His Dwelling Place, because one of the primer goals of the Body of Christ is to become His Dwelling Place. Metatron Messiah is the Prince of the Dwelling Presence while the Bride of Christ is the place that God dwells in the New Jerusalem (Revelation 21:3).

Recall in the "Journey to Become His Bride: Hanukkah Battles" Chapter that we expose that the most detestable practice in God's eyes is when His people turn their backs to His Dwelling Place and worship the sun. God has encoded a clue in Scripture to what this fourth and most detestable practice is. Those who have ears to hear, its *"about twenty-five" (Ezekiel 8:16)*. The most detestable practice in God's eyes that makes him go away from His Sanctuary is about the 25th of December and its worship of the sun god(s). I believe the reason God calls sun god worship the most abominable or detestable practice is not only does Christmas tether God's people to the fallen 3-D world and its constraint of time when eternity has been put in our hearts when we accept Jesus Christ as our Lord and Savior; but it grievously connects us to the false Messiah – Metatron Mithra – which prohibits Christmas keepers from becoming His Dwelling Place and excludes them from joining the fullness of the Messiah bodily – Metatron Messiah.

So, Metatron Messiah is the Prince of the Dwelling Presence of God, which means that he is Prince of the Shekinah Glory. Shekinah is the dwelling presence of God. Christian mystics tell us that shekinah is not found among sinners, and it's a divine rainbow that radiates colors both ways – in heaven and on earth. Please refer to the "Shekinah and the Sabbath" Chapter in the *MEL GEL Study Guide* => https://www.amazon.com/dp/0578188538/.

The fullness of the Messiah bodily radiates His *shekinah* glory. The fullness of the Messiah bodily is His Dwelling Place on earth, as it is in heaven.

*****

8 – THE GOOD SHEPHERD OF HANUKKAH

As I have read the passage about Yeshua's works during Hanukkah (John 8:12 - John 10:42), I have actually been amazed at how the re-dedication of the altar with its pull to be crucified in union with Christ appears time and again. To be lights of the world, we really do need to press into daily crucifixion along with daily communion and daily word. "Then Jesus spoke to them again, saying, *"I am the light of the world. He who follows Me shall not walk in darkness, but have the light of life" (John 8:12 NKJV)*.

Did you know that our DNA communicates with, and is created from, light itself? Scientists are saying that light appears to be a fundamental part of our being. It's hard-coded into our very bodies to function directly with, and through light. On top of that, we can affect light with our intentions alone, so let's make sure our intentions reflect the perfect will of the Father.

The term the "Light the World" has several dimensions. One is speaking about those who follow Him having the light of life, because following Him is mentioned three times in John Chapter 10 and it's connected to His sheep following the Good Shepherd:

"⁴ And when he brings out his own sheep, he goes before them; and the sheep FOLLOW him, for they know his voice. ⁵ Yet they will by no means FOLLOW a stranger, but will flee from him, for they do not know the voice of strangers." (John 10:4-5 KJV).

"My sheep hear My voice, and I know them, and they FOLLOW Me" (John 10:27 NKJV).

The Hanukkah Passage that speaks of the Good Shepherd (John 10:1-21) tells us two specific things about Yeshua our Good Shepherd:

[1] The Good Shepherd knows His sheep and are known by them (John 10:14).

[2] The Good Shepherd gives His life for His sheep (John 10:11).

Like Yeshua, we are found in the form of a man: therefore, we need to take note of *Philippians 2:8 - "And being found in appearance as a man, He humbled Himself and became obedient to the point of death, even the death of the cross."* If we walk in the same manner as Yeshua, we will follow Him in our own death, burial and resurrection process. The cross is not the end, but a means to an end. We need to seriously take note of Yeshua's very words:

- *"And whoever does not bear his cross and come after Me cannot be My disciple" (Luke 14:27 NKJV).*

- *"Then Jesus said to His disciples, "If anyone desires to come after Me, let him deny himself, and take up his cross, and FOLLOW Me" (Matthew 16:24 NKJV).*

Did you know that the Greek root for the word "CRUCIFIED" tells us to be crucified is TO STAND or TO ABIDE or TO PRESENT? It is not a coincidence that Yeshua was crucified standing. When you have done everything to stand, stand therefore.

When you are crucified in union with Christ, you are set on higher ground where the cross is firm; and I AM that I AM is lifted up and draws all people upon Himself (John 8:28; Galatians 2:20; Ephesians 6:13-14).

It's significant that Yeshua governmentally declares "I AM" twelve times during Hanukkah before we read about Yeshua celebrating Hanukkah walking in Solomon's Colonnade (Solomon's Porch):

[1] *"Then Jesus spoke to them again, saying,* **"I AM the light of the world.** *He who follows Me shall not walk in darkness, but have the light of life" (John 8:12 NKJV).*

[2 & 3] *"And He said to them, "You are from beneath;* **I AM from above.** *You are of this world;* **I AM not of this world"** *(John 8:23 NKJV).*

[4] *"Then Jesus said to them, "When you lift up the Son of Man, then* **you will know that I AM**, *and I do nothing of Myself; but as My Father taught Me, I speak these things" (John 8:28 NKJV).*

[5] *"Jesus said to them, 'Most assuredly, I say to you,* **before Abraham was, I AM'"** *(John 8:58 NKJV).*

[6 & 7] *"As long as* **I AM in the world, I AM the light of the world"** *(John 9:5 NKJV).*

[8] *"Then Jesus said to them again, 'Most assuredly, I say to you,* **I AM the door of the sheep'"** *(John 10:7 NKJV).*

[9] **"I AM the door.** *If anyone enters by Me, he will be saved, and will go in and out and find pasture" (John 10:9 NKJV).*

[10] *"The thief cometh not, but for to steal, and to kill, and to destroy:* **I AM come that they might have life**, *and that they might have it more* **abundantly.**" *(John 10:10 KJV).*

[11] *"I AM the good shepherd.* The good shepherd gives His life for the sheep" (John 10:11 NKJV).

[12] *"I AM the good shepherd;* and I know My sheep, and am known by My own" (John 10:14 NKJV).

All the passages that speak of Solomon's Colonnade tell us it's a place of miracles. It was the place where a beggar, who had been crippled from birth, held on to Peter and John and was healed (Acts 3:11). It's also the place where the apostles performed many miracles, signs, and wonders among the people.

The church, universally, was a supernatural community prior to the pagan feast being integrated into its calendar. Daily, even several times a day, miracles occurred. Yeshua set the precedence when He walked in Solomon's Colonnade during this feast declaring the miracles done by God's Kingdom has come upon them. Please note that one of Hanukkah's names is the Feast of Miracles.

Acts 5:12 also informs us that all the believers met together at Solomon's Colonnade. Please do not underestimate that Scripture records Yeshua walked in the Temple in Solomon's Porch during Hanukkah. If you want to be made into the same image as Yeshua, you will walk as He walked.

In fact, when my family came out of the Yuletide Season based in Babylon, Yeshua told me to do what He did when I forlornly asked Him what to do to replace the big hole that was in our family after we had laid down Christmas. Biblical Feasts will be the crux for the manifestation of one flock and one shepherd (John 10:16), or in other words the fullness of the Heavenly One New Man in the Messiah on earth – Metatron.

After the reference to Yeshua celebrating Hanukkah walking in Solomon's Colonnade (John 10:22-23), Yeshua declares one more "I AM" statement making a governmental declaration into one of full government (13 = 12 disciples + Yeshua): *"^{35} If He called them gods, to whom the Word of God came (and the Scripture cannot be broken), ^{36} do you say of Him whom the Father sanctified and sent into the world, 'You are blaspheming,' because I said,* **'I AM the Son of God'***? (John 10:35-36* NKJV*).* Hebrews 7:3 tells us that those that are made after the Order of Melchizedek are made like unto the Son of God. Therefore, in John 10:36 we can see a reference to a people that all creation is waiting for:

- *"For the earnest expectation of the creature waiteth for the manifestation of the sons of God" (Romans 8:19* KJV*).*

- *"For the anxious longing of the creation waits eagerly for the revealing of the sons of God" (Romans 8:19* NASB*).*

- *"For [even the whole] creation (all nature) waits expectantly and longs earnestly for God's sons to be made known [waits for the revealing, the disclosing of their sonship]" (Romans 8:19* Amplified*).*

These are the mature sons of the Most High God that the Father sanctifies and sends into the world.

Yeshua is passing by all of us "born blind" right now. Everyone please raise your hand and say that you have been born blind in some ways. Some Pharisees in John 9:40 asked: "Are we blind also?" What was Yeshua's answer? *"If you were blind, you would have no sin; but now you say, 'We see.' Therefore, your sin remains" (John 9:40).* It is always a good idea to humble yourself and admit that you have blind spots, because all of us do. We aren't even aware of what they are. Hence, why they are called blind spots. If we humble ourselves, His promise is that we will see, and we will be the sheep of His pasture.

Yeshua is sending all who have been "born blind from birth" to wash in the Pool of Siloam during Hanukkah. Siloam means "sent one." Once we can truly say: *"One thing I know: that though I was blind, now I see" (John 9:25),* our Heavenly Father will send us as blazing new wine into the world as the light of the world. I don't know about you, but I want to be a light of the world that is fully turned on.

*****

9 – BEAUTY AND THE BEAST: CHRIST'S BRIDE AND THE ANTICHRIST

Recall that the story of Hanukkah begins in the Book of Daniel 300 years before the first event took place. Another book is in here somewhere, because this chapter is simply going to focus on understanding what the Pattern Son has to say about the Antichrist and His Bride.

Chapters 23-24 of the Book of Matthew happen on an afternoon when Yeshua steps out of the Temple in Jerusalem giving the Pharisees almost no recourse but to kill Him. The Bible tells us that thousands of people were following Yeshua before He went up to Jerusalem. When Yeshua was on the Temple Mount this day, there were thousands of His disciples with Him as well as hundreds of thousands of people. This is when Yeshua lays the Pharisees bare. He tells His disciples do not follow the Pharisees, and calls them all sorts of names. Please refer to Matthew Chapter 23 verses 1-2, 13, 14, 15, 16-17, 21, 23-33.

As you can tell, Matthew 23 is a heavy passage. By the time that Yeshua storms out of the Temple with His disciples, He had completely exposed the religious leaders of His day calling them sons of hell and a brood of vipers. Yeshua leaves telling the Scribes and Pharisees that they are not going to see Him again until they break their own rule against saying the Name: *"For I say to you, you shall see Me no more till you say, 'Blessed is He who comes in the name of the LORD!'"* *(Matthew 23:39 NKJV)*.

As Yeshua and His disciples are on their way out, His nervous disciples pointed out the beautiful work being done on Herod's Temple. Then Yeshua remarks: *"Assuredly, I say to you, not one stone shall be left here upon another, that shall not be thrown down." (Matthew 24:2 NKJV)*. After Yeshua said that, no one opened their mouths as they walked down the Temple Mount, down the Kidron Valley, across the brook until they arrived on the Mount of Olives. Once they all sat down, the disciples asked Him: *"Tell us, when will these things be? And what will be the sign of Your coming, and of the end of the age?" (Matthew 24:3 NKJV)*. The first thing that Yeshua counsels them is: *"Take heed that no one deceives you" (Matthew 24:4 NKJV)*. Everything in Matthew 24 is in regard to taking heed that no one deceives you. Many are going to come in the Name of Yeshua, and they are going to deceive many. *"But he who endures to the end shall be saved" (Matthew 24:13 NKJV)*.

Following verse 13 of Matthew 24, we are told that the gospel of the kingdom shall be preached to all the world, then the end shall come when you see the Abomination of Desolation spoken of by Daniel standing in the Holy Place (Matthew 24:14-15), then shall be the great tribulation such as the world has never seen (Matthew 24:21).

Yeshua says "whoever reads, let him understand" in verse 15: *"Therefore when you see the 'abomination of desolation,' spoken of by Daniel the prophet, standing in the holy place" (whoever reads, let him understand)."* He says this because He knew that the Abomination of Desolation spoken of in Daniel was prophetically fulfilled by Antiochus Epiphanes IV in 165-168 BC, yet Yeshua says this will be the marker when the end shall be.

We need to look at the meaning of the word "end" in Matthew 24:3 and Matthew 24:13 to understand what Yeshua is talking about. The word "end" in *Matthew 24:3 - "What will be the sign of Your coming, and of the end of the age?"* is the Greek word *synteleia*. Synteleia is like a picture of a tail of a dog. The word "end" in *Matthew 24:13 - "But he who endures to the end shall be saved"* is the Greek word *telos*, which is like the very tip of a dog's tail. Therefore, when we see the Abomination of Desolation take place, it's the beginning of the end when the world will experience the greatest tribulation that it has ever seen, and except those days be shortened, no flesh would be saved.

Paul uses the same example of the Abomination of Desolation in his *midrash* on the Book of Daniel. A *midrash* is going into Scripture and grabbing principles, understanding and concepts:

"¹³ But I do not want you to be ignorant, brethren, concerning those who have fallen asleep, lest you sorrow as others who have no hope. ¹⁴ For if we believe that Jesus died and rose again, even so God will bring with Him those who sleep in Jesus. ¹⁵ For this we say to you by the word of the Lord, that we who are alive and remain until the coming of the Lord will by no means precede those who are asleep. ¹⁶ For the Lord Himself will descend from heaven with a shout, with the voice of an archangel, and with the trumpet of God. And the dead in Christ will rise first. ¹⁷ Then we who are alive and remain shall be caught up together with them in the clouds to meet the Lord in the air. And thus we shall always be with the Lord. ¹⁸ Therefore comfort one another with these words" (1 Thessalonians 4:13-18 NKJV).

"*Sleep in Yeshua*" means those who are dead while "caught up" is the Latin word *raturo* or the Greek word *harpazō* where the dead are raised an incorruptible body, then we who are alive will put on immortality (1 Corinthians 15). This happens at the Last Trump. His Last Trump happens to be one of the Fall Feasts of the Lord called the Feast of Trumpets (*Yom Teruah*).

The Feasts of the Lord in the Bible are called shadows of good things to come that let believers know the time of His coming will be in a particular season. We will not know the day or hour, but the first day of the seventh month on God's calendar is *Yom Teruah*, and it is said to happen on a day and hour where no man knows the day or hour. Believers are not supposed to be in darkness that the day should overtake us like a thief. We are children of the light. We need to pay attention. Watch and pray.

Paul's *midrash* of Daniel continues in 2 Thessalonians 2, which repeats things spoken about in Daniel 8, 11, and 12:

"¹ Now, brethren, concerning the coming of our Lord Jesus Christ and our gathering together to Him, ² we ask you, not to be soon shaken in mind or troubled, either by spirit or by word or by letter, as if from us, as though the day of Christ had come. ³ Let no one deceive you by any means; for that Day will not come unless the falling away comes first, and the man of sin is revealed, the son of perdition, ⁴ who opposes and exalts himself above all that is called God or that is worshiped, so that he sits as God in the temple of God, showing himself that he is God. ⁵ Do you not remember that when I was still with you I told you these things? ⁶ And now you know what is restraining, that he may be revealed in his own time. ⁷ For the mystery of lawlessness is already at work; only He who now restrains will do so until He is taken out of the way. ⁸ And then the lawless one will be revealed, whom the Lord will consume with the breath of His mouth and destroy with the brightness of His coming" (2 Thessalonians 2:1-8 NKJV).

Verse 3 of Second Thessalonians 2 says *"that Day will not come unless the falling away comes first."* The "falling away" is the Greek word *apostasia*, which means a rebellious stand. The man of sin is revealed (*apokalypto*). The son of perdition is the same as in Daniel Chapter 8 and 11. He *"opposes and exalts himself above all that is called God or that sits worshiped, so he sits as God in the temple of God showing himself that he is God."* The Abomination of Desolation is not the end, but the beginning of the end. It is when the *telos* begins. And after the tribulation, we will see the sign of the Son of Man in heaven.

> "⁹ *The coming of the lawless one is according to the working of Satan, with all power, signs, and lying wonders,* ¹⁰ *and with all unrighteous deception among those who perish, because they did not receive the love of the truth, that they might be saved.* ¹¹ *And for this reason God will send them strong delusion, that they should believe the lie,* ¹² *that they all may be condemned who did not believe the truth but had pleasure in unrighteousness" (2 Thessalonians 2:9-12 NJKV).*

Those who receive the love of the truth will be saved. Personally, I'd like to simply focus on the Way and the Truth and the Life – Yeshua – and love Him only. Bridal hearts have many promises, not the least of which is that lovers of truth will be saved in the last days. The love of the truth is offered to everyone as a gift. Whatever we love, whether it is love, money, or truth, we can't seem to get enough of. If we love His truth, we will get it. You should know that "truth" will take an eternity to learn: *"And this is eternal life, that they may know You, the only true God, and Jesus Christ whom You have sent" (John 17:3).* God Himself is going to be sending those who do not love the truth a strong delusion that they might believe a lie. That word "send" is the Greek word *pempō*, which means to send one home to where they're comfortable. God is basically giving people the delusion they want.

Bridal hearts will want to be sent home into Yeshua's loving arms. I am not just talking about when we die. I am talking about every single minute of every single day. His pure and spotless Bride will exemplify the theme that's woven throughout Hanukkah, which is co-crucifixion with her Beloved. Never forget that a Burnt Offering is called an *olah* in Hebrew, which means to "go up." One of the central themes of the first five books of the Word of God (Torah) is the man who is sent ascends and descends. The Ancient Hebrew Word Picture for the word *olah* tells us that His Burnt Offering is that which the Shepherd brings forth. Our Great

Shepherd Yeshua brought the most perfect sacrifice for sins – Himself. Then, while we are being sanctified and purified by the Father, our Great Shepherd will choose what will best crucify our sin nature (flesh) to raise one's spiritual level.

Every time we make His specified spiritual sacrifice, it will cause us who are being made after the Order of Melchizedek to decrease in our own strength and increase in the way of eternal life. His complete Bridal Baptism of Fire of our Kingdom of Self will cause His Continual Living Sacrifices to operate wholly and fully in the Kingdom of God. Kings and priests of the Order of Melchizedek are indeed overcomers who lead their inner fire bride forth through a series of battles for purity. Can you hear the Maccabee call? "Whoever is zealous for God's Word and is steadfast in the Covenant, let him follow me!" This is the Blazing New Wine of Hanukkah that will bring about the Bridal Restoration of DNA.

*****

10 – GENERAL GUIDELINES TO CELEBRATING HANUKKAH

Hanukkah is an annual eight-day celebration that celebrates the overthrow of pagan sun god worship in God's Temple and the rededication of His Altar in Is-real. I am not minimizing this holiday's application to Israel when I say Is-real, I'm trying to touch-on a specific point for everyone. Hanukkah is about purifying your body and your altar, so you can be a part of His pure and spotless Bride.

During this celebration, I see those who have overcome overwhelming odds to take a righteous stand against the world-dominating force as "Maccabees." The name "Maccabees" means hammer, like the instrument used to drive the nails into Yeshua's hands and feet. I also personally see the Maccabee hammer, as a gavel in a judge's chamber that vibrates at the frequency of freedom.

Even though the eight-day miracle of oil is suspect, the menorah (lampstand) itself is from God's Temple; and since Hanukkah was known as the Feast of Lights in Yeshua's Day, in my mind and spirit the custom of kindling a Hanukkah menorah passes God's sniff test. We simply must remember that the historical miracle it symbolizes is the eight-day re-dedication of the Altar and the cleansing of His Temple. We can also celebrate the fact of Yeshua's miracle of touching us who were born blind from birth about Christmas, but now we see. Having offered this Golden Calf as a burnt offering (which is a symbolic offering to the LORD that is burnt up in its entirety, so there is nothing to go back to), we go to the Pool of Siloam (Sent One) to wash our eyes. Now Hanukkah represents us ascending and descending for the purpose of being sent out as blazing new wine into the world as the light of the world.

The main prophetic reading for Hanukkah is *Zechariah 4:6 "Not by might, nor by power, but by my spirit, says the Lord of hosts."* Instead of publicizing the menorah miracle, we are making known the altar miracle of the re-dedication of our hearts to worshiping the One True God, as He has prescribed in His Word. The Feast of Dedication is all about I AM being lifted up, so He can draw all men unto Himself (John 8:28).

Another book will have to be written about Hanukah, because the three themes of the traditional Hanukkah still hold true when put upon God's Altar and seen through the eyes of Yeshua. Hanukkah is the Feast of Dedication (first and foremost), the Feast of Lights, and the Feast of Miracles. Many people celebrate Yeshua being conceived on Hanukkah, but since God chose to hide this fact we should take note and simply celebrate the things that are made known to us. The sheep of the Good Shepherd's pasture know His voice, and they will not celebrate another.

Please remember that Yeshua walks in Solomon's Colonnade – the place where believers meet – during Hanukkah: *"²² And it was Jerusalem the Feast of Dedication, and it was winter. ²³ And Jesus walked in the Temple in Solomon's Porch" (John 10:22-23 KJV).*

On this note, I'd like to share the simple way my family celebrates Hanukkah.

The main focus of our Hanukkah celebration centers on lighting the Hanukkah menorah and having a festive meal with family and friends. I have found that everything I loved about Christmas has a place in our Hanukkah celebrations without any stress or strain. The peace on earth sought by all men during Christmas essentially resides in all the Biblical Feasts, including Hanukkah.

MEALS AND DECORATIONS

My family takes turns hosting a Hanukkah dinner. We have found it difficult to meet all eight days, so we gather together when we can. Even though we try to cook something special during this time, I remember having mac-n-cheese in remembrance of the Maccabees and our own struggle for freedom. It's now an annual tradition in our home that my husband makes a prime rib one of the nights.

To keep things simple, I made Hanukkah meals the focus of my decorating skills. Fine linens, special plates, and napkin holders are the order of the days in our home. I always place our *Hanukkiah* (i.e., Hanukkah menorah) in the center of our table. If you don't have a *Hanukkiah*, tea candles will work. Personally, I like fresh flowers too. The rest of the dining area is decorated with signs and decorative cutouts I've collected. I have also gotten some special simple surprises at times for each place setting, like a piece of chocolate in the shape of the menorah. Plenty of candles are placed throughout the house. We have given small gifts throughout the years, especially since we laid down Christmas when my son was 5-years-old. My son has gotten used to his yearly supply of socks and pajamas with each being given on a separate night. I've notice that the gifts are getting much less frequent and people don't even seem to mind. Personally, one of my love languages is giving, so I really enjoy giving the perfect gift to someone; but we were also convicted about getting rid of materialism. I try to decorate with the cool colors of blue and purple with some white thrown in. We hang snowflakes in front of our main window, and have also hung white lights out side too, but in recent years we have not. Your creative imagination can guide you as you search to honor what was done during the Maccabean years, Yeshua's years on earth and your own personal story of overcoming.

UNDERSTANDING THE LIGHTING OF THE CANDLES

When we light the Hanukkah menorah, we "do" a devotion.

In the next chapter I've included one set of devotions for Hanukkah in this book. I have also published another book called *Let There Be Light! Hanukkah Meditations* => https://www.amazon.com/dp/0998598208/. *Let There Be Light! Hanukkah Meditations* is a Hanukkah guide to contemplation for people focused on the Kingdom of God and His righteousness (Matthew 6:33). These Hanukkah meditations can double as devotional readings throughout the eight days of Hanukkah. Eight sets of eight-day meditations/devotions are included as well as a guide for the nightly blessing and kindling of lights.

Back to lightning the Hanukkah menorah and delving into a devotional reading. First, my family kindles the Hanukkah lights for that night, and then we read the devotion and discuss it. Usually our best moments during Hanukkah happen during these discussions or when we breaking bread together. It's really all about Yeshua and His believers celebrating Him and one another.

When we kindle our Hanukkah menorah each night, we start with one candle on the right outermost edge from the one lighting the candle, and add one candle each night. I don't believe that we need to be religious about "how to" kindle the Hanukkah lights, the importance is that we light them in honor of Yeshua's celebration of this holiday and us joining Him in it. My family likes to start from the right to the left, because that is how Hebrews read. I've heard of other people who start with all eight candles and decrease it each night. To each their own; but personally, I like my light symbolically increasing during the Feast of Re-dedication of my heart.

You will notice on a *Hanukkiah* that there's one candle holder that is either higher or set apart. You can simulate this with tea lights too. The set apart candle is called the *shamash* or servant candle. It's symbolic of Yeshua not coming to be served but to serve as well as Him being literal The Light of the World that lights the other lights of the world (us):

- *"⁴⁴ And whoever wishes to be first among you shall be slave of all. ⁴⁵ For even the Son of Man did not come to be served, but to serve, and to give His life a ransom for many"* (Mark 10:44-45 NASB).

- *"Then Jesus spoke to them again, saying, 'I am the light of the world. He who follows Me shall not walk in darkness, but have the light of life"* (John 8:12 NKJV).

- *"As long as I am in the world, I am the light of the world"* (John 9:5 KJV).

On the first night of Hanukkah, after sundown, the *shamash* candle is lit, which in turn is used to kindle the first candle on the Menorah. The second night, we light the *shamash* again and use it to light the two right candles. This continues through the eight nights of the Hanukkah.

The following is a diagram showing the kindling of the Hanukkiah to increase the light during the eight-days of Hanukkah:

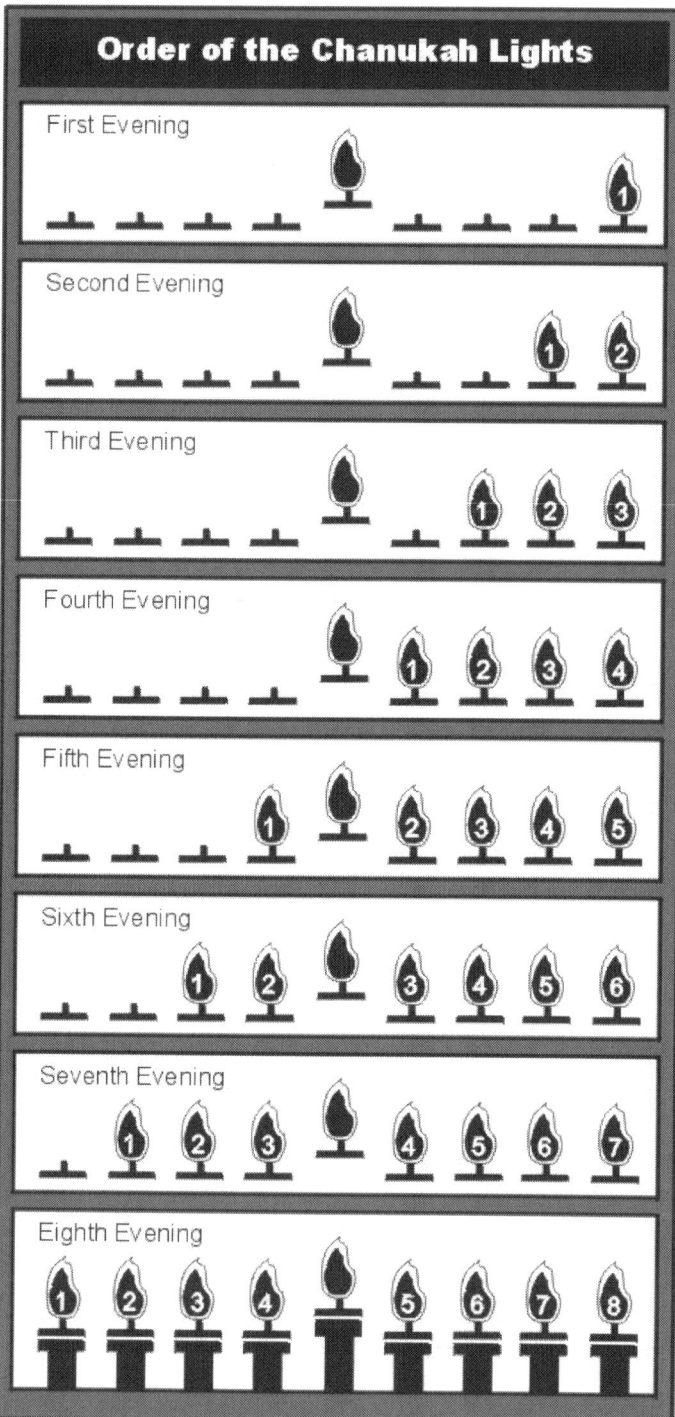

MEANING OF THE CANDLES

The following are some possible meanings of the candles culled from *Yeshua Ha'Mashiach Ministries*. For those in need of an extremely short devotion during Hanukkah, this may be sufficient for you. I would suggest asking participates what each day's message means to them personally.

FIRST CANDLE - The first candle of Hanukkah describes creative light, the very light of God, as it was in the beginning: *"³ And God said, Let there be light: and there was light. ⁴ And God saw the light, that it was good; and God divided the light from the darkness" (Genesis 1:3-4 KJV)*.

SECOND CANDLE - The second candle reveals that God is the source of Israel's light: *"²¹ And the LORD went before them by day in a pillar of a cloud, to lead them the way; and by night in a pillar of fire, to give them light; to go by day and night: ²² He took not away the pillar of the cloud by day, nor the pillar of fire by night, from before the people" (Exodus 13:21-22 KJV)*.

THIRD CANDLE - The third candle reminds us that God Himself is the source of our own individual light: *"[A Psalm of David.] The LORD is my light and my salvation; whom shall I fear? The LORD is the strength of my life; of whom shall I be afraid?" (Psalm 27:1 KJV). "For You will light my lamp, the LORD, My God will light up my darkness" (Psalm 18:28 HNV)*.

FOURTH CANDLE - The fourth candle describes the light that comes from God's Word: *"¹⁰⁵ Your word is a lamp to my feet and a light to my path. ¹³⁰ The entrance of Your words gives light; It gives understanding to the simple" (Psalms 119:105, 130 NKJV)*.

FIFTH CANDLE - The fifth candle represents the greatest grace and light of all, our Messiah Yeshua: *"⁴ In Him was life, and the life was the light of men. ⁵ And the light shines in the darkness, and the darkness did not comprehend it" (John 1:4-5 NKJV). "Jesus spoke to the people once more and said, 'I am the light of the world. If you follow me, you won't have to walk in darkness, because you will have the light that leads to life'" (John 8:12 NLT). "I have seen your salvation, which you have prepared for all people. He is a light to reveal God to the nations, and he is the glory of your people Israel!" (Luke:30-32 NLT). "For God, who said, "Let there be light in the darkness," has made this light shine in our hearts so we could know the glory of God that is seen in the face of Jesus Christ" (2 Corinthians 4:6 NLT).*

SIXTH CANDLE - The sixth candle represents those being made in the Messiah's image being the light of the world: *"¹⁴ You are the light of the world like a city on a hilltop that cannot be hidden. ¹⁵ No one lights a lamp and then puts it under a basket. Instead, a lamp is placed on a stand, where it gives light to everyone in the house. ¹⁶ In the same way, let your good deeds shine out for all to see, so that everyone will praise your heavenly Father" (Matthew 5:14-16 NLT).*

SEVENTH CANDLE - The seventh candle speaks of the future glory of Israel (Is-real) being restored and our light shining in the darkness: *" Arise, shine; For your light has come! And the glory of the LORD is risen upon you. ² For behold, the darkness shall cover the earth, And deep darkness the people; But the LORD will arise over you, And His glory will be seen upon you" (Isaiah 60:1-2 NKJV).*

EIGHTH CANDLE - The eighth candle illuminates the glorious eternal dwelling place of His Bride, the New Jerusalem: *"²² I saw no temple in the city, for the Lord God Almighty and the Lamb are its temple. ²³ And the city has no need of sun or moon, for the glory of God illuminates the city, and the Lamb is its light. ²⁴ The nations will walk in its light, and the kings of the world will enter the city in all their glory. ²⁵ Its gates will never be closed at the end of day because there is no night there. ²⁶ And all the nations will bring their glory and honor into the city. ²⁷ Nothing evil will be allowed to enter, nor anyone who practices shameful idolatry and dishonesty but only those whose names are written in the Lamb's Book of Life" (Revelation 21:22-27 NLT).*

HANUKKAH BLESSING OVER THE CANDLES

As the candles are being kindled, a blessing is spoken over them. The first night a special blessing is usually said to open the festive season with another blessing following it. You can say your own blessing that's related to the re-dedication of your heart and the cleansing of your temple (body) – or – you can use one of these:

<u>First Night Blessing</u>:

Blessed are You O Lord our God, King of the universe, who granted us life, sustained us and permitted us to reach this season.

Baruch Ata Adonai Elohaynu Melech ha-olam, she-he-che-yanu v'kee-ma-nu v'hi-gee-ah-nu laz-man ha-zeh.

<u>Traditional Blessing</u>:

Blessed are You O Lord our God, King of the universe, who has sanctified us with Your commandments, and commanded us to light Hanukah lights.

Baruch Ata Adonai Elohaynu Melech ha-olam, ah-sher kid-shah-nu b'mitz-voh-tayv v'tzee-vah-nu l'had-leek ner shel Hanukah.

Blessed are You O Lord our God, King of the universe, who performed miracles for our fathers in those days at this season.

Baruch Ata Adonai Elohaynu Melech ha-olam, she-ah-sah ni-seem la-ah-vo-tay-nu ba-ya-meem ha-hem baz-man ha-zeh.

Building Up Faith Blessing:

Blessed are You O Lord our God, King of the universe, who has given us holidays, customs, and times of happiness, to increase the knowledge of God and to build us up in our most holy faith.

Baruch Ata Adonai Elohaynu Melech ha-olam, ah-sher nah-tan lah-nu cha-gim, min-ha-gim, oo-mo-ah-dim l'sim-cha, l'hag-deel et da-at Adonai, v'liv-not oh-tah-nu b'emunah ki-do-shah v'na-ah-lah.

Blessed are You O Lord our God, King of the universe, who performed miracles for our fathers in those days at this season.

Baruch Ata Adonai Elohaynu Melech ha-olam, she-ah-sah ni-seem la-ah-vo-tay-nu ba-ya-meem ha-hem baz-man ha-zeh.

Re-dedication of the Altar Blessing:

Blessed are You O Lord our God, King of the universe, you are worthy, worthy, worthy of pure and holy worship. We re-dedicate our hearts solely to You, our First Love. We choose from our very depths to purify our temples as You – the Good Shepherd – chooses. We also declare that we are the man that is sent to the pool of living waters that ascends and descends through the Revelation 4:1 door as your sons.

*****

11 – HANUKKAH DEVOTIONS

READING NIGHT 1 – "Walking As Yeshua Did"

"²² Then came the Feast of Dedication at Jerusalem. It was winter, ²³ and Jesus was in the temple area walking in Solomon's Colonnade" (John 10:22-23 NIV).

The Feast of Dedication is another term for Hanukkah, so is the Feast of Light and the Feast of Miracles. Because Hebrew is a pictorial language, it can have several different phonetic spellings for the same word in English. Hence, sometimes we see Hanukkah spelled with an "H" and sometimes with a "C-H".

When anyone asks why a Christian would celebrate Hanukkah, the simplest and most direct answer is that Jesus did. *"Jesus gave them this answer: 'I tell you the truth, the Son can do nothing by Himself; he can do only what He sees His Father doing, because whatever the Father does the Son also does'" (John 5:19).* So, when Jesus celebrated Hanukkah on earth, significantly, His Heavenly Father participated also. Stop and really think about that. Our precious Heavenly Father not only approved of Hanukkah, but joined in the festivities. In fact, the days of Hanukkah were designated as a festival of praise and thanksgiving, because the

Jewish people recognized the annual return of the same kind of spiritual force that resulted in the original miracle of winning back their temple by overcoming pagan sun god worship. The eight days has to do with the eight days required to purify God's Altar, which is symbolic of our purifying our hearts.

The light of the Menorah in God's Temple is symbolic of the light of God's Presence. It was a priestly task to light it after they went to the Brazen Altar and the Brazen Laver, which prophetically speaks of being cleansed by fire and by water.

DISCUSSION QUESTIONS:

1) When asked why you celebrate Hanukkah, have you ever responded: "Because Yeshua (Jesus) did?" If so, what was their response?

2) What caused you to personally win the battle(s) of overcoming pagan sun god worship (i.e., Christmas)?

3) What are the changes you've seen during this season since you've come out of Babylon and laid down Christmas?

4) The Bible tells us *"make sure that the light you think you have is not actually darkness" (Luke 11:35 NLT)*. Give example of how the light you think you have can be darkness?

*****

READING NIGHT 2 – "Priests Cleansing Our Temples"

"But you are a chosen people, a royal priesthood, a holy nation, a people belonging to God, that you may declare the praises of Him who called you out of the darkness into His wonderful light" (1 Peter 2:9).

"^{19} Or do you not know that your body is the temple of the Holy Spirit, who lives in you and was given to you by God? You do not belong to yourself, ^{20} for God bought you with a high price. So you must honor God with your body" (1 Corinthians 6:19-20 NLT).

Hanukkah celebrates the purification of God's Temple, which was the preeminent house of worship in Jerusalem. The Bible also tells us that believers are the temple of the Holy Spirit. The flame of the Holy Spirit burns inside and out of us, so we may be the light of the world.

It was the priests that cleansed the Temple. When we review the below characteristics of the first earthly priesthood (Levitical priesthood), we can see the original requirements of the Lord's that are still necessary for His royal priesthood today. These priestly characteristics will show us areas in our lives that can use some improvement (i.e., cleansing). Let us look at the Levites to gain some understanding about the priesthood that believers belong to, and the behavior expected of God's holy nation. The Tribe of Levi was chosen by God to be set apart for intimate relationship with God (i.e., religious service):

[1] The Levites were set apart, because they were willing to pay the price to go against the flow. They radically obeyed the LORD (Exodus 32). They took a painful stand of righteousness – sword against their brothers.

[2] The Levites were God centered (Numbers 3). The Levites camped around the Presence of God, not around a person,

doctrine, group, etc.

[3] They gave up the right to a "normal" life... the LORD Himself became their inheritance.

[4] They had cities of refuge, where broken-hearted, hurting people had a safe place to come.

[5] The Levites' first ministry was/is to the LORD (Ezekiel 44:10-16).

[6] They led continual worship in the Tabernacle/Temple. There was a special song for each day as well as specific songs for festivals, sacrifices and offerings. Jewish tradition says that when the LORD "spoke" the world into existence that He actually sung.

[7] The Levites brought the Presence of God back to Jerusalem and all cities (1 Chronicles 15). God's people radically obey Him, and their lives are centered on Him.

DISCUSSION QUESTIONS:

1) Who dwells in you?

2) Do you ever feel that the light of God within you is burning dimly? And why?

3) What way(s) can you endeavor to cleanse your temple (body)?

4) What characteristic of the Levitical Priesthood speaks to you the most, and why?

*****

READING NIGHT 3 – "Eyes to See"

"²⁶ Go to this people and say, 'You will be ever hearing but never understanding; you will be ever seeing but never perceiving.' ²⁷ For this people's heart has become calloused; they hardly hear with their ears, and they have closed their eyes. Otherwise they might see with their eyes, hear with their ears, understand with their hearts and turn, and I would heal them'" (Acts 28:26-27 NIV).

WINDOWS OF THE SOUL: *"The eye is the lamp of the body. If your eyes are good, your whole body will be full of light" (Matthew 6:22 NIV).* The eye is the organ of sight. The human eyeball measures only about one inch in diameter, yet the eye can see objects as far away as a star and as tiny as a grain of sand and can quickly adjust its focus between the two. Our eyes are two-way windows. They show you the world, but also show others your feelings. Raised upper lids signal surprise. Pupils grow wide with wonder, interest, or fear. You might wink to let someone know you're kidding and perhaps blink when nervous. You may gaze into the eyes of those you love, but look away when embarrassed or ashamed. Did you know that your fingerprints have forty unique features, but your iris has 266?

HOW WE SEE: The first step in seeing is light bouncing off every object in your sight. The Bible says when we are in sin, we are in darkness and we can't see (i.e., blind):

- *"¹ Surely the arm of the LORD is not too short to save, nor his ear too dull to hear ² But your iniquities have separated you from your God; your sins have hidden His face from you, so that He will not hear. ³ For your hands are stained with blood, your fingers with guilt. Your lips have spoken lies, and your tongue mutters wicked things. ⁴ No one calls for justice; no one pleads his case with integrity. They rely on empty arguments and speak lies; they conceive trouble and give birth to evil. ... ⁷ Their feet rush into sin;*

they are swift to shed innocent blood. They pursue evil schemes; acts of violence mark their ways. [8] The way of peace they do not know; there is no justice in their paths. They have turned them into crooked roads; no one who walks along them will know peace. [9] So justice is far from us, and righteousness does not reach us. We look for light, but all is darkness; for brightness, but we walk in deep shadows" (Isaiah 59:1-4, 7- 9 NIV).

- *"[13] For He has rescued us from the dominion of darkness and brought us into the kingdom of the Son He loves, [14] in whom we have redemption, the forgiveness of sins" (Colossians 1:13-14 NIV).*

- *"[19] This is the verdict: Light has come into the world, but people loved darkness instead of light because their deeds were evil. [20] Everyone who does evil hates the light, and will not come into the light for fear that his deeds will be exposed. [21] But whoever lives by the truth comes into the light, so that it may be seen plainly that what they have done has been done in the sight of God" (John 3:19-21 NIV).*

DISCUSSION QUESTIONS:

1) What effect does light have on darkness?

2) What will happen if you blow out this candle?

3) Did you know that you can't see for one-half hour a day? Why? (Answer: Because you're blinking.)

4) How might we have a calloused heart where we are ever seeing but not perceiving? (Hint: These are areas in people's lives where we have chosen our own way.)

*****

READING NIGHT 4 – "What Do You See?"

"Not by might, nor by power, but by My Spirit, says the Lord of hosts" (Zechariah 4:6 NKJV).

The quintessential verse of Hanukkah is Zechariah 4:6. Let's look at this powerful verse as it relates to the Golden Lampstand (i.e., Menorah) in God's Temple from the lowly perspective of an almond. The word for "almond tree" in Hebrew literally sounds like the Hebrew word for "watching." *"¹¹ Moreover the word of the LORD came to me, saying, 'Jeremiah, what do you see?' And I said, 'I see a branch of an almond tree.' ¹² Then LORD said to me, 'You have seen well, for I am ready to perform My word" (Jeremiah 1:11-12 NKJV).*

An almond tree is a deciduous tree having pink flowers and fruit (i.e., nut). An almond is a kernel. A kernel is defined as a grain or seed; or the central or important part of a subject or plan or problem. But get this, the seed of the almond is also its edible fruit. What an incredible picture of the Spirit of the Living God enabling us to be able to sow and reap at the same time.

The Golden Lampstand in Exodus 25 is a symbol of Jesus as Light of the World as well as His believers being the light of the world. In the Hebraic culture the almond tree is symbolic of the tree of life. Thus, we can see an Old Testament picture in the Golden Lampstand of Jesus being the light and life of the world. Jesus uttered this Messianic statement on the Mount of Olives: *"I am the light of the world; he who follows Me shall not walk in darkness, but shall have the light of life" (John 8:12 NASB).*

A menorah has seven branches with accompanying lamps. They were called lamps, because they contained the oil and wicks that produced the flame. Significantly, the Golden Lampstand's illumination was created by man-made wicks, oil, and flame. The cups of the lamps that hold the oil for the Golden Lampstand are shaped like almond flowers with both buds and blossoms. When we associate Jeremiah 1:11-12 with the menorah picture, we can see one aspect of the menorah. It symbolizes the light of God's Presence watching over His Word to see that it is fulfilled. By the way, full almond blossoms symbolize life blooming while the almond buds symbolize the hope of new or renewed life. When things look dark and wintry do not despair, it is only a season for spring is near. The almond tree is the first one to bloom in Jerusalem in the spring of the year.

Zechariah 4:1 shows the angel of the Lord waking up this person and asking him the same question we started out with: "What do you see?" In *Zechariah 4:2* the man answers, *"I see a solid gold lampstand... where there is an additional bowl which causes the lampstand to yield a ceaseless supply of oil..."* Then *Zechariah 4:6* says *"Not by might, nor by power, but by My Spirit, says the Lord of hosts."* The two olive trees supplying the ceaseless oil to the lampstand in Zechariah 4:13-14 can be interpreted as being the One New Man in Christ (Jews and Gentiles in the Messiah).

DISCUSSION QUESTIONS:

1) The ceaseless supply of oil is symbolic of what? (Hint: Zechariah 4:6)

2) What encouragement can, or do, you get when you think of God watching over His Word to perform it?

3) How are you a container (lamp) for God's Presence (Spirit)?

4) How can you become a better lamp to the world? (Hint: Matthew 5:14; Psalm 119:105; Proverbs 6:23; 2 Peter 1:19)

*****

READING NIGHT 5 - "Pure & Pressed Like Gold"

"Command the Israelites to bring you clear oil of pressed olives for the light so that the lamps may be kept burning" (Exodus 27:20).

"[10] That I may know Him, and the power of His resurrection and the fellowship of His suffering, being conformed to His death; [11] in order that I may attain to the resurrection of the dead. ... [14] I press on toward the goal for the prize of the upward call of God in Christ Jesus" (Philippians 3:10-11, 14 NASB).

Let's examine the symbolism of the Lampstand in light of Yeshua being the Light of the World. The Golden Lampstand was only fed by the purest of olive oil (Exodus 27:20-21). In fact, the oil that lit the Temple Menorah had to be pressed, not crushed. Do you feel hard pressed at times? Remember that the Lord disciplines the ones He loves. To even harvest the olives, their trees must be battered with sticks. Then the olives are pressed or squeezed, depending on its use.

The sense of Exodus 27:20 is that the oil for the menorah had to be absolutely pure from the start; therefore, the oil was made meticulously by pressing each olive gently until one drop of pure oil emerged. What a picture of the care the Lord our God takes in our lives. *"[5] For we do not preach ourselves but Christ Jesus as Lord, and ourselves as your bond-servant for Jesus' sake. [6] For God who said, 'Light shall shine out of darkness,' is the One who has shone in our hearts to give the light of knowledge of the glory of God in the face of Christ. [7] But we have this treasure in earthen vessels, so that the surpassing greatness of the power will be of God and not from ourselves; [8] we are afflicted in every way, but not crushed; perplexed, but not despairing; [9] persecuted, but not forsaken; struck down, but not destroyed; [10] always carrying about in the body the dying of Jesus, so that the life of Jesus may be manifested in our body" (2 Corinthians 4:5-10 NASB).*

Exodus 27:20 says that the Golden Lampstand is to be lit continually. It was continual in the sense that it was kindled every single day without exception, being lit from evening until morning.

Another fascinating fact about the very intricate Golden Lampstand is that it was made from one solid gold ingot. This was not just an average gold ingot, but a 125-pounder, which represents indivisibility. It speaks of a person having one set of values and only one. Everything on and in the menorah had to be hammered out of the gold ingot, including the almond bud and blossom lamps. Nothing could be made separately, nothing. It would have been easier to make the pieces of the menorah separately, and then attach them; but God absolutely forbid His Temple Menorah to made in a piece-mill fashion. You and all of mankind have been made in God's own image (Genesis 1:26). Even though God perfectly made us as He designed and desires, we are still being formed into the image of the Son. Take heart everyone. The Bible tells us, *"But He knows the way I take; when He has tried me, I shall come forth as gold" (Job 23:10* NASB*).*

DISCUSSION QUESTIONS:

1) Why was the Golden Lampstand lit at sundown?

2) Do you ever feel like the Lord is meticulously pressing out one drop of pure anointing oil out of you? Tell us about one difficult circumstance where God took His time to bring forth gold in your life.

3) Can you think of any other reasons why the Golden Lampstand was fabricated out of one solid ingot of gold; and nothing could be made separately, and then attached?

*****

READING NIGHT 6 – "The True Light of Love"

"⁷ Dear friends, I am not writing a new commandment for it is an old one you have always had, right from the beginning. This commandment to love one another is the same message you heard before. ⁸ Yet it is also new. This commandment is true in Christ and is true among you, because the darkness is disappearing and the true light is already shining" (1 John 2:7-8 NLT).

"The one who loves his brother abides in the light and there is no cause for stumbling in him" (1 John 2:10 NASB).

Our Lord of Light, Love and Life is Jesus Christ (Messiah Yeshua). These three concepts – light, love, and life – go hand-in-hand in God's Word. When we accept Jesus Christ of Nazareth as our Lord and Savior, we begin our journey to become like Him, which is the exact representation of our heavenly Father. *"¹ See how great a love the Father has bestowed on us, that we should be called the children of God; and such we are. For this reason the world does not know us, because it did not know Him. ² Beloved, now we are children of God, and it has not appeared as yet what we will be. We know that when He appears, we will be like Him, because we will see Him just as He is" (1 John 3:1-2 NASB).* Divine love is the Father's incredible gift to all of us: *"Every good and perfect gift is from above, coming down from the Father of the heavenly lights, who does not change like shifting shadows" (James 1:17).* The Bible even says: *"¹⁵ Whoever confesses that Jesus is the Son of God, God abides in him and he in God. ¹⁶ We have come to know and have believed the love which God has for us. God is love, and the one who abides in love abides in God, and God abides in him" (1 John 4:15-16 NASB).*

Several years ago, I had Jesus come to me in a vision. I saw Him take my hand and heard Him say, "Come with Me. I have something to show you." Jesus began to explain, "Just as the physical realm of earth was founded on the waters, so is its spiritual realm founded on My Father's love. I began to see these iridescent shards of light shoot past me. I was amazed, especially since I had never thought of what the spiritual world was founded on ever before. The first thing I did was research if the earth was truly founded on the waters. I discovered that the Bible tells us that it was: *"For he laid the earth's foundation on the seas and built it on the ocean depths" (Psalm 24:2 NLT)*. The next thing I contemplated was divine love. It would take pages upon pages to even scratch the surface of this subject. So, let's just let the Bible speak for itself: *"[38] For I am convinced that neither death nor life, neither angels nor demons, neither the present nor the future, nor any powers, [39] neither height nor depth, nor anything else in all creation, will be able to separate us from the love of God that is in Christ Jesus our Lord" (Romans 8:38-39 NIV)*. Indeed, God is love. *"[7] Beloved, let us love one another, for love is from God; and everyone who loves is born of God and knows God. [8] The one who does not love does not know God, for God is love" (1 John 4:7-8 NASB)*.

DISCUSSION QUESTIONS:

1) Do you know what the greatest commandment is? (Hint: Matthew 22:37-39)

2) Two of the most important eternal things on earth are people and God's Word. How are people and God's Word related to divine love? (Hint: Galatians 5:13-14; 1 John 5:2-3).

3) What does it mean that we abide in the light when we love one another?

4) Tell us how you know God loves you or someone else.

*****

READING NIGHT 7 – "The Place of Miracles"

"The apostles performed many miraculous signs and wonders among the people. And all the believers used to meet together in Solomon's Colonnade" (Acts 5:12 NIV).

Yeshua walked in Solomon's Colonnade during the feast of Hanukkah, declaring to the Jews that His miraculous works plainly revealed He was the Messiah. Israel's priests had previously concluded that when they heard the testimony of someone being healed of the incurable disease of leprosy, it would be an obvious sign of the Messiah – that He had come. And not only that, but the Messiah also would restore the sight of someone born blind. One born lame would walk. When John the Baptist asked Jesus: Are you the One? Yeshua sent back the message: Tell John the blind see, the leper is cleansed, the lame walk and the captives are set free (Matthew 11:4-5).

All the passages that speak of Solomon's Colonnade tell us it's a place of miracles. Acts 5:12 informs us that all the believers met together at Solomon's Colonnade. It's the place where the apostles performed many miracles, signs, and wonders among the people. It is also the place where a beggar, who had been crippled from birth, held on to Peter and John and was healed (Acts 3:11).

Solomon's Colonnade is also called Solomon's Porch. It was built by Solomon on the east side of the temple. From this side, the glory is supposed to fill God's temple. A porch or portico is a covered area adjoining an entrance to a building and usually has a separate roof. Spiritually speaking, it represents the place where a believer already has entered the temple (i.e., a relationship with God), but not the building (i.e., become a permanent dwelling place for God).

The celebration of Hanukkah holds several keys for end-time believers. Hanukkah is celebrated in winter when things look asleep, just as all ten virgins in Matthew 25 were asleep because *"the Bridegroom was a long time in coming" (Matthew 25:5)*. By the way, both the wise and foolish virgins are representative of believers. Hanukkah emphasizes God's people celebrating both a miraculous military victory over heathen oppressors, by a small, ragtag righteous remnant as well as cleaning out and re-dedicating their Temple to the Lord.

Notice how *Acts 5:12* articulates: *"And all the believers used to meet together in Solomon's Colonnade."* I believe that this statement is prophetic. I see eternity looking back into earth's time-space continuum and the heavenly throng's acknowledgement of it. All the believers in the Lord Jesus Christ meet in Solomon's Colonnade in a spiritual sense when they celebrate the Biblical feast of Hanukkah in Zion.

DISCUSSION QUESTIONS:

1) What's the name of the place in the Temple area where believers met? (Answer: Solomon's Colonnade)

2) What went on there? (Answer: Miracles, signs and wonders)

3) Can you tell us of any miracles you've seen or experienced?

*****

READING NIGHT 8 – "Will You Be Betrothed?"

Hanukkah is celebrated in winter when things look asleep, just as all ten virgins in Matthew 25 were asleep because *"the Bridegroom was a long time in coming" (Matthew 25:5)*. By the way, both the wise and foolish virgins are representative of believers.

Hanukkah is not one of the seven feasts of the Lord specified in Leviticus 23, but it is one of the two winter feasts mentioned in the Bible – Hanukkah (John 10:22-23) and Purim (Book of Esther). If we operate on the premise that the entire Bible is inspired by God (2 Timothy 3:16-17), we must contemplate why these feasts are in God's Word. Are they mentioned positively or negatively? Positively. Does God discourage or encourage their celebration? Definitely not discouraged. In fact, Yeshua celebrated these feasts as a Jew when He walked here on this earth. I don't know about you, but I want to do what Jesus did. Jesus celebrated Passover (*Pesach*), the Feast of Unleavened Bread (*Hag Ha Matzah*), the Feast of First Fruits (*Bikkurim*), Pentecost (*Shavuot*), the Feast of Trumpets (*Yom Teruah*), the Day of Atonement (*Yom Kippur*), the Feast of Tabernacles (*Sukkot*), the Feast of Dedication (*Hanukkah*), and the Feast of Lots (*Purim*). Jesus celebrated the Lord's feasts as a shadow of things to come because they are part of His Word – part of Him. The fulfillment of everything in God's Word, including the feasts of the Lord, is found in the Messiah. Jesus Christ of Nazareth – the Mature Head and His Mature Body – gives definitive form to the Lord's feasts. Just as Yeshua embodies the feasts, so shall we. Yeshua brings the feasts of the Lord into an organized whole, as a prophetic picture of His ministry to His body and the redemption of all creation.

Through the feasts of the Lord, God is telling us that He has ordained an exact, set, and appointed time when He will fulfill definite events in His plan of redemption. Jesus came to earth in the fullness of time, which was the exact time ordained by God

(Galatians 4:2-4). The Lord also has set an exact time when He is appointed to judge the world (Acts 17:31). Technically, God's feasts represent the congregation where God's people are brought together or assembled together for worship as an organized body. In 2 Chronicles 8:13, the primitive root for *mo-ed* is the Hebrew word *ya-ad*, which is defined as fixing an appointment – like writing a critical meeting in your day-timer. But more importantly, this primitive root implies that the Lord is summoning His people to meet Him at His stated time, He is directing us into a certain position, and He is engaging us for marriage (i.e., to be betrothed). Just as *mo-ed* in space refers to the locality where mankind has their appointed place of assembly for an appointed purpose, so *mo-ed* in time is a point in time which summons God's people communally to an appointed activity. As it is written: *"As You summon to a feast day" (Laminations 2:22).* The question remains for Christians: If we aren't celebrating the Feasts of the Lords, can we truly be betrothed to Him?

DISCUSSION QUESTION:

1) How many Biblical feasts can you name? (Answer: Passover (*Pesach*), the Feast of Unleavened Bread (*Hag Ha Matzah*), the Feast of First Fruits (*Bikkurim*), Pentecost (*Shavuot*), the Feast of Trumpets (*Yom Teruah*), the Day of Atonement (*Yom Kippur*), the Feast of Tabernacles (*Sukkot*), the Feast of Dedication (*Hanukkah*), and the Feast of Lots (*Purim*)).

2) Who summons people to the feasts of the Lord? (Answer: God) Why is He summoning us? (Answer: So, we can intimately be united with Him in a marriage like relationship)

3) If we aren't celebrating the Feasts of the Lords, can we truly be betrothed to Him?

*****

If you are interested in more Hanukkah devotions, please check out the *Let There Be Light! Hanukkah Meditations* book => https://www.amazon.com/dp/0998598208.

12 – INFORMAL BIBLIOGRAPHY

Due to the desire to keep this book as concise as possible all reference materials will be generally listed on this page:

1. *5000 Questions and Answers on Chanukah* by Jeffrey M. Cohen

2. *Apocrypha, The* by Cambridge at The University Press

3. *Catholic Encyclopedia, The*, http://www.newadvent.org/cathen/

4. *Chanukah - Its History, Observance, And Significance* Published by Mesorah Publications, Ltd

5. *First Maccabees Second Maccabees* by Alphonse P. Spilly, C.PP.S

6. *Holy Bible* (KJV, NASB, NKJV, NLT)

7. *Judas Maccabaeus - The Jewish Struggle against the Seleucids* by Bezalel Bar-Kochva

8. *Messianic Jewish Candle Lighting Ceremony For Hanukah*, http://www.yeshuahamashiach.org/Hanakah_Instructions.htm

9. *Order of Melchizedek, The* (mp3) by Ian Clayton,

http://resources.sonofthunder.org/

10. *SANTA-TIZING: What's wrong with Christmas and how to clean it up* by Robin Main, https://www.amazon.com/SANTA-TIZING-Whats-wrong-Christmas-clean/dp/1607911159

11. *The Real Story of Chanukah: Dedicated to the Death* by Kevin Geoffrey

12. *Yom Teruah - How the Day of Shouting Became Rosh Hashanah* by Nehemia Gordon http://www.karaite-korner.org/yom_teruah.shtml

*****

ABOUT THE AUTHOR

Robin Main is a prophetic artist, author, speaker and teacher who equips people to be the unique and beautiful creation that they have been created to be. She flows in love, revelation and wisdom with her SPECIALTY being kingdom enlightenment.

Her MISSION is to enlighten the nations by venturing to educate and restore the sons of the Living God.

Her CALL is a clarion one to mature sons and the pure and spotless Bride who will indeed be without spot or wrinkle.

Her ULTIMATE DESIRE is that everyone be rooted and grounded in love, so they can truly know the height, width, breadth and depth of the Father's love.

Made in the USA
Middletown, DE
24 March 2018